Glimpses of Tibetan Divination

Prognostication in History

Edited by

Chia-Feng Chang (*Taiwan National University*)
Michael Lackner (*Friedrich-Alexander-University Erlangen-Nürnberg*)
Klaus Herbers (*Friedrich-Alexander-University Erlangen-Nürnberg*)
Alexander Fidora (*University of Barcelona*)

VOLUME 2

The titles published in this series are listed at *brill.com/prhi*

Glimpses of Tibetan Divination

Past and Present

Edited by

Petra Maurer
Donatella Rossi
Rolf Scheuermann

BRILL

LEIDEN | BOSTON

Cover illustration: Chinese divination, *thangka* section. The Museum of the Five Continents (previously the Völkerkunde Museum), Munich, reproduced by permission.

Library of Congress Cataloging-in-Publication Data

Names: Maurer, Petra H., editor. | Rossi, Donatella, editor. | Scheuermann, Rolf, editor.
Title: Glimpses of Tibetan divination : past and present / edited by Petra Maurer, Donatella Rossi, Rolf Scheuermann.
Description: Leiden ; Boston : Brill, [2019] | Series: Prognostication in history, 2589-4404 ; Volume 2 | Includes bibliographical references and index.
Identifiers: LCCN 2019030666 (print) | LCCN 2019030667 (ebook) |
ISBN 9789004407374 (hardback) | ISBN 9789004410688 (ebook)
Subjects: LCSH: Divination–Tibet Region. | Tibet Region–Religious life and customs.
Classification: LCC BF1773.2.T5 G55 2019 (print) | LCC BF1773.2.T5 (ebook) |
DDC 133.309515–dc23
LC record available at https://lccn.loc.gov/2019030666
LC ebook record available at https://lccn.loc.gov/2019030667

Typeface for the Latin, Greek, and Cyrillic scripts: "Brill". See and download: brill.com/brill-typeface.

ISSN 2589-4404
ISBN 978-90-04-40737-4 (hardback)
ISBN 978-90-04-41068-8 (e-book)

Copyright 2020 by Koninklijke Brill NV, Leiden, The Netherlands.
Koninklijke Brill NV incorporates the imprints Brill, Brill Hes & De Graaf, Brill Nijhoff, Brill Rodopi, Brill Sense, Hotei Publishing, mentis Verlag, Verlag Ferdinand Schöningh and Wilhelm Fink Verlag.
All rights reserved. No part of this publication may be reproduced, translated, stored in a retrieval system, or transmitted in any form or by any means, electronic, mechanical, photocopying, recording or otherwise, without prior written permission from the publisher.
Authorization to photocopy items for internal or personal use is granted by Koninklijke Brill NV provided that the appropriate fees are paid directly to The Copyright Clearance Center, 222 Rosewood Drive, Suite 910, Danvers, MA 01923, USA. Fees are subject to change.

This book is printed on acid-free paper and produced in a sustainable manner.

Contents

Preface VII
Background History of the Volume XXII
On the Contributions Contained in This Volume XXV
List of Figures and Tables XXIX
Notes on Contributors XXX

1 A Case of Prophecy in Post-imperial Tibet 1
   Per Kværne

2 Three Dice, Four Faces, and Sixty-Four Combinations: Early Tibetan
   Dice Divination by the Numbers 11
   Brandon Dotson

3 A Preliminary Analysis of Old Tibetan Dice Divination Texts 49
   Ai Nishida

4 Divinations Padampa Did or Did Not Do, or Did or Did Not Write 73
   Dan Martin

5 Landscaping Time, Timing Landscapes: The Role of Time in the *sa
   dpyad* Tradition 89
   Petra Maurer

6 Signs and Portents in Nature and in Dreams: What They Mean
   and What Can Be Done about Them 118
   Charles Ramble

7 Identifying the Magical Displays of the Lords of the World:
   The Oneiromancy of the *gSal byed byang bu* 136
   Donatella Rossi

8 Vibhūticandra's *Svapnohana* and the Examination of Dreams 161
   Rolf Scheuermann

9 Prognosis, Prophylaxis, and Trumps: Comparative Remarks on Several
   Common Forms of Tibetan Cleromancy 181
   Alexander K. Smith

10 The Role of Lamyn Gegeen Blo bzang bstan 'dzin rgyal mtshan in the Dissemination of Tibetan Astrology, Divination and Prognostication in Mongolia   198
    Agata Bareja-Starzýnska

Index   213

Preface

The desire to know the future, to seek answers to questions both spoken and those left unsaid, is a deep-seated human instinct. In evolutionary terms, its origins may lie in the quest for survival itself, in the need to be healed, and in the necessity of effectively fulfilling the social and economic obligations of life such as the planting of fields and harvesting and so on. The human propensity to look into the future, and to try to see what it holds in store for us, might be one of the many psychological features that distinguish humans from other animals.

Rather than having recourse to long and intense critical examination of the possibilities available—weighing the pros and cons of different courses of action for example—which still leave a large element of contingency when it comes to outcomes, it was (and to a large extent still is) very common for Tibetans to consult a diviner, an astrologer or an oracle as means of giving respite from these tensions of uncertainty and offering guidance on how to proceed.

In Tibetan societies past and present, consulting a diviner was and still is as socially acceptable as consulting a healer or a doctor. Such consultations were not considered strange, and such prognostications were not derided as superstition. Such practices have stood the test of time—they have been in use for centuries—and they continue to be widespread today. Nor were such services restricted to people of a particular social status. Diviners were and are accessible to all and anyone can consult them. Going to a diviner when one has a question about the future was (and is) as natural as going to a healer when one contracts a disease. In Tibetan society, only the State Oracles were restricted for use by the government alone, and ordinary people could not approach them with requests for prognostication.

Over the centuries, Tibetans developed many practices of prognostication and adapted many others from neighboring cultures and religions. In this way, Tibetan divination evolved into a vast field of ritual expertise that has been largely neglected in Tibetan Studies. Focused as they tend to be on Tibetan history and Buddhism, scholars have often skirted the activities and beliefs associated with the daily lives and simple needs of Tibetans. This disregard is especially surprising given the popularity of prognostication in Tibet. Prognostication permeates many spheres of life, reveals many fields of knowledge, and lays open many aspects and layers of Tibetan society and culture.

Why study divination? Divinatory techniques and predictions can offer insights into the cultural influences of neighboring countries. They open up a wide field of knowledge on myth, religion, ritual, and culture; on demons and gods, flora and fauna, on secular and sacral activities, on material culture and religious objects, and even on how to live and to die. They can help explain the structure of houses, and the choice of location for cemeteries. However, there is more.

Divination techniques and prognostication can inform us about the structure of society, about its social classes and gendered roles, while at the same time giving us access to the inner lives of people, to the secrets of human emotion and feeling, and to the hopes and fears of the people. Such techniques and predictions may thus be considered a mirror of society, helping us reach a deeper understanding of culture. People are guided by the wish to know the future, to know about the forces that might influence their activities, to know in advance if an upcoming event or project will succeed or fail. Like a game, divination is all about loss and gain. Depending on the technique, predictions can even help achieve specific goals in life and avoid certain dangers. They offer people guidance through life, helping them find answers, achieve emotional stability and to embolden faith, in much the same way that prayer can make misery and pain more bearable.

The events for which diviners were consulted can range from regularly performed everyday activities to particular events such as marriage or a building project that might be performed only once in a lifetime. The questions raised can range from simple to very complex. Some questions may require only a straightforward "yes" or "no" answer; others, concerning the outcome of a particular course of action, can be answered simply with a "good" or "bad", with various shades in between. Alternatively, a client may ask for a range of details and options concerning the future.

Depending on the question presented and the method employed, the information returned about the upcoming activities and events might be closely related to the aspect of timing. To guarantee the success of an activity, the client may be enjoined to embark on the project only at a suitable time, for timing can often be *the* decisive factor for a favorable outcome or a successful achievement. Just as the questions posed about the future can be very varied, so too can the means for finding answers to them.

1 Techniques

All techniques examine and analyze the current situation and the circumstances of the request in the present. Many techniques—including the medical

PREFACE   IX

practice of pulse diagnosis—also examine the past. With pulse diagnosis, a Tibetan healer can read past events like a broken bone for example. As an attempt to survey the various divination techniques, one might distinguish them as falling into the following categories.

First, there are those forms of divination without any specific object, such as divination through dreams (*rmi lam*) or oneiromancy,[1] or through omens that occur spontaneously, such as portents of death. 'Objectless' divination requires profound knowledge on how to interpret the manifold signs and omens that can appear to the diviner in these ways. Oracles and prophets might also be subsumed under this category, as their predictions follow an intuitive knowledge, or else information transmitted by divine agents.

The next category of prognostications concerns those in which divination occurs through the medium of an object that exists naturally or arises by itself. Among these are the interpretation of clear visions that occur on the surface of any clear and even object, such as a lake, the blue sky or a mirror (*pra*), and the interpretation of topography as a branch of geomancy. Dreams are similar to a landscape or a lake, vectors of hidden knowledge disguised in images that require interpretation. Other signs that occur naturally or arise of their own accord are phenomena in nature such as the blowing of the wind—the examination of the flickering of a butter lamp (*mar me brtag pa*), the shape and direction of a plume of smoke (*spos kyi dud pa*), the whorls on a horse's pelage (*gtsug*),[2] the marks on a human body, physical reactions in one's body such as sneezing or the twinkling of the eyes, or animal calls such as the cawing of crows, and so on. The diviner interprets these omens by the signs, patterns, shapes and the events themselves. No further or extraneous calculation is required.

A third category subsumes those divination techniques which interpret patterns using a particular object. This includes methods such as scapulimancy (*sog mo*, divination with shoulder-blades), divination with rosaries (*mo 'phreng*), with arrows (*mda' mo*, in Tibetan culture there are at least two kinds of arrow divination), with pebbles (*lde'u 'phrul* which probably goes back to geomancy, i.e. "the art of dotting"), with dice (*sho mo*), with cords (*ju thig*), and so on.

Chinese divination or calculation (*nag rtsis*) should be regarded as a further separate category. The diviner merely calculates the future of his client by establishing a relationship between the past and the present. Any prediction

---

1 See Ramble, Rossi, and Scheuermann in this volume.
2 See Maurer, Petra. *Handschriften zur tibetischen Hippiatrie und Hipplogie* (Bonn: VGH Wissenschaftsverlag, 2001), 170–179.

depends on aspects and dimensions in their relation to time, and this kind of prognostication is a purely technical procedure.

The main purpose of all these techniques is to avoid unfavorable or unpleasant situations and avert damage, calamity, hindrance or disease. Means of preventing harm can include ritual practices (*gto*) and yogic exercises (for example to avoid death) as well as other rituals to overcome and defeat the demon perpetrators of whatever harm is threatened.

The manner in which the various techniques were preserved in Tibet suggests many cultural influences. For example, the Chinese origin of the so-called Chinese calculation or divination (*nag rtsis*) is very clear. Divination with dice was popular in India and Central Asia, but was also widespread in the Islamic tradition.[3] Prognostication involving animals, such as the calls of birds and the whorls on a horse's coat occur extensively in India. The use of knotted cords is likely to be of Bon origin as also may be divination by means of counting beads on a "rosary". This simple practice is performed by laymen and monks, and is very popular in Tibetan communities. Most if not all of these divinatory practises however are of multi-cultural origin and/or influence and not based on originally Buddhist concepts. It was the 5th Dalai Lama who integrated divination into Buddhism and Buddhist concepts such as *rten 'brel* (dependant origination) were obviously consecutively superimposed.

2 Terminology

The manifold influences and forms of Tibetan divination are visible through the diverse terminology applied to them. It seems that except *pra*, the various terms point to other cultural backgrounds rather than referring to a specific technique. The terms *phya, mo* and *pra* already appear in Old Tibetan sources and also in Bon literature, whereas *rtsis* might be of later origin.[4]

A person who predicts the future can be a monk or a layperson, male or female. With the exception of oracles, the technique is not defined by the person who performs it, but rather the designation of the specialist is defined by the method he or she uses. So, for example, the term *rtsis pa* or *rtsis mkhan* refers to an astrologer, diviner or "calculator". In this context it denotes simply the individual who performs the so-called Chinese calculation (*nag rtsis*) by

---

3 See Dotson in this volume.

4 Karmay, Samten G. "The Appearance of the Little Black-headed Man," in *The Arrow and the Spindle. Studies in the History, Myths, Rituals and Beliefs in Tibet* (Kathmandu: Mandala Book Point, 2009), 247.

PREFACE   XI

means of reading the zodiac signs, the elements and other dimensions such as *spar kha*, *sme ba*, *srog*, *lus*, *dbang thang* and *klung rta*. It goes without saying that the calculation of planets is also included. Planets such as Rāhu (*gza'*) are regarded as the cause of hindrances and diseases, a further illustration of the relationship between medicine and divination.

The focus in calculation is particularly on time and timing. The relationship between all the relevant elements and dimensions assigned to the person is correlated to the current time, or to the point in time of the undertaking to be assessed, and thus its advisability (or not) is determined and a suitable time is suggested. That means that the relationship between the past—that is, the birth year of the client—and the future or present, depending on the timing, is the decisive factor. The calculation for occasions such as a marriage, for example, is more complex, as two people are involved. In this case, the diviner has to calculate the relationship of each of the two people's elements to each other, and the relationship of both to the fixed timing. As above, he correlates the past with the fixed time. To complicate the system further, certain planets, directions, months, days, *spar kha* and so on are assessed as negative.[5]

Another term is *mo pa* or *mo mkhan*, denoting an individual who performs *mo* divination. A *phya mkhan* performs a *phya* divination, also called *phya ken tse*, the diviner of Bon. Another special term is *pra mkhan*, in which *pra* denotes a form of divination performed on the clear surface of something such as a lake, the blue sky, or a mirror. The terms *phyva* (!) and *pra* denote at the same time the result, *phyva* the "good fortune" or "luck". The meaning of *pra*, however, seems to be unspecific with regard to the predicted result.

This is not a comprehensive list; there are many other local terms, such as *'on po* in Ladakh. This term denotes a diviner and ritual specialist who also administers medical treatment. Better known is the term *emchi* for a traditional healer, a term which originates in the Mongolian language.

3 Activities, Events, and Questions

Divination serves the general purpose of improving human life. As such, no human activities or events are excluded from the possibility of forecasting. Each and any undertaking can be prognosticated. Written sources such as the

---

5 Tseng, Teming. *Sino-tibetische Divinationskalkulationen (Nag rtis), dargestellt anhand des Werkes dPag-bsam ljon-shing von Blo bzang tshul khrims rgya mtsho* (Halle: International Institute for Tibetan and Buddhist Studies, 2005), 151 ff.

Vaiḍūrya dkar po and the *dPag bsam ljon shing* present an insight into the manifold undertakings concerning which a diviner can be called upon to prognosticate. As for the client and the diviner, there are no restrictions or rules with regard to social status, gender, age, and so on. The main criteria for the decision to consult a diviner are the significance the client attributes the event as well as its possible consequences.

What concerns can motivate prognostication? As mentioned above, the desire to remain healthy or to be healed is undoubtedly one, and prognostication is particularly common when choosing the treatment of diseases with an unknown origin. This might stand at the source of the culture of divination for timing life-sustaining activities, since Tibetan traditional society considered demons—whose activities are influenced by time and place—as the causes of obstacles and calamities such as disease, bad crops and natural disasters such as floods, earthquake, and the loss of a harvest.

A good harvest depends on the timing of related activities. The day when the fields should be plowed or the crop gathered in has to be auspicious in order to avoid damage by unsuitable weather conditions and to ensure the most abundant yield. The activity of demons moving at the time can, therefore, influence nearly every activity, and precautions must be taken to offset such influences. This is true of any undertaking, from setting out on a journey in the hope of avoiding robbery or other misfortune and reaching one's destination safely, embarking on a business venture in such a way as to ensure maximum profits, to choosing the time and place for a wedding or the construction of a building.

The questions asked depend on the event or planned enterprise concerned. The client's fears of loss and failure and/or his wishes to make gains or succeed are the basic concern. Below, I will illustrate this with a small series of questions that a client might ask. These correlate with particular techniques applied and are based on a singular possible undertaking or event.

The simplest form of question a client might ask is "should I act or not? Should I go on the journey? Should I stay back? Should I embark on this business venture?" Such questions can be answered by a "yes", a "no", or "it does not matter/is irrelevant".

If the answer is no, then the client may inquire about the reason for the negative response. An unsuitable timing could lead to the undertaking being postponed. If the expected negative influences are not too serious, then a ritual may be enough to deflect calamity. If the obstacles are serious, however, the client might be advised to abandon the plan altogether. If the obstacles do not forbid the activity itself, then the client may consult the diviner again after a certain period of time has elapsed.

PREFACE   XIII

If the answer is a "yes", then the client could still ask for the best timing: "Should I go now? Should I go tomorrow? Should I go in two weeks?"

Activities that involve more than one person are more complicated: a question such as "Should I marry or not?" is more difficult to answer since it involves the elements and dimensions of the couple. If the result of a *rtsis* prognostication is very negative owing to the incompatibility of the couple's elements, then the marriage might be canceled. In any case, improvement of the situation is possible through the performance of rituals. A positive relation between the couple's elements moreover, would nevertheless require the calculation of the right timing.

More comprehensive questions are those that ask for the expected end result of a plan: "Will it be positive or negative"? The possible answers are: "yes" or "no" or "moderate". A negative answer due to unsuitable timing can lead to a postponement. Against other obstacles such as demons, the diviner might recommend a ritual.

Another scenario is the wish to achieve a specific outcome. The client might be striving for a specific result or attempting to avoid loss or failure. Alternatively, the client might ask for the interpretation of a certain portent, or request advice as to the best means by which he might optimize his chances of fulfilling whatever he is striving for. The questions he asks could, for example, include the following: "Where should I construct the house in order to ensure the safety of my family? What does it mean if the place looks like the heart of an elephant? What consequences follow from owning a horse that has a whorl in its forehead?"

Such requests for detailed predictions can be responded to by examining a particular area, interpreting the whorls in the horse's hair, or analysing dreams or other omens. Topomancy—the analysis of an area's shapes and forms—involves not only a broad variety of images that allow precise predictions with regard to specific circumstances.[6] It also declares particular shapes as carrying particular omens. The simple discernment of shapes in a physical area of space allows assessment of the place as positive or negative. The patterns assessed are based, for example, on the tools of daily life, on sacred objects, on human, animal or demonic body-forms and other things. Particular patterns can be exploited, so that the person in question might achieve specific qualities, such as becoming a hero. For example, a place where one becomes a hero looks like the chest of a lion. Others are said to ward off death.

---

6   See Maurer in this volume.

The interpretation of portents of death in the *Mṛtyuvañcanopadeśa*[7] is similar to texts on geomancy and dream interpretation. Detailed and complex images of events, bodily impulses and physical defects, and dreams are seen as signs of impending death. These omens also offer the healer the possibility of diagnosing a patient's disease. This Buddhist text, which is undoubtedly influenced by concepts foreign to Buddhism, furthermore aims at preparing the patient for death. The signs allow the healer to recognize death's approach and to prognosticate an expected time of its arrival. Moreover, it gives the patient the opportunity to prepare himself for his death through spiritual practice. Alternatively, he can try to have rituals performed to cheat death.

Other complex questions that might be posed include questions about the days on which diseases or other calamities (*keg*) might be encountered in the coming year. What are the times of such illnesses and calamities? With regard to health, a healer will answer such questions by feeling and interpreting the patient's pulse. Other matters (aside from healing/disease) would be the task of a diviner. The portents of death and the predictions in the geomantic texts concerning health again point to a key aspect in prognostication: the importance of time and timing.

4 Time and Timing

Manifold and multi-layered questions require manifold and multi-layered techniques for answering them. Time and timing are the most significant factors in Chinese calculation (*nag rtsis*) but are also very prominent in other forms of divination. The success of an undertaking often depends on the right timing when the activity is begun. Generally, the timing of events or activities can follow the Tibetan calendar where auspicious and inauspicious days for specific undertakings are marked. The more significant a particular undertaking is for a client, the more likely he is to consult a diviner to obtain the specific auspicious time on which to begin.

Time and timing are not only significant factors for the client and the patient but can also influence the activity of the diviner. Texts on geomancy, for example, recommend that the diviner perform a simple pre-divination to determine whether the day for the examination of an area is auspicious or not. Thus, a diviner may perform a smoke divination to ascertain whether the time is right

---

7 See Schneider, Johannes. *Vāgīśvarakīrtis Mṛtyuvañcanopadeśa, eine buddhistische Lehrschrift zur Abwehr des Todes* (Wien: Österreichische Akademie der Wissenschaften, 2010).

for undertaking an examination of the land. Particular weather phenomena such as the direction in which the smoke blows can indicate if the day is suitable or not.

On a more general level, prognostication for the whole populace or nation correlates with time, such as in the horse races that were performed in Tibet until the 1950s.[8] A further possibility is prognostication with regard to circumstances that can concern a region or a nation such as wars. There are texts on divination for wars; on such occasions the Tibetan government consulted the state oracles. A failed or incorrect prognostication could lead to an oracle being discharged.

The centrality of timing to the culture of divination calls on us to reflect on the concepts of time and its division in traditional Tibetan society. Peasants and nomads in the formerly agricultural and pastoral society had a simple system to measure time; they followed natural processes and cycles. The seasons determined their activities. Sun, moon, and other planets determined their daily and monthly routines. The seasons of the year determined the timing of specific activities: the plowing and sowing of the fields, the harvest, and the collection of herbs. The life and the death of cattle in Tibet and other Himalayan mountain areas depended on the seasons; cattle were moved from summer and winter pastures. Late summer and autumn were the seasons for sharing and slaughtering. Moreover, the needs of the cattle divided the times of the day, i.e., the feeding in the morning and the milking in the evening. In traditional societies, such natural divisions of time had a much greater impact on daily life than they have in modern societies, in which although time can be measured exactly, it can also be ignored. The seasons and the cycles of day and night were significant to the organization of life throughout the year. The needs of humans and animals structured time.

Time-correlated systems and concepts in Tibet, however, were made more complex by another factor that relates to both locality and religion, namely the hindrances and obstacles presented by demons or demonic forces. Tibetan culture knows numerous demons such as the "lord of the ground" (*sa bdag*), who moves through time and place. This idea influences all plans for any kind of fieldwork, journey, building construction, and so on. On top of the natural and demon-related time-constraints, there were also other units used to structure

---

8   Richardson, Hugh. *Ceremonies of the Lhasa Year* (London: Serindia Publications, 1993), 52 ff. For a survey on horse races, see Petra Maurer, Pferderennen und ihre Bedeutung in Tibet, in *Nepalica-Tibetica. Festgabe for Christoph Cüppers*, eds. Franz-Karl Ehrhard und Petra Maurer (Andiast: International Institute for Tibetan and Buddhist Studies, 2013), vol. 2, 57–74.

time as in other societies: years, months, weeks, days, and hours. As in China and India, Tibetans also recognized a sixth unit that a diviner can calculate: the unit of two hours that also denotes the "time of the day" like dawn (*nam langs*), sunrise (*nyi shar*), morning (*nyi dros*), and so on. And as already explained, these units—years, months and so on—were directly related to other factors: the elements, the directions, divinatory dimensions called *sme ba* and *spar kha*, the zodiac signs, and personal elements such as *rus khams* or *rus chen*.

Moreover, another time system came from India, namely the astronomical system known as *grub rtsis*. It is different again, and compartmentalizes time as follows: the day is divided into sixty units called *chu tshod*; *chu tshod* are divided into sixty *chu srang*, and the *chu srang* into six breaths (*dbugs*). Thus, 21,600 breaths make one day of the week.

5   Theoretical Background

Divinatory techniques try to answer questions by correlating time and place. I, therefore, present below a brief survey of the theoretical structure of time and place. These elements form alike the basis of both medical and divinatory concepts.

The primary causes (*rgyu*) for the world are contained in the world—in the environment that is determined by the four elements. 'Phags pa (1235–1280), the nephew of Sa skya Paṇḍita (1182–1251), explains in his *Shes bya rab gsal* (Fol. 2) that the composition of the physical world is based upon the four elements earth (*sa*), water (*chu*), fire (*me*), and wind (*rlung*). These are commonly the elements referred to in medicine: the human body is composed of them. A fifth element, ether (*nam mkha'*), may be added. These elements are related to the three humors (*nyes pa gsum*) wind (*rlung*), bile (*mkhris pa*), and phlegm (*bad kan*) which, together with the elements, constitute the balance of any particular body. There is, however, an exception with regard to the correlation between human body and element. *sDe srid* Sangs rgyas rgya mtsho, for example, follows a Chinese concept in assigning the organs to the Chinese elements too.

The elements that feature in divination are usually considered as being five in number, and originate in China: they are earth (*sa*), water (*chu*), fire (*me*), wood (*shing*), and iron or metal (*lcags*). These five elements form, among other dimensions, the components of time. They are regarded as factors which influence the life of a person through their correlation. They exist largely beyond our control. With divination techniques, however, their negative influences can be calculated and/or prognosticated, and thereby their effects mitigated or

PREFACE   XVII

enhanced. A change in human behavior, or a change in plan, can allow a person to avoid the negative influence that might otherwise threaten an undertaking. Furthermore, rituals can help to mitigate or even prevent damage.

The other, so-called secondary, causes (*rkyen*) are, in medical tradition, considered factors such as demons, behavior, seasons, and nutrition. In divination, they are very similar: demons, behavior, and timing. A change in behavior, or in food, or in medical treatment, can improve a body's condition and thus benefit health. The same is valid for social or economic conditions. A change in behavior or a change of plans can improve a current situation and influence upcoming events. If the plans are fixed and unchangeable, then a ritual might serve as a remedy of last resort.

These reflections bring us to the Tibetan conceptualization of the world (or universe) as the "vessel" (*snod*) and living beings as its content or essence (*bcud*). The vessel itself is composed of time and space and consists of six elements. It affects human lives and the variability of its composition can lead to conditions that have to be improved or changed. This is true both with regard to the microcosmic level of the body (the area with which medicine is concerned) and with regard to the macrocosmic level (with which divination is concerned).

Despite these shared theoretical concepts, divination—in contrast to medicine—is not included in the traditional five major sciences (*rig gnas che ba lnga*); astronomy and mathematics of Indian origin (*skar rtsis*) are a part of the five minor sciences (*rig gnas chung ba lnga*). However, in his *Vaiḍūrya dkar po*, Sangs rgyas rgya mtsho (1653–1705) distinguishes eighteen sciences in all, included among which are astrology (*skar rtsis*) and Chinese divination (*nag rtsis*).[9]

6   Prognostication and Medical Practice

Apart from gaining knowledge about the future, the shared purpose of both prognostication and medicine is to improve life. Intentions behind the wish to consult a healer and a diviner are identical yet different at the same time. A patient usually consults a healer when he is sick—even though the stage of a disease depends very much on the sensitivity of the patient who wants to avoid real physical damage to the body and be healed.

---

9 Sangs rgyas rgya mtsho, *Phug lugs rtsis kyi legs bshad bai ḍūrya dkar po* (Pe cin: Krung go'i bod rig pa dpe skrun khang, 1997), smad cha, 447.

On the other hand, a client consults a diviner, usually beforehand, so as to avoid any kind of damage in the future. Both methods originate in the wish for happiness, contentment, and fulfillment in life. They might be achieved by diagnosis and prescription: just as medical treatment can heal the body, a ritual can turn back or block threatening forces and change the future for the better. Both medical patient and divination client seek information: the patient about his health, the client about the conditions and circumstances of places and times. The aim of both is to prevent damage to one's own life or to those of relatives and friends. It might even be the one and the same person who diagnoses a disease and prognosticates the future. Especially in rural areas, diviners can be oracles—the line between oracles and shamans is also not clear—so a diviner can fulfill the function of a healer and vice versa. Tibetan society has institutionalized this connection by establishing the Medical-Astrological-Institute (*sman rtsis khang*) in Lhasa and, in the 1960s, in its exile community in the Indian hill station Dharamsala.

With regard to the prognostication practices used in medicine and divination, the methods of examination are also comparable. The examination of a patient's body with the pulse or urine analysis is comparable to the examination of the land through observations of the shapes of mountains and rocks and the flow of rivers. Both look at the current states and use them to try to prognosticate the future. Furthermore, pulse diagnosis is not only applied to diagnose health issues but is also used as a means of prognostication for predicting a family's position in society, its wealth, upcoming visits of guests, and so on.

For medical purposes, the subtleness of pulse diagnosis allows early diagnosis of illnesses that may be threatening a client's health. An early diagnosis gives the opportunity for healing through simple means such as a change in daily behavior or diet. Similarly, prognostication offers the chance to avoid harm by changing plans or the timing of planned activities.

Both healer and diviner examine the present while also looking at the past. Both predict the future and make suggestions accordingly, the healer with regard to the patient's health and the diviner with regard to other activities. If present circumstances and conditions suggest that an intervention would be beneficial, the healer and/or diviner can perform rituals or prescribe medicines. Further evidence for the perceived equivalence of the two kinds of services is in the method of payment: in both cases, it is not fixed or mandatory. Both patient and client can show their gratitude with whatever offering, gift, or money they chose to dedicate.

Healer and diviner, patient and client—though for the latter it seems of less significance—should observe similar ethical rules such as abstaining from

PREFACE   XIX

alcoholic drinks and sexual intercourse, especially before an examination. For
the best results, both techniques require the right timing: the best time for a
pulse diagnosis is early morning, and likewise the texts recommend, for example, that the best time for an examination of land or a *mo*-divination is also the
morning.

A healer's or diviner's activity may be broken down into the following four
steps:

- examination of the current status: for example through pulse diagnosis (for
  a healer) or examination of a piece of land (for a geomantic diviner)
- interpretation, analyses, and diagnosis of the current status quality based on
  this examination
- prognostication of the future
- prescription, which might involve medical treatment and/or a ritual.[10]

7   Oracles and Prophets

The correlation between medicine and prognostication is also apparent in the
similar activities of oracles, prophets, and shamans whose terms and functions
are hard to differentiate. One of the best-known examples of the Tibetan culture of prediction is the Tibetan state oracle, which has a very high status. These
"public services" are not unique to Buddhism but are also found in Bon.[11]

The prediction of an oracle is based on the idea that a deity—in the case of
the state oracle the deity Pehar—uses a person's body as a medium (*lus g.yar*)
and speaks through it. During his performance, the Tibetan state oracle (as do
many other oracles) wears ceremonial regalia which include a helmet and a
mirror. The state oracle is employed by the government and consulted for state
affairs and at times of war.[12] The Fourteenth Dalai Lama even consulted the
state oracle before his flight from Tibet. Even though he himself did a *mo* divination that indicated he should stay, he nevertheless left when the state oracle
told him to go.

The terminology applied is manifold and depends on the oracles' status: the
state oracle of gNas chung is called *sku rten pa*, "the one whose body serves as
support", and *chos rje*, "master of dharma". This oracle is usually a monk with a
certain training.

---

10   Samten G. Karmay, *The Appearance of the Little Black-headed Man*, 246.
11   See Kvaerne in this volume.
12   Nebesky-Wojkowitz, René de. *Oracles and Demons of Tibet*. The Cult and Iconography of
      the Tibetan Protective Deities (The Hague: Mouton & Co, 1956), 410.

Other terms are *lus khog* or *sku khog, lha bka', lha pa* and *lha 'bab* (*mkhan*). The term *lha pa* is also applied for shamans. Important oracles in Tibet—such as the oracles of gNas chung, dGa' gdong, and lHa mo chos skyong—are usually male. Other important oracles acknowledged by the Tibetan government could be male or female.[13] One of the important female oracles, for example, was the 'Bras spungs rten ma, an official of the fourth rank (*rim bzhi*) in the Tibetan government, who was allowed to practice in the temple of 'Bras spungs and the residence of the Dalai Lama. An oracle's prognostication is similar to the utterance of a prophet (*lung bstan mkhan*): oracle and prophet predict the future. Their prediction is based on intuitive knowledge. As for the oracle, the knowledge can be supplied by a deity, the prophet's knowledge is based on insight. Both their predictions can concern any sphere of life.

8   Final Remarks and Acknowledgements

This short survey is not meant to present a survey on the current studies on divination. The volume on Tibetan prognostication itself is not intended as a complete survey of all techniques, as this would involve too many factors that cannot be dealt with here. However, the articles do show the diversity and multi-cultural influences on divination in Tibet. The anthropological view presented here is based on my observations and experiences while staying in Tibetan communities and living with Tibetan families.

I will therefore take the opportunity to thank all those who accompanied me while studying these subjects. I owe special thanks to the Tibetan traditional healers of horses and humans, and the many diviners in India, Nepal, China, and Tibet who took their time to share their knowledge with me. I also wish to thank those who allowed me to observe their treatments as well as those who diagnosed and treated me or performed a *mo, phya* or *rtsis* divination on my behalf. I thank them for their patience in listening to my questions and enabling the philological work. Their knowing guided me through the process of understanding and translating the texts. And their not-knowing was sometimes a great relief and kept me going by relieving the frustrations of my own ignorance.

Special thanks are due to the late Dunchu Sonam Dorje of the Medical-Astrological-Institute in Dharamsala, who lost his life too early. He shared his

---

13   For a study of modern female oracles, see Hildegard Diemberger. Female Oracles in Modern Tibet, in *Women in Tibet*, eds. Janet Gyatso and Hanna Havnevik (London: Hurst and Company, 2005), 113–168.

PREFACE

immense knowledge on the Tibetan techniques of Chinese calculation. He was kind enough to tell me only after several months that I had upset him by asking too many questions, because as his student he had expected me to listen and not to ask.

Furthermore, I would like to thank Dieter Schuh, who was my main teacher in Tibetan Studies, for sharing his extraordinary knowledge in practically all fields, including his language skills. Guiding me over many years, he was an excellent and patient teacher. It was he who introduced me to horse medicine and Chinese calculation. His philological expertise helped me to persevere with difficult material, while his vast understanding of traditional mathematics helped me to gain an insight into the Chinese calculation methods preserved in Tibet.

I would like to thank the IKGF in Erlangen for offering me a fellowship in 2017, which allowed me to leave my daily routine of the "Tibetisches Wörter-buch" at the Bavarian Academy of Sciences and Humanities for some time and dedicate my time to this very interesting field of Tibetan Studies.

Finally, I would particularly like to express my special thanks to my two co-editors Donatella Rossi und Rolf Scheuermann. Without their contributions, this volume would not have been completed.

Petra Maurer
Munich, February 2019

Background History of the Volume

A few years ago, the Director of the IsIAO Library, Prof. Francesco D'Arelli, and Prof. Elena De Rossi Filibeck, supervisor of the Giuseppe Tucci Tibetan Fund,[1] invited me to take care of the Bon volumes included in the Fund. A specific interest in divination was elicited by the contents of a miscellaneous volume (no. 514 in the *Catalogue*) featuring a conspicuous number of topics linked to divination, such as prophetic visions, dream visions, dream dialogues, prophetic encounters, and so on.[2]

Apart from the intrinsic value of the texts subsumed under Vol. 514, the fact that the seventy eight Bon volumes of the Fund represent an important *locus* of research became even more apparent; they would also benefit from a more contextualized and in-depth cataloguing as well as digitalization, given the age of the manuscripts. These issues were brought up during the conference held at the School of Oriental and African Studies of the University of London in 2011.[3] On that occasion, I also presented a letter written by the XXXIII Abbot of (New) Menri Monastery, the late Ven. Lungtok Tenpai Nyima (Lung rtogs bsTan pa'i Nyi ma, 1929–2017),[4] encouraging the implementation of a corresponding project. However, in 2012, the Institute and its Library were shut down due to administrative reasons. After a long period of quiescence and total inaccessibility, the entire ex IsIAO Library was incorporated in the Italian National Library's asset (2017);[5] hopefully, it will soon be available to interested scholars.

---

1 See her *Catalogue of the Tucci Tibetan Fund in the Library of IsIAO*, 2 vols. (Rome: Istituto Italiano per l'Africa e l'Oriente, 2003). The Fund contains more than 2500 manuscripts collected by Giuseppe Tucci during four expeditions, two in Western Tibet (1933 and 1935) and two in Central Tibet (1937 and 1948).

2 Cfr. D. Rossi "A Brief Note on the Bonpo Texts of the Giuseppe Tucci Fund Preserved at the Library of IsIAO", in *Bon. The Everlasting Religion of Tibet. Tibetan Studies in Honour of Professor David L. Snellgrove. Papers Presented at the International Conference on Bon 22–27 June 2008, Shenten Dargye Ling, Château de la Modetais, Blou, France, New Horizons of Bon Studies 2*, eds. Samten Gyaltsen Karmay and Donatella Rossi (*East and West*, 59, 1–4, 2009), 337–345.

3 *Bon, Shangshung, and Early Tibet. An International Conference Celebrating 60 Years of Tibetan Studies at SOAS, 50 Years of Bonpo Studies in the West, and the Founding of the London Shangshung Institute for Tibetan Studies, 9–10 September 2011*.

4 For his biography up to 1994 see Bya 'phur Nam mkha' rGyal mtshan, *Bon gyi gong sa chen po skyabs rje lung rtogs bstan pa'i nyi ma dpal bzang po'i rnam par thar pa kun bzang dgyes pa'i mchod sprin* (Dolanji HP: Kyongtul Tenzin Namgyal, Bon Monastic Centre, 1994). A full hagiography under the coordination of Geshe Nyima Woser Choe-khorTshang is in the making.

5 http://www.bncrm.beniculturali.it/ last accessed 01/04/2019.

In 2014, thanks to the remarkable mission of the International Consortium for Research in the Humanities (IKGF), it was possible for me to spend one year in Erlangen (March 2014-February 2015). One of the aims consisted in the preliminary study of the monumental divination work compiled in 1885 by the distinguished scholar Mi pham (Mi pham 'Jam dbyangs rNam rgyal rGya mtsho, 1846–1912), titled *Srid pa 'phrul gyi ju thig gi dpyad don snang gsal sgron me*,[6] which revealed how complex and interdisciplinary the ancient *Ju thig* divination system is; it also raised questions, among others, concerning the semiotics and semantics of divination, the ethical role of the diviner, and so on.[7]

During that timeframe, Prof. Michael Lackner proposed the visit of a Tibetan *Ju thig* divination expert. The choice indisputably fell upon Ven. Menri Ponlop Trinley Nyima (sMan ri dPon slob 'Phrin las Nyi ma, Dolpo, 1962). During his brief yet intense stay, we organized (1) a reading session for the Consortium fellows introducing the *Ju thig* system and its techniques, with particular reference to the abridged form based on the use of consecrated pebbles;[8] (2) a public event held at the IKGF premises on a general introduction to Tibetan astrology and mantic praxes, followed by the construction of a multi-colored apotropaic structure (*gtor ma*) for balancing the elements of the area; (3) a public lecture at the Erlangen-Nürnberg University on a *Brief Introduction to Bon and its Worldview* (*Bon gyi skor la ngo sprod mdor bsdus*),[9] which included the performance of a purification and offering ritual (*gCod*); (4) an interview, during which he explained the origin and traditions of the *Ju thig* divination system, the abridged form mentioned above as well as the most peculiar one involving the use of ropes, the special manufacturing of the latter, and the liturgy and ceremony connected to that system. He also performed a live *Ju thig* divination using the ropes. The whole interview was filmed, translated into English, and subtitled. It can be directly viewed on the IKGF website.[10] (5) We also

---

6   Ed. Sonam Topgay Kazi (Sikkim, Gangtok, 1974), 849 *folia*.

7   Cfr. D. Rossi "Alcune Riflessioni sull'Interrelazione fra la Semantica e la Divinazione", in *From Bhakti to Bon. Festschrift for Per Kværne*, eds. Hanna Havnevik and Charles Ramble (Oslo: The Institute for Comparative Research in Human Culture, Novus Press, 2015), 449–462.

8   The text of reference is titled *Ma sangs 'phrul gyi rdel mo mngon shes rno gsal gyi sgron me zhes bya ba bzhugs pa legs so*. Ven. Ponlop Trinley Nyima was gracious enough to allow the xeroxing of his personal manuscript, a copy of which is deposited at the IKGF Library.

9   Simultaneously translated by Dr. Rolf Scheuermann.

10   http://www.ikgf.uni-erlangen.de/videos/documentaries/, *Practice of Divination: The Tibetan Zhang Zhung Ju thig Divination System* (2014), length: 38min 43 sec.

worked together on a introductory reading and translation of the Dunhuang divination text known as Pelliot Tibétain 1047.[11]

After the visit of Ven. Menri Ponlop, I convened a workshop on divination upon Prof. Lackner's request (December 2–3, 2014). The workshop was titled *Divination in Tibet and Mongolia. Past and Present.* The discussion group featured nine participants: Agata Bareja-Starzyńska, Per Kværne, Dan Martin, Petra Maurer, Charles Ramble, Donatella Rossi, Mona Schrempf, Dieter Schuh, Alexander K. Smith. The workshop was the first of its kind. It was aimed at establishing a blueprint for a trans-disciplinary and cross cultural discourse on the nature and history of divination in Tibet and Mongolia. Later on, Prof. Petra Maurer (IKGF Fellow, 2017) and myself decided to take the matter further and convened a Tibetan Divination Panel at the XIV IATS Seminar (2016) featuring six participants: Agata Bareja-Starzyńska, Petra Maurer, Eric Mortensen, Ai Nishida, Donatella Rossi, Rolf Scheuermann, Alexander K. Smith (IKGF Fellow, 2017–2018).

The finalized articles herein contained represent a collection of the topics dealt with and discussed during the above-mentioned events, with the addition of an article by Prof. Brandon Dotson (IKGF Fellow, 2015–2016 and 2017). It is hoped that they will contribute to kindle interest in the subject-matter and fuel further research studies that may lead to the identification and assessment of a 'cultural history' of the Tibetan mantic tradition in its vast and polyhedral declinations.

Gratefulness is expressed to Prof. Michael Lackner for his solicitude and to the IKGF Editorial Board for having endorsed the publication of this Volume in the distinguished IKGF Brill Series *Prognostication in History*; to the IKGF Administrative Coordinator Frau Petra Hahm and to the staff for their outstanding support; and to the co-editors for their always stimulating input and learned insight.

Donatella Rossi
Roma, February 2019

---

11   Cf. Ariane Macdonald-Spanien, "Une lecture des Pelliot Tibétain 1286, 1287, 1038, 1047, et 1290. Essai sur la formation et l'emploi des mythes politiques dans la religion royale de Sroṅ-bcan sgam-po", in *Études Tibétaines dédiées à la mémoire de Marcelle Lalou* (Paris: Adrien Maisonneuve, 1971), 190–391.

On the Contributions Contained in This Volume

Prognostication responds to a need for orientation concerning the uncertainties of the past, present or future and there are numerous witnesses of techniques designed to support individuals in their decision-making processes throughout the history of humankind. The Tibetan repertoire of divinatory techniques is also rich and immensely varied. Accordingly, the specimen of practices discussed in this volume—many of which are still in use today—merely serve as examples that offer glimpses of divination in Tibet.

As previously mentioned, almost all of the contributions contained in this volume are based on papers presented during one of two individual academic events: (1) the contributions by Per Kværne, Dan Martin, Petra Maurer, Charles Ramble, and Alexander K. Smith result from papers presented during the international workshop entitled "Divination in Tibet and Mongolia. Past and Present" at the International Consortium for Research in the Humanities, Erlangen, December 2–3, 2014, convened by Donatella Rossi; (2) the contributions by Agata Bareja-Starzyńska, Ai Nishida, Donatella Rossi, and Rolf Scheuermann evolved from papers presented during the follow-up panel entitled "Tibetan Divination" at the fourteenth seminar of the International Association for Tibetan Studies, Bergen, June 22, 2016, convened by Petra Maurer and Donatella Rossi. The only exception is the article by Brandon Dotson who was invited to contribute to this volume during his fellowship at the International Consortium for Research in the Humanities in Erlangen in 2015/16.

The first essay, by **Per Kværne**, examines an early prophecy by the Bon priest Dran pa Nam mkha' which is said to have occurred in the eighth century. This prognostication is recorded in the anonymous *Grags pa gling grags* of the twelfth or thirteenth century and foretells the negative consequences that would result from the Tibetan emperor Khri srong lDe btsan's decision to favor Buddhism over the Bon religion. Based on a cross-cultural examination of the concept of the "prophet", Kværne discusses this notion in the context of a Tibetan case study, which shares some similarities with the eschatological narrative of Maitreya in the sense that it depicts a general religious and political deterioration and the future coming of Dran pa Nam mkha'.

Another form of divination popular in Tibet that involves the interpretation of patterns is dice divination, which is the focus of **Brandon Dotson**'s contribution. After investigating the material culture of dice divination by exploring the *paśaka* dice used in Tibet during the eighth to tenth centuries, it examines the specific procedures of the practices and the organization of divination manuals during this period. In doing so, this paper centers primarily on numerical considerations of the material, procedures and *omina*, including a comparative perspective that regards possible transfers and cross-contacts with related practices of the neighboring cultural spheres, which allows us to gain a better understanding of these early forms of dice divination practiced in Tibet.

Ai Nishida's contribution is also devoted to the topic of early dice divination and concentrates primarily on an in-depth textual study of Dunhuang and Silk Road materials. The paper identifies and describes twenty-three dice divination manuals, for which it offers a typology based on the characteristics of the texts, such as their structure and the composition of omens. In this way, the study provides fresh insights into the process of the text production of early Tibetan dice divination manuals, suggesting that these were prepared in two consecutive phases and involved the co-production of a group of diviners.

The following paper, by **Dan Martin**, investigates four divination practices attributed to the eleventh-century South Indian luminary Pha dam pa Sang rgyas, who is said to have visited Tibet on several occasions. This contribution tackles the question of to what degree it is appropriate to associate these four practices, which all interpret patterns using particular objects (five finger divination, arrow divination, stone divination, and Tibetan rosary divination) with the Indian master. The four techniques described in their respective manuals are compared with the literary accounts describing Pha dam pa practicing divination during his lifetime, which suggests that the techniques attributed to him do not correspond to the divinations that he is known to have practiced.

Petra Maurer explores *sa dpyad* or Tibetan geomancy, a form of divination that involves a combination of several techniques that are used to examine naturally existing patterns in the landscape in order to determine the suitable site for construction. Following a comprehensive introduction to the Tibetan *sa dpyad* tradition, that includes a comparative perspective, the essay concentrates particularly on temporal concepts, that play a major role in the decision-making process. Thus, it demonstrates that *sa dpyad* reflects a complex and heterogeneous set of techniques, in which various notions and dimensions of time and location are harmonized to specify the optimum time and location for an event or construction.

The contribution by **Charles Ramble** begins with an overview of the ancient *ju thig* divination of the Bon tradition that is performed with ropes (or pebbles), but also discusses a number of further techniques found in Bon and Buddhist sources that examine naturally occurring patterns, such as the examination of dreams, signs that indicate future rebirths, portents of death, rainbows, loud noises and miscellaneous signs. With the aid of these examples, it investigates the underlying forces of cause and effect that are considered to manifest themselves through the signs.

A further essay that deals with the examination of signs is a study by **Donatella Rossi**, which introduces the *gSal byed byang bu*, an undated and anonymous oneiromantic manual that is contained in a collection of Bon treatises preserved in the Giuseppe Tucci Fund. In addition to a first Tibetan edition and English translation, it offers a close examination of the work's content and assesses its role within the larger framework of the Bon religious discourse in general, and divination practice in particular.

The next contribution, by **Rolf Scheuermann**, is also devoted to an oneiromantic text, the *Svapnohana (rMi lam brtag pa*, Tôh. no. 1749) by Vibhūticandra, an Indian Buddhist master of the twelfth to thirteenth centuries. Through an examination of the signs described in this work, it demonstrates that the *Svapnohana* firmly stands in an Indian tradition of oneiromantic texts which, even though contained in the Tibetan bsTan 'gyur, may not specifically qualify as 'Buddhist.'

Alexander K. Smith deals with the large group of cleromantic practices common in Tibet. They involve techniques to produce and interpret randomly-generated patterns. The paper introduces several forms of cleromancy on the basis of the recent Anthropological and Tibetological literature in the field and discusses the structure of prognostics involved in a particular form of lithomancy or pebble divination practiced in the Tibetan Bon tradition. It concludes with comparative remarks based on textual evidence as well as on information gathered during fieldwork.

The last section, by **Agata Bareja-Starzyńska**, broadens the scope of this volume as it describes the transmission of Tibetan astrological and divinatory techniques to Mongolia. For this endeavor, the activities of the influential seventeenth-century dGe lugs pa scholar Lamyn Gegeen Blo bzang bstan 'dzin rgyal mtshan, who studied in Tibet with several important masters of his time, serves as an example. The paper offers an overview of his life, education and major works on astrology and divination that had an influence on the development of Tibetan astrology and divination in Mongolia.

In sum, this short survey is the first volume that assembles the expertise of a group of eminent scholars in the field to present individual papers that reflect the current state of research regarding numerous issues that deal with traditional forms of prognostication in the Tibetan cultural sphere. As such, it does not claim to be either comprehensive or systematic, but nevertheless brings to light a hitherto relatively understudied area of Tibetan Studies. In this way, it may serve as a starting point for future endeavors that will eventually treat the subject in even greater detail.

Finally, this volume would not have been possible without the support of the International Consortium for Research in the Humanities (IKGF) "Fate, Freedom and Prognostication. Strategies for Coping with the Future in East Asia and Europe" at the Friedrich-Alexander-University Erlangen-Nürnberg, which is funded by the Federal Ministry of Education and Research (BMBF). I would also like to extend my sincere gratitude to my co-editors, Petra Maurer and Donatella Rossi, the directors of the IKGF, Michael Lackner and Klaus Herbers, and the IKGF scholarly community, particularly Petra Hahm and Philipp Hünnebeck who helped to organize the first workshop at Erlangen, as well as Michael Lüdke who guided us through the publication process. Furthermore, I am indebted to Sue Casson and Alanah Marx for meticulously proofreading the manuscript.

Rolf Scheuermann
Erlangen, February 2019

Figures and Tables

Figures

2.1   TibHT 33, a damaged fragment with pips at the head of each oracular response; Depositum der Berlin-Brandenburgischen Akademie der Wissenschaften in der Staatsbibliothek zu Berlin—Preussischer Kulturbesitz Orientabteilung   15

2.2a–b   All four faces of two bone dice from Taxila; after Marshall, *Taxila*, plate 200, nos. 93 and 97   16

2.3   Four *astragaloi* showing all four sides. Photograph by Brandon Dotson   20

2.4   Second of three sets of "wheels" or *lun* used in the system of divination found in the *Zhancha jing* or "Divination *Sūtra*"; photograph by Beverley Foulks McGuire, reproduced with permission   20

5.1   Chinese divination, *thangka* section. The Museum of the Five Continents (previously the Völkerkunde Museum), Munich, reproduced by permission   100

5.2   Schematic exemplification of Figure 5.1, Chinese divination, *thangka* section   101

7.1   Folio 1 (first half, *recto*) of the *gSal byed byang bu*, cm. 60×9. Photograph by Donatella Rossi, gratefully reproduced with permission of the IsIAO President, Prof. Gherardo Gnoli (1937–2012)   142

7.2   Folio 1 (first half, *recto*) of the *gSal byed byang bu*, cm. 60×9. Photograph by Donatella Rossi, gratefully reproduced with permission of the IsIAO President, Prof. Gherardo Gnoli (1937–2012)   143

Tables

3.1   A general list of Old Tibetan dice divination texts   51

3.2   Comparative table of verses, triads, and results   59

3.3   An example of verse contrast   60

Notes on Contributors

Per Kværne

Per Kværne, b. 1945, obtained his MA in Sanskrit from the University of Oslo in 1970. From 1975 he was Professor of History of Religion at the same university until his retirement in 2007. While his doctoral thesis, published in 1977 and reprinted several times, was on the late Indian Buddhist tantric songs of the Caryāgīti, his main field of research has been the Tibetan Bön religion, on which he has published extensively, e.g. *The Bon Religion of Tibet. The Iconography of a Living Tradition*, 1995. He has also published on Western 19th century landscape art ("Singing Songs of the Scotish Heart": William McTaggart 1835–1910, 2007). He is a member of the Norwegian Academy of Science and Letters, Oslo, and the Accademia Ambrosiana, Milano.

Brandon Dotson

Brandon Dotson is an associate professor of Buddhist Studies at Georgetown University. He did his graduate training at Oxford University (2007) and has worked and taught at Oxford, the School of Oriental and African Studies, and Ludwig-Maximilians University of Munich. His most recent books *are Kingship, Ritual, and Narrative in Tibet and the Surrounding Cultural Area* (edited volume, 2015) and *Codicology, Paleography, and Orthography of Early Tibetan Documents* (co-authored with Agnieszka Helman-Ważny, 2016).

Ai Nishida Iwata

Ai Nishida received her BA, MA, and a Ph.D. degree from Kobe City University of Foreign Studies. Having worked as Research Fellow of the Japan Society for the Promotion of Science, she is now a Visiting Fellow of the Kobe City University of Foreign Studies. Her primary field of research is Old Tibetan manuscripts from Dunhuang and East Turkestan.

Dan Martin

Over two and a half decades ago, Dan Martin received a doctoral degree in Tibetan Studies at Indiana University with a dissertation on the Bonpo treasure revealer Shenchen Luga. He is presently semi-retired but still working on two different books and a number of other projects. He is best known for a bio-bibliographical resource called "Tibskrit" made available in digital format only, and under constant revision.

Petra Maurer

Petra Maurer is professor at the Ludwig Maximilians-University in Munich and works at the "Tibetische Wörterbuch" in the Bavarian Academy of Sciences and Humanities. She received her doctoral degree in Tibetan Studies at the Rheinische-Friedrich-Wilhelms-University in Bonn and habilitated in Munich. She teaches Tibetan language, culture and religion at the Ludwig-Maximilians-University in Munich and has taught at Bonn University. Among her major publications are the *Wörterbuch der Tibetischen Schriftsprache*, (co-authored with Johannes Schneider), *Handschriften zur tibetischen Hippiatrie und Hippologie* und *Die Grundlagen der tibetischen Geomantie dargestellt anhand des 32. Kapitels des Vaiḍūrya dkar po* von *sde srid Sangs rgyas rgya mtsho* (1653–1705).

Charles Ramble

Charles Ramble is Directeur d'études (Professor of Tibetan History and Philology) at the École Pratique des Hautes Études, PSL Research University, Paris, a position he has held since 2009, and a member of East Asian Civilisations Research Centre. From 2000 to 2010 he was the Lecturer in Tibetan and Himalayan Studies at the University of Oxford, where he continues to hold a position as University Research Lecturer. His publications include *The Navel of the Demoness: Tibetan Buddhism and Civil Religion in Highland Nepal* (2008), and several volumes in a series entitled *Tibetan Sources for a Social History of Mustang* (2008, 2016, 2017). His research interests include Tibetan social history, Bon, biographical writing, and Tibetan ritual literature and performance.

Donatella Rossi

Donatella Rossi is Chair of Religions and Philosophies of East Asia and of Tibetan Language and Culture at the Department of Oriental Studies, Faculty of Letters and Philosophy, Sapienza University of Rome, and Research Partner of the International Consortium for Research in the Humanities of the University of Erlangen-Nuremberg (IKGF). Her research interests are focused on the Bon religion.

Rolf Scheuermann

Having earned a doctorate in Tibetan and Buddhist Studies from the University of Vienna (2016), Rolf Scheuermann currently works as a Research Coordinator at the International Consortium for Research in the Humanities "Fate Freedom and Prognostication," University of Erlangen-Nuremberg. From 2017–2018, he substituted the Professor of Central Asian Studies at the Department of Indology and Central Asian Studies, University of Leipzig. His research centers mainly on Tibetan Buddhist philosophy and religion, particularly in the context of the early bKa' brgyud tradition.

Alexander K. Smith

After finishing a BA in Western Philosophy and Religious Studies at American University (Washington, D.C.), Alexander developed an interest in Tibetan linguistics, religion, and culture. This led him to apply and be accepted to the Faculty of Oriental Studies at Oxford University, where he completed an MPhil in Tibetan Studies. Having focused on Classical and Modern Tibetan, he then pursued a Ph.D. at the École Pratique des Hautes Études (EPHE, Paris), where he specialized in the study of Bon ritual and divinatory manuscripts. At the moment, he is a visiting research fellow at the Internationales Kolleg für Geisteswissenschaftliche Forschung (Friedrich-Alexander-Universität, Erlangen-Nüremburg).

Agata Bareja-Starzynska

Agata Bareja-Starzyńska, Dr. Habil. Mongolist and Tibetologist, Head of the Department of Turkish Studies and Inner Asian Peoples of the Faculty of Oriental Studies at the University of Warsaw, Poland. Her scholarly interests focus on Buddhism in Mongolia and Tibet, Mongolian-Tibetan relations, Mongolian and Tibetan Buddhist literature. Her publications include Polish translation of the *Ciqula kereglegci*, a 16th Century Mongolian Buddhist Treatise (Warsaw 2006), co-edition of Mongolia related materials kept in Prof. W. Kotwicz's Archives in Poland (*In the Heart of Mongolia*, Cracow 2012) and *The Biography of the First Khalkha Jetsundampa Zanabazar by Zaya Pandita Luvsanprinlei. Studies, Annotated Translation, Transliteration and Facsimile* (Warsaw 2015).

CHAPTER 1

A Case of Prophecy in Post-imperial Tibet

Per Kværne

Their tongue is as an arrow shot out; it speaketh deceit; one speaketh peaceably to his neighbour with his mouth, but in heart he layeth his wait. Shall I not visit them for these things? saith the Lord: shall not my soul be avenged on such a nation as this? For the mountains will I take up a weeping and wailing, and for the habitations of the wilderness a lamentation, because they are burned up, so that none can pass through them; neither can men hear the voice of the cattle; both the fowl of the heavens and the beast are fled; they are gone. And I will make Jerusalem heaps, and a den of dragons; and I will make the cities of Judah desolate, without an inhabitant. [...] Therefore thus saith the Lord of hosts, the God of Israel; Behold, I will feed them, even this people, with wormwood, and give them water of gall to drink. I will scatter them also among the heathen [...] and I will send a sword after them, till I have consumed them.[1]

Speaking in the seventh century BCE, the prophet Jeremiah castigated his contemporaries, or, according to Jewish and Christian belief, God castigated and warned His faithless people through the prophet Jeremiah. Jeremiah is an archetypal prophet, pitilessly lashing out, as God's mouthpiece, at the sin and faithlessness of his fellow Israelites.

While the present focus is Tibet, we might still start by asking: what, in fact, is a prophet? And, following from that: is it appropriate to use this term with regard to a particular person, whether historical or otherwise, in Tibet?

"The Greek term *pro-phêtês* was a cultic functionary who 'spoke for' a god; that is [...] he delivered divine messages in association with a sanctuary where the god had made its presence known."[2] The term was taken up by Christian translators of the Hebrew Bible to refer to various Israelite religious specialists and has thus become a central concept in the Christian tradition. With the development of Comparative Religion as a field of systematic research, the term 'prophet' was extended to include various founders of religions in the Mid-

---

1 Jeremiah, 9: 8–11, 15–16; King James the Sixth translation of the Bible (1611).
2 Sheppard and Herbrechtsmeier, "Prophecy," 8.

dle East and Western Asia, such as Jesus and Mohammed, but also Zarathushtra (at least as conceived by the later Zoroastrian tradition) and Mani, thus establishing what one might call the classic image of a prophet. One attempt (among others) to define a prophet in this sense singles out five defining features:

1. "They all conceived of their activity as the result of a personal divine commission."
2. Some of the pronouncements of these prophets were regarded as "uniquely heaven-sent, sacred, and binding upon people in perpetuity."
3. These pronouncements were regarded by later tradition as universal truths.
4. Prophets were social critics.
5. "Prophets helped both to maintain and to reform religious tradition."[3]

It could be added that some of them, for example, Mani and Mohammed, "understood themselves explicitly as successors to a line of prophets."[4]

This 'classic' image of prophets was subsequently extended to include more recent founders of religion, such as Joseph Smith, who founded the Church of Latter-Days Saints, or modern leaders of various Pentecostal and charismatic movements "who consider themselves capable of receiving the spirit and speaking as divine agents."[5] Finally, Western imperialism has had an impact on numerous indigenous cultures in Africa, the Americas, and the Pacific region, giving rise to movements of revivalism and nativism, generally initiated and led by charismatic individuals, sometimes closely resembling, or even inspired by, the more classic prophets. Examples of such movements are the ghost dance among Native Americans, the cargo cults in Melanesia, and the Iglesia ni Cristo (Church of Christ) in the Philippines.

Modern prophets have been studied by anthropologists and comparative religionists, resulting in an understanding of prophets as individuals who express the interests and concerns of their communities, rather than the somewhat romantic ideal of "individualists crying to deaf ears from the loneliness of the desert."[6]

Turning to the topic of this paper, we shall focus on twelfth and thirteenth-century Tibet, more specifically the Bon (*bon*) religion at that time. Just a few words to recapitulate the setting: After the collapse of the Tibetan Empire in the ninth century CE, a religious tradition arose known as Bon in opposition to Buddhism which was consolidating its position in Tibetan society. The term

---

3 Ibid., 9–10.
4 Ibid., 11.
5 Ibid., 13.
6 Ibid., 13.

bon, well documented in the period of the Tibetan Empire as a term for various types of ritual experts, now came to designate a coherent, although constantly developing religion, heavily influenced by, yet distinct from Buddhism. Often referred to as "Eternal Bon" (*g.yung drung bon*) by its adherents, it has survived in Tibet as well as in exile until today.

I shall single out an episode from a Bon text that according to Anne-Marie Blondeau[7] probably dates from the late twelfth or possibly the early thirteenth century. This text, which is still unpublished in a Western edition, will be referred to by its short title, *Grags pa gling grags* (the exact significance of which has not yet been precisely determined).[8] While covering a wide range of cosmological and mythological topics, the second half of the text focuses on a personage, Dran pa Nam mkha', regarded by the "Eternal Bon" tradition as one of its most important representatives during the reign of the Tibetan emperor Khri srong lDe btsan (742–c. 800 CE), a firm supporter of Buddhism.

After being unsuccessful in his efforts to persuade the emperor to continue to adhere to Bon, the religion of his ancestors, Dran pa Nam mkha', so the *Grags pa gling grags* maintains, accepts Buddhism, the new faith introduced from India, although in a gesture of defiance he insists—in the manner, as he says, of former Buddhas—on ordaining himself. While the other Bon priests are given the choice—should they refuse to change their religion—between exile or death, Dran pa Nam mkha' chooses to become a Buddhist and to remain in Tibet, but at the same time he utters a prophecy (*lung bstan*) outlining the dire consequences of the emperor's evil policy. He does so, however, only because the emperor himself asks about the consequences of his actions:

> O sovereign king, listen well!
> Because the true (Doctrine of) Supernatural Speech [i.e. Bon] has been
>   suppressed,
> retribution will appear both in this life and in the future.
> At this (present) time, the life-span (*sku tshe*) of the lord will be short
> and the ministers will have narrow thoughts.
> The life-span of the princes will be short
> and they will not dwell in the center (of Tibet).
> One (or the other) saying,
> 'I shall assume the position of king (*rgyal sa*)',

---

7 Blondeau, "Identification de la tradition."
8 The Tibetan text, based on four manuscripts, together with a complete translation, will be published together with a full translation of the *Grags pa gling grags*.

the (royal) order (*bka'*) will have no authority
and will be dispersed like leaves of a tree.
The queens, too, will be unfaithful,
and step over the bodies (of their husbands).
The monks will be without shame
and internal strife will arise.
The inhabitants of Tibet will break the laws and scoff at their lord.
Here in Tibet there will be many manifestations of demons (*bdud kyi
sprul pa*).

Dran pa Nam mkha' goes on to outline the disastrous consequences which the suppression of Bon will have for Tibetan society, and especially for Buddhism:

Even the king's own descendants (*gdung rgyud*)
will be scattered like stars all over the earth.
Lords and subjects will be mixed,
evil people will assume the appearance (*cha lugs*) of kings.
At that time, many demons of disease (*ngams kyi 'dre*)
will cause great suffering to people.
As for the retribution that will befall the monks,
they will be greater than (those afflicting) the lord's own lineage:
ordained monks will not adhere to the Discipline (*khrims*),
'senior monks' (*gnas bstan*) will be generals.
Not staying in caves and hermitages,
they will enclose the monasteries with fortifications;
fighting among themselves,
they will destroy the doctrine of the Buddha.

We note that the picture presented here is far from that of eighth century Tibet. Instead—and allowing for the inevitable exaggerations—it reflects a later situation where Buddhist monasteries were rapidly increasing their economic and political power and at the same time were engaged in bitter conflicts. Dran pa Nam mkha' goes on to describe the moral degeneration of the Buddhist monks:

The monks (*btsun pa*) will take wives
and challenge the king [...].
All the tantric adepts (*sngags pa*)
will contend with each other in magic,
and become village priests (*grong chog/phyog(s) mkhan po*).
The armies of the border peoples

will issue forth like the autumn harvest;
the inhabitants of Tibet will be oppressed and enslaved [...].
Monks will consort with women,
women will be covered by skins and prepare beer (*skyo chu*).
At that time, many manifestations of female demons will appear.

Skipping parts of this long prophecy, we shall see what final catastrophes are in store for Tibet. Again we note that the collapse of monastic discipline and the subsequent implosion of the fabric of society are at the center of concern:

Thereafter, after seventeen royal generations,
people from (beyond) the borders will look towards Tibet.
At the time when the span of life will be only fifty years,
the inhabitants of Tibet will act just as they like.
Thereafter, after nineteen generations,
a demon of disease will come from China to Tibet;
it will enter the hearts of monks (*btsun pa*), women, and laymen (*skye bo*):
the monks will take pride in their appearance,
women will run after men, laymen will put on yellow robes.
As a sign of the spirit of disease,
they will put on sleeves
which are not in accordance with (clerical) robes,
they will don grey hats [...].
The land will be filled with monastic estates (*sa gzhi gnas gzhi*) (numerous) like the stars (of the sky).
At that time, few monks will adhere to (monastic) law,
tantric adepts who keep their vows will be difficult to find,
laymen who have a sense of shame will be rare.

Finally, the very earth itself will be overwhelmed by disasters:

At that time, the time of a demon of disease will come to Tibet;
from the east to the west a glow of fire will appear.
As a sign of the sap of the earth escaping to the hills, earthquakes will occur.
The essence of the grain will gradually diminish;
as a sign of the harvest diminishing,
one's own fields will be established as monastic lands (*gnas gzhi*).

From the east, a red glow of flames will fill one half of the sky.
There will be illness (*nad*) among people
and disease (*yams*) among cattle,
(so that) about one half will perish.

True, Dran pa Nam mkha' does not speak on behalf of a deity. He speaks on his own behalf—or rather, he speaks with the confidence that comes from having understood certain moral laws that are, if anything, as unalterable as natural laws. Nevertheless, the insistency, indeed the passion of his words, justifies, in my opinion, characterizing him as a prophet.

At this point, I would like to make two side remarks, which cannot, however, be further developed here. The first is that it might perhaps be worthwhile to compare Dran pa Nam mkha's prophecy with the ordinance (*bka' shog*) of the king of Pu hrangs, *lha bla ma* Ye shes 'od, discussed by Samten G. Karmay.[9] Although this document is only attested in full in a late sixteenth to early seventeenth-century source,[10] it may well go back, at least in substance, to the late tenth or early eleventh century.

My second remark concerns Dan Martin's article, "The Star King and the Four Children of Pehar: Popular Religious Movements of 11th- to 12th-century Tibet."[11] Whether the religious milieus discussed in these two articles were characterized by prophecy, is an open question. Both articles, however, deal with milieus that were outside the monastic and politically ascendant institutions, in other words outside the centers of power which in the eleventh and twelfth centuries were beginning the process of constructing what might be called the 'mainstream' narrative of Tibetan history, a narrative that is still accepted by most Tibetans today.

It may be useful at this point to consider some of the anthropological work that is relevant to the phenomenon of prophecy. A basic work in this regard is Ioan M. Lewis' *Ecstatic Religion* (1971). Although Lewis does not deal explicitly with prophecy, the basic idea of this work is that "ecstatic religious behavior is a means of expression used by disenfranchised groups who find standard channels of communication closed to them."[12] The same may surely be said about prophets, many of whom, down through the ages, have been said to have

---

9   Karmay, "The Ordinance". This text, too, attacks "village abbots" (*grong gi mkhan po*), and the entire message of karmic retribution for deviant and degenerate practices is quite similar to the diatribes of Dran pa Nam mkha'.

10   Ibid., 151.

11   Martin, "The Star King."

12   Sheppard and Herbrechtsmeier, "Prophecy," 13.

spoken in a state of ecstasy, as evidenced, among innumerable examples, by the *Revelation of Saint John* or by Mohammed receiving the *Quran* through an angel.

Dran pa Nam mkha' shows no sign of being a religious ecstatic, but insofar as he is a literary mouthpiece for a thirteenth-century Bon author or milieu, his warnings and diatribes would make sense as the expression of the frustration of a religious group that by that time was in the process of becoming increasingly disenfranchised and marginalized, at least in Central and Western Tibet.

Other anthropologists, among them Victor Turner,[13] "see prophets as appearing in periods of transition between societies organized along lines of kinship and clan affiliation and those structured according to more highly complex groupings that accompany the rise of states."[14] In Tibet the thirteenth century could certainly be seen as such a period of transition. Whatever its antecedents as an imperial court religion in the seventh to ninth centuries may have been, the Bon religion in the thirteenth century was intimately connected with certain clans whose power was limited to specific localities, their religious institutions generally being no more than small chapels or hermitages, whereas it could be argued that the dominant trend in Buddhism in Tibet at that time was for more influential clans to be allied with, or even to work through, powerful monasteries evolving in the direction of state-like polities. A case in point would be the 'Khon clan and the Sa skya monastery which was under its control.

In other words, leaving on one side the question of the historicity of Dran pa Nam mkha', I suggest that we should see the prophetic utterances ascribed to him in the *Grags pa gling grags* as expressions of the frustration that its (anonymous) author may have felt at the slow but inevitable marginalization of the Bon religion in the thirteenth century, viewed as all the more intolerable when compared to what was claimed (rightly or wrongly) to have been its flourishing condition as the unchallenged court religion during most of the Tibetan Empire. So while Buddhists were busy in the thirteenth century constructing a Tibetan national history in which the coming of Buddhism was regarded as the turning point in the history of Tibet, bringing with it not only spiritual riches, but also all sorts of other social and material benefits, the Bonpos were at the same time producing their own historical narrative, according to which the introduction of Buddhism was a catastrophe and the emperors' abandoning

---

13   Turner, "Religious Specialists."
14   Sheppard and Herbrechtsmeier, 13.

their ancestral religion, that is Bon, led to the political and spiritual collapse of Tibet—a narrative that was diametrically opposed to that construed by Buddhists.[15]

Yet at the end of day the Bonpos must have understood that Buddhism had come to stay, and that there could be no revival of the ancient empire, nor a Bon restoration. An indication of this is the conciliatory note that Dran pa Nam mkha' strikes with regard to an ideal vision of Buddhism, as opposed to the perceived laxness and immorality of contemporary Buddhist monks. This is evident in his advice to the Emperor as to how the disastrous effects of the latter's actions could to some extent be mitigated:

> Enforce the royal laws (*rgyal khrims*) with authority!
> All the monks (*btsun pa*) must carefully observe the monastic discipline (*'dul khrims*)!
> All the laymen (*skye bo*) must show modesty and shame!
> Establish (a ban on) hunting in mountains and valleys!
> Proclaim the supreme message (*gsung rab*) of the profound Transmitted Word!
> Expel the many demons of disease (*ngams kyi 'dre*) by means of rituals!
> Bring offerings to the *klu* who live below the ground!
> Then there will be to some extent a happy year, a happy month,
> and the doctrine of Dharma (*chos*) will not disappear.

However, while decline will, in the end, still be inevitable, there is hope at a point of time in the distant future—if not for everyone, at least for the chosen few. Dran pa Nam mkha' himself will go into hiding, but in due course, an emanation will appear among the barbarian populations (*mtha' 'khob*) at the borders of Tibet. This emanation will be neither Bonpo nor Buddhist, thus abolishing all religious strife:

> When the time is ripe for my Doctrine,
> although remaining hidden,
> I shall send forth a non-hidden emanation.

---

15 The "decline narrative" in literary sources dating from the early centuries of Buddhism in Tibet has been discussed at some length by Doney, *Transforming Tibetan Kingship*, especially pp. 157 et seq. To explore the intertextuality of the Buddhist and Bon sources with regard to such narratives, projected back to the Imperial period in Tibet, would be a useful task for future research.

> 3 139 years from now my emanation will appear
> in the land of the border barbarians (*mtha' 'khob yul*),
> who will understand the teachings of Bon.
> He will have great wisdom, but few worldly interests;
> he will be neither Buddhist monk,
> nor Bonpo, nor layman (*ban min bon min skye'o min*),
> but have the appearance of a madman (*snyon pa'i cha byad*).

Finally, Dran pa Nam mkha' himself will come out of hiding, although he will not be seen by one and all:

> I, Dran pa, will not go beyond suffering,
> having obtained the supernatural power of (prolonging) life.
> Wandering about in the world,
> I shall bless the fortunate ones.
> Examining and secretly observing the fortunate ones,
> I shall give instruction.

As a redeemer destined to appear in the future, Dran pa Nam mkha' is different from the Buddhist idea of Maitreya, the coming Buddha. Maitreya will descend into a womb, to be born in this world when the present process of degeneration has run its course and a new golden age has dawned. He will then proclaim the eternal Dharma to one and all, in the same way as innumerable former Buddhas. In the *Grags pa gling grags*, however, we are dealing with a different concept, namely that of a teacher who has achieved the power to prolong his life, and eventually will wander about, unseen by the crowd. He is a redeemer who will not be recognized by humanity at large, but only by the few whom he identifies in secret, and teaches and blesses in secret. On a strictly comparative as opposed to historical basis, one can see similarities to certain aspects of mythical figures in other religious traditions, such as the "hidden *mahdī*" of Shia Islam, or Kāśyapa, the disciple of Buddha Siddhārtha Gautama who is believed to remain hidden in a state of hibernation inside Mount Kukkuṭapāda until the time when Maitreya is born, when it will be his task to "convey to Maitreya the robe that is the symbol of the lineage of his predecessors".[16]

Fascinating as such comparisons may be, I must admit my ignorance at this point, and I would be grateful if there is a prophet or a diviner, or, even better,

---

16   Nattier, "The Meaning," 46, n. 60.

a scholar, among the readers who can throw light on the notion of the future manifestation of Dran pa Nam mkha'.

References

Blondeau, Anne-Marie. "Identification de la tradition appelée *bsGrags-pa Bon-lugs*." In *Indo-Tibetan Studies. Papers in Honour and Appreciation of Professor David L. Snellgrove's Contribution to Indo-Tibetan Studies*, ed. Tadeusz Skorupski, pp. 37–54. Tring: The Institute of Buddhist Studies, 1990.

Doney, Lewis J.A. *Transforming Tibetan Kingship. The Portrayal of Khri Srong sde brtsan in the Early Buddhist Histories*. PhD thesis. School of Oriental and African Studies, University of London, 2011.

Karmay, Samten G. "The Ordinance of Lha bla-ma Ye-shes-'od." In *Tibetan Studies in Honour of Hugh Richardson*, ed. Michael Aris and Aung San Suu Kyi, pp. 150–162. Warminster: Aris & Phillips, 1980.

Lewis, Ioan M. *Ecstatic Religion*. Harmondsworth: Penguin Books, 1971.

Martin, Dan. "The Star King and the Four Children of Pehar: Popular Religious Movements of 11th- to 12th-Century Tibet." *Acta Orientalia Academiae Scientiarum Hung.* 49, no. 1–2 (1996), pp. 171–195.

Nattier, Jan. "The Meaning of the Maitreya Myth. A Typological Survey." In *Maitreya, the Future Buddha*, ed. Alan Sponberg and Helen Hardacre, pp. 23–47. Cambridge: Cambridge University Press, 1988.

Sheppard, Gerald T. and William E. Herbrechtsmeier. "Prophecy. An Overview." In *The Encyclopedia of Religion*, ed. Mircea Eliade, vol. 12, pp. 8–14. New York: Macmillan Publishing Company, 1987.

Turner, Victor. "Religious Specialists: Anthropological Study." In *International Encyclopedia of the Social Sciences*, ed. David L. Sills and Robert K. Merton, vol. 13, pp. 437–444. New York: Macmillan, 1968.

CHAPTER 2

Three Dice, Four Faces, and Sixty-Four Combinations: Early Tibetan Dice Divination by the Numbers

Brandon Dotson

There is a wide variety of dice divination traditions in Tibetan culture.[1] The most prevalent form uses cubical, six-sided dice marked with pips from one to six in the usual fashion. Other forms of Tibetan Buddhist dice divination mark the faces of such a die with the syllables of a mantra. A separate tradition of dice divination uses a rectangular (technically "cuboid") four-sided die, known in Sanskrit as a *pāśaka*. This tradition of divination is known largely from twenty-odd eighth-to-tenth-century manuscripts from Dunhuang, Turfan, and Mazār Tāgh, and does not easily classify as belonging to either the Buddhist or the Bon religions. Despite some differences, these early dice divination practices share a number of common features with later Tibetan divination traditions, including the preponderance of female divinities and the relevance of the oracular responses to a person's "fortune" (*phya*).[2]

---

1 The research going into this chapter was supported by a visiting fellowship during 2015–2016, and again during the summer of 2017 at the International Consortium for Research in the Humanities, "Fate, Freedom and Prognostication: Strategies for Coping with the Future in East Asia and Europe," at the University of Erlangen-Nuremberg, generously funded by the German Federal Ministry of Education and Research (BMBF). This work is indebted to conversations with many of the fellows who were active during my time at the consortium, including Charles Burnett, Constance Cook, Esther-Maria Guggenmos, Zhao Lu, and Jan-Ulrich Sobisch. I have also benefitted from exchanges with Daniel Michon and Ai Nishida. I am grateful to Michael Willis at the British Museum and Sam van Schaik at the British Library for affording me access to dice and to divination books. I would also like to thank the good people of the mathematics message board at stackexchange.com for fielding my questions on probability and multinomial distribution, and express my gratitude to Andrea Bréard for offering comments and corrections to a draft of this essay. Any errors or misunderstandings found here are entirely my own.

2 See Brandon Dotson, "The Call of the Cuckoo to the Thin Sheep of Spring: Healing and Fortune in Old Tibetan Dice Divination Texts," in *Tibetan and Himalayan Healing: An Anthology for Anthony Aris*, ed. Charles Ramble and Ulrike Roesler (Kathmandu: Vajra Publications, 2015), 147–160 and idem, "Hunting for Fortune: Wild Animals, Goddesses and the Play of Perspectives in Early Tibetan Dice Divination," in *Animals and Religion on the Tibetan Plateau*, ed. Geoff Barstow (Special issue of *Études Mongoles & Sibériennes, Centrasiatiques & Tibétaines*, 50 [2019]): 1–26.

© KONINKLIJKE BRILL NV, LEIDEN, 2020 | DOI:10.1163/9789004410688_003

One major task for those who would take stock of Tibetan divination texts from the eighth or ninth century to the present is to compare our twenty-some extant Old Tibetan dice divination texts and to tease out their similarities and differences and place them in the context of Tibetan dice divination more generally. This approach is exemplified by the excellent work of Ai Nishida.[3] A related task is to perform a similar operation in relation to neighboring and possibly related traditions from India, China, the Islamic World, and elsewhere. The most ambitious work of this type was undertaken in more recent times by Michel Strickmann, but even from the very beginning of the study of Old Tibetan dice divination texts, scholars such as A.H. Francke and F.W. Thomas have compared these Tibetan texts with the *Pāśakakevalī* and the *Bower Manuscript* from the Indic world, and the *Irq Bitig* of the Turks, all of which employ a similar system of divination with three four-sided dice and with recourse to books containing sixty-four oracular responses.[4] Such comparative studies can be extremely fruitful for mapping the specific contours of different economies of fortune. Of course this also raises questions of transmission, and of whether or not Tibet's dice divination traditions derive, for example, from India, China, the Islamic World, the Greco-Roman world, or elsewhere. Within Tibetan dice divination, it also concerns continuity and innovation, and other similar issues that are difficult to negotiate amid the thick description and careful study of oracular responses that are often replete with allusive and archaic language.

Apart from delving into the fascinating contents of Old Tibetan dice divination texts with their gods, animals, evocative scenes, prescribed rituals, and so forth, one can also consider Tibetan dice divination from a different perspective, and at a slightly greater remove, by taking account of its material culture, its procedures, and the general organization of divination books. This is the task of the present contribution, which uses numbers to try to get some purchase on

---

3 See Ai Nishida 西田爱, "古チベット卜語サイコロ占い文書の研究 (A Study of Old Tibetan Dice Divination)," 日本西藏学会夕輯 (*Report of the Japanese Association for Tibetan Studies*) 54 (2008): 63–77. This is now superseded by idem, "A Preliminary Analysis of Old Tibetan Dice Divination Texts," in *Glimpses of Tibetan Divination: Past and Present*, ed. Petra Maurer, Donatella Rossi, and Rolf Scheuermann (Leiden: Brill, 2019), 49–72.

4 Michel Strickmann, *Chinese Poetry and Prophecy: The Written Oracle in East Asia* (Stanford: Stanford University Press, 2005); A.H. Francke, "Tibetische Handschriftenfunde aus Turfan," *Sitzungsberichte der Preussischen Akademie der Wissenschaften, philosophisch-historische Klasse* 3 (1924): 5–20; idem, "Drei weitere Blätter des tibetischen Losbuches von Turfan," *Sitzungsberichte der Preussischen Akademie der Wissenschaften, philosophisch-historische Klasse* 7 (1928): 110–118; and F.W. Thomas, *Ancient Folk-Literature from North-Eastern Tibet* (Berlin: Akademie Verlag, 1957), 113–157.

THREE DICE, FOUR FACES, AND SIXTY-FOUR COMBINATIONS

a tradition of dice divination that was current in Tibet from at least the eighth to the tenth century, and which experienced an apparently later, Buddhist revival from around the fourteenth century CE. Among these numbers are the number of faces of a divination die, the number of times the dice are cast, the method by which the pips of the dice are combined or added, the number of oracular responses in a divination book, and the balance of good responses to bad or mixed ones.[5] While the contents of the oracular responses are highly adaptable to the concerns of their users, be they Indian, Turk, Arab, Persian, Chinese, or Tibetan, and be they Buddhist or non-Buddhist, the numerical elements constitute the "bones" of the system, and as such are more resistant to change and therefore more indicative if one hopes to assess the transmission of this tradition to Tibet, or indeed the history of this method of divination more generally. To explore this premise, this chapter examines the material culture of dice in comparison with possibly related systems of divination, and also considers the methods of combining numbers or symbols to arrive at an oracular response, along with the organization of responses within a divination book, and the balance of fortune imagined thereby.

1   *Pāśaka* Dice, Their Four Faces, and Related Objects

Most forms of Tibetan dice divination are performed with recourse to three cubical six-sided dice. These dice have their pips arranged such that opposing faces add up to seven, with one and six, two and five, and three and four opposing. The principle that a die should have such "balanced" opposing faces is very widespread, whether the dice are used in games or in rituals, and this is often accorded cosmological significance. In the Greco-Roman world, there may be a neo-Pythagorean or neo-Platonic source for associating the balanced opposing faces of a six-sided die with the number of heavenly bodies and the number of days in the week. One also finds justification for the principle of balanced opposing faces in Islamic commentaries.[6]

---

5   Each entry in an Old Tibetan dice divination text typically consists of four elements. These are: 1) combination of pips or symbols; 2) imagistic utterance, sometimes in verse, and sometimes from the mouth of a god; 3) interpretation, stating the response's relevance to various activities such as trade; and 4) a succinct evaluation or summation. The Tibetan term *mo*, "divination" refers in such texts to the summation and also to the entry as a whole. The generality of this term and the quasi-tautologies it creates in translation (e.g., "sixty-four divinations in a divination book") militate against adopting emic terminology in this instance.

6   Anna Contadini, "Islamic Ivory Chess Pieces, Draughtsmen and Dice in the Ashmolean

14   DOTSON

The type of early Tibetan dice divination that concerns us here does not use cubical six-sided dice, but rather employs rectangular, four-sided long dice with one to four pips, known in Sanskrit as a *pāśaka*. The rarity of such dice posed problems for the first scholars to investigate Old Tibetan dice divination texts in any detail. In a pioneering article published in 1924, A.H. Francke made notes on various manuscripts recovered from Turfan and offered transliterations and translations of two manuscript fragments from Turfan that he believed to have come from a single divination text, along with one fragment from Mazār Tāgh recovered by Aurel Stein.[7] This latter was housed in the Oriental Collection of the British Museum among hundreds of other fragments that Francke observed during his time compiling a catalog in London from 1914 to 1918.[8] In his remarks on these dice divination fragments, Francke noted the presence of small circles at the head of each paragraph, and identified this as a defining feature of dice divination texts.[9]

Francke correctly identified these circles as representations of dice pips. Unfortunately, he was unaware of the form of die known in Sanskrit as a *pāśaka*. As a result, Francke was left to imagine what a four-sided die would look like. To do so, he speculated that a six-sided die was used, with the fifth face of the cube being blank and the sixth face occupied by a St. Andrew's Cross, that is, an "X."[10] Francke's mistake is perfectly understandable from the perspective of someone who had never seen a long die, a stick die, or a *pāśaka*. Were one to ask someone to describe a four-sided die today, s/he would likely describe the pyramidal four-sided die used by game enthusiasts. Fortunately, *pāśaka* dice have come to be fairly well known through Heinrich Lüders' study of dice in ancient India, which described the die as typically being seven cm × one cm × one cm, that is, of dimensions that allow it to land under normal circumstances only on one of its four wide faces, and not on either of its two narrow ends.[11]

     Museum," in *Islamic Art in the Ashmolean Museum*, ed. James Allan (Oxford: Oxford University Press, 1995), 127–129; 146, n. 65.

7   Francke, "Tibetische Handschriftenfunde aus Turfan," 5–20. The two Turfan fragments that Francke translated were catalogued by Manfred Taube in 1980, and are now found under the shelfmarks TibHT 33 and TibHT 32; Manfred Taube, *Die Tibetica der Berliner Turfansammlung* (Berlin: Akademie Verlag, 1980). The Mazār Tāgh fragment is Or.15000/67, number 129 in Takeuchi's catalog; Tsuguhito Takeuchi, *Old Tibetan Manuscripts from East Turkestan in the Stein Collection of the British Library* (London: The British Library and the Toyo Bunko, 1998), 41.

8   Ibid., xxiv. The catalog was never published, and was superseded by Takeuchi's catalog.

9   Francke, "Tibetische Handschriftenfunde aus Turfan," 7.

10   Francke, "Tibetische Handschriftenfunde aus Turfan," 12.

11   Heinrich Lüders, *Das Würfelspiel im alten Indien* (Berlin: Weidmannsche Buchhandlung, 1907).

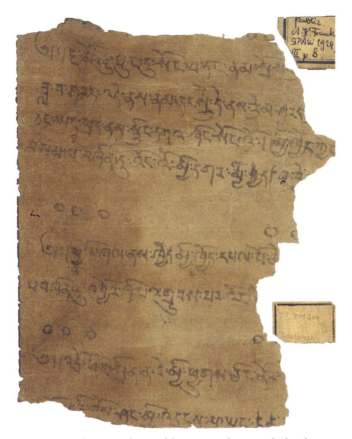

FIGURE 2.1 TibHT 33, a damaged fragment with pips at the head of each oracular response; Depositum der Berlin-Brandenburgischen Akademie der Wissenschaften in der Staatsbibliothek zu Berlin—Preussischer Kulturbesitz Orientabteilung

Francke in fact rectified his oversight in a second article in the same journal's 1928 issue, where he correctly described the dice used for divination with reference to Lüders' study and to a die from Niya photographed in Aurel Stein's *Ancient Khotan*.[12] This photograph displayed only one face of the die, but in another of Stein's publications, *Serindia*, one can see another *pāśaka* from Niya,

---

12 A.H. Francke, "Drei weitere Blätter des tibetischen Losbuches von Turfan," *Sitzungsberichte der Preussischen Akademie der Wissenschaften, philosophisch-historische Klasse* 7 (1928): 113–115; Marc Aurel Stein, *Ancient Khotan: Detailed Report of Archaeological Explorations in Chinese Turkestan*. Volume III: Plates (Oxford: Clarendon Press, 1907), plate LXXIV, N. XV. 004.

FIGURES 2.2A–B
All four faces of two bone dice from Taxila; after Marshall, *Taxila*, plate 200, nos. 93 and 97.

where faces with three and two pips are visible.[13] Images of four of the seventeen *pāśaka* dice recovered from John Marshall's excavation of Taxila in the Punjab, Pakistan, show all four faces of each *pāśaka*. Some of these, such as figure 2.2b, have more finely decorated and stylized pips and more elaborate borders at their narrow ends.[14]

These dice are long and even and very well made. They generally correspond to the typical proportions of a *pāśaka* as described by Lüders as being seven cm long by one cm wide by one cm deep.[15] These dice contrast with the die from Niya that Stein published in *Ancient Khotan* in that the latter evidently has uneven sides, and appears to be shorter and thicker. Surveying these and other *pāśaka* dice unearthed from Central Asia, the Punjab, Khyber, and elsewhere, and attending to the measurements supplied by Marshall for the seventeen Taxila dice he documented, it is evident that one can divide the dice into two basic groups based on size: there are those approximately seven to nine cm long, and there are those around four cm long.

Pāśaka dice are also distinguished by their different styles of pips and by their ornamentation. Some dice, for example, have wider, shallower pips with small points making a circle around the outside, while others have small deep pips with one or more shallow concentric circles drawn around them. The rep-

---

13   Marc Aurel Stein, *Serindia: Detailed Report of Explorations in Central Asia and Westernmost China*. Volume IV: Plates (Oxford: Clarendon Press, 1921), plate XXXVI, L. B. IV. v. 0034.

14   See John Hubert Marshall, *Taxila: An Illustrated Account of Archaeological Excavations Carried Out at Taxila under the Orders of the Government of India Between the Years 1913 and 1934* (Cambridge: Cambridge University Press, 1951), plate 200, nos. 92, 93, 97, and 98. The dates of these objects are uncertain, but Taxila was in decline by the seventh century, and all but abandoned by the turn of the second millennium. For the material cultural context of these dice, which points to their use in divination, see Daniel Michon, *Archaeology and Religion in Early Northwest India: History, Theory, Practice* (New Delhi: Routledge, 2015), 152–200.

15   Lüders, *Das Würfelspiel im alten Indien*, 17.

THREE DICE, FOUR FACES, AND SIXTY-FOUR COMBINATIONS

resentations of dice pips drawn on the pages of Old Tibetan dice divination texts similarly range from simple circles, as in figure 2.1, to concentric circles similar to those adorning the die in figure 2.2a. Some dice feature more ornate pips, such as the die in figure 2.2b where each circular pip encloses three small circles. The most ornately decorated pips on a *pāśaka* die are found on a die that comes not from India or Central Asia, but from the Near East. This is one of two bone *pāśaka* dice kept in the Nasser D. Khalili Collection of Islamic Art (acc. no. MXD 205), whose pips enclose carvings of scorpions and birds.[16] Their provenances and dates are unknown, though Fustat has been mentioned as a possible find spot.[17] These are not the only *pāśaka* dice to be found in an Islamic, or possibly pre-Islamic context. There is also a *pāśaka* die kept in the Louvre (acc. no. MAO 483), dated from the seventh to ninth centuries, and provenanced to Egypt. This die, like the die from Taxila in figure 2.2a, has pips consisting of a central pip or hole with two concentric circles, the inner one deeper than the outer. Both dice also share the feature of having incisions cut in lines around their ends, creating a segmented appearance at either end of the die; there are three such lines cut into the Louvre die, and two in the Taxila die. This type of ornamentation is found on several longer *pāśaka* dice, but is so far yet to be observed on the shorter variety. Among other forms of ornamentation found outside the pips, we can also mention the small circles arrayed in patterns on the four sides of the other *pāśaka* die in the Khalili collection, acc. no. MXD 172.

The date of manufacture of each of these dice is uncertain, and it is clear that the date ranges assigned to them are largely educated guesses. Attestations in the material cultural record stretch back to as early as the third millennium BCE, since *pāśaka* dice have been excavated from both upper and lower levels at Mohenjo Daro.[18] The seventeen *pāśaka* dice from Taxila, as well as others from the Punjab, Khyber, and Uzbekhistan, likely date from the Parthian and Kushan periods. The Khotanese dice may also belong to the Kushan period or

---

16 The die is assigned acc. no. MXD 205, and the other die is MXD 172. These are a bit longer than other extant dice at 8.2×1.7×1.7 cm and 9.2×1.4×1.4 cm; Emilie Savage-Smith, "Divination," in *Science, Tools, and Magic: the Nasser D. Khalili Collection of Islamic Art, Volume XII* (Oxford: the Nour Foundation and Oxford University Press, 1997), 150, 158; Finkel, "Dice in India and Beyond," 41, plates 2:4 and 2:5. Finkel's article contains images of further *pāśaka* dice.

17 Savage-Smith, "Divination," 158.

18 E.J.H. Mackay, *Further Excavations and Mohenjo-Daro*, vol. 2 (New Delhi: Government of India Press, 1937), plates 138 and 143; and Irving Finkel, "Dice in India and Beyond," in *Asian Games: the Art of Contest*, ed. Colin Mackenzie and Irving Finkel (New York: Asia Society, 2004), 40.

later, and the dice from the Near East likely date to the early Islamic period. These latter dice are evidently connected to the transmission of *pāśaka* dice divination from the Indic to the Islamic world. There, it is often referred to as the method of Ja'far al-Ṣādiq (c. 702–765), and is transmitted in Turkish and Persian divination books known as *Fāl-namāh*, and in Arabic divination books known as *Kitāb al-Fāl*. We will return to these Islamic traditions below.

There is a further feature of *pāśaka* dice that is perhaps even more significant than those pertaining to their material, size, pips, and ornamentation. As noted above, it is an enduring and widespread principle that the sums of the opposing faces of a die be numerically balanced. It is particularly interesting, therefore, that the majority of the dice for which the published images suffice, or which I have been able to visit in person, have pips that proceed one, two, three, four, wending around the die in succession. This is unbalanced in that one and three oppose, and two and four oppose. (In a balanced arrangement, one and four would oppose and two and three would oppose, with the sum of the opposing faces thus adding up to five.) Besides this serial arrangement of pips, there are also other unbalanced arrangements that have been attested, such as a die from the Punjab whose pips proceed one, three, two, four around the four faces of the die (British Museum no. 1979,6–27.21). Balanced *pāśaka* dice may indeed exist, but they have not been attested thus far.

Before considering the meaning of this imbalance, it should be mentioned that the unbalanced faces of these *pāśaka* dice contrast with those of a very similar, and much more famous object used almost exclusively in gaming. This is another form of the *pāśaka* die, chiefly employed in the games of *caupur* and *pachisi*.[19] Most such dice have faces that are marked one, two, five, and six, with opposing faces adding up to seven.[20] Similarly, rectangular dice used in chess and perhaps in the game of *nard* in the Islamic world are marked with one, two, five, and six pips in the form of small circles, almost identical to dice used in *caupur* and *pachisi*.[21] While such dice were used for *pachisi* in India up until recent times, it appears that as far as the Islamic world is concerned, they are only present in the archeological record from approximately the ninth through eleventh centuries.[22]

---

19   On *pachisi*, see Irving Finkel, "Round and Round the Houses: the Game of *Pachisi*," in *Asian Games: the Art of Contest*, ed. Colin Mackenzie and Irving Finkel (New York: Asia Society, 2004), 47–58.

20   Lüders, *Das Würfelspiel im alten Indien*, 17. Lüders also mentions a die with sides of one, three, four, and six pips, respectively. Irving Finkel associates these with South India; Finkel, "Dice in India and Beyond," 40.

21   Contadini, "Islamic Ivory Chess Pieces, Draughtsmen and Dice in the Ashmolean Museum," 127–129.

22   Ibid., 129.

The contrast between the two types of *pāśaka* dice raises some interesting questions. Do they occur in the same cultural contexts? Is one strictly for gaming? Do the balanced opposing faces of the *"pachisi-type pāśaka"* allude to a sense of orderliness and fairness, and to an as it were "un-weighted" die? Reciprocally, do the "unbalanced" faces of "divination-type *pāśaka*" suggest an object designed to cheat fate? Or, if the sequential arrangement of the faces (one, two, three, four) is indeed normative for such dice, does this express some cosmological significance similar to how the sum of seven might evoke the seven heavenly bodies, the days of the week and so forth? To the latter question we can venture an affirmative answer by recalling that the four Vedic world ages or *yuga*-s take their names from the terms for dice rolls. These are usually known as *kṛta, tretā, dvāpara,* and *kali* and are associated, in descending order, with the numbers four, three, two, and one.[23] The names of the dice throws can also be associated with the cardinal directions, and thus have spatial as well as temporal reference points.[24] On the symbolism of dice in India, Don Handelman and David Shulman write, "[t]he dice in Indian games take different shapes—nuts, cubes, rectangles. But regardless of their form, the dice themselves are little models of the cosmos, within the modeling of the dice game."[25] With such a cosmological backdrop, it is surely fitting that one number should follow after another in sequence around the four faces of an Indian *pāśaka*.

Before moving on to the method of combining the pips in order to arrive at an oracular response, it will be useful to introduce two more objects that will figure in some of the divination traditions discussed below. One, the *astragalos*, or sheep's knuckle, is ubiquitous, but is most closely associated with the Greco-Roman world. It displays the principle of balanced opposing faces that add up to seven. The other, the *lun* (輪) or "wheel" is essentially a teetotum or spinning top, used in Chinese Buddhist divination.

The *astragalos* (Greek; Latin *talus*) is the knucklebone of a sheep, used all over the world in both games and divination. The ubiquity of the sheep's knuckle and its use in both gaming and divination contrasts with the relative obscurity of the rectangular die or *pāśaka*. An *astragalos* has four sides, but due

---

23　See Lüders, *Das Würfelspiel im alten Indien,* 38–51; M.P.V. Kane, *History of Dharmaśāstra,* volume 3 (Poona: Bhandarkar Oriental Research Institute, 1946), 886–888; and Luis González-Reimann, "The Ancient Vedic Dice Game and the Names of the Four World Ages in Hinduism," in *World Archaeoastronomy,* ed. Anthony F. Aveni (Cambridge: Cambridge University Press, 1988), 195.

24　Lüders, *Das Würfelspiel im alten Indien,* 38.

25　Don Handelman and David Shulman, *God Inside Out: Śiva's Game of Dice* (Oxford: Oxford University Press, 1997), 66.

FIGURE 2.3
Four *astragaloi* showing all four sides
PHOTOGRAPH BY BRANDON DOTSON

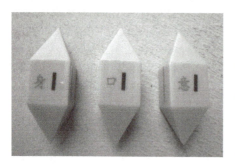

FIGURE 2.4
Second of three sets of "wheels" or *lun* used in the system of divination found in the *Zhancha jing* or "Divination *Sūtra*"
PHOTOGRAPH BY BEVERLEY FOULKS MCGUIRE, REPRODUCED WITH PERMISSION

to the composition and shape of the bone each of the four sides does not come up with equal probability, since there are broad and narrow sides, and convex and concave sides.[26]

In the Greco-Roman tradition the four sides are valued one, three, four, and six, with the opposing sides adding up to seven.[27] This is obviously quite different from the sequential pips of the *pāśaka* used in Indian, Turk, and early Tibetan dice divination, and we will examine their divergent methods of combining pips or values in detail below.

The third and final object to introduce is referred to as a "wheel" (*lun* 輪), and is used in a Chinese Buddhist form of divination found in the sixth-century apocryphal sutra, the *Zhancha shan'e yebao jing* or "Divination *Sūtra*" (T. 839).[28] This object has four faces, and is somewhere between a *pāśaka* and a teetotum

---

26   Fritz Graf, "Rolling the Dice for an Answer," in *Mantikê: Studies in Ancient Divination*, ed. Sarah Iles Johnston and Peter T. Struck (Leiden: Brill, 2005), 60; Stewart Culin, *Chess and Playing Cards: Catalogue of Games and Implements for Divination Exhibited by the United States National Museum* (Philadelphia: University of Pennsylvania Press, 1896), 826–831.
27   The convex broad side is three, the concave broad side is four, the flat narrow side is one, and the "indented" narrow side is six; Culin, *Chess and Playing Cards*, 827.
28   Strickmann, *Chinese Poetry and Prophecy*, 80.

THREE DICE, FOUR FACES, AND SIXTY-FOUR COMBINATIONS   21

in that both ends are pointed, with no rod or stick to facilitate spinning, as in the case of a true teetotum like a *dreidel*. Nevertheless, the pointed ends act like a spinning axis.

Apart from their different form, the sides of these *lun* are marked in a wider variety of ways than is a *pāśaka*. In fact, three sets of these "wheels" (*lun*) are employed in the system of divination described in the *Zhancha shan'e yebao jing*. In the first set, each of the ten "wheels" is inscribed with one of the ten good acts, with the opposing evil act inscribed on the opposite face. The other two faces are left blank. Casting all ten "wheels" reveals one's past actions. The second set of "wheels" reveals the depth of karmic actions of body, speech, and mind. Each face is inscribed with a line, where the length and thickness (short and thin; long and thin; short and thick; long and thick) indicate the strength of past karmic residues. The third and final set of "wheels" is six in number. Each "wheel" is inscribed with numbers on three faces, with one face blank.[29] The numbers proceed from one to eighteen, e.g., one, two, three, blank on the first "wheel"; four, five, six, blank on the second "wheel," and so on up to eighteen. All six "wheels" are spun, and the resulting numbers are added together to make a sum from zero to sixty-three. This is repeated twice more, such that there are eighteen rolls in total, with all of the sums added together to return a number from zero to 189.[30] These numbers index oracular responses in the *Zhancha jing*, where 1–160 pertain to the present, 161–171 to the past, and 172–189 to the future.[31] We will return to this text in examining various methods for combining pips and symbols to arrive at an oracular response in the section that follows.

To conclude this brief survey of the types of *pāśaka* dice relevant to early Tibetan dice divination, and their contextualization alongside similar objects,

---

29   The use of blank faces, so notable in these sets of "wheels," also seems to be found in South Indian dice, and in *pāśaka* dice from Mohenjo-Daro that have faces of one, two, three, and zero; see Finkel, "Dice in India and Beyond," 40; and E.J.H. Mackay, *Further Excavations and Mohenjo-Daro*, vol. 2 (New Delhi: Government of India Press, 1937), plates 138 and 143. One notes that the fourth face of these dice from Mohenjo-Daro bears two long black lines, which in their turn create two light-colored lines, so I hesitate to agree with Finkel that the side is blank or represents zero.

30   This summary of the *Zhancha jing* draws on Whalen Lai, "The *Chan-ch'a ching*: Religion and Magic in Medieval China," in *Chinese Buddhist Apocrypha*, ed. Robert Buswell (Honolulu: University of Hawai'i Press, 1990), 175–206 and Beverley Foulks McGuire, *Living Karma: The Religious Practices of Ouyi Zhixu* (New York: Columbia University Press, 2014), 42–45. See also Kuo Liying, "Divination, jeux de hazard et purification dans le bouddhisme chinois: Autour d'un sutra apocryphe chinois, le *Zhanchajing*," in *Bouddhisme et cultures locales: Quelques cas de réciproques adaptations*, ed. Fukui Fumimasa and Gérard Fussman (Paris: École Française d'Extrême-Orient, 1994), 145–167.

31   Lai, "The *Chan-ch'a ching*," 181–182.

we must admit that the archeological record of *pāśaka* dice is less than optimal, with uncertain dates and provenances for many finds. A more concerted survey of the material culture of these dice would likely clarify this sketchy picture. Such a survey of museums and collections, including those in India and Pakistan, could more fully establish the normative arrangement of the faces of these dice, and further clarify their distribution, their variations in size, decoration, and so forth. This would need also to be complemented by a material-cultural study of the relevant dice divination books (*Pāśakakevalī*, *Fālnamāh*, *Kitāb al-Fāl*, and *mo dpe*) in Sanskrit, Tibetan, Turkish, Persian, Arabic, and Chinese. The brief presentation of these *pāśaka* dice here is meant largely to highlight the peculiarity of their "unbalanced" arrangement of pips and its possible mythological and cosmological justification, and to offer some preliminary remarks on their typology in terms of size (e.g., seven-to-nine cm and four cm), decoration (e.g., concentric circles, dots, lines cut at the ends), and distribution (Indic Central Asia, Indus Valley, and the Near East).

2   Combining Pips and Indexing Responses

By itself, it is possible for a given roll of the dice to be synonymous with an oracular response. This would be true for a tradition with strong numerological beliefs such that some combinations of numbers or symbols would always be auspicious or inauspicious. It would also be true of divining communities who are so familiar with the responses that they know the meaning immediately upon seeing how the dice fall, how the hexagram is constructed, or which number one receives when a stick shakes loose in East Asian lot divination (*chouqian* 抽籤). It appears to be the case in early Tibetan dice divination, however, that the oracular responses stand at a remove from the dice rolls, which exist in relation to them in the manner of an index. How dice roll combinations index responses was likely taken for granted by diviners and their clients, but there are in fact several different methods by which one can combine the numbers and symbols generated by randomizing technologies such as dice. In other words, the relationship between a combination of dice rolls, a hexagram in *Yijing* divination, or a stick shaken loose in East Asian lot divination and the responses that they index in a book, on a slip of paper, in the individual memory of a diviner, or in the collective memory of a divining community displays a good deal of variation. It is here, in the translating or combining of these randomized letters, numbers, and symbols to index an oracular response, that we find methods that in their specificity constitute one of the defining features of a given divination system.

Looking at Tibetan dice divination in comparative context, we can observe three common ways of combining pips, numbers, or symbols. The first, simplest method is that used in a common form of Tibetan dice divination, using three six-sided dice, often associated with dPal ldan lha mo in her form as dMag zor rgyal mo.[32] Here three dice are thrown, and one simply adds the pips on the dice, giving sixteen possible combinations numbered three to eighteen. In doing so, the order in which the dice fall does not matter, and one attends only to the sum such that 3/3/3 indexes the same oracular response as 4/3/2, e.g., number nine in a dice divination book. Assuming sequential pips as in a common six-sided die numbered from one to six, the number of possible outcomes is given by the formula $(SxN)-(S-1)$, where N = the number of sides of a die or object and S = the number of dice or objects cast. Thus there are sixteen possible outcomes, numbered from three to eighteen. These outcomes are not equally probable, however, since only one combination of pips (1/1/1) can add up to three, for instance, whereas several different combinations can add up to ten (e.g., 5/4/1 or 4/4/2). As a result, one has a .5% chance of rolling a three or an eighteen, but has a 12.5% chance of rolling a ten or an eleven.

Where a die or object has a blank side, or where the pips, numbers, letters, or values do not proceed sequentially (e.g., as in the case of an *astragalos*'s sides having the values of one, three, four, and six), the formula must be adjusted.

A second common method of combination also adds the objects' pips or numbers and pays little or no attention to the order in which the dice or objects fall. This is true of the *Sortes Sanctorum*, and of many other forms of Greco-Roman cleromancy practiced with *astragaloi*.[33] Recall here that the four sides of the sheep knuckle have the values one, three, four, and six. Here one does not distinguish order, such that a roll of 1/3/3/4/4/ and one of 1/4/4/3/3, both adding up to the same sum, direct one to the same oracular response. Although order does not matter, different combinations index different responses: 3/3/3/1/1 and 4/4/1/1/1, for example, each add up to eleven, but they index separate responses within a divination book or on a stele. One can calculate the num-

---

32 See, for example, *dPal ldan lha mo dmag zor rgyal mo'i sgo nas sho brtags tshul kun gsal me long*, in the *gSung 'bum* of dKon mchog 'jigs med dbang po (1728–1791), Vol. 10: 432–452 (Bla brang bkra shis 'kyil, 1999); TBRC W2122; http://tbrc.org/link?RID=O01DG03|O01DG034JW 33976$W2122. Published also in Tshe ring and 'Brug rgyal mkhar, eds., *Mo dpe dang sa dpyad rmi lam brtags thabs* (Gansu: Gansu Nationalities Publishing House, 1997), 1–24.

33 See, for example, Graf, "Rolling the Dice for an Answer"; and Jacqueline Champeaux, "'Sorts' antiques et médiévaux: les lettres et les chiffres," in *Au miroir de la culture antique: mélanges offerts au président René Marache par ses collègues, ses étudiants et ses amis* (Rennes: Presses Universitaires de Rennes, 1992), 67–89. Note that some authors, including Strickmann, refer to the *Sortes Sanctorum* as the *Sortes Apostolorum*.

ber of possible outcomes within a tradition using this system of combination with recourse to the formula $(S+N-1)!/[S!(N-1)!]$. In the Greco-Roman tradition of casting five *astragaloi*, where each side is numbered one, three, four, or six, one can add the numbers from a single throw to arrive at a number between five and thirty. Within this range, wherein one distinguishes different combinations of numbers but ignores their order, there are fifty-six possible combinations corresponding to fifty-six oracular responses.[34] Using the same method of combination, three six-sided dice can also index fifty-six responses. Here, as in the first method, the outcomes do not fall with equal probability.

The third method does not add pips, but rather combines them by attending to the order in which the dice or objects were thrown, or by otherwise distinguishing one die from another.[35] This is the method employed in divination with *pāśaka* dice. Here, a roll of 1/3/1 indexes a separate response from a roll of 1/1/3. The relevant formula for calculating the number of outcomes is N^S where once again N = the number of sides of a die or object and S = the number of dice or objects cast. Using this method of combination, each outcome and its attendant response is equally probable.

In early Tibetan dice divination, in the *Pāśakakevalī*, in the two divination texts in the *Bower Manuscript*, and in the *Irq Bitig*, the number of possible outcomes is expressed as $4^3 = 64$. This is also the case in the *Moxishouluo bu* 摩醯首羅卜 (S. 5614) or *Maheśvara's Method of Divination*, a Chinese Dunhuang manuscript whose oracular responses each begin with a combination of three numbers from one to four.[36] The same method works with letters substituted

---

34 The oracles proceed 5, 7, 8, 9, 10 (2), 11 (2), 12 (2), 13 (3), 14 (3), 15 (4), 16 (4), 17 (4), 18 (4), 19 (4), 20 (4), 21 (3), 22 (3), 23 (2), 24 (2), 25 (2), 26, 27, 28, and 30.

35 Lüders believed that each of three *pāśaka*-s was marked with a different royal symbol—a discus, an elephant, and a pot; Lüders, *Das Würfelspiel im alten Indien*, 22.

36 Marc Kalinowski, "La divination par les nombres dans les manuscrits de Dunhuang," in *Nombres, astres, plantes et viscères: sept essais sur l'histoire des sciences et des techniques en Asie orientale*, ed. Isabelle Ang and Pierre-Étienne Will (Paris: Institute des Hautes Etudes Chinoises, 1994), 63–64; see, more recently, idem., "Cléromancie," in *Divination et société dans la Chine médiévale: Étude des manuscrits de Dunhuang de la Bibliothèque nationale de France et de la British Library*, ed. Marc Kalinowski (Paris: Bibliothèque nationale de France, 2003), 320; 352–353; Strickmann, *Chinese Poetry and Prophecy*, 138–139; Wang Jingbo 王晶波, *Dunhuang zhanbu wenxian yu shehui shenghuo* 敦煌占卜文獻與社會生活 (Lanzhou: Gansu jiaoyu, 2011), 116–118. The key phrase in the text concerning its method reads 擲頭投子, which could certainly be understood as referring to the casting of a die. Wang, almost as if channeling A.H. Francke's comment from 1924, assumed a six-sided die with two blank sides. Kalinowski thought it could be either dice or draughtsmen. Whatever the method, it is repeated three times to arrive at a combination of three numbers

THREE DICE, FOUR FACES, AND SIXTY-FOUR COMBINATIONS   25

for pips or written numbers, and we see this in a later Tibetan Buddhist tradition of divination with lettered *pāśaka* dice whose faces are marked *A, WA, YA*, and *DA*. The text, attributed to Śāntideva (late-seventh to mid-eighth century CE) is found in the *bsTan 'gyur* and in other sources, and appears to have been translated into Tibetan in the fourteenth century.[37] Michel Strickmann stated that *A, WA, YA*, and *DA* are Tibetan renderings of the first four letters of the Greek alphabet, α, β, γ, and δ, a claim from which Strickmann concluded that the tradition has a Hellenistic origin, perhaps as early as the time of Alexander.[38] The same method of combination, also using letters instead of pips, is found in Islamic divination books known as *Kitāb al-Fāl* and *Fāl-namāh*, where each of the sixty-four oracular responses is indexed by a combination of four letters of the Arabic alphabet.[39]

---

   between one and four, and these combinations index oracular responses associated with Buddhist and Chinese gods and spirits, and each response ends with a summation, e.g., "very auspicious" 大吉.

37 The text is often known as the "Divination Calculation of Mañjuśrī" (Mo rtsis 'jam pa'i dbyangs). See Zhi ba lha, Go tam shrI, and Nyi ma rgyal mtshan (trans.), "Mo rtsis 'jam pa'i dbyangs," in *bsTan 'gyur* (*dpe bsdur ma*). TBRC W1PD95844. 114: 1282–1297. dPe cin: Krung go'i bod rig pa'i dpe skrun khang, 1994–2008. http://tbrc.org/link?RID=O2MS16391|O2MS 163914CZ190851$W1PD95844; Bo dong paN chen Phyogs las rnam rgyal, 'Jigs med 'bangs, "dPal ldan zhi ba lhas gsungs pa'i sho 'gyed pa'i mo rtsis bstan pa," in *gSung 'bum/Phyogs las rnam rgyal*. TBRC W22103. 2: 191–212. New Delhi: Tibet House, 1969–1981. http://tbrc.org/ link?RID=O22103|O221031KG67774$W22103. The Tibetan translator of this work is Thar pa lotsawa Nyi ma rgyal mtshan, a teacher of Bu ston Rin chen grub (1290–1364) based at gSang phu ne'u thog Monastery.

38 Strickmann, *Chinese Poetry and Prophecy*, 117. The use of Tibetanized Greek (or other, e.g., Arabic or Aramaic) letters instead of pips argues in favor of this being a later transmission of this same tradition of dice divination into Tibet, possibly through Hellenized Islamic intermediaries. This is a point that Strickmann also considers, and which merits further investigation. My proposal, against Strickmann's, is that this tradition originated in India, from whence it traveled both to Central Asia and to the Islamic World.

39 Ibid., 122; Gustav Flügel, "Die Loosbücher der Muhammadaner," *Berichte über die Verhandlungen der Königliche Sächsischen Gesellschaft der Wissenschaften zu Leipzig, Philologisch-Historische Klasse 13* (1861): 48; J.-A. Decourdemanche, *Le Miroir de l'avenir. Recueil de sept traités de divination traduit du turc* (Paris: Bibliotheque orientale Elzevirienne 1899), 5–7. See also Alexander Nicoll, *Bibliothecae Bodleianae Codicum Manuscriptorum Orientalium Catalogi* (Oxford, 1835), 276. The 19th-century Turkish text translated by Decourdemanche apparently uses the first four letters of the Arabic alphabet, a, b, j, and d (ا ب ج and د). The text in the late-14th-century Arabic compilation "Book of Wonders" (*Kitāb al-Bulhān*; MS. Bodl. Or. 133, folios 131a–163a) kept in the Bodleian Library, by contrast, uses the letters j, ', f, and r (ج ع ف and ر), in that order evidently spelling the name of the text's supposed author, Ja'far al-Ṣādiq (c. 702–765). Among other relevant divination texts attributed to Ja'far al-Ṣādiq we can add a "Treatise on *qur'ah* [Divination with Lettered Dice]" kept in the Bodleian Library under the shelfmark MS. Bodl. Or. 812, as well as MS. Bodl. Or. 815,

In a later Tibetan dice divination tradition that, like "Śāntideva's method," is associated with Mañjuśrī, a similar technique of combination is used with recourse to two six-sided dice whose faces are marked *A, RA, PA, TSA, NA,* and *DHI.* Here a roll of *RA TSA* indexes a separate response from a roll of *TSA RA,* and there are 36 responses in all ($6^2 = 36$).[40]

This method of combining pips or symbols works with other objects besides dice. The sixty-four hexagrams of the *Yijing,* for example, which consist of six sets of two possible combinations (a straight or a broken line or milfoil stalk), could be described as $2^6 = 64$. More specifically, since a hexagram is in fact a combination of two of the eight trigrams, the formula for possible outcomes is $2^3 = 8$ trigrams, and, combining two trigrams to make a hexagram, $8^2 = 64$ hexagrams.[41]

The same method of combination, albeit with different objects and with 125 possible outcomes, is used in the *Lingqi jing,* or "Book of Empowered Draughtsmen," a Daoist divination text originating between 280 and 289 CE.[42] Here one casts twelve draughtsmen (essentially coins with one side blank), four of which are marked "above" 上, four of which are marked "middle," 中 and four of which are marked "below" 下. The results are added, such that one can have between zero and four of each of these three categories. These first sixty-four combinations, referred to as *gua* 卦, ("trigrams" or "mantic figures") are the same as what one finds in *pāśaka* divination, proceeding 1/1/1 to 4/4/4. The difference is that one can also have a blank, which results when one or more of the groups of four draughtsmen comes up with four blanks. The combinations from sixty-five to 125 each incorporate one blank, e.g. "1/-/1" or two blanks, e.g., "-/1/-". With the advent of the number zero in China, these blanks came to be represented

---

and a Turkish divination book with sixty-four oracular responses that also uses alphabetical combinations from the first four letters of the Old Arabic alphabet; Flügel, "Die Loosbücher der Muhammadaner," 52. There are no doubt many more, but a survey of these is beyond the scope of this article. The genre designations *Kitāb al-Fāl* and *Fāl-namāh* can in fact include many other forms of divination, most of which are more common than divination with dice (*qur'ah*).

40   For a popular adaptation of a version of this tradition from the *gSung 'bum* of Mi pham rgya mtsho (1846–1912), see Jay Goldberg and Lobsang Dakpa, trans., *Mo: Tibetan Divination System* (Ithaca: Snow Lion, 1990).

41   For these and similar *Yijing* calculations by the Qing literatus Chen Houyao (1648–1722), see Andrea Bréard, "How to Quantify the Value of Domino Combinations? Divination and Shifting Rationalities in Late Imperial China," in *Coping with the Future: Theories and Practices of Divination in East Asia,* ed. Michael Lackner (Leiden: Brill, 2017), 516–517.

42   See Carol Morgan, "An introduction to the *Lingqi jing*," *Journal of Chinese Religions* 23 (1993): 97–120.

as zeros, and the final combination "o/o/o" was added as well.[43] Mathematically, the number of possible outcomes and attendant oracular responses can be summarized as $5^3 = 125$.

These are not the only three methods used for combining numbers or symbols in dice divination and related forms of cleromancy, but other methods are often a variation of them. The *Zhancha shan'e yebao jing*, for example, essentially follows the first method noted above, of simply adding the numbers together. Its use of blank faces obviates the need to start the oracular responses at a number higher than one, as in, for example, later Tibetan dice divination with three six-sided dice, where the first response is indexed by the sum of three $(1+1+1)$. It is intriguing that in the *Zhancha jing* zero (or blank) also indexes a response, and therefore has a value. The tripling of the dice-casting (here "wheel-turning") procedure in the *Zhancha jing* should not obscure the fact that when it is performed just once the result is sixty-four possible outcomes, numbered zero to sixty-three. This number of oracular responses by itself does not prove any connection either with early Tibetan dice divination or with the *Yijing*. Indeed the *Zhancha jing*'s somewhat unique method of combination, like the physical form of its "wheels," marks its difference from both of these traditions.

The methods for combining numbers can certainly be subject to innovation, and the *Zhancha jing*'s system could be an example of such. At the same time, the methods of combination in a given divination system appear to remain largely static, and to follow certain internal rules, such that it can be taken as a defining feature of each particular method of divination. The method of combination, as we have seen, is in fact less given to change than the materials employed. The faces of a *pāśaka* die, for example, can bear pips, numbers, or letters. Beyond that, and despite our emphasis on the material culture of divination, one can even say that the dice themselves are less the determining factor of "*pāśaka* divination" or of "early Tibetan dice divination" than is the method of combination. The introduction to the Turkish *Fāl-namāh* translated by Decourdemanche, for example, prescribes that one use a pyramidal four-sided die, or, in the absence of a die, that one write the first four letters of the alphabet on four identical slips of paper to be placed face down and then drawn and replaced like lots in order to create a combination and index a response.[44] Indeed one could easily perform early Tibetan dice divination with other technologies than *pāśaka* dice, such as using draughtsmen, sorting stalks, counting

---

43   Ibid., 98–99.
44   Decourdemanche, *Le Miroir de l'avenir*, 5–7.

beads off a *māla* in the same manner used in *māla* divination today, or by the separation of pebbles into three piles of one to four pebbles each.[45] Similarly, one can construct the hexagrams of the *Yijing* with milfoil stalks, but one can equally use coins or other means. One should therefore not be too insistent on assuming that the material culture of a given divination system is static, nor that the combinations (e.g., whether of pips, letters, or numbers) in a divination book necessarily dictate the form of the object, e.g., a *pāśaka*, used to arrive at such a combination.

The differences between these three principal methods of combining letters, numbers, or symbols are clear enough that one could not mistake the method of combination in the *Sortes Sanctorum* for that employed in *pāśaka* divination. Similarly, one could not mistake the latter's method of combination for that of simply adding the numbers, as in the case of Tibetan divination with three six-sided dice to index sixteen oracular responses numbered three to eighteen. Using these same objects—three six-sided dice,—the "*Sortes Sanctorum* method" of combination would yield fifty-six responses, while the "*pāśaka* divination method" would yield 216 responses. Furthermore, within the many traditions whose number of possible outcomes is given by the formula N^S, there are also some clear differences. The choice of numbers, letters, or pips is one. Perhaps the most fundamental difference involves the number of objects involved. It should be obvious that using two six-sided dice to arrive at one of thirty-six responses ($6^2 = 36$) is *prima facie* different from one using three four-sided dice to arrive at one of sixty-four responses ($4^3 = 64$). By the same rationale, moreover, combining coin flips or milfoil stalks to arrive at one of eight possible combinations (e.g., trigrams), and then combining one such combination with another to make one of sixty-four possible combinations (e.g., hexagrams) also represents a different method than that of *pāśaka* divination's three four-sided dice, even if the number of possible outcomes is the same. While it might be flippant to call it simply coincidence that both the *Yijing* and *pāśaka* divination have sixty-four responses, it should be the argument for mutual influence or connection that bears the burden of proof. The default assumption should be that 4^3 arrived at the answer "64" independently of $(2^3)^2$.

---

45   Chime Radha, "Tibet," in *Oracles and Divination*, ed. Michael Loewe and Carmen Blacker (Boulder: Shambhala Publications, 1981), 14–17; Alexander K. Smith, "Remarks Concerning the Methodology and Symbolism of Bon Pebble Divination," *Etudes mongoles et siberiennes, centrasiatiques et tibetaines* 42 (2011): 5.

3   Arranging Oracular Responses

Alongside dice, divination books are the other major material cultural element of dice divination. One might assume that a dice divination book should be easily navigable. Indeed, this principle is partly evident when one merely glances at a dice divination book, even without reading the words or knowing the language. The patterned representation of pips, letters, or numbers, set apart from the text, immediately catches the eye. In many such books, the representation of the pips, numbers, or letters stands at the head of each oracular response as its own line of "text" following a blank line that offsets it from the previous response in the manner of a paragraph. Alongside legal texts and official letters, dice divination is in fact one of the few Tibetan genres that makes such ample and meaningful use of blank space on the written page.[46]

With respect to the arrangement of the oracular responses in a text, we can observe that these may be ordered from combinations of higher numbers to lower numbers, e.g., proceeding from 4/4/4 to 1/1/1 in more or less descending order, or they may be organized inversely, in ascending order. A further alternative is a more chaotic arrangement in which no order is apparent.

A particularly rigorous method of ordering the responses is found in Indic dice divination texts including the *Pāśakakevalī* and the divination text in part IV of the circa-sixth-century *Bower Manuscript*.[47] This is the arranging of groups of responses in named, numerically similar subgroups, called *āya*-s. In the divination text in part IV of the *Bower Manuscript*, the responses are indexed by Brāhmī numerals. Following an opening invocation, the first four responses are 4/4/4, 3/3/3, 2/2/2, and 1/1/1. Each of these triplets has its own name, e.g., 4/4/4 is called a *cāṇṭayaṇṭa*,[48] 3/3/3 is a *navikkī*, and 2/2/2 is a *paṭ-*

---

46   On the similarities between the *mise en page* of Old Tibetan dice divination texts and legal codes from Dunhuang, see Brandon Dotson, "Introducing Early Tibetan Law: Codes and Cases," in *Secular Law and Order in the Tibetan Highland*, ed. Dieter Schuh (Andiast: International Institute for Tibetan and Buddhist Studies, 2015), 282–283.

47   A.F. Rudolf Hoernle, *The Bower Manuscript; Facsimile Leaves, Nagari Transcript, Romanised Transliteration and English Translation with Notes* (Calcutta: Supt. Govt. Print. India, 1897), 192–202; for a detailed study of the named combinations or *āya*-s, see Lüders, *Das Würfelspiel im alten Indien*, 29–37. On the date of the *Bower Manuscript*, recovered from Kucha, see Lore Sander, "Origin and Date of the Bower Manuscript: a New Approach," in *Investigating Indian Art: Proceedings of a Symposium on the Development of Early Buddhist and Hindu Iconography held by the Museum of India Art Berlin May 1986*, ed. M. Yaldiz and W. Lobo, (Berlin: Museum für Indische Kunst, 1987), 313–323.

48   Conjectural; see Hoernle, *The Bower Manuscript*, 197, n. 3; and Lüders, *Das Würfelspiel im alten Indien*, 30.

ṭabandha, and 1/1/1 a *kālaviddhi*.[49] Such an opening is certainly fitting from the perspective of Vedic cosmology and the connection between the dice rolls and the world ages or *yuga*-s, which follow each other in descending order until the world's destruction. This sentiment might inform the arrangement of oracular responses in descending order more generally within a dice divination book.

The text goes on to list fifty-five more responses for a total of fifty-nine; it does not reach sixty-four due to its repeating one combination and omitting six. Following the first four triplets, this tradition groups the remaining responses into sixteen groups of *āya*-s consisting of either three or six responses each. The first group, for example, is called the three *śāpaṭa*-s: the first *śāpaṭa* is 4/4/3, the second *śāpaṭa* is 4/3/4, and the third *śāpaṭa* is 3/4/4. This group contains all three possible combinations of two fours and one three. Similarly, the next group, the three *mālī*-s, comprise the three possible combinations of two threes and one four: 3/4/3, 3/3/4, and 4/3/3. The ten other groups (twelve in total) that include three dice combinations all follow this same principle, and each includes one repeated number. The four groups that contain six combinations each are made up of combinations of three different numbers. The first of these, which follows the three *mālī*-s, is the six *vahula*-s: 3/2/4, 4/3/2, 2/4/3, 4/2/3, 3/4/2, and 2/3/4.[50] The six *bhadrā*-s, six *śakti*-s, and six *dundubhī*-s are similarly comprised of combinations of one, two, and four, of one, three, and four, and of one, two, and three, respectively.[51]

As noted by Lüders, this tradition of named combinations is also relevant to the *Pāśakakevalī*.[52] As a method of organizing the oracular responses, the creation of named subgroups of combinations based on the numbers combined certainly marks this tradition off from those texts that include no such subgroups. It also entails a creation of yet more numbers: within the sixty-four responses, there are four *āya* groups of triplets, and sixteen further *āya* groups that can be further subdivided into twelve groups of three responses, and four groups of six, making twenty named groups in all.

Despite the sense of order that this subgrouping imposes, the internal organization of the named *āya*-s is fluid. The three *mālī*-s (3/4/3, 3/3/4, 4/3/3), for instance, are arranged in neither ascending nor descending order. This is typical of the internal ordering of nearly all the named subgroups. In addition, the ordering of the subgroups with respect to one another proceeds in descending order, but it does so with a few twists and turns. If one were to add their

---

49   Hoernle, *The Bower Manuscript*, 198.

50   The latter combination is missing in the text, which only names five *vahula*-s.

51   Hoernle, *The Bower Manuscript*, 199–200.

52   Lüders, *Das Würfelspiel im alten Indien*, 30.

THREE DICE, FOUR FACES, AND SIXTY-FOUR COMBINATIONS 31

sums, then the first non-triplet group, the *śāpaṭa-s* (4/4/3, 4/3/4, 3/4/4), would be eleven, and the last group, the *kharī-s* (1/1/2, 1/2/1, 2/1/1), would be four. But between these two poles it is not an orderly descent, but rather proceeds 10, 9, 9, 7, 8, 6, 10, 8, 8, 6, 7, 7, 5, 5.

In the fragmentary version of the *Pāśakakevalī* preserved in part v of the *Bower Manuscript*, the extant responses do not refer to names of the *āya-s*, but they are nevertheless arrayed within the *āya* groupings of numerically similar combinations. The first three responses, for example, are 4/4/1, 1/4/4, and 4/1/4, but without any reference to these being the three *kūṭa-s*.[53] There are some further indicative differences with regard to this text's more elaborated contents, its attention to time, and to confirmatory "tokens" often consisting of marks on the querent's body. Attending here only to numerical and organizational elements, we can observe that the responses are usually indexed by both numerals and by written numbers, e.g., "4/1/4: Four, one in the middle, four at the end."[54] The oracular responses here do not begin with the same four triplets as in the divination text in part IV of the *Bower Manuscript*, but appear to generally proceed in a similar fashion from higher to lower combinations.[55]

The most consistent and logical arrangement of oracular responses appears in the 19th-century Turkish *Fāl-namāh* attributed to Jaʿfar al-Ṣādiq that J.-A. Decourdemanche translated into French. This employs the first four letters of the Arabic alphabet instead of numbers or pips, and it proceeds in ascending order from ١/١/١ (a/a/a) to د./د./د. (d/d/d) in the following pattern: a/a/a, a/a/b, a/a/c, a/a/d, a/b/a, a/b/b, a/b/c, a/b/d, a/c/a, a/c/b, a/c/c, a/c/d, a/d/a, a/d/b, a/d/c, a/d/d, b/a/a, b/a/b ...[56] This progression in ascending order from a first divination of 1/1/1 to the final divination of 4/4/4 is also found in many later versions of the *Pāśakakevalī*.[57]

In the Tibetan Buddhist *Mo rtsis ʾjam paʾi dbyangs* and similar texts that use combinations of the letters *A, WA, YA,* and *DA,* borrowed from the first four letters of the Greek or Aramaic alphabet, there is also a progression in ascending order.[58] Here, however, the text begins with *A/A/A,* but does not end with *DA/DA/DA.* Rather, the triplets effectively act as "headings" of four sections—though they are not distinguished as such by page setting—such that *A/A/A* is

---

53 Hoernle, *The Bower Manuscript*, 210.

54 Ibid., 210.

55 Ibid., 203–213.

56 Decourdemanche, *Le Miroir de l'avenir*, 6–7.

57 See the table in Francke, "Drei weitere Blätter des tibetischen Losbuches von Turfan," 115. Cf. Albrecht Weber, "Über ein indisches Würfel-Orakel," *Monatsberichte der Königlichen Akademie der Wissenschaften zu Berlin* (1860): 158–180.

58 See Zhi ba lha, et al, "Mo rtsis ʾjam paʾi dbyangs."

followed by all combinations beginning with *A*, after which the triplet *WA/WA/WA* introduces all combinations beginning with *WA*, and so on in the same fashion for the "*YA* combinations" and "*DA* combinations" following *YA/YA/YA* and *DA/DA/DA*, respectively. Internally, the combinations in these "sections" proceed in no particular order, and the text ends with the final response *DA/WA/YA*. This is very similar to the order followed in the Arabic dice divination text in the "Book of Wonders" (*Kitāb al-Bulhān*; MS. Bodl. Or. 133, folios 131a–163a) kept in the Bodleian Library, which also uses the triplets as section headings. It proceeds more carefully in each section, however, first listing those combinations with two repeated letters before moving onto those combinations where each letter is different.

The ordering of the oracular responses in the *Mo rtsis 'jam pa'i dbyangs* is essentially the inverse of what one finds in most Old Tibetan dice divination texts in that in the latter texts the triplets also act as "section headings," but proceed in descending rather than ascending order. The "typical" pattern, if we may call it such, is seen in IOL Tib J 739, IOL Tib J 740, and PT 1052. The first divination is 4/4/4, followed by all possible combinations beginning with 4, e.g., 4/4/3, 4/2/4, etc. After that comes 3/3/3 and all combinations beginning with 3; then 2/2/2 and all combinations beginning with 2, and then 1/1/1 and all combinations beginning with 1. The internal order, that is to say, how the responses progress from 4/4/4 to 3/3/3, and so forth, is variable. One can find even greater variation in a text like Or.8210/S.155, but the responses are still generally organized in descending order.

One interesting counterpoint is found in BD 14599, a Dunhuang dice divination text kept in Beijing which begins with the four descending triplets, just like we find in the divination text in part IV of the *Bower Manuscript*. However, its remaining five extant responses, 2/3/2, 4/2/2, 4/3/1, 4/3/3, and 1/4/3, proceed in no discernible order, and the text appears to be left incomplete, since it is followed by blank space to the end of the scroll.

Turning to those texts whose oracular responses are arranged in neither ascending nor descending order, one can cite the apparent chaos of the tenth-century *Irq Bitig*. It begins with the four triplets, but these occur in the order 2/2/2, 4/4/4, 3/3/3, 1/1/1. The responses that follow seem to proceed in no particular order, beginning with 2/4/2, and ending with 3/3/2.[59] These combinations,

---

59 See the table in Thomas, *Ancient Folk-Literature from North-Eastern Tibet*, 142. Cf. Vilhelm Thomsen, "Dr. M.A. Stein's Manuscripts in Turkish 'Runic' Script from Miran and Tun-huang," *Journal of the Royal Asiatic Society* (1912): 181–227; and Talat Tekin, *Irk Bitig: the Book of Omens* (Wiesbaden: Otto Harrassowitz, 1994), 8–26. On the structure and date of the *Irq Bitig*, see Volker Rybatski and Hu Hong, "The Irq Bitig, the Book of Divination: New Discov-

as in the Tibetan divination texts, are represented by pips rather than numbers. The *Moxishouluo bu*, or *Maheśvara's Method of Divination*, begins in a similar manner to the first divination text in the *Bower Manuscript*, which also makes reference to *Maheśvara*, among other gods. Also in common with the *Bower Manuscript*, the *Moxishouluo bu*'s responses are indexed by numbers, and it begins with the four triplets. The order of the first four are inverted, however, in that they go in ascending rather than descending order, 1/1/1, 2/2/2, 3/3/3, and 4/4/4. The *Moxishouluo bu* then proceeds fairly chaotically, 2/4/1, 2/1/4, 4/1/3, 1/4/2, etc., ending with 3/1/2.[60] A few of the responses appear in pairs, e.g. 2/1/4 follows 2/4/1, but otherwise there is no trace of anything like the *āya*-s of Indic dice divination books.

The *Lingqi jing*, by contrast, arranges its oracular responses in thirty-one groups of four, in ascending order. The first four are 1/1/1, 1/1/2, 1/1/3, and 1/1/4. The next four proceed 1/2/1 to 1/4/1, and the sixteenth group goes from 4/4/1 to 4/4/4.[61] The next fifteen groups of four employ one or two blanks, e.g., "1/-/1" or "-/1/-." These blanks, as noted above, came to be represented as zeros, probably from the thirteenth century on, and to these thirty-one groups of four combinations a final combination or numerical trigram, 0/0/0 was added to make 125 in all. It is noteworthy here that the blanks come after the first sixty-four responses, and that the text uses groups of four rather than groups of five. It comes most likely as a result of the fact that the system initially had only 124 combinations/ trigrams. At the same time, it seems to set the blank or zero apart, and one wonders if this might have been a secondary development from a core of sixty-four oracular responses.

The organization of oracular responses within a dice divination book is variable, and it is through this variation that we can often see differences between traditions, as well as some possible traces of transmission. Ascending versus descending order, the presence or absence of triplets at the beginning of the text, and the use of named groups of combinations linked together by their numerical components are all prospectively meaningful when considering how these diverse texts might be grouped. An interesting marker of difference between Old Tibetan dice divination texts and the later, Tibetan Buddhist tradition of divination with *pāśaka*-s is that the latter tradition arrays its responses in ascending, rather than descending order. This, in addition to

---

eries Concerning its Structure and Content," in *Interpreting the Turkic Runiform Sources and the Position of the Altai Corpus*, ed. Irina Nevskaya and Marcel Erdal (Berlin: Klaus Schwarz Verlag, 2015), 149–173.

60   Kalinowski, "Cléromancie," 352; 368.

61   Morgan, "An Introduction to the *Lingqi jing*," 99.

using letters instead of pips, advertises the difference between the two traditions even before one has examined the contents of their respective responses.

One of the features that unites nearly all of the divination texts we have mentioned is that they skip and/or repeat numerical combinations and/or responses. Our only complete Old Tibetan dice divination text, IOL Tib J 740, omits two responses, and the nearly complete IOL Tib J 739 omits seven. The *Irq Bitiq* both omits and repeats combinations in order to arrive at a total of sixty-five instead of sixty-four responses. The *Moxishouluo bu* similarly has sixty-five responses due to repetition and omission. Even the use of named *āya* subgroups did not save the first divination text in the *Bower Manuscript* from omitting six responses and repeating one. This sense of omission and repetition mirrors the contents of the oracular responses themselves, which feature overlapping formulae and motifs, and which are often written in unstable or semi-literate orthographies.

This sense of disorder and incompleteness is directly opposed to the principle that a divination book should be easily navigable. It conjures a setting in which a diviner might scan his or her book for a client's combination only to find that it is missing from the text or that it is repeated. While this is not impossible, it does seem farcical and highly improbable. More likely, this disorder tells us something about the context of these texts. One possibility is that it displays a distance from their users and a degradation of knowledge and of tradition. Another possibility is that these texts are artefacts of a process of textualizing oral traditions. As such, they would be artificial productions and not records of actual divination performances, and would therefore be subject to all of the attendant consequences that such a "command performance" entails.[62] They might be insurance against loss of tradition, but they might equally be "props" for oral performance—present but rarely consulted—in the manner of so many ritual texts in the contemporary Tibetan cultural area. In this case

---

62   On these dynamics in the context of the textualization of oral literature in general, and epic in particular, see Lauri Honko, "Text as Process and Practice: the Textualization of Oral Epics," in *Textualization of Oral Epics*, ed. Lauri Honko (Berlin: Mouton de Gruyter, 2000), 3–54. In a Himalayan ritual context, see, for example, Martin Gaenszle, "Scripturalisation of Ritual in Eastern Nepal," in *Ritual, Heritage, and Identity: the Politics of Culture and Performance in a Globalized World*, ed. Christiane Brosius and Karin M. Polit (London: Routledge, 2011), 281–297. My position contrasts with that of F.W. Thomas and Volker Rybatski, who propose that Tibetan and Turkish dice divination texts, respectively, were records of divinatory séances; Thomas, *Ancient Folk-Literature from North-Eastern Tibet*, 117; Volker Rybatski, "The Old Turkic Irq Bitig and Divination in Central Asia," In *Trans-Turkic Studies: Festschrift in Honour of Marcel Erdal*, ed. Matthias Keppler, Mark Kirchner, and Peter Zieme (Istanbul, 2010), 89–90.

the oracular responses would be preserved in the mind of the diviner, and their disorder in his or her text would be a non-issue. Of course this is only to touch upon the relationship between the oral and the written in these divination rituals, an important topic that requires more extensive treatment than I can offer here.

4   The Balance of Fortune

A fundamental question that one might ask of a given divination system is how likely it is to return an auspicious result. Many oracular responses involve serious peril, such as predictions of imminent misfortune and death, so a prospective client might be concerned to know the likelihood of an inauspicious result, and also what sorts of correcting rituals might be available should this happen. Ignoring the matter of correcting rituals for now, it can be stated that each oracular response in early Tibetan dice divination ends with a succinct evaluation or summation. This typically takes the form of the phrase "a good divination" (*mo bzang ngo*), "a bad divination" (*mo ngan no* or *mo ngan to*), or "a middling [that is to say, 'mixed'] divination" (*mo 'bring ngo*). Evaluations of "good" and "bad" are present in nearly all of the *Irq Bitig*'s responses, and the *Moxishouluo bu* also ends each response with an evaluation, though not always in such straightforward terms as "good" and "bad." Such evaluations make it very easy to add up the number of good, bad, and mixed responses in order to arrive at the "balance of fortune" of a given divination text. This balance is comparatively transparent in the case of *pāśaka* divination and systems that use a similar method of combination where order matters, since each outcome is equally probable. When considering the balance of fortune for those divination methods that use one of the other systems of combination described above, such as adding the pips of three six-sided dice to arrive at one of sixteen possible outcomes numbered three to eighteen, one must keep in mind that the outcomes are not equally probable.

Across *pāśaka* divination texts the greater outlook of fortune is weighted in favor of good, rather than bad outcomes. The *Irq Bitig* has thirty-nine good responses, nineteen bad, and seven that lack any evaluation or summation. The *Moxishouluo bu* also has a very favorable balance of fortune, with by far the highest number being "very auspicious" 大吉, and only five responses being clearly inauspicious as opposed to auspicious or neutral (*ping* 平). Calculating the balance of fortune in Old Tibetan dice divination texts from Dunhuang, Turfan, and Mazār Tāgh is complicated by the fact that only one of our texts is complete, with the twenty-odd other fragmentary texts ranging from a few damaged lines to over two hundred lines.[63] Furthermore, our one complete text and another nearly complete text are imperfect in the sense that one, IOL Tib J 740, has two missing responses, while the other, IOL Tib J 739, lacks seven. The former has forty good responses, fifteen bad, six mixed or middling (*'bring*), one "basis" (*gzhi*),[64] and two missing. The latter text has thirty-seven good responses, fourteen bad, six mixed or middling, six missing, and one incomplete, with the manuscript ending in the middle of the response at the end of the final extant page.[65] Their balance of fortune, or the cosmology of fortune imagined by these divination texts, is almost identical, and is obviously weighted in favor of a good outcome.

Those texts that lack explicit evaluations at the end of each response still exhibit a balance of fortune. The responses of the dice divination texts in the *Bower Manuscript*, the Turkish *Fāl-namāh* translated by Decourdemanche, and the Tibetan Buddhist *Mo rtsis 'jam pa'i dbyangs*, for example, lack summations, but one can easily identify based on their contents which of the responses are good, bad, or mixed. One might refer to these as their "implicit evaluations." Identifying these and looking to their balances of fortune, one later version of the *Pāśakakevalī*, as noted by Francke, has forty-two good responses, eleven bad, and eleven mixed.[66] The first dice divination text in the *Bower Manuscript* has thirty-one good responses, nine bad, and fourteen mixed. Decourdemanche's Turkish *Fāl-namāh* does not, strictly speaking, have any bad responses, since even those that begin inauspicious end favorably. The ratio of unremittingly good responses to those that start out bad but then turn out good is almost a perfect 2 : 1 ratio at 43 to 21.[67]

This general picture of a 2 : 1 ratio of good responses to bad or mixed responses is complicated by the fact that the probability of receiving a good response is not always as straightforward as simply casting the dice and receiving a good, bad, or mixed response. While this may be the case in the *Moxishouluo bu*, where one is permitted to stop after receiving a good result, and where one is allowed to try up to three times, at least one early Tibetan dice div-

---

63   See the table of twenty divination texts in Ai Nishida, "古チベット語サイコロ占い文書の研究," 64; and the twenty-three in idem, "A Preliminary Analysis of Old Tibetan Dice Divination Texts."

64   On the meaning of *gzhi*, see below.

65   This is to oversimplify as follows: 37 on balance good (35 *bzang rab*; 1 *bzang*; 1 *bzang bar 'ong*); 6 on balance middling or mixed (3 *'bring*; 1 *'bring smad*; 1 *dgra bya la bzang rab*; 1 *rang bzo ba la ngan dra bya la bzang*); 14 on balance bad (9 *ngan rab*; 2 *ngan*; 2 *ngo lon gyis* or *ngo yogs gyis*; 1 *bag zon bya*).

66   A.H. Francke, "Drei weitere Blätter des tibetischen Losbuches von Turfan," 115–116.

67   Decourdemanche, *Le Miroir de l'avenir*.

ination text makes use of the "rule of three." Here one does not simply roll the dice once and receive one response but rather performs the process three times to receive three responses. This method is stated explicitly in the only extant preamble to an Old Tibetan dice divination text. This is found in the tenth-century codex IOL Tib J 739, which provides both an invocation and some brief instructions for performing the divination. Casting for three oracular responses instead of one changes the odds of receiving a given outcome. It also means that the diviner will read out three separate responses to the client, each with its own images, verses, and applications. This offers three opportunities for the client to read him or herself into the responses and for the diviner to construct a narrative relating the specific responses and their verses to the question at hand and to the client.

The method for arriving at three different oracular responses given in the preamble to IOL Tib J 739 states that if one should receive three good or three bad responses in succession, then this is definitive, and one should not cast dice for a further response. Should one have two bad responses and one good, it is permissible to cast the dice once more for a further response. In the inverse case, however, the verse states, "Two being good, with one bad, this being middling, set it [aside] on the *gzhi* / as *gzhi*."[68] We will return to this important term below. This statement in the preamble to IOL Tib J 739 allows us to calculate the probabilities of the four outcomes (three good, two good and one bad, one good and two bad, or three bad). As noted above, IOL Tib J 739 has thirty-seven good responses, fourteen bad, six mixed, one incomplete, and six missing. "Filling in" the missing and incomplete responses by distributing them roughly proportionally in order to calculate the probabilities of each possible outcome, there would be forty-one good responses, seventeen bad, and six mixed. Using these numbers, the probabilities of getting the four outcomes mentioned in IOL Tib J 739's preamble are as follows:

> Three good (GGG) = 26%
> Two good, one bad (GGB; result is *"gzhi"*) = 33%
> Two bad, one good (BBG) = 13.5%[69]
> Three bad (BBB) = 2%

---

68   *bzang gnyis ni ngan gcig dang / 'bring gis ni gzhi' la zhog*; IOL Tib J 739, 3v1–2.

69   One casts the dice for a further response if one receives a combination of BBG. It appears that this is not another "round" in the sense that one does not start over and cast for three fresh responses, but rather casts the dice just once more for a fourth response. Unfortunately, the text is not at all clear on what one is to do with that fourth response. Is it to be

This leaves out any combinations that include middling or mixed (*'bring*) responses, which make up about a quarter of all possible outcomes. Unfortunately, the preamble to IOL Tib J 739 is completely silent on how these mixed responses figure into interpreting the outcome. It is likely that the method involved, whatever it may be, was simply taken for granted. To complete the calculation, the probabilities of the remaining six possible outcomes would be as follows:

GGM = 11.5%
GMB = 9.5%
MMG = 1.7%
MMB = 0.7%
MMM = 0.1%
BBM = 2%

As a result of the rule of three, it is highly unlikely that one would receive three bad responses in a row, even when, at first glance, the presence of seventeen bad divination responses in a book of sixty-four might seem hazardous. Similarly, it is not as easy to get three good responses in a row as it is to roll the dice once for a single good response. Perhaps the most striking fact is that according to this method, one third of divination outcomes—those that return two good responses and one bad—yield a result that is referred to as *gzhi*, a term that usually means "basis" or "foundation."

The specific point of reference of *gzhi* in this context—material or not—remains to be determined, but an investigation of the term's appearance in a variety of divination texts reveals its meaning. In IOL Tib J 740, the combination 2/3/1 returns a divination whose value is *gzhi*.[70] The interpretation preceding this evaluation/ summation is generally good. In Or.8210/S.155, the combination 3/1/2 indexes a divination from the mouth of the god Ram tshir concerning one's good and bad dreams: if one has a good dream, then things will turn out just as in the dream, and if one has a bad dream, one should worship the gods to

---

added to the previous three, such that one has a BBGB, BBGG, or BBGM, or is to be taken on its own (G, B, or M) as definitive? In the latter case, the probabilities would be transparent, and the chance of a good outcome favorable.

70   *rtsod purte ltang rIng gi zhal nas lamdu 'gro ba' la btab na don grub / nor nyed khyIm na 'dug pa la btab na khyIm na myI 'dugste lam rIng por 'groste / mo gzhI'o*; IOL Tib J 740, ll. 177–180; Brandon Dotson, "Divination and Law in the Tibetan Empire: the Role of Dice in the Legislation of Loans, Interest, Marital Law and Troop Conscription," in *Contributions to the Cultural History of Early Tibet*, ed. Matthew T. Kapstein and Brandon Dotson (Leiden: Brill, 2007), 24.

THREE DICE, FOUR FACES, AND SIXTY-FOUR COMBINATIONS   39

overcome it. The evaluation states, "this divination is *gzhi*" (*mo gzhi* ['o]; ll. 98–99).[71] An oracular response in PT 1047 is more decisive about the meaning of *gzhi*: "if it falls on the *bag*[72] [called] *rdud ryags*, one is unable to speak about the divination board. It is neither good nor is it bad; the divination is just *gzhi*."[73] On this point, Ariane Macdonald offered a tentative hypothesis: "faut-il comprendre que ce n'est qu'une base, qu'aucune divinité n'est venue animer en l'interprétant?"[74] It is clear from this, and also from the passage in the preamble translated above ("two being good, with one bad, this being middling, set it [aside] on the *gzhi* / as *gzhi*"), that *gzhi* is neither good nor bad. In this verse it is equivalent to "middling" or "mixed" (*'bring*), but in IOL Tib J 740 the term *'bring* co-occurs with *gzhi* such that one must assume they are not completely synonymous. PT 1047's explanation clarifies the difference: while *'bring* is a mixed response, *gzhi* is meaningless, and essentially falls outside of the divination system as a null result.

The existence, and indeed the high probability of a null result is a very interesting circumstance, and one that seems counterintuitive if one assumes that divination's purpose is to always give one direction, if not certainty, about the past, present, or future. The *gzhi* outcome, by allowing the divination system to

---

71   *lha raM tshir gyi zhal nas myi khyod gyis rmyi lam bzang po zhig rmyis dang / snying la bsams bzhin [rk]es [ng-] smin pa bzhin 'ongo rmyi lam ngan po rmyis dang mgal pas zhugs la lha rjed chig dang des thubo / mo gzhi[g]o*; Or.8210/S.155, ll. 98–99; Kazushi Iwao, Sam van Schaik, and Tsuguhito Takeuchi, eds., *Old Tibetan Texts in the Stein Collection Or.8210* (Tokyo: the Toyo Bunko, 2012), 18.

72   This term qualifies the sixteen different foreign—possibly Zhang zhung—terms used to refer to the names of the sixteen combinations and/or types of omens in PT 1047, some of which are found in (other) Old Tibetan dice divination texts. This number of responses or combinations, incidentally, could be taken to suggest that three six-sided dice were used in PT 1047's system of divination, which differs from the system of early Tibetan divination described here and represented by the twenty-three Old Tibetan divination texts listed by Nishida. Given the overlap of terminology with Old Tibetan dice divination texts that made use of four-sided *pāśaka*-s, however, it may be more likely that these foreign terms are names for the sixteen *āya*-s or groups of dice combinations that follow the first four triplets.

73   *bag rdud ryags bab na' / / mo shing smrar myi bthub ste bzang pho 'ang ma mchis ngan pang ma mchis te mo / / gzhi tsam*; PT 1047, ll. 242–243; Ariane Macdonald, "Une lecture des Pelliot tibétain 1286, 1287, 1038, et 1290: essai sur la formation et l'emploi des mythes politiques dans la religion royale de Sroṅ bcan Sgam po," in *Études Tibétaines dédiées à la mémoire de Marcelle Lalou* (Paris: Adrien Maisonneuve, 1971), 275. On divination boards in early Tibet, see Brandon Dotson, "A Fragment of an Early Tibetan Divination Board from Mīrān," in *Festschrift für Franz-Karl Ehrhard*, ed. Volker Caumanns, Marta Sernesi, and Nikolai Solmsdorf (Munich: Indus Verlag, 2019), 165–187.

74   Macdonald, "Une lecture des Pelliot tibétain 1286, 1287, 1038, et 1290," 275, n. 324.

essentially reject a query, recalls George Park's observation that "[a]n important aspect of divination as institutionalized procedure is just this—that it provides 'resistance' in its own right to any client's proposal."[75] Similarly, Robert Parker writes that "divination fails in its function if its objectivity is not convincingly demonstrated. Though clients seldom go away with an answer that is unsatisfactory, the possibility must always be present."[76] This principle of resistance is easily recognized in East Asian divination from the well-known tradition of casting two crescent-shaped blocks or *bei* (杯), often in conjunction with lot divination (*chouqian* 抽籤): when they land with both flat sides down this means "no"; when they land one up and one down this means "yes"; but when they land with both flat sides up this means "the gods are laughing."[77] The null result in early Tibetan dice divination appears to offer a clear example of a similar form of resistance. Here the dice, asserting themselves as a technology not entirely beholden to its users, might also draw on the sense of play so strongly implied by their medium.

This is one possible reading, and our sources do not tell us precisely how a null result was interpreted, that is, whether or not this might be viewed as indicating the absence of *sman* goddesses in the ritual proceedings, as Macdonald suggests, or whether it may be due to any perceived ritual shortcomings on the part of the diviner and/or the client. Whatever the case, the possibility of a null result within a system of divination injects further uncertainty and chance into an already aleatory technology. Cross-culturally, it may also be the case that the presence and/or the frequency of a null result or a similar concept within a divination system is indicative of its transmission history. The frequency of a null outcome in early Tibetan dice divination is in any case a fascinating element that helpfully problematizes common assumptions about the place of certainty in the ritual transaction of divination.

---

75 George K. Park, "Divination and its Social Contexts," *Journal of the Royal Anthropological Institute* 93.2 (1963): 198.

76 Robert Parker, "Greek States and Greek Oracles," in *Crux: Essays Presented to GEM de Ste. Croix on his 75th Birthday*, ed. P.A. Cartledge and F.D. Harvey (Sidmouth: Duckworth Press, 1985), 78.

77 See, for example, Emily Martin Ahern, *Chinese Ritual and Politics* (Cambridge: Cambridge University Press, 1981), 45–49.

5 Conclusions

The remarkable variation and adaptability that we have observed in this system of dice divination would be notably amplified were we to consider the diverse contents of all the relevant Sanskrit, Tibetan, Chinese, Sogdian, Turkish, Persian, and Arabic texts. The oracular responses are subject to the poetic inclinations and cultural and religious norms of their users. So it is that we find *devatas*, the Maruts, virgins, and sexual pleasure in the *Bower Manuscript* and the *Pāśakakevalī*; quotations from the *Quran* in Turkish, Persian, and Arabic *Kitāb al-Fāl and Fāl-namāh*; mountains, yaks, and local gods in Old Tibetan divination texts; Buddhist, Daoist and local deities in the *Moxishouluo bu*, and an impressive bestiary of animals in the *Irq Bitig*. Similarly, divining communities insert their own interpretations that are particularly suited to the local ritual economy, and to their specific concepts of fortune, luck, and fate. It is clearly here, in the character and content of the responses and interpretations where the technology of dice divination is particularly adaptable to its host culture, and also to the concerns of whatever religion might try to absorb dice divination into its repertoire.

The pantheons of gods who speak the oracular responses or who are somehow associated with them, the poetics of the responses, the contours of how they are interpreted for fortune, marriage, hunting, trade, and so forth, along with the responses' place within the wider ritual economy constitute the "meat," so to speak, of dice divination. The "bones" of this method of divination—the numbers that we have examined here—are, on the other hand, less given to adaptation, and constitute its defining elements. These are the number of faces of a die, the symbols on each face, the number of times the dice (or other objects) are cast, the number of oracular responses in a divination book, their method of arrangement, and the probability of receiving a good, bad, mixed, or null result.

The four-sided *pāśaka* die, with its deep Indic past and its relevance to Vedic cosmologies, represents this system's Indic "signature," but it is not the *sine qua non* of this method of divination. Other randomizing techniques such as drawing lots, casting draughtsmen, using pebbles, or using a pyramidal die can easily be substituted in order to arrive at a combination of three numbers, letters, or pips from one to four. Even so, the *pāśaka* dice themselves display a variety of forms. The most widespread form of the *pāśaka* die is that used for the games of *pachisi* and *caupur*, with faces of one, two, five, and six pips. Among those *pāśaka* dice with faces of one, two, three, and four pips, there are those of the "standard" length of seven to nine cm, and there are the more squat and compact four-cm-long *pāśaka* dice such as that published by Aurel Stein in *Ancient*

Khotan and those kept in the British Museum. Further distinguishing features include the incision of lines at the ends of the long sides of the die, the style of the pips, and the presence or absence of decorative motifs within or around the pips. The material culture of these dice is fascinating, and the archeological record, as imperfect as it is, may in time help answer questions about the chronology of the transmission of this system of divination.

The symbols incised on the dice and/or their corresponding representations in dice divination books also show a good deal of variation. The *Bower Manuscript*, the *Pāśakakevalī*, and the *Moxishouluo bu* all use numbers. At the time when our extant divination manuscripts were written down, in the ninth and tenth centuries, the Tibetans did not yet use written numerals, and it is therefore perhaps unsurprising that they represented the dice rolls "pictorially" with drawings of the same pips that appear on extant *pāśaka* dice from India, Central Asia, and elsewhere. This is also the practice of the Runic Turkish *Irq Bitig*. In the Islamic World, letters were preferred, with the responses being most often indexed by the first four letters of the Arabic alphabet. The use of the first four letters of an alphabet—whether Greek, Arabic, or Aramaic—appears to have been transmitted into Tibet somewhat later, and absorbed into the Buddhist canon in the thirteenth or fourteenth century. The relevant Tibetan Buddhist text, attributed to Śāntideva, provides instructions for making the die, and marking its faces with the letters *A, WA, YA,* and *DA*. This means that there was no need to "translate" the pips of the fallen dice into the letters or numbers in a divination book, something which may have been a common practice in some traditions of Indic and Islamic (and Chinese) *pāśaka* divination.

If one cannot insist on the four faces of the *pāśaka* die, or even on this object itself as central to this form of divination, what then is its defining characteristic? At its most basic, "*pāśaka* divination," or "early Tibetan dice divination" might be defined as belonging to a system that combines three groups of four symbols to arrive at one of sixty-four outcomes or responses. Or, in shorthand, $4^3 = 64$. The method of combination, which does not add the values of the pips, but rather combines them, distinguishes it immediately from divination systems such as that of the *Sortes Sanctorum* and from later Tibetan dice divination with three six-sided dice. The radically different method of combining the relevant numbers or symbols, even more so than the differing number of oracular responses—sixty-four in *pāśaka* divination, fifty-six in the *Sortes Sanctorum*, and sixteen in later Tibetan dice divination—renders it unlikely that any one of these traditions stands as an ancestor in relation to the other(s). Even within those divination systems that use the same method of combining numbers or symbols, we have noted that the *Yijing* arrives at sixty-four responses through a method that is different enough from *pāśaka* divination's method to make their shared number of responses seem less a mark of transmission than a testament to the resonance of the number sixty-four in diverse cultural settings.

The arranging of the sixty-four responses within a divination book is also an area where one can see similarities and differences across traditions, some of which are surely relevant to the question of transmission. Indic dice divination texts, for instance, often make use of named subgroups of numerically related dice rolls, referred to as *āya*-s. Some texts begin with ascending or descending triplets, e.g., 4/4/4, 3/3/3, 2/2/2, 1/1/1, while others do not. More generally, some texts give the responses in ascending order from lowest to highest, others arrange them in descending order, and still others display no discernible order whatsoever. The arrangement of responses in descending order might, like the unbalanced faces of the *pāśaka* die, be explained with reference to the Vedic cosmology of the world ages or *yuga*-s—*kṛta, tretā, dvāpara*, and *kali*—which succeed each other in descending order.

While this review is by no means exhaustive, nearly all of the dice divination texts consulted here include repeated and/or omitted combinations and/or responses, and very few feature the expected total of sixty-four responses. This, along with the semi-literate orthography of many of these manuscripts, tells us something about their context, and suggests a practice-based tradition wherein there lies a dynamic tension between oral and textual transmission.

The overall balance of fortune is generally favorable. A two-to-one ratio of good responses to bad responses appears to be somewhat typical across traditions, but the actual probabilities of the various outcomes must be calculated based on their distributions and on other factors. In at least one tradition of early Tibetan dice divination and in those other traditions that, following the "rule of three," require that one roll the dice for three responses rather than just one, the probabilities are not as straightforward. This rule of three that we see in the casting of three *pāśaka* dice, or of one *pāśaka* three times, and the three-fold repetition of this process to arrive at three responses, is also far from unique and can be found in many forms of divination across a variety of cultures. It raises problems for how one interprets a situation in which a querent receives anything other than all good responses or all bad responses, and it also makes receiving a bad outcome far less probable. Unfortunately, the methods for addressing such situations where one has a mixture of responses seem to have gone without saying, such that the processes involved are rarely specified in the texts. In the only Old Tibetan dice divination text that begins with invocations and instructions, we find this question partially addressed, but the answer also reveals something very intriguing. This is the "null divination" (*gzhi*), which is neither good, bad, nor mixed, but simply meaningless.

This refusal of the dice to play along is almost the purest expression of divination: it represents an aleatory technique that, beyond addressing queries with opaque verses or archaic speech from the mouths of gods, also sometimes chooses simply to remain mute.

Individually, it may be the case that none of these numbers is particularly indicative. Taken together, however, this constellation of numbers constitutes the defining feature of early Tibetan dice divination, and is indicative for determining its transmission across cultures. The preliminary indications point to a transmission from the Indic world, where we find the oldest *pāśaka* dice, the oldest attested tradition of their use in gaming and divination, and a cosmological justification for the peculiarly "unbalanced" arrangement of their pips, which wend around the die in sequence. This form of divination seems to have been transmitted to the north and west to Persian and Arabian cultures, and to the north and east to Turkish, Tibetan, and Chinese cultures. The dates of these transmissions are uncertain, but the Turkish, Tibetan, and Chinese divination manuscripts from Dunhuang, Turfan, and Mazār Tāgh date from the late-eighth to mid-tenth centuries, with the birch-bark *Bower Manuscript* from Kucha dating to approximately the sixth century. The later, Tibetan Buddhist tradition of divination with *pāśaka* dice marked with Tibetan transcriptions of the first four letters of the Greek, Aramaic, or Arabic alphabet would appear to be a retransmission, possibly via the Islamic World. These are only preliminary hypotheses, however, and the precise vectors of transmission remain to be determined through detailed study of divination books in Sanskrit, Turkish, Persian, Arabic, Tibetan, and Chinese, along with a more concerted survey of the material culture of *pāśaka* dice. Such an undertaking would add flesh to the bare bones of the system of dice divination sketched here through an investigation of its numbers.

References

Ahern, Emily Martin. *Chinese Ritual and Politics*. Cambridge: Cambridge University Press, 1981.

Bréard, Andrea. "How to Quantify the Value of Domino Combinations? Divination and Shifting Rationalities in Late Imperial China." In *Coping with the Future: Theories and Practices of Divination in East Asia*, ed. Michael Lackner, pp. 499–529. Leiden: Brill, 2017.

Champeaux, Jacqueline. " 'Sorts' antiques et médiévaux: les lettres et les chiffres." In *Au miroir de la culture antique: mélanges offerts au président René Marache par ses collègues, ses étudiants et ses amis*, pp. 67–89. Rennes: Presses Universitaires de Rennes, 1992.

Contadini, Anna. "Islamic Ivory Chess Pieces, Draughtsmen and Dice in the Ashmolean Museum." In *Islamic Art in the Ashmolean Museum*, ed. James Allan, pp. 111–154. Oxford: Oxford University Press, 1995.

Culin, Stewart. *Chess and Playing Cards: Catalogue of Games and Implements for Divination Exhibited by the United States National Museum*. Philadelphia: University of Pennsylvania Press, 1896.

Decourdemanche, J.-A. *Le Miroir de l'avenir. Recueil de sept traités de divination traduit du turc*. Paris: Bibliotheque orientale Elzevirienne 1899.

Dotson, Brandon. "Divination and Law in the Tibetan Empire: the Role of Dice in the Legislation of Loans, Interest, Marital Law and Troop Conscription." In *Contributions to the Cultural History of Early Tibet*, ed. Matthew T. Kapstein and Brandon Dotson, pp. 3–77. Leiden: Brill, 2007.

Dotson, Brandon. "The Call of the Cuckoo to the Thin Sheep of Spring: Healing and Fortune in Old Tibetan Dice Divination Texts." In *Tibetan and Himalayan Healing: An Anthology for Anthony Aris*, ed. Charles Ramble and Ulrike Roesler, pp. 147–160. Kathmandu: Vajra Publications, 2015.

Dotson, Brandon. "Introducing Early Tibetan Law: Codes and Cases." In *Secular Law and Order in the Tibetan Highland*, ed. Dieter Schuh. Monumenta Tibetica Historica Abteilung III Band 13, pp. 267–314. Andiast: International Institute for Tibetan and Buddhist Studies, 2015.

Dotson, Brandon. "A Fragment of an Early Tibetan Divination Board from Mīrān." In *Unearthing Himalayan Treasures: Festschrift for Franz-Karl Ehrhard*, ed. Volker Caumanns, Marta Sernesi, and Nikolai Solmsdorf, pp. 165–187. Marburg: Indica et Tibetica Verlag, 2019.

Dotson, Brandon. "Hunting for Fortune: Wild Animals, Goddesses and the Play of Perspectives in Early Tibetan Dice Divination." In *Animals and Religion on the Tibetan Plateau*, ed. Geoff Barstow (Special issue of *Études Mongoles & Sibériennes, Centrasiatiques & Tibétaines* 50 [2019]): 1–26.

Finkel, Irving. "Dice in India and Beyond." In *Asian Games: the Art of Contest*, ed. Colin Mackenzie and Irving Finkel, pp. 38–45. New York: Asia Society, 2004.

Finkel, Irving. "Round and Round the Houses: the Game of *Pachisi*." In *Asian Games: the Art of Contest*, ed. Colin Mackenzie and Irving Finkel, pp. 47–58. New York: Asia Society, 2004.

Flügel, Gustav. "Die Loosbücher der Muhammadaner." *Berichte über die Verhandlungen der Königliche Sächsischen Gesellschaft der Wissenschaften zu Leipzig, Philologisch-Historische Klasse 13* (1861): 24–74.

Francke, A.H. "Tibetische Handschriftenfunde aus Turfan." *Sitzungsberichte der Preussischen Akademie der Wissenschaften, philosophisch-historische Klasse 3* (1924): 5–20.

Francke, A.H. "Drei weitere Blätter des tibetischen Losbuches von Turfan." *Sitzungs-*

berichte der Preussischen Akademie der Wissenschaften, philosophisch-historische Klasse 7 (1928): 110–118.

Gaenszle, Martin. "Scripturalisation of Ritual in Eastern Nepal." In *Ritual, Heritage, and Identity: the Politics of Culture and Performance in a Globalized World,* ed. Christiane Brosius and Karin M. Polit, pp. 281–297. London: Routledge, 2011.

Goldberg, Jay and Lobsang Dakpa, trans. *Mo: Tibetan Divination System.* Ithaca, Snow Lion, 1990.

González-Reimann, Luis. "The Ancient Vedic Dice Game and the Names of the Four World Ages in Hinduism." In *World Archaeoastronomy,* ed. Anthony F. Aveni, pp. 195–202. Cambridge: Cambridge University Press, 1988.

Graf, Fritz. "Rolling the Dice for an Answer." In *Mantikê: Studies in Ancient Divination,* ed. Sarah Iles Johnston and Peter T. Struck, pp. 51–97. Leiden: Brill, 2005.

Handelman, Don and David Shulman. *God Inside Out: Śiva's Game of Dice.* Oxford: Oxford University Press, 1997.

Hoernle, A.F. Rudolf. *The Bower Manuscript; Facsimile Leaves, Nagari Transcript, Romanised Transliteration and English Translation with Notes.* Calcutta: Supt. Govt. Print. India, 1897.

Honko, Lauri. "Text as Process and Practice: the Textualization of Oral Epics." In *Textualization of Oral Epics,* ed. Lauri Honko, pp. 3–54. Berlin: Mouton de Gruyter, 2000.

Iwao, Kazushi, Van Schaik, Sam, and Takeuchi, Tsuguhito. eds. *Old Tibetan Texts in The Stein Collection Or.8210, Studies in Old Tibetan Texts from Central Asia* vol. 1. Tokyo: The Toyo Bunko, 2012.

Kalinowski, Marc. "La divination par les nombres dans les manuscrits de Dunhuang." In *Nombres, astres, plantes et viscères: sept essais sur l'histoire des sciences et des techniques en Asie orientale,* ed. Isabelle Ang and Pierre-Étienne Will, pp. 37–88. Paris: Institute des Hautes Études Chinoises, 1994.

Kalinowski, Marc. "Cléromancie." In *Divination et société dans la Chine médiévale: Étude des manuscrits de Dunhuang de la Bibliothèque nationale de France et de la British Library,* ed. Marc Kalinowski pp. 301–368. Paris: Bibliothèque nationale de France, 2003.

Kane, M.P.V. *History of Dharmaśāstra,* volume 3. Poona: Bhandarkar Oriental Research Institute, 1946.

Lai, Whalen. "The *Chan-ch'a ching*: Religion and Magic in Medieval China." In *Chinese Buddhist Apocrypha,* ed. Robert Buswell, pp. 175–206. Honolulu: University of Hawai'i Press, 1990.

Liying, Kuo. "Divination, jeux de hazard et purification dans le bouddhisme chinois: Autour d'un sutra apocryphe chinois, le *Zhanchajing.*" In *Bouddhisme et cultures locales: Quelques cas de réciproques adaptations,* ed. Fukui Fumimasa and Gérard Fussman, pp. 145–167. Paris: École Française d'Extrême-Orient, 1994.

Lüders, Heinrich. *Das Würfelspiel im Alten Indien*. Berlin: Weidmannsche Buchhandlung, 1907.

Macdonald, Ariane. Une lecture des Pelliot tibétain 1286, 1287, 1038, et 1290: essai sur la formation et l'emploi des mythes politiques dans la religion royale de Sroṅ bcan Sgam po. *In Études Tibétaines dédiées à la mémoire de Marcelle Lalou*, pp. 190–391. Paris: Adrien Maisonneuve, 1971.

Mackay, E.J.H. *Further Excavations and Mohenjo-Daro*, vol. 2. New Delhi: Government of India Press, 1937.

Marshall, John Hubert. *Taxila: An Illustrated Account of Archaeological Excavations Carried Out at Taxila under the Orders of the Government of India Between the Years 1913 and 1934*. Cambridge: Cambridge University Press, 1951.

McGuire, Beverley Foulks. *Living Karma: The Religious Practices of Ouyi Zhixu*. New York: Columbia University Press, 2014.

Michon, Daniel. *Archaeology and Religion in Early Northwest India: History, Theory, Practice*. New Delhi: Routledge, 2015.

Morgan, Carol. "An Introduction to the *Lingqi jing*." *Journal of Chinese Religions* 23 (1993): 97–120.

Nicoll, Alexander. *Bibliothecae Bodleianae Codicum Manuscriptorum Orientalium Catalogi*. Oxford, 1835.

Nishida, Ai 西田愛. "古チベット語サイコロ占い文書の研究 (A Study of Old Tibetan Dice Divination)." 日本西藏学会夕輯 (*Report of the Japanese Association for Tibetan Studies*) 54 (2008): 63–77.

Nishida, Ai 西田愛. "A Preliminary Analysis of Old Tibetan Dice Divination Texts," in *Glimpses of Tibetan Divination: Past and Present*, ed. Petra Maurer, Donatella Rossi, and Rolf Scheuermann, 49–72. Leiden: Brill, 2019.

Park, George K. "Divination and its Social Contexts." *Journal of the Royal Anthropological Institute* 93, no. 2 (1963): 195–209.

Parker, Robert. "Greek States and Greek Oracles." In *Crux: Essays Presented to G.E.M. de Ste. Croix on his 75th Birthday*, ed. P.A. Cartledge and F.D. Harvey, pp. 76–108. Sidmouth: Duckworth Press, 1985.

Radha, Chime. "Tibet." In *Oracles and Divination*, ed. Michael Loewe and Carmen Blacker, pp. 3–37. Boulder: Shambhala Publications, 1981.

Rybatski, Volker. "The Old Turkic Irq Bitig and Divination in Central Asia." In *Trans-Turkic Studies: Festschrift in Honour of Marcel Erdal*, ed. Matthias Keppler, Mark Kirchner, and Peter Zieme, pp. 79–102. Istanbul, 2010.

Rybatski, Volker and Hu Hong. "The Irq Bitig, the Book of Divination: New Discoveries Concerning its Structure and Content." In *Interpreting the Turkic Runiform Sources and the Position of the Altai Corpus*, ed. Irina Nevskaya and Marcel Erdal, pp. 149–173. Berlin: Klaus Schwarz Verlag, 2015.

Sander, Lore. "Origin and Date of the Bower Manuscript: a New Approach." In *Investigating Indian Art: Proceedings of a Symposium on the Development of Early Buddhist and Hindu Iconography held by the Museum of India Art Berlin May 1986, ed. M. Yaldiz and W. Lobo, pp. 313–323. Berlin: Museum für Indische Kunst, 1987.

Savage-Smith, Emilie. "Divination." In *Science, Tools, and Magic: the Nasser D. Khalili Collection of Islamic Art, Volume XII*, pp. 148–159. Oxford: the Nour Foundation and Oxford University Press, 1997.

Smith, Alexander K. "Remarks Concerning the Methodology and Symbolism of Bon Pebble Divination." *Études mongoles et sibériennes, centrasiatiques et tibétaines* 42 (2011): 2–15.

Stein, Marc Aurel. *Ancient Khotan: Detailed Report of Archaeological Explorations in Chinese Turkestan*. Volume II: Plates. Oxford: Clarendon Press, 1907.

Stein, Marc Aurel. *Serindia: Detailed Report of Explorations in Central Asia and Westernmost China*. Volume IV: Plates. Oxford: Clarendon Press, 1921.

Strickmann, Michel. *Chinese Poetry and Prophecy: the Written Oracle in East Asia*. Stanford: Stanford University Press, 2005.

Takeuchi, Tsuguhito. *Old Tibetan Manuscripts from East Turkestan in the Stein Collection of the British Library* vol. II Descriptive catalogue. Tokyo/London: The Centre for East Asian Cultural Studies for Unesco, The Toyo Bunko, and The British Library, 1998.

Taube, Manfred. *Die Tibetica der Berliner Turfansammlung*. Berlin: Akademie-Verlag, 1980.

Tekin, Talat. *Irk Bitig: the Book of Omens*. Wiesbaden: Otto Harrassowitz, 1994.

Thomas, Fredrick William. *Ancient Folk-Literature from North-Eastern Tibet*. Berlin: Akademie-Verlag, 1957.

Thomsen, Vilhelm. "Dr. M.A. Stein's Manuscripts in Turkish 'Runic' Script from Miran and Tun-huang." *Journal of the Royal Asiatic Society* (1912): 181–227.

Wang Jingbo 王晶波. *Dunhuang zhanbu wenxian yu shehui shenghuo* 敦煌占卜文獻與社會生活. Lanzhou: Gansu jiaoyu, 2011.

Weber, Albrecht. "Über ein indisches Würfel-Orakel." *Monatsberichte der Königlichen Akademie der Wissenschaften zu Berlin* (1860): 158–180.

CHAPTER 3

A Preliminary Analysis of Old Tibetan Dice Divination Texts

Ai Nishida

1 Introduction

Among the Old Tibetan divination texts retrieved from Dunhuang and other sites along the Silk Road in East Turkestan, dice divination texts predominate in terms of both number and diversity of provenance. A.H. Francke conducted pioneering studies of these texts as early as 1924. With the aid of preceding publications concerning the Sanskrit treatise on dice divination, he disclosed that six fragmental manuscripts preserved within the Berlin Turfan Collection containing Old Tibetan paleographical features pertained to the same genre; namely, dice divination. He published the transliterations and German translations of the manuscripts and identified several similarities between these Tibetan texts and a Turkic text found in Dunhuang.[1]

In 1957, subsequent to Francke's work, F.W. Thomas furnished plentiful data on other Old Tibetan dice divination texts maintained at the British Library.[2] Thomas's perceptive views of dice divination, explicated in his *Introduction* and *Addendum*, as well as his transliteration and translation of IOL Tib J 738, enlightened readers about the general outline of Old Tibetan dice divination. At the beginning of the twenty-first century, B. Dotson opened up a new field concerning these texts. Through his close investigation of IOL Tib J 740, which consists of two texts, the first a dice divination text and the second "a set of questions and answers concerning legal processes", he revealed that "the local magistrates employed divination dice and divination manuals to decide legal disputes."[3] Contributions by other pioneering scholars included the translation of single Old Tibetan dice divination texts[4] or brief outlines of

---

1   Francke 1924 and 1928.
2   IOL Tib J 738, IOL Tib J 739, and IOL Tib J 740.
3   Dotson 2007: 59.
4   For example, Wang and Chen published the transliterations and Chinese translations of P.t.1046B, IOL Tib J 738.2, and IOL Tib J 738.3 (Wang and Chen 1987: 154–161; Idem 1988: 105–122). Following Kalsang Yangjen's study, which includes the transliteration and translation of

---

© KONINKLIJKE BRILL NV, LEIDEN, 2020 | DOI:10.1163/9789004410688_004

these.[5] Nevertheless, a comprehensive image of Old Tibetan dice divination texts together with their fundamental perspectives have yet to be provided: for example, how many documents remain available? How are they interrelated? When were they written? And who wrote them? In order to answer these questions, I first classified relevant texts contained in various collections as exhaustively as possible and then examined the original manuscripts in order to extract stereotypical expressions. T. Takeuchi has demonstrated the efficacy of such methodology when working on Old Tibetan letters and contracts.[6]

In what follows, I shall present (1) a general list of the Old Tibetan dice divination texts that I have found so far, indicating their requisition number, form, physical condition, provenance, and the number of extant lines; (2) an outline of the Old Tibetan dice divination texts based on a preliminary attempt; (3) formulae drawn from the texts; (4) their mutual relations; and (5) the process of producing the texts.

2　General Information

I have found twenty-three dice divination texts so far, which I present in the following list. For the sake of convenience, the texts are numbered in succession. Furthermore, I use the following abbreviations to describe the physical condition of the texts:

complete:　text remains complete.
om (B):　　beginning of the text is lost due to damage.
om (E):　　end of the text is lost due to damage.
om (B, E):　beginning and end of the text are lost due to damage.

IOL Tib J 740, Chen remarked on the similarity of the content of P.t.1046B and IOL Tib J 740 (Chen 2011: 108). The majority of these Chinese contributions were collected into *Tibetan Documents from Dunhuang, Volume for Culture*, 2011, edited by Zheng and Huang. Transliterations for IOL Tib J 738, IOL Tib J 739, IOL Tib J 740, P.t.1043, P.t.1046B, P.t.1051, and P.t.1052 are presented in Imaeda et al. eds., 2007. They are also accessible through the OTDO website (https://otdo.aa-ken.jp).

5　A. Macdonald Spanien briefly mentioned several dice divination texts in her eminent article (A. Macdonald Spanien 1971: 285–286). Z. Yamaguchi provided an outline and partial translations of P.t.1051, and I myself have presented a tentative view, based on my preliminary survey of these texts (Yamaguchi 1985: 535; Idem 1987: 177–179; Nishida 2008 and 2018).

6　Takeuchi 1990, 1995. For details on the methodology used for studying Old Tibetan texts, see Takeuchi 1995: 1–5.

A PRELIMINARY ANALYSIS OF OLD TIBETAN DICE DIVINATION TEXTS

TABLE 3.1 A general list of Old Tibetan dice divination texts

Text no.	Requisition no.	Form	Physical condition	Provenance	No. of lines
1	IOL Tib J 738	scroll	om (B, E)	Dunhuang	90 + 33 + 162
2	IOL Tib J 739	codex	om (E)		374
3	IOL Tib J 740	scroll	complete		237 + 122
4	IOL Tib J 743	scroll	om (B, E)		32
5	IOL Tib J 745	scroll	complete		33
6	Or.8210/S.155	scroll	om (B, E)		188 + 8
7	Or.15000/67	fragment	om (B, E)	Mazār Tāgh	12
8	Or.15000/76	fragment	om (B, E)		9
9	P.t. 1043	scroll	om (B)	Dunhuang	100
10	P.t. 1046B	scroll	om (B, E)		41
11	P.t. 1049	scroll	om (B)		8
12	P.t. 1051	scroll	om (B, E)		73
13	P.t. 1052	scroll	om (B)		261 + 11
14	Tu 8 + Tu 12	fragment	om (B, E)	Turfan	14
15	Tu 11	fragment	om (B, E)		11
16	Tu 55	fragment	om (B, E)		5
17	Tu 56	fragment	om (B, E)		11
18	SI O 145	fragment	om (B, E)	Dunhuang	14
19	Dx. 7759	fragment	om (B, E)		7
20	Dx. 8542	fragment	om (B, E)		7
21	BD 14600 + 14599	scroll	om (B)		23 + 46
22	BD 14599	scroll	complete		34
23	Otani 6004	fragment	om (B, E)		5

Generally speaking, the Merkmals used for dating Old Tibetan manuscripts, such as particular official titles or seals, substantial colophons, and dated texts on the *recto* side, can hardly be expected in divination texts.[7] As for their paleography, Van Schaik suggested that one dice divination manuscript is consistent with the writing style of the imperial period;[8] nevertheless, other texts seem to represent the semi-cursive style, which probably dates to the late imperial and post-imperial periods. At the same time, several features dictate their possible earliest and latest dates. As seen in the list above, Text 2 is solely in codex form. This form generally dates from the late ninth century onward, which implies that Text 2 was perhaps compiled after the collapse of the Tibetan empire. On the other hand, Texts 7 and 8 were brought from Mazār Tāgh, which means that they were produced during the period of the Tibetan domination of the Khotan area; that is to say, 790c.–850c. Taking these points into account, I suggest that these dice divination texts were produced during the significant time-span of the imperial period and its immediate aftermath. This may also be confirmed by the quantity of the texts and their broad provenance, as well as the abundance of paleography, despite the fact that they all belong to the same genre of texts.

3 Outline of Old Tibetan Dice Divination Texts

Let us recall the procedure of Old Tibetan dice divination, as shown in the studies mentioned above. Presumably, a single four-sided oblong die was used for this divination method. Between one and four die-eyes were depicted on each of the rectangular sides. This kind of die was found among East Turkestan ruins.[9] By means of three tosses of a die, one can obtain a set of die-marks that consist of three die-eyes; this yields sixty-four prospective combinations of die-marks, i.e., omens, as a result.[10] In divination manuscripts, these die-eyes are depicted as small circles arranged in a line or "in geometrical shapes," sepa-

---

7   For these Merkmals, see Takeuchi 2012: 205–206.

8   Van Schaik identified the writing style of Text 3 as the "square style", one of the peculiar types of paleography of the imperial period (Van Schaik 2013: 121–122, 130). I assume that Texts 1, 5, and 12 display the archaic writing style, which nevertheless does not preclude the possibility of a post-imperial period dating.

9   For instance N.004 *Ancient Khotan* Pl. LXXIV, and L. B. IV. V.0034 in *Serindia* Pl. XXXVI (Stein 1907 and 1921).

10 Unfortunately, even an extensive complete text (Text 3) contains sixty-two omens, due to the absence of 4/1/2 and 4/3/2.

A PRELIMINARY ANALYSIS OF OLD TIBETAN DICE DIVINATION TEXTS

rated by punctuation lines:[11] for example, the combination ⊚⊚ / ⊚ / ⊚⊚⊚⊚ means that a die appears as 2, 1, and 4, respectively.[12] In some cases, they are sketched in red or in the form of double or triple circles but, in other cases, they are simply presented in black with a single circle, which may reflect the original shape and color of the die-mark itself.

Usually, a dice divination text exclusively comprises descriptions of omens; it is worth mentioning in this regard that a metrical introductory part precedes the omens in Text 2. The first omen is led by the last paragraph of the introductory part as follows:[13]

cho lo ni bzang gsuM na /
bzang gis ni bskyar myi 'tshal /
bzang gnyis ni ngan gcig dang /
'bring gis ni gzhi' la zhog //
ngan gnyis ni bzang la gcig la /
gcig tsham ni bskyar te btab
cho lo ni ngan gsuM na /
bskyar kyang ni don ma mchis /
mo gdab pa ni @@@@ / @@@@ @@@@[14] //

If the dice fall in good three times,
[the result is] good and [you] don't need [to try] again.
[If the dice fall in] good twice and once in bad,
[the result is] midway (/fair) and leave it as [a result of] average.
[If the dice fall in] bad twice and once in good,
[you can try] the [divination] cast only once again.
If the dice fall in bad three times,

---

11   Thomas 1957: 115.

12   Each omen requires the discrimination of the order of die-eyes in a set of die-marks: for example, 1/2/3, 2/1/3, and 3/2/1 lead different omens. Therefore, it seems that a set of die-marks did not result from a single toss of three dice, but from three tosses of a single die.

13   I use the translation system of the Old Tibetan Documents Online, in addition to borrowing the following *signes critiques* for my translation from Takeuchi 1995: 137–138.
[abc]   supplements by the translator.
[...]   illegible or missing.
(abc)   translator's note.
(*lit.* abc)   literal translation of the corresponding passage in the text.
See Imaeda et al., 2007: xxxi–xxxiii; and Takeuchi 1995: 137–138.

14   I use "@" for the transliteration of die-eyes.

no benefit will be gained even if [you try] again.
[The omen led by] the divination will be [as follows]: 4 /4 [/] 4

This short paragraph reveals an interesting aspect with regard to the interpretation of the result, which appears to be evaluated not by a single triad or omen but by counting three triads or omens together. If that is true, one would need to obtain three omens by tossing a single die no less than nine times. Moreover, in the case of two of the omens being bad and one good, another extra omen is allowed, perhaps to enhance the divination's accuracy or leave open the possibility of converting the divination result into an auspicious one.

Through an extensive investigation of the original manuscripts, the following new information was brought to light:

1) texts were (occasionally) compiled by more than one person;
2) die-marks were inserted in the final phase of the text composition.

Concerning the first remark, I have so far identified changes of handwriting in three texts: Text 3 (ll. 114, 120), Text 6 (ll. 95, 101, 148), and Text 9 (l. 94).[15] In terms of the second remark, Text 6 is worth mentioning because the die-marks are written in narrow blank spaces between the end of one omen and the beginning of the following one or they are placed in between the lines, and sometimes the marks seem to be placed in the middle of an omen rather than in the headline. This may clearly explain the peculiarity of Texts 5 and 12, in which no die-marks are depicted, even though their formulae and contents explicitly identify them as dice divination texts. The most plausible explanation is that these two texts represent a stage in the production process and are thus incomplete divination manuals.

It may be hypothesized that dice divination texts were composed step by step, possibly by groups of professionals; such a hypothesis may contrast with Thomas's suggestion, according to which, "the text is a collection of actual *responsa*, compiled by a professional from his own or other records with a view to use in prospective 'home-luck' and 'life-luck' practice."[16]

4 Composition of the Omen

As Chen pointed out, all eleven omens recorded in Text 10 present an analogy to a group of omens in Text 3,[17] wherein the equivalent set of die-marks draws

---

15 Although not very clear, the change of handwriting can be seen at l. 25 in Text 5.
16 Thomas 1957: 117.
17 See footnote 4 and Nishida 2018.

A PRELIMINARY ANALYSIS OF OLD TIBETAN DICE DIVINATION TEXTS

similar oracles and almost identical consequences, i.e., final evaluations such as *mo bzang* "auspicious" or *mo ngan* "inauspicious". If that is the case, can we forecast the omens by memorizing a certain text? Unfortunately, it does not work that way. A survey of the texts led me to posit that we can never predict an omen from a set of die-marks; in other words, those identical triads usually lead to different final evaluations in different texts, apart from the two texts mentioned above.[18] Then, how are the final evaluations deduced? Do they depend on the arbitrary choice of individual practitioners or writers of the divination text? In spite of Thomas's view that "textual identity in the Mss. is hardly to be expected: they are likely to have been personal hand-books of practitioners, whose experience and interests will have fostered a measure of independence,"[19] I shall argue and demonstrate, by analyzing the composition of the texts, that they were not merely personal or individual elaborations—even though the correlation between triads and final evaluations appears arbitrary—because they were probably produced by groups of professionals and because they share a certain fixed pattern for drawing the final evaluations.

Let us consider the composition of the omen. Omens are either related in verse form, with metrical descriptions consisting of six syllables, or written in prose. I will respectively indicate these as ⟨Type-1⟩ and ⟨Type-2⟩.

⟨Type-1⟩[20] Text 1, 2, 4, 7, 8, 12, 13
⟨Type-2⟩   Text 3, 5, 6, 9, 10, 11, 14, 15, 16, 17, 18, 19, 20, 21, 22, 23

The contents of both types can be summarized in the following four entries:
(a) set of die-marks,
(b) verse in ⟨Type-1⟩ / the name of the divinity in ⟨Type-2⟩,
(c) commentary,
(d) result.
Before discussing the details, let us first consider omens from both types of texts:

---

18   In my opinion, as for Texts 3 and 10, one is not a copy of the other, since the sequence of the omens is not identical and they sometimes show very radical differences in terms of spelling and expressions; nevertheless, it cannot be excluded *a priori* that they were based on the same model.

19   Thomas 1957: 140.

20   Note that the verses are consistently absent in Text 4. Nevertheless, I regard this text as a variant of the ⟨Type-1⟩ texts, since it has (b-2) descriptions documented among ⟨Type-1⟩ omens instead of (b-3) which are particular to ⟨Type-2⟩ omens. I shall discuss (b-2) and (b-3) below.

56   NISHIDA

[1] ⟨Type-1⟩: Text 1–3, ll. 113–118.

[Transliteration]
(a)   *@ / @@@ / @@ /*
(b)   *kye ngang ngur nI gser ma g.yu //*
        mthIng brang nI chab gI rkyen /
        men tog nI hva lo then //
        ne'u sIng ni spang kyi rgyan //
        spang rgyan nI mthon ste bkra //
        bzang ldan[*ni] lus [*la]'tshogs //
        blta sdug nI dmyIg lam bkra //
        spos drI nI gangs na gda' //[21]
(c)   *mo 'dI nI khyIm phya dang srog phya la btab na // lhad dpal bzang po 'am*
        sman dkar mo zhIg yod pas // de la mchod 'phras legs par byas na // khyed
        la 'go zhing 'dug pas / rIgs bshor na sod /rje blas zhus na gnang / don gnyer
        na grub / 'dron po la btab na 'ong // nad pa la btab na sos / gsol shags byas
        na gnang // bor lag byung na rnyed // tshong byas na khe phyIn //
(d)   *mo 'dI la btab kyang bzang //*

[Translation]
(a)   1/3/2
(b)   Oh! The gold and turquoise color[22] of geese and ducks, [as well as their] azure [color] adorn the footpath[23] [along] the water (/stream).

---

21   Similar verses recur in the same text (Text 1–2), and Text 13.
       [Text 1–2] ll. 29–30.
       @@@@ / @@@ / @@@ kye g.y[u] mtsho nI ngur 'phyo ba // mtsho sman nI gnyan gyI
       drIn // men tog nI hva lo mtshon // ne'u sing nI spang gyI rgyan // spang rgyan nI m[tsho?]
       [---]n nI lus la 'tshogs //
       [Text 13] ll. 222–231.
       @ / @@@ / @
       $// ngang ngun ni gser ma g.yu [rgya?] mtsho nI mtsho 'i rgyan / men togs nI sna tshogs
       gyang / snor ma ni gling la mdzes / pug ron nI phyugs gcig mo / 'da' ga dar ni sno la 'tshal
       dri gshin [*ni] snor ma gling / [---] ri ni shangsu gda' / lha mtsho mi glIng gi [-]in /
22   *gser ma g.yu*: the syllable *ma* between the color terms *gser* "gold" and *g.yu* "turquoise"
       remains unclear. In P.t.1136, an example shows *ma g.yu* compared with *gser* (*gser rta'I gser*
       ma ron dang ma g.yu rta'i g.yu ma ron gnyis l. 21). An example in IOL Tib J 734 mirrors *ma*
       g.yu (mother turquoise) with *pha dung* (father conch-shell: *pha dung gyI glang po dang /*
       ma g.yu'i 'pra mo gnyIs smos ste l. 3r119). In the former case, *ma g.yu* may be interpreted as
       a color compound, while we should regard *ma* as "the mother (turquoise)" in contrast to
       pha "father" in the latter case. Here, I prefer to apply the former example and leave it as a
       color term, a type of turquoise.
23   *mthIng brang nI chab gI rkyen*: This sentence may be understood as "[as well as their] azure

A PRELIMINARY ANALYSIS OF OLD TIBETAN DICE DIVINATION TEXTS · 57

As for the flower, [I /you] pick [the flower of the] hollyhock.
A meadow is the adornment of a hallowed ground.[24]
The adornment of a hallowed ground [grows on the] high and blooming.
[I /you] gather [the objects] possessing fine [nature] onto [my /your] body.
Even if [I /you] face suffering, a view [that comes into] the eyes is beautiful.
Every scent of incense, there exists.

(c)   This divination, if cast for home-luck and life-luck, there exists a [divinity] lHad dpal bzang po or a [divinity] sMan dkar mo, and if [you] devote an offering fruit (/rice) properly to him (/her),[25] [you will be] possessed (/supported) by [him /her].[26]
If [you] chase wild animals,[27] [you will] kill [them].
If [you] request an official work,[28] [it will be] granted.
If [you] endeavor for profit, [it will be] accomplished.
If cast for a person you are waiting for,[29] [he/she will] come.
If cast for a sick person, [he/she will] recover.

---

chests are the adornment of the stream" by taking *brang* as "chest, breast" but, as far as I am aware, neither geese nor ducks have azure chests; hence, I read *brang* as *'phrang*, "a footpath."

24   *spang rgyan*: Dotson stated that *spang snar* is found in numerous ritual and divination texts, and defined it as "a hallowed ground sometimes used for hunting" (Dotson 2013: 63, no. 7.) Here, I adopt his reading and consider *spang* as an abbreviated form of *spang snar* on account of the metrical limitation.

25   *'phras*: *'phras* "stroke, blow, kick" does not fit the context here, so I consider it to be *'bras*, which probably means "rice" or "fruit" dedicated to the divinity. According to the texts from East Turkestan, in the course of a ceremony of *sku bla*, *'bras* is listed as a victual offering together with wheat (*khar* and *gnag*). Likewise, some fruit or vegetables (= *'bras bu*), such as a kind of persimmon (*sta dka'* = *sta ka*) or radish (*lha phug* = *la phug*), appear as offering objects to entertain the *sku bla*. See Thomas 1951: 386, no. 79 and 387, no. 81, and Nishida 2016: 267–268.

26   *'go zhing 'dug*: *'go* usually means "to stain, to dirty, to infect", which is thought to be an unfavorable situation for the person concerned but, here, the subject is a divinity and this situation causes a good prognosis. In this respect, I understand it by denoting the situation as "a divinity sticks to the person" or, more precisely, "a divinity is on the person's side". See also Dotson 2017.

27   *rigs*: This should be the abbreviation for *ri dags* as prevalent among dice divination texts.

28   *rje blas*: I adopted Takeuchi's rendering of "an official work, duty" (Takeuchi 1995: 266–267). For a detailed discussion on *rje blas*, see Uebach and Zeisler (2008).

29   *'dron po*: Thomas renders *'dron po* as "a traveler" by regarding it as *'gron po* (Thomas 1957). In divination texts, the appearance of *'dron po* is always seen as a good prognostic. In this regard, I prefer to regard *'dron po* as a traveler, a stranger, or an outsider who is desired should appear, and interpret it as "a person you are waiting for".

If [you] make a petition, [it will be] granted.
[As for] a lost property, [it will be] regained.
If [you] operate a business, [you will] make a profit.

(d)   This omen, for [whatever is] cast, [it is] good.

[2] ⟨Type-2⟩: Text 3, ll. 5–9.

[Transliteration]
(a)   *@@@@ / @ / @@@@*
(b)   *$: / / lam lha'I zhal nas*
(c)   *myI khyod lhas thugs rje gzIgste / zhal ces btab na yang thar / tshong bya na yang tshong rgyal / snying la bdag 'dzangs snyam ma sem par lha la phyag 'tshol [dang] snyIng la bsam ba' bzhIn 'ongste*
(d)   *mo bzango /*

[Translation]
(a)   4/1/4
(b)   [The omen] from the mouth of [the divinity] Lam lha [is as follows]:
(c)   [for] you, a human being, the divinity will feel compassion so that, even if
       [you] receive a [legal] decision, [you will be] released.
       Even if [you] operate a business, [you will] succeed in [your] business.
       Pay respect to the divinity without thinking yourself as clever in your mind,[30] [and everything] will appear just as you expect in your mind.
(d)   [So that this] omen is good.

4.1   *Type-1 Texts*

A close investigation of the ⟨Type-1⟩ texts revealed that several verses are ubiquitous across the text diversity; in other words, ⟨Type-1⟩ texts sometimes share verses, with slight differences. In fact, all of the verses in Text 12—which records eleven omens without die-marks—are relevant to the other ⟨Type-1⟩ texts. A comparison of the relevant verses is shown in Table 2 below, together with their triads and results. The horizontal column in the table represents the line numbers in the texts, whose omens have equivalent verses: namely, we come across similar verses in ll. 3–5 in Text 12, ll. 15v1–4 in Text 2, and ll. r86–93 in Text 13. Note that the triads never agree, with one exception,[31] and that, instead, equivalent

---

30   *snying la bdag 'dzangs snyam ma sem par*: I read this expression as *snying la bdag mdzangs snyam du ma sems par*.

31   The exception is an omen in Texts 2 and 13 that represents the identical triads 2/3/3 where

A PRELIMINARY ANALYSIS OF OLD TIBETAN DICE DIVINATION TEXTS   59

TABLE 3.2   Comparative table of verses, triads, and results

Text 12	Text 1	Text 2	Text 13
(ll. 3–5) good?		(ll. 15v1–4) 2/1/1: very good	(ll. r86–93) 2/4/3: good
(ll. 11–12) good	(ll. 3v4–5) 4/3/4: very good	(ll. 11v5–8) 2/2/2: very good	
(ll. 19–20) *instructions only*	(ll. 3v13–14) 3/4/4: bad		
(ll. 26–27) very good	(ll. 3v18–19) 4/2/2: good		
(ll. 32–33) very good	(ll. 3v22–23) 4/2/1: good		
(ll. 38–40) good	(ll. 3v27–28) 4/1/4: good	(ll. 8r9–13) 3/4/3: very good	(ll. r43–48) 3/1/2: *not stated*
(ll. 45–47) very good			(ll. r26–33) [3]/1/3: good
(ll. 52–55) not good	(ll. 3v31–34) 2/3/3: bad	(ll. 14r1–5) 2/1/3: very bad	(ll. r122–129) 2/3/2: bad
(ll. 59–60) *instructions only*	(ll. 3v37–38) 2/3/2: bad		
(ll. 65–66) good	(ll. 3v42–44) 2/3/1: good	(ll. 13v2–15) 2/3/3: very good	(ll. r115–121) 2/3/3: good
(ll. 70–72) *text omitting*		(ll. 7v11–8r2) 3/3/4: very good	

or relevant verses are likely to result in the same or similar final evaluation. Hence, I conceive the verse in an omen as functioning as a key to trigger its result, yet the triads still differ from one text to another.

The following table presents an example of contrasting verses from four texts in which discrepant descriptions are shown in bold font, regardless of spelling variants. For the benefit of the reader, final evaluations are also provided.

This table clearly illustrates the significance of grasping the concept of the verse by examining not a single text but all of the corresponding texts simultaneously. An unintelligible word in a text, such as *sbam* in Text 1 or *sbrang*

(b) verses and (d) result correspond with each other. Nevertheless, the relevant omen in Text 1 still signifies 2/3/1.

60 NISHIDA

TABLE 3.3 An example of verse contrast

Text 1–3 (ll. 27–31) (4/1/4)	Text 2 (ll. 8r9–14) (3/4/3)	Text 12 (ll. 38–44) (no die-marks)	Text 13 (ll. 43–49) (3/1/2)
kye byang rI nI phang pung na //	*kye bya rog ni phang phung la /*	*byang rI ni phang bung la*	*byang ri ni phang pung la /*
dngos gI nI phung rkorko	*dgos kyis ni na rgo rko /*	*dgos kyIs nI khongs bskyos na /*	*gtos gyi ni sa bskor na /*
gser gI nI sbam dang mjal	*g[s]er gi ni sbrang dang mjal*	*gser kyis nI sbram dang 'dzal ////*	*gser ri ni sbram dang mjal /*
		rom po ni rja ra na	*rom po nI sja ra na /*
	gor ma ni brtsed brtsed na /	*gor la nI bcod btab na //*	*gor la nI gtsod 'debs 'debs*
	mu men ni prag bzhin ma /	*nu myen ni 'phra zhig rnyed //*	*[ru?] myen ni sbram zhig rnyed /*
		gsar la ni g.yus spras zhing	*gser sbram ni g.yu spras zhIng*
dga' yIs nI tvag kyIs blangs		*bzang mtha' ni lho 'i dkor*	*rin chen nI brtsigs pa la*
snam phrag tu sur gis stsal //	*'od bzangs ni lha me lham /*	*myi spyad nI phang su bgyis //*	*'od bzangs nI lamse lams*
bzang //	*bzang rab bo //*	*bzang ngo //*	

in Text 2, can thus be ascertained as a word known from the other two texts: *sbram*, more precisely *gser (gi) sbram*, "an unwrough gold" or "a gold ingot".[32]

The verse in dice divination texts not only presents us with spelling variations but also with the interchangeability of sections of verses. It should be underlined that these verses were certainly based on a source; otherwise, they would have been concurrent with early Tibetan culture, instead of representing an arbitrary elaboration by each practitioner. Dotson rightly pointed out that several verses in a dice divination text, which are also found in the Old Tibetan Chronicle as well as in ritual texts, refer to the traditional depiction of hunting.[33] The view expressed by Dotson—that the depiction of hunting stems

32 This word is yet to be solved, since we can find the following expressions in Text 21: *gser gyi sram dang mjald* "[you] will meet with a golden otter" and *sbal dang mjald* "[you] will meet with a frog". These examples suggest the possibility that *sbam* is a confusing spelling that mixes *sram* with *sbram* or *sbal*.

33 Dotson 2013: 63–64. He offers examples from Text 2 (ll. 2v6–7 and 17r10–17v6), the Old

A PRELIMINARY ANALYSIS OF OLD TIBETAN DICE DIVINATION TEXTS 61

from a traditional stereotypical image—may well support my point. Notwith-
standing its absence from the above examples, the stereotypical expression A
gyi mo la bab te "[it] falls down on the omen of A", sometimes appears between
(b) and (c) in ⟨Type-1⟩ texts, to which I refer as (b-2) hereafter.[34]

In some cases (d-1), an instruction is added before the final evaluation (d-2).
The following excerpt shows an example of these constituents:

[3] Text 12, ll. 3–10.

[Transliteration]

(a)   *$ / /:/:/ /*[35]

(b-1)   *mu sman nI zhal na re //*
          lha rI ni byang ri gnyis //
          gnyI ga nI gzed gi ri //
          sman ri nI gtsug sdings // las //
          mgrin phran nI rtse 'jos shing //
          gzed po nI stong sgo ru //
          mu sman nI chab la gshegs //
          gzed po nI gsol pa la //
          sha 'bri nI gcig gnang na //
          sman dag nI gang las gnang //
          da dung nI lan ma thob //
          ya rus nI lha mchod la //
          mar du ni sri gnon cig //[36]

Tibetan Chronicle (P.t.1287, ll. 412–416), and funerary texts (P.t.1136, ll. 40–41, and P.t.1134, ll. 111–112), in the latter of which the depiction is not written in verse. I prefer to add another example from Text 1–2 (ll. 20–21); the following two examples also seem to be relevant: Text 1–1 (ll. 8–10, which recurs at ll. 21–23) and Text 7 (ll. 7–10).

34   In addition, the following stereotypical expression is still extant in both ⟨Type-1⟩ and ⟨Type-2⟩ texts: X *gyi ngo* "[this is] the prognostic of X." *ngo* primarily means "face, counte-nance" but in divination texts it seems better to render it as "prognostic", which probably derives from "likelihood, prospect, and probability" registered in the dictionary (Jäschke 1881: 129).

35   As noted above, this text does not include any die-marks, but just blank spaces.

36   Similar verses recur in Text 2 and Text 13.
     [Text 2] ll. 15v1–4.
     @@ / @ / @ / kye lha re ni sman ri gnyis / gnyis ka ni dpal gyi shari / lho ri ni byang ri nyis / gnyis ka ni sman gyi ri / rtags tsan nib yang btsun nyis /
     [Text 13] ll. r86–r93.
     @@ / @@@@ / @@@ [---] // lho ri nI byang ri gnyis gnyis ka nI [srib?] ri gnyis gnyis ka nI / gzed gyi ri // sman ri ni gtsu[g?] sdings na / [mgrin?] rtse 'jos zhing mu sman ni 'phan bsrol te // mu sman nI chab la gshegs / bsar gyis srong bskor [---] du / sha 'bri nI snar la gnang / mu sman nI 'ban la sla /

(b-2)	*'di nI je'u gnam sman myI dmyis pa'I mo la bab ste* //
(c-1)	*snga na sman chen po zhig gis srung srung ba las / myi khyod la bdag gis ngan pa'I bgegs ched po zhig byas te // sman dang lha myI dgyes ste // 'dri*[37] *yul gdon nam yul gang yang ma shegs pa cig du zhugs te // da dung khyer te thob pa nI ma yin* //
(d-1)	*mo phya dag gdam cing bon byas ni* [*bgegs*] *brtsal te / sman dang lha dpal mchod na bzang ngo // de ltar ma byas na mo ngan no* //
(c-2)(d-2)	*mo 'dI gzhan la ngan // ri dags shor nab dang dor gnyer ba*[38] *dang / gnyen bya ba la btab na grub ste bzang rab bo* //

[Translation]

(a)	
(b-1)	[The divinity] Mu sman says:
	both the divine mountain and the north mountain are the mountains of [a divinity] gZed [po].
	[The divinity] sMan [comes down] from the high peak [of] the mountain to the mountain foot[39] and enjoy [himself].
	gZed po [comes down?] to the thousand doors(?),[40] [the divinity] Mu sman comes [down] to the river.
	If [you] ask gZed po to grant flesh of a female Yak, sMan will grant you whatever [you wish].
	However, [you] have not received an answer yet, and [you should] respect [the divinity] lHa in the upper regions, and in the lower regions [you should] suppress [the evil spirit] Sri.
(b-2)	This falls down on the omen of *Je'u gnam sman myI dmyis pa*.
(c-1)	A great [divinity] sMan has been protecting you before.
	However, on you, a human being, [there is] a worse obstruction made by yourself, so that [the divinity] sMan and [the divinity] lHa are unhappy.

---

37   *'dri*: This should be an error for *'dre*.

38   *dor gnyer ba*: This must be read as *don gnyer ba*.

39   *mgrin phran*: *mgrin* usually means throat, neck, or voice; however, considering the reference to a mountain, I regard it as a metaphor denoting the "foot" or "ridge" of a mountain by comparing a mountain to the human head. For *phran*, I adopt Jäschke's second rendering of "part of the body" and interpret this passage as "the mountain foot or ridge".

40   *stong sgo ru*: This remains unclear.

A PRELIMINARY ANALYSIS OF OLD TIBETAN DICE DIVINATION TEXTS   63

To where [the demons such as] 'Dre and gDon, who never leave their land and remain *en masse*, still more [demons] will be carried.

There will be nothing(?) to obtain.

(d-1)　　　If [you] [receive] advice(?) [led by] the divination, and perform Bon, the obstruction will be removed.[41]

If [you] devote an offering [ritual] to [the divinity] sMan and [the divinity]

lHa dpal, [it] will be auspicious.

If [you] don't do like that, [this] omen will be bad.

(c-2) (d-2)　This omen, for whatever else [it is] bad, [although] if cast for [your] desire to chase wild animals,[42] endeavoring a profit, and marriage, it will be accomplished.

[It] is very good.

In some cases, the (c) commentary and (d) result appear to be misaligned and overlapping, as is the case with this example while, in other cases, the final evaluations are not clearly stated. Furthermore, the gist of the omen (c-1) is occasionally provided alongside specific topics—home-luck, life-luck, lost property, and so on—which I refer to as (c-2); they are listed in the stereotypical expression: B *la btab na*, "if cast for B".

It is less clear for the element "A" in (b-2), due to the abundance of varieties, some of which can be assumed to be Tibetan words that are otherwise expected to be words drawn from other languages. They are likely to be designated as a title or representation of the omen in question, often side by side with the name of a kind of spiritual entity. In order to comprehend these opaque expressions, it is necessary to collect the analogs instead of interpreting haphazardly. Accordingly, I hesitate either to translate or discuss their origin here, as we have hitherto few examples at hand. Nevertheless, it may be worth mentioning that they manifestly reflect the cultural world of early Tibet, and the inconsistent spellings or plentiful variations might be attributed to their origin, as these

---

41　　*bgegs brtsal te*: A similar expression recurs in Text 12, *bgegs stsol cig* (l. 17). I prefer to translate it as "to remove the obstruction" according to Jäschke's view: *stsol ba* is sometimes incorrect for *bsal ba* (*sel ba*) "to clean, to remove," which should fit the context here.

42　　*ri dags shor nab*: *ri dags shor* means "to chase wild animals," but *nab* is unclear here. For the time being, I will read it as *rnab pa*, "to desire, to covet," but it remains unsatisfactory (*Bod rgya tshig mdzod chen mo*: 1562).

64 NISHIDA

elements, probably related to spiritual entities, belonged to an oral cultural tradition rather than the literary world.

Fortunately, we recognize the identical or relevant "A" in Texts 1 and 12:

'dre ma ha	*| 'dre ma ha*[43]
then dbang nyId	*| theb la nyen*[44]
yul sa dga' la yan	*| 'das la yan*[45]
sman rgod shele	*| sman rgod da chen*[46]

Except for the first entity, they may seem to be irrelevant. Yet, once we notice that these parallel "A" entities are strikingly accompanied by similar verses as shown in Table 2 above, we cannot help but anticipate their correspondence. If true, (b-2), i.e., a type of omen title also bounds to the final evaluation in a similar way as (b-1), i.e., the verse.

With regard to the instruction (d-1), the previous example provides three indications: "[receive] advice from the divination (or consult a diviner?)," "perform Bon," which seemingly infers a kind of ritual or treatment intended to banish evil spirits, and "devote an offering [ritual] to the divinity." Apart from these, "perform a ceremony (*cho ga gyis zhig*)" or "carry out a ritual (*rim gro byo shig*)" are commonplace in order to overcome an inauspicious omen.

The composition of ⟨Type-1⟩ omens can be summarized as follows:
(a) set of die-marks,
(b) key terms:
  (b-1) verse of six syllables
  (b-2) title (A *gyi mo la bab te*),
(c) commentary:
  (c-1) gist of the omen
  (c-2) specific topics (B *la btab na*),
(d) result:
  (d-1) instruction (*cho ga gyis zhig* /*rim gro byo shig* / *lha mchod gyis*)
  (d-2) final evaluation

---

43 Text 1–3: l. 14 and Text 12: l. 20.
44 Text 1–3: ll. 19–20 and Text 12: l. 27.
45 Text 1–3: l. 23 and Text 12: l. 34.
46 Text 1–3: l. 38 and Text 12: l. 61.

4.2 Type-2 Texts

Let us now consider ⟨Type-2⟩ texts. As shown in the above example [2], ⟨Type-2⟩ texts do not use verses in (b), but usually begin with a stereotypical expression, such as C *gyi zhal nas*, C *gyi mchid nas*, or C *na re* "[the omen from] the mouth/word of C," or "C says," denoting that the omen in question was emitted by the divinity "C." Various kinds of names fall into the "C" category, yet most appear only once and merely overlap across texts. However, I have identified a few examples of "C" that recur in more than one text. In the majority of cases, those omens result in consistent final evaluations. For example, the divinity lHa Mu tsa myed appears in three texts and results in good omens in at least two of them;[47] likewise, lHa dByar mo thang invariably results in good omens.[48] Note that the identity of the triads is hardly observed here.

Thomas pointed out that, among the divinities who uttered the prognostication, there are some who are quite famous: 'O [l]de gung rgyal, "a legendary early Tibetan king;" dByar mo thang, "a famous site in north eastern Tibet;" and Thang lha ya bzhur and Yar lha sham pho, "a Yar lung god," "(those) actually known as local deities in pre-Buddhist Tibet." According to his view "these particulars are quite consonant with the supposition of a Bonpo appurtenance of the text."[49] Dotson attracted our attention to further divinities in Text 3; namely, Sha med gang dkar and lHe'u rje zin tags, who "are called upon as witnesses in the song of Emperor 'Dus srong in the Old Tibetan Chronicle," and Sla bo sla sras, who "is mentioned as 'lord' (*rje*) Bla bo bla sras in the Dunhuang ritual text IOL Tib J 734." It is worth repeating his remark regarding how those three divinities survived in later sources.[50] Let us consider yet another divinity, lHa mu tsa med, who impressively appears as Mu tsa med in an Old Zhangzhung manuscript (P.t.1251).[51] Thomas's suggestion of "Bon po appurtenance of the text" may be supported by this coincidence.

In some cases, subsequent to the stereotypical expression C *gyi zhal nas*, a kind of narrative or a maxim is inserted. For example, a ⟨Type-2⟩ text offers a kind of maxim; *myi chungu kha ma che rtag du rta chungu kha ma drag myi la ngan dus ma che / myi nus pa la kha ma drag*.[52] This may function as recalling

---

47 Text 3: l. 119, Text 6: l. 27, and Text 9: l. 21. In the last text, the final evaluation is not stated.
48 Text 3: l. 86, Text 6: l. 113, and Text 22: l. 65.
49 Thomas 1957: 140–141.
50 Dotson 2007: 24–25.
51 All of the Old Zhangzhung manuscripts are probably medical in nature but their details remain unknown (Takeuchi and Nishida 2009.) lHa mu tsa med/myed is possibly bound to both medical treatment and divination.
52 Text 10 ll. 5–8. This recurs in Text 3: *myI chungu la kha ma che rta chungu la kha ma dag myi / la ngan dus ma che / myI nus pa la kha ma drag* (ll. 180–183).

the scenery of the omen to one's mind, or as envisaging the omen. Interestingly, the Old Tibetan Chronicle exhibits an analog expression in the conversation where the mother of lHa bu ru la skyes responds to his question about his parentage.[53]

Other than these, I have come across the equivalent narrative in three texts:

[4] Text 21, ll. 21–26.

[Transliteration]
(a)   *@@ @@ @*
(b-3)   *$ // lha myI mgon mched bun gi zhal nas*
(b-4)   *rgyal po zhig mtso'I gling na bzhugs na rkyal yang myI shes / ji ltar byasna mtsho'i gling nas tar snyam sems shIng 'dug 'dug nas / bya ngang mo chu na 'dug pa bzungsthe rgyal / po'I zhal nas myI g.yung drung na 'dug gyang ta mar myi skyid cheste shI 'ang khor bar nyon myi mongs gyis nam sros gyang nyi ma myi shard myi srid ches gsung ste bya ngang mo la zhon de song na' / mtsho'i pa roldu pyinde /dga' ba dang skyid pa dang nor pyugs yul dang prade dga'o*
(c-1)   *myi khyod gyang de dang mtshung te mtar legs par 'ongo*
(d-2)   *mo bzango /*

[Translation]
(a)   2/2/1
(b-3)   [The omen] from the mouth of [the divinity] lHa myI mgon mched bun [is as follows]:
(b-4)   A king stayed on a lake island (= an island floating on a lake).
          He did not know how to swim, and [he] was staying [there] wondering how he could escape from the lake island.
          Thereupon, the king caught a goose on the lake and said: Even if a person lives within eternity, he/she will die due to the great misfortune.
          However, within the orb of transmigration, there is no misery, so that [it is like that even if] the sun sets it rises [again],[54] a person will [eventually] flourish, he said.

---

53   *ma 'I mchid nas / myI'u chung kha ma che shig / rte 'u cung kha ma drag nga myi shes shes byas na* / (P.t.1288 ll. 29–30), "A quoi sa mere répondit 'Petit enfant, n' aie pas bouche trop grande! Ne l'a pas si forte un poulain. Je ne sais pas'." (Bacot et al. 1940–1946: 125.) The mother's admonition is possibly used to trigger the final evaluation of this omen, *mo ngan*, with great adequacy.

54   *nam sros gyang nyi ma myi shard*: referring to the parallel sentence in Text 6: *re shig nam*

A PRELIMINARY ANALYSIS OF OLD TIBETAN DICE DIVINATION TEXTS   67

[He] left, riding on the goose, and arrived at the other side of the lake.

Then [he] met with the land of bliss, happiness and affluence, and [he grew] delighted.

(c-1)   You, a human being, are just like this [narrative]: it will finally get better.

(d-2)   [This] omen is good.

This narrative is likely to denote that a current bad situation will improve subsequently. This perspective can be ascertained in similar narratives from the other two texts, Texts 6 and 14; they consistently result in *mo bzang*, auspiciousness. Consequently, these narratives are also closely related to the final evaluation; in other words, for the purpose of presenting the gist of the omen, these narratives are referred to.[55]

As shown in the example [2] above, other stereotypical expressions appear in ⟨Type-2⟩ texts: *lhas (/lha ngas) thugs dgongs mdzad de*, "the divinity, (I myself), will be considerate [of you]," or *lhas thugs rje gzigs ste* "the divinity will feel compassion [for you]," which I would like to categorize as (c-1) constituent, the gist of the omen. Following these stereotypical phrases, conventional descriptions are given and then a bad situation is converted into a better one.

Another typical expression is *myi khyod de dang 'dra ste* or *myi khyod kyang de dang mtshung te*, "you, a human being, are just like this," which we have seen in the preceding example. Occasionally, these expressions are succeeded by

---

 sros gyang phyIs nam nangs bzhIn tu lan yod do "like a situation that even if the sun sets for a while it rises later [again], [you will] obtain a response," I adopt *nyi ma shard* rather than *nyi ma myi shard* here.

55 The triads between the omens including the equivalent narrative are coincident with Texts 6 and 21, but not with Text 14.

 [Text 6] ll. 130–133.

 @@ @@ @

 $ /:/ *rgyal po zhig mtsho'i glang la bzhug ste nam zhIg dang mtsho dI' las thar ram myI thar sem zhIng bzhug pa la* [*lhas*] *thugs dgong mdzade mtsho'i nang nas gru* [*c*]*ig phyung nas rgyalpo gru'i nang du zhug te cang ma nyes par mtsho'i* [*pha*] [---] [*phyin*] *te myI khyod de mtshung ste snyIng 'tshar mong kyong re shig nam sros gyang phyIs nam nangs bzhIn tu lan yod do mo bza*[*ng*]

 [Test 14] ll. 5–8.

 @ @@@ @@@

 $ /:/ *rgyal po chen po* [---] *mtsho'i gleng na bzhugste / mtsho' la nam thard zhes myi* [---] *zhing bzhugs pa // las l*[*h*]*as thugs dgongs mdzade /* [*rl*]*ug gyis mtsho 'i rked du* [---] *gshegs* [---]*s bltams thugs dgye g*[*i*]*s myi khyod gsol ba yang gnango // mo bzango*

instructions such as *lha la phyag 'tshol zhig* "pay respect to the divinity!" or *lha mchod gyis*, "devote an offering [ritual] to the divinity!" If one follows these indications, one will obtain an auspicious omen or at least prevail against inauspiciousness, otherwise the person will receive a bad omen as a result. Strikingly, *lha la phyag 'tshol zhig* appears exclusively in ⟨Type-2⟩ texts, as far as I know, but the indication for performing *cho ga* or *rim gro* can instead be observed invariably among ⟨Type-1⟩ texts.[56] These instructions help us to guess whether or not the omen with ambiguous descriptions will be bad—even when the final evaluation is not clearly stated—since they are only supplied for inauspicious omens. Hence, the composition of ⟨Type-2⟩ texts can be summarized as follows:

(a) set of die-marks,
(b) key terms:
  (b-3) divinity
    (C *gyi zhal nas*, C *gyi mchid nas*, C *na re*)
  (b-4) narrative / maxim,
(c) commentary:
  (c-1) gist of the omen
    (*lhas thugs dgongs mdzad de, lhas thugs rje gzigs ste*)
  (c-2) specific topics (B *la btab na*),
(d) result:
  (d-1) instruction
    (*lha mchod gyis, lha la phyag 'tshol zhig*)
  (d-2) final evaluation

5 Conclusion

By analyzing the stereotypical expressions of the dice divination texts presented here, several points have been brought to light. First, they have distinctive formulae composed of four categories: (a) set of die-marks, (b) key terms, (c) commentary, and (d) result. Category (b) can be subdivided into four constituents, according to which all of the texts are roughly classified into two groups. One group contains (b-1) verse and/or (b-2) title (A *gyi mo la bab te*), and the other group has (b-3) divinity (C *gyi zhal nas*) and/or (b-4) narrative or maxim. Depending on each group, (d-1) respective instructions are

---

56 In contrast, *lha mchod cig* and *lha brjod cig* are commonplace in both.

shown in the case of inauspicious omens. It is most striking that category (b) is always closely connected with the divination results; in other words, it always functions as a key to trigger the divination result even when die-marks are consistently irrelevant to them.

On these grounds, I surmise the process of producing the divination texts according to the following two phases:

1) Preparation of the drafts substantiating the divination results by means of prevalent verses, the names of effective divinities, well-known narratives or maxims. All of these are crucial for envisaging the prognostics and are supposed to be rooted in the cultural tradition of early Tibet or to reflect the multi-ethnic and multi-cultural *milieus* where local divinities particular to various districts as well as the divinities derived from other cultural backgrounds predominate. During this phase, a comprehensive commentary is supplemented in order to respond to the needs in the actual case of the divination. All of these preparations were probably accomplished not by a single professional but by a group of professionals.

2) Insertion of the sets of die-marks within the appropriate blank spaces prepared beforehand. This may well explain both the disorder of the sequence of the triads, which otherwise only causes the inconvenience of finding the omen at stake in an extensive text, and the defective texts, which contain no descriptions of die-marks.

Another question may be raised as to how the die-marks were assigned to the respective omens but I am, as yet, unqualified to discuss the matter since further research is necessary in that regard. Nevertheless, I believe that my attempt constitutes a first step toward reconsidering the Old Tibetan dice divination texts.

References

Bacot, Jacques, Thomas, Fredlic William, and Toussaint, Gustave-Charles. *Documents de Touen-houang relatifs à l'histoire du Tibet*. Paris: Librairie Orientaliste Paul Geuthner, 1940–1946.

Chen Jian 陳践. 『P.T.1046 骰卜』 [= P.T.1046 Dice Divination]. In 『敦煌吐蕃文献选辑』 [= *Tibetan Documents from Dunhuang, Volume for Culture*], ed. Zheng Binglin 郑炳林 and Huang Weizhong 黄维忠, pp. 108–111. Lanzhou 兰州: 民族出版社 Minzu chubanshe, 2011.

Dotson, Brandon. "Divination and Law in the Tibetan Empire: The Role of Dice in the Legislation of Loans, Interest, Marital Law and Troop Conscription." In *Contribution to the Cultural History of Early Tibet*, ed. M. Kapstein and B. Dotson, pp. 3–77. Leiden / Boston: Brill, 2007.

Dotson, Brandon. "The Princess and the Yak: The Hunt as Narrative Trope and Historical Reality in Early Tibet." In *Scribes, Texts, and Rituals in Early Tibet and Dunhuang*, ed. Brandon Dotson, Kazushi Iwao, and Tsuguhito Takeuchi, pp. 61–85. Wiesbaden: Ludwig Reichert Verlag, 2013.

Dotson, Brandon. "On 'Personal Protective Deities' ('go ba'i lha) and the Old Tibetan Verb 'go." Bulletin of SOAS, vol. 80(3), pp. 525–545, 2017.

Francke, August H. "Tibetische Handschriftenfunde aus Turfan." *Sitzungsberichte der Preussischen Akademie der Wissenschaften*, pp. 5–20, 1924.

Francke, August H. "Drei weitere Blätter des tibetischen Losbuches von Turfan." *Sitzungsberichte der Preussischen Akademie der Wissenschaften*, pp. 110–118, 1928.

Imaeda, Yoshiro et al. eds. *Tibetan Documents from Dunhuang Kept at the Bibliothèque Nationale de France and the British Library, Old Tibetan Documents Online Monograph Series* vol. 1. Tokyo: Research Institute for Languages and Cultures of Asia and Africa, Tokyo University of Foreign Studies, 2007.

Imaeda, Yoshiro. *Histoire du cycle de la naissance et de la mort: Étude d'un texte tibétain de Touen-houang*. Genève/Paris: Librairie Droz, 1981.

Iwao, Kazushi, Van Schaik, Sam, and Takeuchi, Tsuguhito. eds. *Old Tibetan Texts in the Stein Collection Or. 8210, Studies in Old Tibetan Texts from Central Asia*, vol. 1. Tokyo: The Toyo Bunko, 2012.

Jäschke, Heinrich August. *A Tibetan-English Dictionary*. London: The Charge of the secretary of state for India in council, 1881.

Kalsang Yangjen 格桑央京. "敦煌藏文写卷 Ch.9.II.19 号初探" [= *A Preliminary Explanation into the Dunhuang Tibetan Manuscript No. 19 of Ch. 9.II*]. 『中国藏学』 [= *China Tibetology*], vol. 2, pp. 9–17, 2005.

Macdonald-Spanien, Ariane. "Une lecture des Pelliot tibétaine 1286, 1287, 1038; 1047 et 1290, essai sur le formation et l'emploi des mythes politiques dans la religion royale de Sroṅ-bcan sgam-po." In *Etudes tibétaines dédiées à la memoire de Marcelle Lalou*, ed. A. Macdonald, pp. 190–391. Paris: A. Maisonneuve, 1971.

Nishida, Ai 西田愛. "古チベット語サイコロ占い文書の研究" [= A Study on Old Tibetan Dice Divination Texts]. 『日本西藏学会々報第54号』 [= *Report of the Japanese Association for Tibetan Studies* no. 54], pp. 63–77, 2008.

Nishida, Ai "Old Tibetan Scapulimancy." In *Revue d'Etudes Tibétaines*, vol. 37, pp. 262–277, 2016.

Nishida, Ai. "Two Tibetan Dice Divination Texts from Dunhuang: Pelliot tibétain 1046B and IOL Tib J 740." Central Asiatic Journal vol. 61(1), pp. 133–150, 2018.

Stein, Aurel. *Ancient Khotan*. Oxford: Clarendon Press, 1907.

Stein, Aurel. *Serindia*, vol. IV. Oxford: Clarendon Press, 1921.

Stein, Rolf Alfred. "Du récit au rituel dans les manuscrits tibétains de Touen-houang."

In *Etudes tibétaines dédiées à la memoire de Marcelle Lalou*, ed. Ariane Macdonald-Spanien, pp. 479–547. Paris: A. Maisonneuve, 1971.

Taube, Manfred. *Die Tibetica der Berliner Turfansammlung*. Berlin: Akademie-Verlag, 1980.

Takeuchi, Tsuguhito. "A group of Old Tibetan Letters Written under Kuei-i-chün: A Preliminary Study for the Classification of Old Tibetan Letters." *Acta Orientalia Academiae Scientiarum Hungaricae*, 44, ½, pp. 175–190, 1990.

Takeuchi, Tsuguhito. *Old Tibetan Contracts from Central Asia*. Tokyo: 大蔵出版 Daizo Shuppan, 1995.

Takeuchi, Tsuguhito. *Old Tibetan Manuscripts from East Turkestan in the Stein Collection of the British Library*, vol. I, Plate. Tokyo/London: The Centre for East Asian Cultural Studies for Unesco, The Toyo Bunko, and The British Library, 1997.

Takeuchi, Tsuguhito. *Old Tibetan Manuscripts from East Turkestan in the Stein Collection of the British Library*, vol. II, Descriptive Catalogue. Tokyo/London: The Centre for East Asian Cultural Studies for Unesco, The Toyo Bunko, and The British Library, 1998.

Takeuchi, Tsuguhito. "Old Tibetan Buddhist Texts from the Post-Tibetan Imperial Period (Mid-9c. to Late 10c.)." In *Old Tibetan Studies, Dedicated to the Memory of R.E. Emmerick*, ed. Cristina Scherrer-Schaub, pp. 205–214. Leiden: Brill, 2012.

Takeuchi, Tsuguhito and Nishida, Ai. "The Present Stage of Deciphering Old Zhangzhung." *Issues in Tibeto-Burman Historical Linguistics, Senri Ethnological Studies* 75, ed. Yasuhiko Nagano, pp. 151–165, 2009.

Thomas, Fredric William. *Tibetan Literary Texts and Documents Concerning Chinese Turkestan*, vol. 2. London: Royal Asiatic Society, 1951.

Thomas, Fredric William. *Ancient Folk-Literature from North-Eastern Tibet*. Berlin: Akademie-Verlag, 1957.

Uebach, Helga and Zeisler, Bettina. "*rJe-blas, pha-los* and Other Compounds with Suffix *–s* in Old Tibetan Texts." In *Chomolangma, Demawend und Kasbek: Festschrift für Roland Bielmeier zu seinem 65. Geburtstag*. Band 1, ed. Marianne Volkart et al., pp. 309–334. Halle (Saale): VGH Wissenschaftsverlag, 2008.

Wang, Yao and Chen, Jian 王堯・陳踐. 『吐蕃時期的占卜研究』 [= *A Study of the Old Tibetan Divination Documents*]. Hong Kong: 中文大學出版社 Zhongwen daxue chubanshe, 1987.

Wang, Yao and Chen, Jian 王堯・陳踐. 『敦煌吐蕃文書論文集』 [= *Selection of the Old Tibetan Documents*]. Chengdu: 四川民族出版社 Sichuan minzu chubanshe, 1988.

Van Schaik, Sam. "Dating Early Tibetan Manuscripts: A Paleographical Method." In *Scribes, Texts, and Rituals in Early Tibet and Dunhuang*, ed. Brandon Dotson, Kazushi Iwao, and Tsuguhito Takeuchi, pp. 119–135. Wiesbaden: Ludwig Reichert Verlag, 2013.

Weber, Albrecht. "Über ein indisches Würfel-Orakel." In *Monatsberichte Königlichen*

Preus. Akademie der Wissenschaften zu Berlin, pp. 158–180. Berlin: Druckerei der Königlichen Akademie der Wissenschaften, 1859.

Yamaguchi, Zuihō 山口瑞鳳. "チベット語文献" [= Dunhuang Tibetan Documents other than Buddhist Scriptures]. In 『講座敦煌 6 敦煌胡語文献』 [= *Dunhuang Documents other than Chinese Texts*], ed. Z. Yamaguchi, pp. 449–555. Tokyo: 大東出版社 Daito shuppansha, 1985.

Yamaguchi, Zuihō 山口瑞鳳. 『チベット上』 [= *Tibet, the First Volume*]. Tokyo: 東京大学出版社 Tokyo daigaku shuppansha, 1987.

Zheng, Binglin and Huang, Weizhong 郑炳林・黄维忠. eds. 『敦煌吐蕃文献选辑』 [= *Tibetan Documents from Dunhuang, Volume for Culture*]. Lanzhou 兰州: 民族出版社 Minzu chubanshe, 2011.

CHAPTER 4

Divinations Padampa Did or Did Not Do, or Did or Did Not Write*

Dan Martin

There is a widespread notion when it comes to the subject of divination that it is about knowing future events ahead of time. People who look more deeply into the subject are likely to know that it is not so much about finding out the future as it is for *revealing*, more generally, the unknown and thereby *resolving* a situation of indecision. Very often this indecisiveness does indeed come from not knowing what the future will bring. We humans engage in these widely varied practices because we cannot make up our minds in matters belonging to all three times: past, present and future. For example, a divination meant to solve the problem of a lost object may reveal the past event of its losing, the place where it is in the present, as well as where we may be able to locate it in the future. In any case, it told us where to look when we could not decide for ourselves.

I might say that even the Tibetan word we normally translate as *prediction* or *prophecy*, *lung bstan*, shares in this temporal ambiguity. This is especially clear when we consider the negative form of the word, *lung ma bstan pa*, that means something neutral, neither fish nor fowl, indefinite, not well defined, out of order and even perhaps chaotic. The positive word *lung bstan* promises a resolution of this negative situation of ambiguity and uncertainty.[1]

---

* I would like to express my appreciation to the librarians of Leiden (Silvia Compaan-Vermetten), Stuttgart (Kerstin Losert) and Copenhagen (Anne Burchardi) who responded to my arcane inquiries about Padampa texts in their holdings with much warmth and efficiency. I thank very much Rolf Kramer of Munich for pointing me in the right direction to locate the Stuttgart manuscript. I must give thanks to Karma Phuntsho (Thimphu), without whose help I would not have been able to make use of some unique Bhutanese manuscripts, texts that will continue to prove their importance, as well as to Kurtis Schaeffer who first alerted me to their existence.

1 *Lung bstan*, used in the Kanjur and Tanjur texts to translate Sanskrit *vyākaraṇa* as well as in works by Tibetans, is frequent in the most strongly Buddhist contexts, particularly predictions of the future attainment of Buddhahood. But it is also used in prophecies of other future events (including prophetic genres of strongly political tones predicting future disasters). We even find it used in grammatical contexts as a term for the field of Indic grammar as a whole

---

© KONINKLIJKE BRILL NV, LEIDEN, 2020 | DOI:10.1163/9789004410688_005

I should point out, too, that even the most secular sorts of people resort to methods like flipping coins and drawing straws. Divinations may require cosmological concepts that permit their working, views that may not necessarily be religious in nature, yet religions including Buddhism do find practical ways to employ them. Making choices and achieving consensus often prove difficult, and it may be foolish to entirely neglect tools that can be this useful. Bearing this in mind will help keep a more even-handed attitude about a practice we may no longer believe in, or no longer believe in very much.

Still another point should be emphasized. In the past we humans regardless of cultural differences have always been extremely sensitive to signs in our environment that could help us decide what our next steps ought to be. Stars, clouds, shadows and footprints may help determine directions to take, how to prepare for weather conditions, what game to hunt. In the absence of such signs provided by nature we have often sought ways to deliberately provoke them. I think that this is where divination methods enter in. The irony of these methods is in the fact that they present indeterminate situations of their own. We seek methods to overcome indecision such that we *cannot*, by our own volition, predict or predetermine the results. We have no idea how the dice will fall, and we should not. And out of that cloudy indeterminacy comes a more or less clear answer that determines the right path for us to take, where to look for a lost object, which horse to bet on, and so on.

A little indeterminacy in our own approaches may be called for, in the sense that we should be prepared to let down the definitional boundaries, and admit to ourselves that predictability is as much a problem for modern science as for the diviners, or agree that twenty-first-century medical diagnostic procedures may have much in common with, or at least much that is comparable to, divination. When we try to answer our questions about authorship and attribution, we too find ourselves in search of signs, looking for indications that could help us find our way in what can be a field of inquiry as perplexing as it is, to myself at least, fascinating.

My present plan is to look briefly, one at a time, at four different divination manuals connected to the name of Padampa that deal with four different types of divination. Then I will cover everything I can discover about Padampa's personal practice of divination from the earliest sources so far known, identifying which types *they* were. Since I know of few such incidents, this should not take very long. After that, I consider briefly how these divination texts may

---

(although in this case Tibetans translated the term differently). The negative expression *lung ma bstan pa* was used to translate Sanskrit *avyākṛta*.

fit a pattern when taken together with *other* Padampa-attributed texts. Then I will conclude something or another on the basis of these, or at least suggest something interesting enough it could repay further testing. Now I suppose we have more or less determined the path lying ahead of us, so we can get things underway with a little confidence.

1   Introducing Padampa

Since the question always comes up and is foundational for rightly comprehending the authorship ascriptions, we must look briefly at the name problem. Padampa (Pha dam pa) is not in any sense a proper name, or even a name that was used while he was alive. Although some have attempted to sanskritize it, it is a term of respect awarded him by Tibetans, so the attempt is anachronistic and, if we reflect on it, slightly ludicrous. No source tells us what his childhood name, surely an Indic name, would have been. His childhood was spent in south India, so it could have been from a Dravidian tongue, or since he was born into the Brahmin caste, and his parents' names are given in Sanskrit forms, they may well have named him in Sanskrit. The most commonly encountered Indic names are in fact the two ordination names he received at Vikramaśīla Monastery as a thirteen- or fourteen-year-old novice and later on as a full monk. These two names are, respectively, Kamalaśrī and Kamalaśīla. There are other rarely encountered Indic names that are not important for present purposes: Karuṇasiddhi, Ajitanātha and a few others.[2]

Of all the sources on Padampa there is one that stands head and shoulders above all the others because of its provenance. The original title of the *Zhijé Collection*, as restored by myself, may be translated into English as, "Among the Peacemaking Teachings that Lay at the Heart of the Holy Dharma, this is the Text of the Later Oral Transmission known as *The Exceptionally Profound*". The physical manuscript was made in 1246 or so in very large part based on a 1207 golden manuscript. I regard this as the closest thing to contemporary evi-

---

2   Although there may be occasional confusions also in the Tibetan literature, I believe that all of the following names can be understood as different ways Tibetans have referred to the same figure: Pha dam pa, Pha dam pa Sangs rgyas, Dam pa Sangs rgyas, Na gu, Nag gu, rGya gar Na gu, Dam pa rGya gar, Dam pa Nag chung, Dam pa rGya gar Nag chung, A tsa ra Nag po. In the earliest sources, when he is not addressed simply as Dam pa (especially in texts recording words spoken in his presence), he is most likely to be called Dam pa rGya gar, meaning Venerable India[n].

dence about Padampa that we have available to us today in published form. The manuscript originally had four volumes, even if they were published in five.[3]

I have long had the idea to do a cultural history of Padampa Sangyé (d. 1105 or 1117) along lines similar to those drawn by Jan Assmann in his book *Moses the Egyptian*. It is not so much about finding the 'true' biography of a person as it is about the culture that made use of—created or recreated—that biography for its own often quite valid purposes, or at least for understandable purposes. One could also understand this as the afterlife that anyway has to enter into the writing of any biography of a historic figure. After all, the cultural afterlife may help determine why biographies continue to be written and read, and then supplied to us as our textual evidence. What was the person's legacy, what effects did they leave behind in the broader culture? If we can answer this question, it is surely an important part of their biography. Ironically, it can help us *see* the person better by keeping him or her in less sharp focus. Indeed, a biography that ends in death cannot be a complete biography. We have to allow ourselves to imagine Padampa living on until this very moment, and imagine ourselves as implicated in some kind of cultural process that goes on producing images of him (so to speak). With this sort of approach we can seriously entertain Padampa's 'authorship' of works that he very possibly or even very likely had no role in authoring. It seems too simple to label these texts *pseudepigrapha* and then simply reject and ignore them, when a more interesting and productive question may be: To what degree is the attribution of these texts to his authorship appropriate? Is there something about the ways people lead their lives that effectively select which works or sorts of works will be attributed to them in their afterlife?

2   Four Divination Texts

So to get to the business at hand, here is a list of the types of Padampa-attributed divination texts that have been located so far:

---

3   My own restoration (justified elsewhere) of what the partially illegible title must have once said is *Dam chos snying po zhi byed las / brgyud pa phyi ma'i snyan brgyud zab khyad ma*. From now on this collection will be called *Zhijé Collection*. For the published version, see *The Tradition of Pha Dampa Sangyas: A Treasured Collection of His Teachings Transmitted by T[h]ug[s] sras Kun dga'*, Kunsang Tobgey (Thimphu 1979), in five volumes. The texts have been made freely available online, together with a detailed table of contents, at Tibetan Buddhist Resource Center website, although once there it is necessary to search for the artificially made and inaccurate title *Zhi byed snga bar phyi gsum gyi skor*, or follow this link: http://www.tbrc .org/#!rid=W23911.

1. Five Finger Divination—*mdzub mo lnga'i mo*
2. Arrow Divination—*mda' mo*
3. Stone Divination—*rdo mo*
4. Rosary Divination—*'phreng mo*

All four of these may be found within a set of eighteen Tibetan divination practices listed in an article by Jiangbian Jiacuo.[4] So they may be regarded as typical for Tibetan culture, in a general way.

2.1 *Five Finger Divination*

I do have one text for Padampa's Five Finger Divination. I have little to say about it right now, just to say that there *is* one. It involves correspondences between the fingers and the Chinese-style elements of water, iron, earth, fire and wood.[5]

2.2 *Arrow Divination*

The only source I know about for the Arrow Divination text attributed to Padampa has an interesting history of its own.[6] It was a gift, in the eighteenth century, from the Empress of Russia Catherine the Second to the court of the Duchy of Württemberg in Stuttgart.[7] Prior to its arrival in St. Petersburg it is

---

4   These correspond to nos. 4, 7, 10 and 14 in the list given in Jiangbian Jiacuo, "An Investigation", 405–406: 1. String Divination, 2. Bootlace Divination, 3. Bird Divination, 4. Rosary Divination, 5. Tsampa Ball Divination, 6. Shoulder Blade Divination, 7. Pebble Divination, 8. Grain Divination, 9. Drum Divination, 10. Finger Divination, 11. Song Divination, 12. Dream Divination, 13. Oracle Divination, 14. Arrow Divination, 15. Dice Divination, 16. Mirror Divination, 17. Sling Divination, and 18. 'Six Birds' Divination (*bya drug gi mo*). I don't mean to suggest that this list is an exhaustive one, just that it would seem to be rather representative of what divinations one might expect to encounter in Tibetan culture.

5   For the published version of this, see the bibliography under *mDzub mo lnga yi mo*.

6   Schlagintweit, "Verzeichnis der tibetischen Handschriften", 261–262: "Invocation of Nagpo Chenpo by Moving the Arrow." For some more interesting discussion of arrow divinations, and of staff divinations that may work along the similar lines, see Marco Polo, *Travels of Marco Polo*, vol. 2, page 243 (the discussion is by Yule or Cordier, and not by Marco Polo). As one may see here, the main idea of this sort of divination is that the two or more lengthy pieces of wood, after being released, will seem to move on their own in relation to each other and to the directions in space.

7   The text is contained in a booklet with an outer cover having a Guru Rinpoche mantra in place of a title, as well as the seal of the German library, the Württembergische Landesbibliothek, Stuttgart, with the shelfmark "Cod. orient. fol. Nr. 9." Our particular text contained in place of a title the words *Dam pa Sangs rgyas la phyag 'tshal lo*, "Prostrations to Dampa Sangyé". The title appears on the next page: *Dam pa Sangs rgyas kyis mdzad pa'i mda' mo*, "Arrow Divination composed by Dampa Sangyé". The colophon title is: *Dam pa'i mda' mo thong ba gdon gsal mngon shes me long*. Of course "*thong ba gdon gsal*" must be read as *mthong ba don gsal*, and then the title can be translated, "Dampa's Arrow Divination: Mirror of Clairvoyance [that supplies] Clear Significance by [just] Seeing It".

likely to have been in some sort of Mongolian-inhabited region, and given the dates it may be that it was transported to Russia by Peter Simon Pallas (1741–1811).[8]

The name of Dampa Sangyé is the first thing in this text, which is characterized by unusual spellings throughout. The divination is to be done using a white wool blanket (*rnaṃ pu* is *snam bu*) as an altar cover on which a sinistrally turning *yungdrung* has been drawn with rice (*'brus* is to be read as *'bras bu*). The diviner visualizes herself as Dampa, dark brown in color and wearing a fur cloak. His right hand is displaying the possibilities, and there you imagine the decorated arrow and the mirror. There are preliminary practices of food, drink and smoke offerings. The actual practice involves placing "four" arrows (actually, only two arrows are used later on in the text where they are called the *god arrow* and the *ghost arrow*) with their notches together at the center of the altar cloth, with their points sticking into the hollow of the hand and then released. Comparing the behavior of the two arrows determines the reading. Does one fall while the other stands? Does one push the other down? Conclusions can also be drawn from the sounds the arrows make and whether they shake or not.

The text goes on and gives readings for nine folios, ending with a colophon that once again attributes this arrow divination text to Dam pa, meaning of course Padampa. There have been a few writings about Tibetan arrow divinations associated with the legendary epic hero Gesar.[9] For now we will just notice this difference in attribution and go on to look at the next divination text.

2.3 *Stone Divination*

This very brief text I only know in one single version, in two modern publications entitled "Clairvoyance of the Stone Divination."[10] It never actually says it is by Padampa, so one might wonder if we ought to count it as one.[11]

---

8   This was suggested by Emil Schlagintweit in his catalog of 1904 where he describes its contents quite briefly. After I wrote a brief blog about Padampa's Rosary Divination, Rolf Kramer of Munich wrote to inform me that the Stuttgart texts traveled to Marburg and Munich in the 1960s, and probably had not been touched for the last fifty years. He also said that it was very likely the text is still situated in Stuttgart. He suggested I write to the library and request a copy, and I received a very prompt response.

9   Jiangbian Jiacuo, "An Investigation," as well as the brief treatment of this type as one of many by Chime Radha, "Tibet", 14.

10   See the bibliography under *rDo mo'i mo'i mngon shes*.

11   However, this very type of stone divination, described in Bawden, "Some Mongolian Divinatory Practices", 7, is ascribed as follows: "These [sic!] originator of this process is said to be one Pa(a)damba". (Surely Padampa, later on spelled "Padamba," is the one intended

However, it does start with a homage to Padampa, and a request (to him, evidently) for the clear clairvoyance that comes from knowledge of Stone Divination.

The diviner imagines herself as Padampa (just as in the Arrow Divination text), then says, "Somebody bring a stone!" The bringing of the stone is analyzed in two ways, first by the direction from which the stone is brought. This is interpreted according to the spirits and fates that are associated with those directions, and this also determines the choice of rituals in favor of the indicated spirits. Secondly, the stone is examined for its color, and this again is interpreted along similar lines, including recommendations for acts of worship or ritual. Interpretations are provided for five simple colors and two combinations. A bare reference is made to round-shaped rocks that are guaranteed to result in wish fulfillment. Round and red stones would be regarded as yielding the most favorable results.

2.4 *Rosary Divination*

Rosary Divination is widely rumored to be the most commonly performed divination in Tibetan culture, and this makes sense since so many Tibetans constantly have them close at hand. The particular manuscript attributed to him is one with the title *Pha dam pa sangs rgyas kyi 'phrungs mo*, found in the university library of Leiden. A full transcription of this text has been provided online.[12]

We might notice the strange spelling *'phrungs mo* in the title, later on spelled *'phrengs mo*. Notice also *theg mar* in place of *thog mar* in the first line. This careless orthography is typical of many divination manuals I have seen, but I see it as a point in their favor if we are in fact wanting to learn about popular laypeople's practices back before there were automated spellcheckers. We just have to get used to it. To paraphrase the text, it says that you first say the Buddhist refuge, followed by a three-part mantra that is given. After that you blow on the rosary to 'mantraize' it, and imagine your right hand as Śāriputra, your left as Maudgalyāyana.

---

here, but he is credited with the origins of the practice, and not with the authorship of any particular text, it would seem.)

12   In an entry for the blog Tibeto-logic (tibeto-logic.blogspot.co) dated May 31, 2013, entitled "Phadampa's Rosary Divination". The location details for the manuscript are these: "Leiden University Library, Collection Institute Kern, 2740/M 463". One may notice the very brief but useful treatment of Rosary Divination in Namkhai Norbu, *Light of Kailash*, vol. 1, 203–204.

80   MARTIN

The continuation does not make complete sense to me, but here is a rough translation anyway:

> [2r] Divide the rosary in two (not three) halves at some point, and stack the beads three by three. If the result is *one* on top of *one*, it means that xxxxx (something cut off [or punished?] will continue?). It means that the dry mountain has water bursting out of it. It means that the dried up tree has leaves sprouting on it. It means that running away results in freedom. It means that an issueless woman bears a child. [2v] It means the poor man finds wealth.[13]

This certainly bears comparison with another divination manual. This other manual, attributed to Atiśa, has a little different title.[14] It starts with the words *'Phreng mo*, so you know it is a rosary divination. It has an homage to the Three Precious followed by 108 repetitions of the Maṇi Mantra. It then gives a brief history of the Rosary Divination emphasizing its Indian-ness. Once, it says, while Jowo Je was on his way to Tibet from India he received a prophetic utterance from Tārā, "Atiśa, when you travel in the dark continent of Tibet, you will need to orient the wicked Tibetans with no faith in 'it' toward higher perceptions, so I am granting this divination to you".

> The Atiśa Rosary Divination—
> It is important to know [2r] how to count off in threes after dividing [the rosary] in two ... If *one* follows *one*: The matter is decided yet the merits are unclear. On the dry tree leaves grow. On the dry mountain water bursts forth. To the dry woman is born a child. The poor man finds wealth. The childless get children.

---

13   *'phrengs ba gsum du cad gsum dus rtsegs la// gcig thog du gcig byung na// thebs pa chad pa thung pa'i ngo// ri skam po la chu sdol pa'i ngo// shing skam po la lo 'dabs skyes pa'i ngos// bro nas thar pa'i ngo// rab chad ma la bu skyes pa'i ngo// [2v] dbul po la nor snyed pa'i ngo.*

14   It was filmed by Karma Phuntsho as part of the "Endangered Archives" project in Bhutan: Atiśa, *'Phreng mo mngon shes gtod ma.* Another copy: Atiśa, *Sgrol mas jo bo rje la lung bstan pa'i 'phreng mo,* never exactly says that Atiśa composed it, just that it was ordained by Tārā upon his departure for Tibet. Another copy with a slightly different title is: Atiśa, *sGrol mas a ti shar lung bstan pa'i phreng mo.* There is yet another copy, untitled, with an *incipit* reading *rJe btsun sgrol mas jo bo rje dpal ldan a ti sha la lung bstan pa'i 'phreng mo.* Clearly, the majority of known versions of this text attribute it to Atiśa rather than to Padampa. I learned *via* the internet that a text of this nature by Atiśa has been translated into French by one Lilian Too, with the title *L'Oracle des 21 Tara: Divination Mo transmise à Atisha par*

DIVINATIONS PADAMPA DID OR DID NOT DO, OR DID OR DID NOT WRITE   81

We can ignore the remainder for the time being since I believe it is enough to show the different beginnings of the Padampa and the Atiśa texts. It is extremely clear how much they have in common in their readings of the results, as you see in this sample. Indeed, we know of a third example attributed to yet another author that also has parallels in the prognostics section.[15]

3   Incidents of Divination Padampa Himself Performed

Now we will have a look at the few clear incidents of the teaching or practice of divination found in the *Zhijé Collection*. The physical manuscript, made in 1246 or so, I regard as providing the closest to contemporary evidence about Padampa that we have, although later manuscripts are just now emerging from Bhutan, and potentially much more important manuscripts are listed in the Drepung catalog and will likely be made available someday. In the meantime, I think we can make some provisional judgments that eventually may be tested further. In the *Zhijé Collection* I find only one incident of Padampa's clear and unambiguous practice of a divination.[16] Although the *Zhijé History* neglects to mention it, we find him teaching a divination system to one of his followers in a newly available historical work of comparable age. Let's look at these two things briefly.

3.1   *The Sixty-Four Pebble Divination*

This is a fascinating topic even if I do not know much about it. That does not matter so much after all, since Alexander K. Smith has published some fine essays on the topic.[17] It has been noticed a few times that Padampa had some

---

la déesse Tara, published in 2013. Long ago, Bawden, "Some Mongolian Divinatory Practices", 26–28, made some comments about an Atiśa Rosary Divination text in Mongolian language.

15   Thu'u bkwan III Blo bzang chos kyi nyi ma, *Phreng mo 'debs tshul.*

16   See Martin, "Ritual Indigenization", which concerns Padampa's employment of an indigenous Tibetan shamanic rite performed in order to determine the source of a woman disciple's severe ailments. This could count as an incident of divination, but it is never clarified by what particular method the divination is supposed to be effected, or at least it remains unclear to me.

17   Smith, "Remarks concerning the Methodology", and Smith, "Prognostic Structure". The latter publication is especially significant for us since it supplies the title of a divination text attributed to 'Brug lha and translates an account of how 'Brug lha passed the same divination practices to both Padampa (here called Dam pa rGya gar) and to A da lHa sras. The latter was responsible for the Bon transmission. It is interesting that, just like the Chinese classic text on yarrow-stalk divination, the I Ching, and just like some four-sided Dice Div-

82 MARTIN

contacts with the Bonpo Tertön by the name of Druglha ('Brug lha), and that he even received teachings from him about pebble divination. Their contact is known and recorded in a Bon pebble divination manual that was used by Namkhai Norbu.[18] In the Zhijé literature itself, we find that this teaching was only passed on and preserved in the Intermediate Transmission, and not in the Later Transmission period meaning the teachings given at Tingri.[19] So we should not expect them to be contained in the *Zhijé Collection*, and indeed they cannot be found there.

Some Bhutanese manuscripts have surfaced recently, but I have not yet had a chance to study them closely. One of them belongs precisely to the Intermediate Transmission lineage that is supposed to include these divinatory teachings.[20] Although no separately titled divination manuals have been located therein, we do find some significant references to the divination teachings.

It would be great to learn about a pebble divination text explicitly attributed to the authorship of Padampa, but so far I am not aware of one. The stone

---

    inations known to both Tibetans and Turks (in the *Irk Bitig*), Padampa's Pebble Divination is known to have 64 (one text says 60) possible results. See Dotson, "Call of the Cuckoo," Yakovlev, "Divination", and especially Strickmann, *Chinese Poetry and Prophecy*, 112–118. Strickmann argued that such systems are quite ancient in India, yet possibly of Greek origin. The Turkic divination system *kumalak* as described by Yakovlev very closely resembles Tibetan pebble divination, and this similarity merits serious investigation.

18   Namkhai, *Drung Deu and Bon*, 25. I should point out, since it could create difficulties, that in the translated account, 'Brug lha is called "Jedrug," and Padampa is called "Pha Tampa". Waddell, *Tibetan Buddhism*, 466–470, has an early discussion of different types of pebble divination. There is a mention of rMa receiving the 'Sixty-Arrangement Pebble Guidance' (*bkod pa drug cu'i rde'u khrid*) in Khams smyon's biography of Padampa, at page 168 (and notice mention of Khro tshang 'Brug lha at pages 38 and 83, in both cases in the form "*bon po* Khra tshang 'Brug lha"). This same source is translated in Molk, *Lion of Siddhas*, 29–174, with relevant pages here being 57 and 139, where "Bönpo Falcon Nest Dragon Deva" translates *bon po* Khra tshang 'Brug lha. The most pertinent source is *Zhijé History* by Zhig po Rin chen shes rab (1171–1245), as contained in the *Zhijé Collection*, vol. 4, 324–432, at page 343. In dGe ye's 1474 history, page 63 (folio 42 *recto*), we note the curious difference that here Khra tshang 'Brug lha is given teachings by Padampa rather than the other way around. John Bellezza's *Antiquities of Northern Tibet*, 133, tells of a local oral tradition in Byang thang explaining the origins of two *chortens* that the two of them built there.

19   Roerich, *Blue Annals*, 873, ought to be copying from the just-mentioned *Zhijé History*, but when we look there at what ought to be the corresponding passage what we find (at *Zhijé Collection*, vol. 4, page 346) is quite laconic and without any mention of the Pebble Divination. Indeed, when Khra tshang 'Brug bla is mentioned a few pages earlier (page 343) there is also no mention of any divination teaching.

20   This text with the front title *brGyud pa bar pa'i lo rgyus kyi rim pa* was filmed by the British Library Endangered Archives project of Karma Phuntsho in Bhutan, "Dramatse Thorbu 041".

DIVINATIONS PADAMPA DID OR DID NOT DO, OR DID OR DID NOT WRITE   83

divination text we spoke of before is obviously not at all the same kind of divination, as it works along very different lines. Observe that here Padampa is very much an Indian, but at the same time overtly receiving an indigenously Tibetan tradition and then passing it on to a Tibetan (to be preserved for posterity *via* the rMa lineage of the Intermediate Tradition of Zhijé). This makes much sense in a situation of cultural exchange that better explains what was happening in early Zhijé than does the usual picture of unidirectional India-to-Tibet traffic.

3.2   *The Bamboo and Feather Divination Incident*

Another time Dampa said, "Inhabitants of Langkhor! Gather together! Because there is a big desire for it, we need to do a divination."

> When everyone had gathered there, they seated a girl on a piece of white felt. The Jetsün took a bamboo in his right hand, and in his left hand a feather. Then he pronounced these words, "Oh lord of the sky! Lord of the earth! This sickness has plagued us enough, and now it is too much! We may die! Bring down the divination, bring it down!"
>
> The girl made her selection and [someone] said, "Be on guard not to let the disease spirit enter in. It is ready to overcome both the doctor and the medicine. If not vanquished now, there will be no other chance. If not vanquished, it is liable to bring death again and again. Be strong and act quickly!"[21]

4   Conclusions

I have to say that for myself this has always been a Padampa-centric enterprise. The desire to know more about *him* drives my interest in divination, more than the other way around. So perhaps inevitably I think about all the types of literature, and not only the divination manuals, that have been attributed to him over the centuries. There are two areas besides divination where we may well doubt authorship attributions to Padampa, and I have written about them elsewhere. These are: Tingrian Couplets and medicine texts.[22] The Tin-

---

21   I located a second exemplar and used it for comparison: Drametse Thorbu no. 105, section PHA, *Dam pa'i yon tan gyi zhus lan shing lo rgyas pa*, complete in 36 folios, with the relevant passage at folios 20–21. For an alternative English translation, see Molk, *Lion of the Siddhas*, 249.

22   The Tingrian Couplets were dealt with in a paper given at the Vancouver meeting of the IATS in 2010. The medicine text was subject of a Tibeto-logic blog entry entitled "The Mag-

grian Couplets are by far Padampa's most famous works today. It is hardly even known that the original collections of such couplets are in the *Zhijé Collection*, where twelve of them are from the mouth of Padampa at the time of his death, with another set of 118 spoken by his disciple Kunga at the time of *his* death. If we add these together to make 130 couplets, we find that the collections that circulate today have at most 25%, but more likely only 5 to 10 percent of their couplets in common with those in the *Zhijé Collection*. The collections with the least number of authentifiable verses are the ones that are the most commonly reproduced.

In the case of the medicine text, only recently appearing for the first time in a modern published format, we may say that the *Zhijé Collection* evinces hardly any interest in medicine, except in the later-added parts, and then in only one text.[23] What we have is a late fourteenth-century excavated text full of magical remedies for a long list of physical ailments.[24] Apart from the sources just mentioned, I have only learned recently of a medical text belonging to the rMa lineage of the "Middle Transmission" (*bar brgyud*) of the Zhijé, and await more details.[25] This rMa lineage is the very same as the one involved with the pebble divination we mentioned before.

The simple conclusion is that while at least four divination texts, each with its distinct system of divination, are attributed to Padampa, these practices do not in fact correspond to those he is known to have performed in the earliest sources we have. In the case of one of the four, the Rosary Divination, we have a more frequently attested alternative attribution to Atiśa. This raises doubts about not only this, but the other divination texts attributed to Padampa as well. My position at the moment is that all these practices are local Tibetan popular practices, actually authored by no one in particular, that at some point required ascription to Indian figures such as Padampa and Atiśa. Padampa

---

ical Medical Bag Texts", dated February 12, 2011. The Copenhagen manuscript is listed in Buescher and Tarab, *Catalogue*, vol. 1, 474 (no. 983 or alternatively PP 44). Here we might also mention a tract against beer drinking.

23 This text with significant medical content are not attributed to Padampa, but to a later member of his lineage, after all, being teachings of Pa tshab written down by his disciple rTen ne late in the twelfth century; see *Zhijé Collection*, vol. 4, 213–215, 254–257, 287–291.

24 It was found in around 1370 in a place in Kham known as Klong thang sGrol ma by an obscure *tertön* named Khams ston Shes rab dpal. Manuscripts exist in Copenhagen and in my own personal library, while the first modern publication is this one: *rTen 'brel gyi rtags spyad mkhyud dpyad dkar nag khra gsum rnams*, 1–53 (but note that the *tertön* is nowhere identified in this publication).

25 This is a five-folio manuscript recently reproduced as part of a set of medical manuscripts. Its specific subject would seem to be head injuries, although this is not yet very sure.

might be deemed a more likely choice for such ascriptions than Atiśa, precisely because of his known association with yet another divination practice, the Sixty Pebble Divination.[26]

I suggest that what we are seeing with these authorial ascriptions may be analogous to what is known in quote ascription studies as "Churchillian Drift." In case you want to repeat a famous quote, do not know who is actually being quoted and if it sounds like something an astute politician might say, ascribe it to Churchill. If they are clever words of earthy wisdom in daily life, attach the name Confucius.[27]

Cultural figures live on and on. Although it may *appear* ironic or even somewhat contradictory, we have to take *some kind* of a cultural historical approach, finding out what the culture was doing with its cultural heroes, if we want to better approach the historical realities of that person's life. By not separating the two concerns, for the time being, we may at some future point be better enabled to separate the two concerns. History brings back to mind prior acts of memory, much in the way Jan Assmann described his own way of pursuing history he calls "mnemohistory."[28]

Padampa was one of those towering figures whose spirit went on to haunt people in varied apparitions through Tibet's history, as he continues to do today, only now with an audience scattered throughout the world. It may very well be that awarding ascriptions of authorship to him is one of the ways that image was recovered, reclaimed and reconstituted. My position is: It is not as if these ascriptions came from nothing. Things were there from the very beginning that could have initiated them and later on gotten recovered in order to justify them ('rationalization in hindsight', I would like to call it). Many historians, just like myself, see the need to dig back into the earliest levels of documentation and

---

26 I suppose Atiśa would be a suitable choice primarily because of the prophecy he received from Tārā about his future life in Tibet, and not necessarily because he was directly involved in divination practice.

27 A real example: Confucius said, "Choose a job you love, and you will never have to work a day in your life." This is entirely true, particularly for those who have chosen Tibetology as a way of life, but its attribution to Confucius is false. For more on Churchillian Drift, a coinage of the prominent gnomologist Nigel Rees, an inhabitant of the British Isles as you might have guessed, see McKean, "Wise Words of Maya Angelou". The *drift* of Churchillian Drift is always from the less toward the more famous person. North Americans might prefer to call it Emersonian Drift, as in "Life is a journey, not a destination", usually attributed to Ralph Waldo Emerson, although nothing like it appears anywhere in his collected works.

28 Jan Assmann, *Moses the Egyptian*, especially the introductory chapter. *Nota bene*: Assmann does not present mnemohistory as the only way to do history, but recommends it as one of a spectrum of alternative (and perhaps complementary) approaches.

bring forgotten things to mind. In doing this, we take a vital part in the very same cultural memory processes we are supposed to investigate. We ought to take responsibility for what we do in our quests for the truths of the matters, try to perform our tasks well, have faith, and hope the results will be good ones even if we cannot know what they will be, concealed as they are in a future largely unforeseeable.

References

Assmann, Jan. *Moses the Egyptian: The Memory of Egypt in Western Monotheism*. Cambridge: Harvard University Press, 1997.

Atiśa (d. 1054). *'Phreng mo mngon shes gtod ma* ['Rosary Divination: Bestower of Clairvoyant Knowledge']. Filmed for the British Library's "Endangered Archives" project by Karma Phuntsho. Catalogued as "Yagang Thorbu 057."

Atiśa (d. 1054). *rJe btsun sgrol mas jo bo rje dpal ldan a ti sha la lung bstan pa'i 'phreng mo* ['The Rosary Divination that was Prophesied by Jetsün Drölma to the Venerable Lord Atiśa']. *In bKra shis tshe ring ma'i 'phrul mos gtsos pa'i mo dpe phan bde'i 'byung gnas* ['A Book of Divinations Headed by the Amazing Divination of the Auspicious Long Life Goddess'], n.p. (purchased in Kathmandu in 1993), 63–73.

Atiśa (d. 1054). *sGrol mas a ti shar lung bstan pa'i phreng mo* ['Rosary Divination that was Prophesied by Drölma to Atiśa']. *In 'Phrul mo sna tshogs phan bde'i 'byung gnas* ['Myriad Amazing Divinations, Font of Benefit and Comfort'], 63–73. Delhi: Konchhog Lhadrepa [Dkon mchog lha bris], 1997.

Atiśa (d. 1054). *Sgrol mas jo bo rje la lung bstan pa'i 'phreng mo* ['Rosary Divination that was Prophesied by Drölma to the Venerable Lord']. In *Mo dpe phyogs bsdus snang srid gsal ba'i me long* ['Collection of Divination Texts: A Mirror Showing the Phenomenal World'], 42–49. Mysore: Snga 'gyur mtho slob mdo sngags rig pa'i 'byung gnas gling [Ngagyur Nyingma Institute], 2000.

Bawden, Charles R. "Some Mongolian Divinatory Practices." *Central Asiatic Journal* 46, no. 1 (2002), 5–33.

Bellezza, John Vincent. *Antiquities of Northern Tibet, Pre-Buddhist Archaeological Discoveries on the High Plateau (Findings of the Changthang Circuit Expedition, 1999)*. Delhi: Adroit Publishers, 2001.

Buescher, Hartmut and Tarab Tulku. *Catalogue of Tibetan Manuscripts and Xylographs*. Copenhagen: Det Kongelige Bibliotek, 2000.

Chime Radha Rinpoche. "Tibet." In *Oracles and Divination*, ed. Michael Loewe and Carmen Blacker, 3–37. Boulder: Shambhala, 1981.

dGe ye Tshul khrims seng ge (15th century). *History of Indo-Tibetan Buddhism by dGe ye Tshul khrims seng ge, a Critical and Facsimile Edition of the Tibetan Text with Summary and Index*. Kyoto: Otani University Shin Buddhist Comprehensive Research Institute, 2007.

Dotson, Brandon. "The Call of the Cuckoo to the Thin Sheep of Spring: Healing and Fortune in Old Tibetan Dice Divination Texts." In *Tibetan and Himalayan Healing: An Anthology for Anthony Aris*, ed. Charles Ramble and Ulrike Roesler, 145–158. Kathmandu: Vajra Publications, 2015.

Drepung Catalog—dPal brtsegs bod yig dpe rnying zhib 'jug khang, *'Bras spungs dgon du bzhugs su gsol ba'i dpe rnying dkar chag* ['Handlist of Antique Books Preserved in Drepung Monastery']. Beijing: Mi rigs dpe skrun khang, 2004. In two volumes (pagination continuous).

Jiangbian Jiacuo. "An Investigation of Gesar's Arrow Divination (Gesar mDav mo)." In *Tibetan Studies*, ed. Per Kvaerne, vol. 1, 403–407. Oslo: Institute for Comparative Research in Human Culture, 1994.

Khams smyon Dharma seng ge (flourished late 19th century). *Grub pa'i dbang phyug chen po rje btsun dam pa sangs rgyas kyi rnam par thar pa dngos grub 'od stong 'bar ba'i nyi ma*. In Chos kyi seng ge and Gang pa, *Pha dam pa dang ma cig lab sgron gyi rnam thar* ['Biographies of Padampa and Machig Labdrön'], 1–242. Xining: Mtsho sngon mi rigs dpe skrun khang, 1992.

Khams ston Shes rab dpal (*circa* 14th century), revealer. *rTen 'brel gyi rtags spyad mkhyud dpyad dkar nag khra gsum rnams*. In *Pha dam pa'i mkhyud dpyad sna tshogs*, 1–53. Lhasa: Bod ljongs mi dmangs dpe skrun khang, 2014.

Martin, Dan. "Ritual Indigenization as a Debated Issue in Tibetan Buddhism (11th to Early 13th Centuries)." In *Challenging Paradigms: Buddhism and Nativism, Framing Identity Discourse in Buddhist Environments*, ed. Henk Blezer and Mark Teeuwen, 159–194. Leiden: Brill, 2013.

McKean, Erin. "The Wise Words of Maya Angelou, or Someone, Anyway." *The New York Times*, opinion page, A27. April 10, 2015.

mDzub mo lnga yi mo ['Five Finger Divination']. In *Mo dpe phyogs bsdus snang srid gsal ba'i me long* ['Collection of Divination Texts: A Mirror Showing the Phenomenal World'], 38–39. Mysore: sNga 'gyur mtho slob mdo sngags rig pa'i 'byung gnas gling [Ngagyur Nyingma Institute], 2000. Also contained in: *bKra shis tshe ring ma'i 'phrul mos gtsos pa'i mo dpe phan bde'i 'byung gnas* ['A Book of Divinations Headed by the Miraculous Divination of the Auspicious Long Life Goddess'], n.p., 57–58. Purchased in Kathmandu in 1993.

Molk, David, with Lama Tsering Wangdu Rinpoche, translators. *Lion of Siddhas: The Life and Teachings of Padampa Sangye*. Ithaca: Snow Lion, 2008.

Namkhai Norbu. *Drung Deu and Bön: Narrations, Symbolic Languages and the Bön Tradition in Ancient Tibet*, translated by Adriano Clemente and Andrew Lukianowicz. Dharamsala: Library of Tibetan Works and Archives, 1995.

Namkhai Norbu. *The Light of Kailash: A History of Zhang Zhung and Tibet, Volume One, The Early Period*, translated by Donatella Rossi. Arcidosso: Shang Shung Publications, 2009.

Polo, Marco (1254–1324). *The Travels of Marco Polo: The Complete Yule-Cordier Edition*. Mineola: Dover Publications, 1993. Reprint of the 1929 edition.

rDo mo'i rnam shes ['Super Knowledge of Stone Divination']. In *Mo dpe phyogs bsdus snang srid gsal ba'i me long* ['Collection of Divination Texts: A Mirror Showing the Phenomenal World'], 40–41. Mysore: sNga 'gyur mtho slob mdo sngags rig pa'i 'byung gnas gling [Ngagyur Nyingma Institute], 2000. Also contained in: *bKra shis tshe ring ma'i 'phrul mos gtsos pa'i mo dpe phan bde'i 'byung gnas* ['A Book of Divinations Headed by the Miraculous Divination of the Auspicious Long Life Goddess'], n.p., 59–60. Purchased in Kathmandu in 1993.

Schlagintweit, Emil. "Verzeichnis der tibetischen Handschriften der Königlich Württembergischen Landesbibliothek zu Stuttgart." *Sitzungsberichte der philosophisch-philologischen und historischen Klasse der königliche bayerischen Akademie der Wissenschaften zu München, Jahrgang 1904* (1905), 245–270.

Smith, Alexander K. "Prognostic Structure and the Use of Trumps in Tibetan Pebble Divination." *Magic, Ritual and Witchcraft* 10, no. 1 (Summer 2015), 1–21.

Smith, Alexander K. "Remarks Concerning the Methodology and Symbolism of Bon Pebble Divination." *Études mongoles et sibériennes, centrasiatiques et tibétaines* 42 (2011), 2–15.

Strickmann, Michel. *Chinese Poetry and Prophecy: The Written Oracle in East Asia*, ed. Bernard Faure. Stanford: Stanford University Press, 2005.

Thu'u bkwan III Blo bzang chos kyi nyi ma (1737–1802). *Phreng mo 'debs tshul lkog gyur gsal ba'i me long*. In *Dmangs srol yig cha phyogs bsgrigs*, ed. Tshe ring and 'Brug rgyal mkhar, 125–133. Lanzhou: Kan su'i mi rigs dpe skrun khang, 1997.

Waddell, L. Austine. *Tibetan Buddhism with Its Mystic Cults, Symbolism and Mythology*. New York: Dover Publications, 1972. Reprint of 1895 edition.

Yakovlev, V. "Divination about the Way and the Way of Divination among the Turkic People." A draft English translation of a paper presented at the 51st Permanent International Altaistic Conference held in Bucharest, 2008.

Zhijé Collection—The Tradition of Pha Dampa Sangyas: A Treasured Collection of His Teachings Transmitted by T[h]ug[s] sras Kun dga'. "Reproduced from a unique collection of manuscripts preserved with 'Khrul zhig Rinpoche of Tsa rong Monastery in Dingri, edited with an English introduction to the tradition by B. Nimri Aziz." Thimphu: Kunsang Tobgey, 1979. In five volumes.

CHAPTER 5

Landscaping Time, Timing Landscapes: The Role of Time in the *sa dpyad* Tradition

Petra Maurer

1 Introduction

Divination in Tibet occurs in many forms, but the form that has had the most profound influence on Tibetan culture and the Tibetan's way of life is *sa dpyad*, which is often—and not without problems—translated as *geomancy*. *Sa dpyad* refers to a tradition of beliefs and practices based on a suite of relationships; an expert in *sa dpyad* must understand the relationships between different characteristics of the landscape, the landscape and its elements, and these elements and the area's inhabitants. One of the most important relationships within the tradition and practice of *sa dpyad*, however, is one of the most overlooked: the relationship between time and place. In *sa dpyad*, this relationship is primary and symbiotic. Not only are places understood by the passing of seasons and generations, but time is understood through astrological movements and the relationship between astrological houses and natural elements, the components of places.

Although *sa dpyad* has often been described as merely the reading of and adjustment to the landscape, what a focus on the role of time within the tradition reveals is just how much the *sa dpyad* tradition is dependent on relationships. The technique not just depends on relationships between the various characteristics of a landscape, and not just between the landscape and its inhabitants, but also between these landscapes and temporality. This temporality, moreover, exists on multiple levels. The texts and practices of *sa dpyad* exist within a historical continuum of Tibetan culture; various traditions were imported and reformulated into the Tibetan language, and have been preserved in Tibetan texts. *Sa dpyad* exists, therefore, in historical time. But this is not all. Not only has *sa dpyad* been influenced by the passing of time, it has also helped to construct the Tibetans' understanding of time; for *sa dpyad* includes a paradigm of temporality, a way to measure time. And there is more. *Sa dpyad* not only contains within it a paradigm of time, but as this paradigm is described through the elements and creatures of the natural world, the temporal paradigm itself is used to read this world. The rela-

© KONINKLIJKE BRILL NV, LEIDEN, 2020 | DOI:10.1163/9789004410688_006

tionship between time and place is cyclical, and it describes the cyclical passing of time in place; first, through the seasons, and then through the generations. In this tradition, it is believed that each generation is linked through the "bone-element" (*rus khams*) that is inherited patrilineally, an element descending through time. This bone-element too creates relationships across time; it is positioned within time and it creates an inherited link to one's ancestral place.

The circularity of these relationships and the uses of place and time in the tradition are complex and can be daunting. To understand the relationships between time and place in *sa dpyad* it is first necessary to delve into the meaning of the term itself, its tradition, and the Tibetans' semantic constructions of time. After establishing these perimeters, the connections between time and place within them will become clearer. Through this investigation, not only does the fundamental role of time in the *sa dpyad* tradition become clear, but also the importance the tradition places on all relationships: relations between time and place and other relations in time and place.

2 The Terminology: *feng shui, sa dpyad,* and the Art of Dotting

Although *sa dpyad* is usually translated as 'geomancy', this term does not render the Tibetan exactly.[1] *Sa dpyad* is a field of knowledge, which belongs to *nag rtsis*, a term that refers to Chinese divination,[2] calculation, astrology and astronomy. Accounts on its transmission to Tibet date it in the times of Srong btsan sgam po (ca. 505–649) or, according to the 14th century historiographical source *rGyal rabs gsal ba'i me long*, in the times of his father gNam ri srong btsan (ca. 570–618).[3]

The term geomancy can be interpreted in two different ways: like *sa dpyad*, it can refer to the 'characteristics of the land', that is, the interpretation of topographical features of an area. The technique could also be called topomancy. In the Tibetan context, and this corresponds to the two techniques in Chinese *feng shui* 風水 ("wind water") as well,[4] besides the interpretation of topograph-

---

1 Special thanks to Ruth Gamble for proofreading the English and commenting on the paper.
2 From lat. *divinare*, "to explore the will of God" or more generally "to reveal the hidden or unknown." Divination can also be understood as mantic art to predict the future or prognostication. For further explanations, see the end of section 3.
3 Sørensen, *Royal Genealogies*, 153.
4 Other terms are *di li* 地理 (shape of the land) or *kan yu* 看域 (examination of the ground).

LANDSCAPING TIME, TIMING LANDSCAPES 91

ical features, the diviner or, more colloquially, the astrologer (*rtsis mkhan*) also calculates several dimensions, so *nag rtsis* is of fundamental relevance for the prediction.[5]

"Geomancy" also denotes the analyses of patterns or forms drawn or produced in sand or any other kind of soil. This method of divination was widely spread and practiced for example in medieval Europe, Arab countries, parts of Africa, and northern India. A diviner predicts the future by producing patterns in the soil or sand that are a random arrangement of dots or lines, or dots and lines that are drawn following special rules. The analysis and interpretation of these patterns is a technique to generally predict someone's future. The German term *Punktierkunst*, the 'art of dotting' is another, even more precise term to render this divinatory method. It also spread as far as Tibet where it was performed with pebbles.

The analysis and interpretation of patterns and shapes is applied in both techniques to analyze the current situation and/or to predict the future. Geomancy, however, focuses on the construction of buildings—although the prediction concerns any sphere of human life—, the art of dotting is advice to predict the future more generally. The diviner reads artificially created patterns when he applies the art of dotting, in geomancy, however, he reads naturally existing shapes in the environment. The technique called *sa dpyad*, the 'examination of the land/an area' includes a twofold procedure: first, the diviner examines the topography of an area in order to ascertain a suitable construction site, and second, he assesses the place in question. The literary meaning of the term seems therefore to be quite straightforward. But as we will see later on there is another factor in determining the place for construction: the calculation.

3   The Textual Sources of *sa dpyad* in the Tibetan Tradition

Those texts that describe *sa dpyad*, be it the *Vaiḍūrya dkar po* or 'Blue Beryl' attributed to or compiled by *sDe srid* Sangs rgyas rgya mtsho (1653–1705), the Fifth Dalai Lama's regent;[6] or a chapter in part Ta of the *bKa' mdzod* of Kong sprul blo gros mtha' yas (1813–1899) *Tsi na'i sa dpyad gsar 'gyur lugs kyi sgo*

---

5   For the symbols used in the compass, see Feuchtwang, *Chinese Geomancy*, 18 ff. In "the School of the Compass" in particular places are calculated with the help of elements, the trigrams and the position of stars and so on; see Maurer, *Grundlagen der tibetischen Geomantie*, 21–22.

6   For the convenience of the reader, I will quote from the latest edition of the text, printed in 1997 in China.

'byed 'phrul gyi lde'u mig 'Magical key to opening the gate to Chinese geomancy according to the tradition of the new translations';[7] or the works of Karma chags med (alias Rāgāsya; 1613–1678)[8] like *Sa dpyad nyung ngu rin chen kun 'dus*, 'Small [text] on geomancy that comprises everything precious' contain highly imaginative descriptions of places.

They compare areas as a whole or in part with living beings, such as animals, persons, demons or parts of their bodies or with inanimate objects, such as items of everyday life and objects used in rituals. By learning how to read the environment through its topographical characteristics, the *sa dpyad* expert is able to find a suitable place for the construction of a building, be it a house, a temple or a *chorten*, or for the laying out of a cemetery. The idea behind this reading is that an area is thought to have certain potencies that influence the life of its inhabitants. The influence arises either through the topographical characteristics alone or—and this cannot simply be derived from the term *sa dpyad*—in connection with Chinese divination (*nag rtsis*). The shape of an area, its mountains, its rocks, its fields, the sky seen from a valley, the course of a river, the growth of trees and even the color of fields and rocks are all thought to affect the region's inhabitants and to determine their future. These effects are quite extensive and have an impact not only on the house about to be constructed but also on the health, types of diseases, lifespan, and mode of death of any of its inhabitants, present and future family members, and livestock. It will also have an impact on their wealth, their harvests, and so on.

4 Developments in the Practice of *sa dpyad*

4.1 *Practice of* sa dpyad

As strange as the instructions in those texts reading the landscape[9] may sound to us today, it is prudent to remember that *sa dpyad* was widely practiced in Tibet before the Chinese invaded the country in the 1950s. Students, the future astrologers and diviners (*rtsis pa*) traveled to Lhasa from all over the country

---

7   For a description of its content, see Maurer, *Grundlagen der tibetischen Geomantie*, 71–72.

8   Information on the life of Karma chags med can be found in Schwieger, *Tibetisches Wunschgebet*, 37 ff.

9   The term *landscape* often denotes an area, terrain or country and is used here with the same meaning. It originally denotes a painting with natural scenery and is therefore similarly problematic like the German word *Landschaft* that formed the root for Dutch *landschap*. At the end of the 16th century the term (together with *herring* and *linen*) was transferred from the Netherlands to England where it turned into the colloquial English term *landskip*, see Schama, *Landscape and Memory*, 10. I thank Charles Ramble for this reference.

LANDSCAPING TIME, TIMING LANDSCAPES 93

and even from Sikkim to study with the *rtsis pa* in the Medical-Astrological-Institute (*sman rtsis khang*). They had to learn the basic *nag rtsis* theories, that is they had to acquire a profound knowledge of Chinese divination as this is a requirement for understanding and making calculations in *sa dpyad*. To become an expert in *sa dpyad*, they had to memorize at least chapter 32 of the *Vaiḍūrya dkar po*. The students were also trained in the interpretation of the landscape by modeling areas in sand as they were described in the text. The future astrologers were not asked to create a realistic diagram of an area but rather to express the region by means of comparison: a living being such as a tiger, a *srin*-demon, the heart of a man, a *vajra*, or a pan, to cite just a few examples.

This abstractness made the procedure considerably more difficult. It may be that a person with some artistic abilities could form these figures, but I doubt that all examples mentioned here are that easy to model. How might they have created recognizable shapes such as:

- the bodies of animals, such as a whole bear, the tail of a fox, a pig running downhill, a falcon gliding down onto the earth;
- or demons: such as a *srin*-demoness, or the resting place of a *bse-rags* demon beating his breast; or a part or the whole of a human body, such as the forehead of an old man, an ankle scratched in a furrow, or a widow with a torn blanket;
- even everyday items or sacred objects may be difficult to form: a dried-out puddle of water, a sling, a dented piece of copper, the eight spokes of the wheel of the *Dharma* or a lotus.

Sangs rgyas rgya mtsho reduces the assessment of places into three principles: avoid bad places (*ngan pa spang*), choose good places (*bzang po blang*) for the construction, and perform rituals before and during construction work (*gdab pa'i thabs*).[10] The description of the places with the help of comparisons might raise several questions: how do mountains or rocks with those shapes really look like? Are there any factors that have to be taken into consideration in the assessment of a place? And if so what were they? The answers to these questions are difficult to determine. All these examples of comparisons are assigned to certain categories that are valued as either good or bad, with names such as the "eight augmentations" (*'phel ba brgyad*), the "nineteen protecting areas" (*bskyab pa'i sa bzang bcu dgu*), the eight "bad signs" of an area (*sa yi ltas ngan*

---

10 Sangs rgyas rgya mtsho, *Vaiḍūrya dkar po, smad cha,* 242.3: *de yang spyid don rnam pa gsum / ngan pa spang zhing bzang po blang / gdab pa'i thabs dang gsum yin no//*; see Maurer, *bla ri,* 68.

brgyad) or "eight small obstacles" (*keg phran brgyad*). There is, however, no obvious logical system for recognizing any of them, not even at second sight.[11]

The qualities assigned to some of these patterns seem logical: places resembling a Buddhist symbol, usually regarded as a sign of good luck and fortune, such as a lotus, a *vajra*, or an opened book (*poti*) are of course considered to have a positive impact on the regions' inhabitants, and therefore to mark the site as suitable for construction. The assessment of others remains unclear: it remains unclear, for example, why a cauldron turned upside down (*zangs kha sbub pa*)[12] is considered a negative form and unsuitable for construction while a pan turned upside down (*sla nga kha sbub nang kha gshim*)[13] is considered positive and is supposed to cause harmony within one's family. As these details demonstrate, learning how to interpret the land and recognize patterns in the environment that mark it as suitable or unsuitable for construction is a complex procedure. But it is only one part of *sa dpyad*, and may well be the easiest part. Besides, the components of Tibetan *sa dpyad* also include methods that cannot properly be called "geomancy" in that they move beyond the mere examination of a region's topographical characteristics.

Furthermore, the examination of an area requires the right procedure, starting with the determination of whether it is the right time to examine the site. Before the real *sa dpyad* can start, the diviner must make a fire, and whether it is the right time to examine the site will be determined by the direction in which the incense smoke (*spos kyi dud pa*) blows.[14] If the smoke's direction suggests the time is unsuitable, the diviner has to postpone his analysis.[15] With the examination of smoke from incense, the direction of the smoke is important and predicts, for instance, whether the time for the examination of an area is suitable. This kind of prediction belongs to the divination that can be called *mo* or more precisely *mo rtsis*.[16]

Writing in the 17th century, the aforementioned regent of the Fifth Dalai Lama, *sDe srid* Sangs rgyas rgya mtsho, combines *sa dpyad* with other subjects and different forms of *rtsis* such as astronomy, astrology and different forms of

---

11   See Maurer, *bla ri*, 69 f.

12   Sangs rgyas rgya mtsho, *Vaiḍūrya dkar po, smad cha*, 245.7.

13   Sangs rgyas rgya mtsho, *Vaiḍūrya dkar po, smad cha*, 265.7.

14   Divination with smoke was also used in Babylonian culture, where cedar kindling was burned in a small pot; see Gurney, *Babylonians*, 152 f.

15   The text does not mention the consequences of an examination of the site at the wrong time but my guess is that an examination at the wrong time is either not successful, or its result turns out to be incorrect; see Maurer, *Grundlagen der tibetischen Geomantie*, 168 ff.

16   For more examples of different forms of divination (*mo*), see Ekvall, *Religious Observances*, 262 ff.

divination in his *Vaiḍūrya dkar po*, such as the interpretation of fluttering of the eyes at a certain time of the day or sneezing (*sbrid pa*), buzzing in one's ears or the cawing of a crow (*skya kha*) and so on,[17] methods of predicting the future that can also be called *mo* or *mo rtsis*[18] and are not particularly related to or combined with the calculation of any other dimensions. The use of the term *rtsis* or calculation in these procedures is closely related to the act itself, as for instance with the counting of the beads when performing *'phreng mo*, the divination with a rosary. In other kinds of divination, the term *rtsis* is related to the assessment of patterns and forms as in *sog mo*, the interpretation of cracks in the shoulder blade or in *sa dpyad* where the patterns and shapes in and of the landscape are assessed. In contrast with the calculation that uses other dimensions in close connection to the time as the signs of the year, the *spar kha* and *sme ba*[19] and so on, the time factor plays a subordinate role in *mo rtsis*: the best time to perform *mo* is early morning, which is also the best time for pulse diagnosis. But if the *mo* cannot be done in the early morning, any other time of the day is suitable. The calculation of the dimensions on the other hand needs not be done in early morning, any time is suitable but the time itself is calculated.

Thus, several other chapters of the *Vaiḍūrya dkar po* deal especially with the calculation (*rtsis*) of different spheres or fields of human life. They explain how to calculate marriage (*bag rtsis*), for example, and how to calculate misfortune (*keg rtsis*) and disease (*nad rtsis*) among other topics. The text also explains how to calculate the times of the day (*dus tshod rtsis*), that are suitable for almost any kind of activity. The common link is the calculation of time and timing, which turns out to be an important factor for the determination of the right place.

As can be seen in *sa dpyad*, *mo* and *rtsis* were basically two different methods, that is the examination of patterns and shapes in the land (*mo*) and the calculation (*rtsis*) of the suitable place and/or time for construction. The clear distinction between *mo* and *rtsis* is for instance also found in the Gesar epic, where we read of a *lha rje*—quite a special term for a healer—a *rtsis pa* and a *mo ma*.[20]

---

17 Sangs rgyas rgya mtsho, *Vaiḍūrya dkar po, smad cha*, 26 ff.

18 In the *rGyal rabs gsal ba'i me long* for instance, the term *mo rtsis pa* is used for those who predict the future; see Kuznetsov, *rGyal rabs*, 190; for the translation see Sørensen, *Royal Genealogies*, 425 f.

19 The dimensions *spar kha* and *sme ba* are considered to be related to time and thus they influence the life of a person, for an explanation of their origin, see Maurer, *Grundlagen der tibetischen Geomantie*, 43–44.

20 Stein, *Gesar*, 325.

4.2 *Chinese Divination and* sa dpyad

The reader of texts on *sa dpyad* comes across several terms that are important in Chinese divination more generally. These terms include *rus chen* and *rus khams*, the *bla*-element, *gnam sgo, sa sgo, keg, dur mig, dgu mig* and *rtsub*. They are not explained in the chapter on *sa dpyad* itself.[21] The terms refer to divinatory dimensions that basically depend on the birth year of a person and are used in Chinese divination to calculate the future. For instance, Sangs rgyas rgya mtsho writes in the *Vaidūrya dkar po*: "If one starts with the construction of a temple, a palace or a fortress one has to remove the *keg* [lit. 'hindrances'] and the different kinds of *dgu mig, dur mig* and *rtsub*."[22] Therefore, the reader needs a fundamental knowledge of Chinese divination, as the descriptions that are given would otherwise be completely useless. The questions that arise from the inclusion of calculation of time are: Do these dimensions influence the place for construction, and if so what is their impact? How does one calculate a site?

5 *Sa dpyad* in Time

5.1 *Aspects of Time and Timing*

As the abovementioned dimensions are usually used to calculate the right timing for an undertaking, I would like to start with some general reflections on time and timing in Tibet and Tibetan culture. How was and is time divided in Tibet? And what concepts do we find there?

Traditional Tibetan society was mainly based on agriculture and pastoralism and therefore dominated by peasants and nomads. They used quite a simple system to measure time as they followed the natural processes: the passing of time was determined by the movement of the sun, the moon and the evening star. The seasons of the year (*dus*) determined the timing of specific activities: the ploughing and sowing of the fields, the harvest, the collection of herbs, and the needs of the cattle which were basically yaks, cattle, sheep, and goats. Furthermore, the seasons influenced the movement and the activities of the nomads: in Tibet as in other mountain areas there are summer pastures and winter pastures for grazing and seasons of sharing and slaughtering. The time of the day is further divided by the needs of the cattle, such as the feeding in the morning and the milking in the evening. Time was determined and organized by seasonal and daily activities that were necessary for survival; there was no

---

21   See Maurer, forthcoming.

22   Sangs rgyas rgya mtsho, *Vaidūrya dkar po, smad cha*, 277.11: *gtsug lag pho brang mkhar khang sogs / 'debs par bya ba'i las brtsam dus / keg dang dgu dur rtsub rigs bcos//*.

need of timing. Exact timing only became necessary in modern societies especially due to the use of machines and modern means of transport. And only then, for instance, is the use of a watch required.

This short survey might illustrate that time was measured and divided using pre-modern means and, in a society more or less free from modern acquisitions, seconds or even hours and days have another value. The different relationship with time and timing became evident when, for instance, Tibetans in the Resistance movement met with modern American society in form of the CIA who trained the Tibetan freedom fighters: the Tibetans who were recruited not only had "difficulty quantifying distances and numbers," but they were also not used to watches and had a different concept of time, a fact that caused problems with punctuality.[23] Military operations or even conferences require punctuality as these events otherwise certainly fail. Modern societies only function when the course of time is recognized and accepted and everybody's watch shows the same time. But the measurement, the controlling of time, something very common nowadays, only started about 100 years ago.[24]

5.2 Terms for Time and Temporality

There are two basic terms that denote time in Tibetan: *dus* and *tshe*. According to their entries in Jäschke's Tibetan-English dictionary, they both denote time in a general sense. But the length of the entries and the explanations in Jäschke's dictionary reveal that there are probably semantic differences between the two terms.

His interpretations regarding the term *dus* are quite detailed and enriched with many examples. Jäschke notes seven main possible semantic interpretations of time, the first being "time, in general" and "*dus kyi* means also: happening sometimes." As second interpretation of *dus*, he denotes "the right time, proper season"; as third, the expression *dus gsum*, "the three times," indicating present, past, and future or the three times of the day (morning, noon, evening); or "in *dus gsum gyi sangs rgyas* the Buddhas of the three times often with special reference to metempsychosis, the present, the former, and the future period of life." He gives "season," which might be three or four, depending on the region, as a fourth meaning. Especially his translation with "conjunctures, times, circumstances," "an age" as synonyms for Sanskrit *yuga* and "year" point to a semantic range that is different from *tshe*.[25]

---

23   See Conboy and Morrison, *Secret War*, 48.
24   Standard Time was introduced at the end of the 19th century; on July 1st 1913, the Eiffel Tower sent the first signal transmitted around the world; see Kern, *Time and Space*, 12–14.
25   See Jäschke, *Tibetan Dictionary*, 254–255.

Goldstein translates *dus* with "time," explaining the word with the phrase "*dus gzhan zhig* another time" and "*dbyar dus* summertime." The latter shows clearly a semantic shift to "season." His examples are certainly derived from the explanations given in the *Tshig mdzod chen mo* (TTC) where the second meaning of *dus* is explained by the seasons, that are obviously taken from India: *dpyid dang so ga/ dbyar/ ston/ dgun stod/ dgun smad de dus mtshams la drug yod pas grangs drug mtshon*, "spring, the hot season, summer, autumn, the first part of winter and the second part of winter, these being the six periods, therefore they are shown as six." The second and third meaning given respectively in Goldstein and TTC is the use of *dus* in connection with a verb, and thus used as temporal conjunction, that can be translated with "at the time of, while, when."[26] More detailed explanations for this use and many examples are found in Jäschke.[27]

The term *tshe* that Goldstein renders with "long life" is translated by Jäschke as "time in a gen[eral] sense," explained as a synonym of *dus* and as a temporal conjunction; *tshe* also means "the time of life" or simply "life," and is used for instance in the compound *mi tshe*, "human life, human lifespan," often translated by "life" with respect to a person.[28]

The semantic difference between *tshe* and *dus* might also be found in the fact that the *tshe*-related term *tshes* is used for "the day of the month" or "the day of the week," "date," *tshe tshad* meaning "duration of (one's) life."

Another term which is often employed for *dus* is *dus tshod*, literally "the space or measure of time;" Jäschke explains "*de'i dus tshod la* at that time; also for hour."[29] Texts on divination employ *dus tshod* for the "times of the day," and name the twelve times of the day, as in the *Vaiḍūrya dkar po* and the *dPag bsam ljon shing*.[30]

The semantic use of *tshe tshad*, literally "the measure of life," meaning "lifespan, the duration of life or age" is obviously very different from *dus tshod*. And the term *tshe thar*, which could be translated as "to grant him his life" (Jäschke) or "saving / sparing a life" (Goldstein), also indicates that *dus* and *tshe* are used very differently, although their basic meaning might be "time."

This short explanation might serve as a first illustration of the distinction between *tshe* and *dus*, and a thorough analysis would require a more detailed

---

26 Goldstein, *Modern Tibetan*, 533; TTC 1257.

27 See Jäschke, *Tibetan Dictionary*, 254.

28 Interestingly, the quotes we have up to now collected in the *Wörterbuch der Tibetischen Schriftsprache* (WtS) for the term *tshes pa* are from different sources, such as Nel pa Paṇḍita, *gZer mig, gZi brjid* and the biography of Milarepa, but in all these it appears only in the compound *zla ba tshes pa* that denotes "the moon in the first days."

29 Jäschke, *Tibetan Dictionary* 255.

30 See the explanations in the following paragraph.

examination of written sources. But as far as I can see, the term *dus* seems more to relate to time in general and connect with the aspect of eternity, endlessness and an infinite nature; on the other hand *dus* can, when employed in the sense of *timing* or *period of time*, be determined through the dimensions of *nag rtsis*: *tshe*, however, denotes rather the time in relation to a person, the personal time and the time of one's life; *tshe* comes to an end and is of a finite nature, it is limited and determined by two components: the dimensions in *nag rtsis* and one's *karma* (*las*).[31]

Dus tshod, "the measure of time" or "hour" leads to the word *chu tshod*, which in modern Tibetan language usually expresses "time," as for instance in: "*chu tshod ga re red* what time is it?" It also means "clock" and "hour" and was once adopted to translate "the clepsydra or water clock of ancient India."[32] The clepsydra, literally "theft of water," was the first instrument created to measure time without the use of the sun, based on the observation that water always flows steadily. Some of the oldest found in Egypt date from the 15th century BCE and might also have been in use by Assyrians in Mesopotamia. From the 6th century BCE onwards, water clocks were also known in China but they were not of primary importance; water could be replaced by mercury, which is more stable than water and does not freeze in winter.[33]

The term *chu tshod* has several meanings which are connected to time and space, and here its quantity remains identical: *chu tshod* denotes 1/60 of a natural day (*nyin zhag*), a zodiac day (*khyim zhag*) and of a lunar day (*tshes zhag*). With regard to space, *chu tshod* designates 1/60 of a yoga-section (*sbyor ba*) and 1/60 of a lunar mansion (*rgyu skar*). However, *chu tshod* can render the Sanskrit terms *nāḍī*, *ghaṭī*, *ghatikā* or even *daṇḍa* and thus its exact measure varies.[34]

5.3 *Measures of Time That Are Divisions of the Year, Months, and Days*
Time in Chinese divination can basically be determined through the elements and the signs of the zodiac. The twelve signs of the zodiac and the elements are related to the twelve directions, that is, the four cardinal directions divided into an upper (*stod*) and a lower half (*smad*) and the four intermediate directions. As figure 5.1 shows:

---

31 According to Charles Ramble (personal communication) *tshe* appears especially in texts that deal with longevity almost like a substance and might be compared with petrol in the tank whose amount varies.

32 Jäschke, *Tibetan Dictionary* 158.

33 See Fraser, *Zeit*, 71.

34 See Schuh, *Kalenderrechnung*, 65; Henning, *Kālacakra*, 12 and *WtS, 18. Lieferung*, 243.

FIGURE 5.1
Chinese divination, *thangka* section
THE MUSEUM OF THE FIVE CONTINENTS (PREVIOUSLY THE VÖLKERKUNDE MUSEUM), MUNICH, REPRODUCED BY PERMISSION

(1) the upper east is the tiger, the lower east the hare; the southeast the dragon;
(2) the upper south is the snake, the lower south the horse; the southwest the sheep;
(3) the upper west is the monkey, the lower west the bird, the northwest the dog;
(4) the upper north is the pig, the lower north the mouse, the northeast the ox.

The five elements are also positioned in the directions: the east is related to wood, the south to fire, the west to iron, and the north to water. The four intermediate directions are related to the earth element. Furthermore, the years are distinguished into male (*pho*) and female (*mo*) years and the element related to a year remains the same for two years.[35]

The twelve months are grouped according to the seasons into a first, middle, and last month of spring, summer, autumn, and winter. The relationship between year and month with regard to the signs of the zodiac is as follows: the first year is the mouse year and as the son of the mouse is tiger, the tiger month is the first. As the succession of the signs of the zodiac is fixed, their relation to the months is determined. Tiger, hare, and dragon denote the first, the middle, and the last month of springtime; snake, horse, and sheep the three months of summer; monkey, bird, and dog the three months of autumn; and pig, mouse, and ox the three months of winter.[36]

---

35 For basic explanations on the chronology in Tibet see also Vogel, *Tibetan Chronology*, 224 ff.
36 Sangs rgyas rgya mtsho, *Vaiḍūrya dkar po, stod cha*, 254.21–26: *de dag phyogs la gnas pa'i*

dragon (*'brug*) southeast (*lho shar*)	snake (*sbru sbrul*) upper south (*lho stod*)	element fire (*me*)	horse (*rta*) lower south (*lho smad*)	sheep (*lug*) southwest (*lho nub*)
Hare (*yos*) lower east (*shar smad*)				monkey (*sprel*) upper west (*nub stod*)
element wood (*shing*)		in the middle are the nine *sme ba* and around these the eight *spar kha*		element iron (*lcags*)
tiger (*stag*) upper east (*shar stod*)				bird (*bya*) lower west (*nub smad*)
ox (*glang*) nordeast (*byang shar*)	rat (*byi*) lower north (*byang smad*)	element water (*chu*)	pig (*phag*) upper north (*byang stod*)	dog (*khyi*) northwest (*nub byang*)

FIGURE 5.2 Schematic exemplification of Figure 5.1

The scheme above illustrates the above-mentioned *thangka* section on Chinese divination.[37]

Interestingly, Sangs rgyas rgya mtsho explains the twelve months as coming from the twelve *dar gud*, a term that might be translated as "prosperity and loss" or "flourishing and decline". The expression denotes dimensions of Chinese origin that are meant to explain basic events in a human life that occur to everyone.

---

tshul / shar stod stag la shar smad yod / shar lho 'brug la shar smad sbrul / lho smad rta la lho nub lug / nub stod spre'u nub smad bya / nub byang khyi la byang stod phag / byang smad byi ba byang shar glang / kun kyang 'byung ba sde lngar gans / shar shing lho me nub phyogs lcags / byang chu mtshams bzhi sa yi khams / dar gud rnam pa bcu gnyis las / zla ba bcu gnyis bshad par bya / lo yi thog ma byi ba ste / byi ba'i bu ni stag yin pas /stag go zla ba dang po ste / zla ba dpyid zla ra 'bring tha / stag yos 'brug yin dbyar zla gsum / sbrul rta lug la ston gsum po / sprel bya khyi yin dgun zla gsum / phag byi glang du shes par bya//. See also Tseng, *Divinationskalkulation*, 64–74.

37 See Maurer, *Thangka zur sino-tibetischen Divination*, 232–233. I would like to thank the Museum of the Five Continents (previously the Völkerkunde Museum) in Munich for the permission to reproduce the section of this *thangka*.

The days, too, are seen to be related to the signs of the zodiac. The first day of the first month, which is male (*pho*), is related to tiger (*stag*), while the first day of the second month, which is female (*mo*) is related to monkey (*sprel*).[38] The days are further divided into units of two hours, denoting the "time of the day" which are placed in relation with the signs of the zodiac (*lo rtags*). According to Sangs rgyas rgya mtsho, the relationship between times of the day and the signs of the zodiac is as follows: dawn is calculated as hare, sunrise as dragon, morning as snake, midday as horse, afternoon as sheep, late afternoon as monkey, sunset as bird, evening as dog, night as pig, midnight as mouse, after midnight as ox, and early morning as tiger.[39]

We find those units in China and India as well, but the division into twelve double hours has its origin in Babylonia, and probably the same division was subsequently adopted by Egypt. This system of twelve double hours might have been the source for the Chinese as well. The segmentation of the time of the day in India was different: the day was divided into thirty *muhūrta*.[40] These units of time, like year, month, day, and hour are directly or indirectly connected with other factors that are important for the calculation of the right time to start an undertaking—in German called *Zeitpunkt*, which corresponds to the term "timing" in English. Besides the five elements and the directions, these units are divinatory dimensions related to the aspects that are called *sme ba* and *spar kha*, the signs of the zodiac, and personal elements such as *rus khams* or *rus chen*,[41] to name just a few. According to Tibetan ideas, all these factors determine human life, although nowadays Tibetans are more likely to use watches and to divide the day in 24 hours and the hour in 60 minutes.

One of the systems that found its way to Tibet was used, for instance, in the astronomical systems (*grub rtsis*),[42] and came from India; it was different: the day was divided into 60 units called *chu tshod*, the *chu tshod* into 60 *chu srang*,

---

38 Tseng, *Divinationskalkulation*, 72 f.

39 Sangs rgyas rgya mtsho, *Vaiḍūrya dkar po, stod cha*, 255.4–5: *de nas dus tshod nam langs yos / nyi shar 'brug la nyi dros sbrul / nyi phyed rta la phyed yo lug / myur kha spre'u nyi nub bya / sa srod khyi la srod 'khor phag / nam phyed byi ba phyed yol glang / tho rangs stag gi dus su brtsi//.* The same divisions and relations are given in the *dPag bsam ljon shing*, see also Tseng, *Divinationskalkulation*, 74, 106–107.

40 Jacobi, *Zeitmessung*, 247.

41 For the terms *rus chen* and *rus khams*, see below.

42 The term *grub rtsis* denotes the astronomical system and the calculation of the calendar based on the inaccurate *karaṇa*-calculation of the *Kālacakratantra* and accurate *siddhānta*-calculations (*grub pa'i mtha' rtsis*) of the *Mūlatantra*. These two opposing systems allowed a change of the Kālacakra-Astronomy within Tibet and resulted in the fully established *grub-rtsis*-system in the 15th to 17th century; see Schuh, *Kalenderrechnung*, 560.

LANDSCAPING TIME, TIMING LANDSCAPES 103

and the *chu srang* into six breaths (*dbugs*). 21,600 breaths make a day of the week; but there are also different types of days. The divisions for the year are named in the same way and the underlying idea again shows the close relation between place and time. According to Bu ston, the area the ten planets have to traverse is the result of the multiplication of the 27 lunar mansions (*rgyu skar*, Skt. *nakṣatra*) by 60, that is, 1620 *chu tshod* of the *nakṣatra*. Bu ston clearly distinguishes these *chu tshod* that are connected to the "place," that is the area the planets have to cover, from the 60 *chu tshod* related to time, that is the day.[43]

Sangs rgyas rgya mtsho differentiates the length of *dbugs*, the breath, according to the species of beings, as for instance the human, the *lha min*, and the *yi dvags* and thus reveals another aspect of the relativity of time: the number of human breaths (*dbugs*) during one hour is 360, which makes 21600 every day. Thirty days make a month and twelve months one year. The day (*zhag*) of the *lha min* is equivalent to sixty years for humans. One year of the *lha min* corresponds to 21600 human years. One year of the *yi dvags* corresponds to thirty years of human life.[44]

5.4 *Relations between the Dimensions and Their Influence on Time and Place*

To start with, I would like to present a more general example in order to demonstrate how these relationships between temporality, timing, and elements work: the sheep year 2015 is of the wood element (*shing*). Someone born in a wood year should therefore delay the inception of any construction project, as the coincidence of the same element in different domains—the relationship is called "self" (*rang*), and in this case it is wood/wood—is considered bad. The relationship called "mother" (*ma*) on the other hand is considered positive. Wood is the mother of fire, so a fire year (*me lo*) would therefore be suitable for the construction of a house if its builder had been born in a wood year.

This short simple example shows Chinese influences and how Tibetans developed them: the elements—water (*chu*), fire (*me*), earth (*sa*), wood (*shing*), and iron (*lcags*)—are taken from the Chinese tradition. Tibetans name these

---

43 Schuh, *Kalenderrechnung*, 65–66, 78. For the analysis of the *zhag gsum rnam dbye*, the three kinds of the day, see also Sangs rgyas rgya mtsho, *Vaiḍūrya dkar po, stod cha*, chapter 17, 190 ff.

44 Sangs rgyas rgya mtsho, *Vaiḍūrya dkar po, stod cha*, 10.11–14: *mi yi dbugs grangs sum brgya dang / drug cur chu tshod gcig longs shing / zhag rer nyis khri stong drug brgya /rgyu ba sum cur zla ba dang / zla ba bcu gnyis lor bzhed cing / lha min zhag gcig mi yi lo /drug cu de yi lo gcig la /mi lo nyis khri stong drug brgya /yi dvags lo gcig mi yi lo / sum cu ... //.*

104 MAURER

relations "mother" and "son," "friend" and "enemy" (*ma bu dgra grogs*): the relationship named "self" is a purely Tibetan development and does not occur in Chinese concepts.

6 *Sa dpyad*, Time and "Bones" (Patrilineal Clans)

6.1 *Time, Mountains,* rus chen *and* rus khams

Some further examples might show how the calculation of time is connected with the site: the two terms to be dealt with are *rus chen* and *rus khams*. In Chinese divination the term *rus chen* denotes the type of a person and is derived from ancient clan-names (the Tibetan term *rus*, lit. 'bone', signifies a patrilineal clan). Sangs rgyas rgya mtsho often uses the abbreviated form of the term and writes only *rus*; in chapter 32, which deals with *sa dpyad*, he uses the complete term, *rus chen*:

> At first, there are, with regard to the enemy-mountain of the five elements, common and special [characteristics]. From these [follows the analysis] of the enemy-mountains, their common characteristics. Whatsoever the *rus chen* [of a person building near a mountain] might be, if from the direction of pig and mouse [shapes] like an ankle [or] stirred up earth occur [or] if the mountain points towards the back, this is an area where the paternal relatives are numb with internal fights.[45]

The term *rus chen* is closely related to *rus khams*, which denotes a person's element. They are each five in number, and depend both on the birth year and also on each other: The *rus khams keg* corresponds to the element wood (*shing*); the *rus khams ji* to fire (*me*); the *rus khams kungs* to earth (*sa*); the *rus khams shang* to iron (*lcags*); and the *rus khams 'u* to the element water (*chu*).[46]

---

45 Sangs rgyas rgya mtsho, *Vaiḍūrya dkar po, smad cha*, 243.1–3: *thog mar khams lnga'i dgra ri ni/ thun mong dang ni khyad par las/ thun mong dgra ri'i mtshan nyid ni/ rus chen gang yang rung ba la/ phag dang byi ba'i phyogs nas su/ long bu sa srubs srol dod nas/ phyin ci log tu kha bltas na/ pha tshan nang 'khrug sbrid pa'i sa//.*

46 See Sangs rgyas rgya mtsho, *Vaiḍūrya dkar po, stod cha*, 259.15: *de yang khams la lnga yin te/ keg shing ji me kungs sa dang/ shang lcags 'u chu rus chen lnga//.* In the *dPag bsam ljong shing* two methods to define the *rus khams* were found: According to the "rough" (*rags*) method, the *rus kham* of a person is identical with the *skyes spar*, the *spar kha* of the birth year or the element that corresponds to the direction of the respective signs of the zodiac; see also Tseng, *Divinationskalkulation*, 139.

LANDSCAPING TIME, TIMING LANDSCAPES

Later on, Sangs rgyas rgya mtsho specifies the relations and explains the term with the physiognomic characteristics of a person:

> Furthermore, the rough [method] to examine the shapes of a face. A [person with] a hoarse trembling voice is *keg* wood. [A person who] concentrates his /her breath near the navel is *kungs* earth. [A person who] produces a sound between his /her teeth is *ji* fire. [A person who] raises the tongue in the open mouth when the breath comes through the nose is *shang* iron. [A person who] draws spittle with the lips shut is *'u* and is of the water element.[47]

These terms and their relation go back to Chinese sources and denote the five basic tones in Chinese music (*kong, shang, jiao, zhen* and *yu*).[48] A simpler method to determine the *rus chen* is found in the *dPag bsam ljon shing* where the *rus khams* is defined as the *spar kha* of one's birth year or one's direction (*rang skyes sam rang phyogs*), "namely tiger and hare are [*rus khams*] *keg* and wood[-element], horse and snake are [*rus khams*] *ji* and fire-element, ox, sheep, dog and dragon are [*rus khams*] *kungs* and earth[-element]. Bird and monkey are [*rus khams shang*] and iron[-element] and mouse and pig are [*rus khams 'u*] and water[-element]."

In a passage called "the special characteristics, the five elements' enemy-mountains (*dgra ri*)," the Regent describes mountains considered to be unsuitable if the birth year of the individual who is undertaking the building stands in a certain relation to the element ascribed to a mountain:

> Regarding the particularity, the enemy[-mountain] of the five elements: The enemy[-mountain of a person with the *rus chen*] *keg* are the snow mountain and the rocky mountain. The lake at the snow mountain is the enemy [of a person with the *rus chen*] *ji*. The enemy[-mountain of a person with the *rus chen*] *kungs* are the rocky mountain and the scree slope (*rdza*). Red earth [also called slate and meadow (*spang*)], a [red] mountain and a [red] rock cliff are the enemy [of a person with the *rus chen*]

---

47 See Sangs rgyas rgya mtsho, *Vaiḍūrya dkar po, stod cha*, 260,4–7: *gzhan yang rags pa byad dbyibs brtag / skad 'gags gre ba 'dar keg cing (r. shing)/ lte khung dbugs sdud kungs sa yin /so dbar sgra 'don ji me yin / kha gdangs lce 'phyar sna dbugs 'ong / shang lcags chu sdud mchu 'dzum pa / 'u ni chu yi khams yin no//.*

48 See Tseng, *Divinationskalkulation*, 139–140; lHa mo tshul khrims, *dPag bsam ljon shing*, 36–37: *de yang stag yos keg shing dang / rta sbrul ji ni me khams pa / glang lug khyi 'brug kungs sa te / bya sprel lcags la byi phag chu//.*

shang. Sandy mountain and meadow (*spang sa*) are the enemies [of a person with the *rus chen*]'u. They are the individual enemy[-mountains] of the five elements.[49]

As Sangs rgyas rgya mtsho does not accept the simpler interpretation and explains the identification of the *rus khams* according to the *spar kha* as "an incorrect method" (*rnam par dag pa'i ring lugs min*) of interpretation, the astrologer would also have to judge a person's physiognomy to determine the element and the right places of construction.[50]

Thus the *rus chen* specifies the type of mountain suitable for construction depending on the element of a person. In the first case, the concept behind this theory is not apparent, and it remains unclear how wood and snow or rock correspond. The lake in the second example might correspond to the element water, and fire should therefore be seen as an opposing element, as the enemy of fire is water. In this way Sangs rgyas rgya mtsho establishes a relation between topographical characteristics and the characteristics of a person. This idea does match the third example as well: red is related to fire and the fire-element; the enemy of iron is fire. It remains an open question if the element ascribed is determined through the *spar kha* by birth year or not.

6.2 *Mountains behind Buildings* (rgyab ri)

It might be common knowledge that the mountain behind a building plays a major role for construction. Characteristics assessed in texts are for instance its shape and height. Kong sprul blo gros mtha' yas considers the *rgyab ri* so important that he even dedicates a complete chapter to this topic in his text on Chinese geomancy (*Tsi na'i sa dpyad gsar 'gyur lugs kyi sgo 'byed 'phrul gyi lde'u mig*).[51] Together with the mountain in front of it (*mdun ri*), he describes the mountain behind a building topographically by means of comparison.

In his *Vaiḍūrya dkar po*, Sangs rgyas rgya mtsho does not simply rely on topographical characteristics but explains the position of the *rgyab ri* as depending on the *rus chen*. I quote from the *Vaiḍūrya dkar po*:

---

49   Sangs rgyas rgya mtsho, *Vaiḍūrya dkar po, smad cha*, 243.11–12: *khyad par khams lnga'i dgra ri ni/ keg gi dgra ri gangs ri brag// gangs ri mtsho ni ji yi dgra/ kungs kyi dgra ni brag dang rdza/ sa dmar {g.ya' dang spang zer ba'ang 'dug/} ri brag shang gi dgra/ bye ri spang sa 'u yi drgra/ khams lnga'i dgra ni so so yin//.*

50   Sangs rgyas rgya mtsho, *Vaiḍūrya dkar po, stod cha*, 260.4–5.

51   See especially chapter 1 and 4.

One assumes that the mountain at the back [of a building], assigned [to a person] with the wood-element [and the *rus chen*] *keg* is in the east, the mountain at the back [of a building], assigned [to a person] with the fire-element [and the *rus chen*] *ji* is in the south, the mountain at the back [of a building], assigned [to a person] with the earth-element [and the *rus chen*] *kungs* is in the four intermediate directions, the mountain at the back [of a building], assigned [to a person] with the iron-element [and the *rus chen*] *shang* is in the west, the mountain of someone with the *rus chen 'u*, that is element water, should be in the north.[52]

These statements correspond to the assignment of the directions and the elements: the element iron is assigned to the west and water to the north.

6.3   *Trees and the* rus khams

The *rus khams* on the other hand again plays a major role with respect to the ground for construction and the environment, here the growth of trees: a place is considered suitable for construction and positive for a person with the *rus khams* wood (*shing*) that belongs to the east when a tree grows in the west, which is assigned to iron. The decisive factor here seems to be the relation of elements: wood is the friend of iron, and these elements are regarded as being in a "friend-relation" (*grogs*). For someone with the *rus khams* earth (*sa*), the element is assigned to the intermediate directions, and the tree should grow in the east. The east is assigned to wood; the element earth is considered to be the friend of wood. For someone with the *rus khams* iron, assigned to the west, the tree should be in the south, assigned to the fire element. The element iron is considered the friend of fire.[53]

But if one looks at the other requirements for the position of trees, it remains doubtful if the relation between the elements is really the decisive factor: if a person is of the *rus khams* water (*chu*), the element is assigned to the north, the three directions south, west, and north are considered as positive for the position of a tree. The water element is considered the enemy of fire and son of iron. In general, the relation "self" (*rang*) is considered as negative.

---

52   Sangs rgyas rgya mtsho, *Vaiḍūrya dkar po, smad cha*, 264.7–9: *keg shing khams pa'i rgyab ri shar/ ji me khams pa'i rgyab ri lho/ kungs sa khams pa'i rgyab ri mtshams/ bzhi dang shang lcags khams pa yi/ rgyab ri nub la 'u chu khams/ pa yi rgyab ri byang du 'dod/*

53   Sangs rgyas rgya mtsho, *Vaiḍūrya dkar po, smad cha*, 265.19–20: *chu khams lho nub byang skyes bzang/ shing khams pa la nub skyes dang/ me khams byang skyes sa khams par/ shar skyes lcags khams lho skyes bzang/ des ni dgra bzhi thub pa yin/*

108   MAURER

The relation of trees with the directions might be influenced by Indian concepts on *vāstuvidyā*. Passages 22–25 of the *Gobhila-Gṛhyasūtra* IV, 7 that belong
to the *Sāmaveda* describe trees that are suitable or unsuitable for buildings.
Some types of trees are considered unfavorable for any construction; their position in a particular direction might even cause danger for the inhabitants.
An *Aśvattha*-tree (fig tree, *Ficus religiosa*) growing to the east of a building
is thought to cause fire. No *Plakṣa*-tree (*Ficus infectoria*) should grow to the
southern side of a house as it might cause an early death for the inhabitants.
Therefore, the owner of a house should change the position of trees and bring
offerings to the goddess related to the tree. For the *Aśvattha*-tree they should
make offerings to the sun and for the *Plakṣa*-tree to Yama.[54]

Another possibility for determining the directions are the signs of the zodiac
(*lo rtags*). In the context of so-called enemy-mountains (*dgra ri*), Sangs rgyas
rgya mtsho describes places where the construction leads to certain difficulties
for those who live there. The assessment of the places depends on two factors,
namely the shape of the mountain and its direction:

> Whatever personal element (*rus chen*) [someone building] has, if from
> the direction of the pig and the mouse [formations] looking like an ankle-
> bone [or] like stirred up earth are prominent [or] the mountain points in
> the opposite (*phyin ci log to*) direction, it is a place where the paternal rel-
> atives are blocked by internal quarrels. This is the place where the outer
> hand is pulled to the inside.[55] If wind comes from the ravine between the
> mountains in two directions tiger and hare, that is the place where son
> and grandson often die by the knife. Regarding [the mountain] with a
> cloudy spring in the direction of the two [animals] horse and snake, this is
> an area where one's siblings run off with one's possessions. If a mountain
> resembling a half moon is visible from the direction bird and monkey, this
> is the place where one's bride runs off with one's possessions. If there is [a
> mountain] in the direction of dog and dragon, the two resembling crows
> sitting together, it is an area with significant losses of wealth. If from the
> directions ox and sheep a mountain resembling a helmet with coral[56] is
> visible, it is a place where the subjects run off with the possessions.[57]

---

54   Oldenberg, *Grihya-Sūtras* 121 f.; Skorupski, *Kriyāsaṃgraha*, 20 f.

55   According to Loden Sherab Dagyab, the sentence can be understood in two different ways:
      a person tries to achieve immaterial wealth from someone, or a person not belonging to
      one's family interferes in internal family affairs.

56   Translation of the Tibetan term *rmog byi* according to Kun dga' rin chen, personal com-
      munication.

57   Sangs rgyas rgya mtsho, *Vaiḍūrya dkar po, smad cha*, 243.1–7: *thun mong dgra ri'i mtshan*

LANDSCAPING TIME, TIMING LANDSCAPES

Other than the position of the trees, the direction of natural phenomena is not related to one's personal element and influences the life of the inhabitants in general, depending on its direction. The assessment of the mountain shape to a direction is only through the assignment of the direction to the signs of the zodiac.

6.4   *The Three Doors:* gnam sgo, sa sgo, ri sgo

Much has been written by anthropologists on *gnam sgo* and *sa sgo*.[58] These two terms basically denote unfavorable years calculated in Chinese divination and thus denote unfavorable times for any undertaking; in the case of *sa dpyad*, for the construction of buildings. The term *ri sgo*, however, depends on the shape of a mountain and is not related to Chinese calculation.

Obstacles called *gnam sgo* and *sa sgo* belong to *keg rtsis*, 'the calculation of hindrances', found in chapter 24 of the *Vaiḍūrya dkar po*. These years are believed to have a negative influence on many undertakings in general and the construction of buildings in particular. When they affect the construction they are said to be open. Therefore, their calculation is important for protecting the inhabitants of a building from harm. According to literary sources such as the *dPag bsam ljon shing*, they are the result that the diviner receives when calculating the *gsang ba log men*, which might be translated as "calculation of the secret misfortune."[59]

The calculation of *gnam sgo* and *sa sgo* is explained in different ways with the signs of the zodiac, the *spar kha*, or the *sme ba*. Thus, their calculation becomes quite a complex subject and I would like to reduce the explanation here to the calculation of the year with the help of the signs of the zodiac, the *spar kha*, and the *sme ba* without going into further detail such as the calculation of month and day.[60]

---

    nyid ni/ rus chen gang yang rung ba la/ phag dang byi ba'i phyogs nas su/ long bu sa srubs srol dod nas/ phyin ci log tu kha bltas na/ pha tshan nang 'khrug sbrid pa'i sa/ phyi lag nang du 'dren pa'i sa/ stag yos gnyis kyi phyogs dag nas/ ri bar dong nas rlun byung na/ bu tsha grir shi mang ba'i sa/ rta sbrul gnyis kyi phyogs dag nas/ chu mig lu ma lcag lcig ni/ bu srang nor khyer 'bros pa'i sa/ bya dang spre'u'i sa shed nas/ zla gam 'dra ba'i ri byung na/ mna' mas nor khyer 'bros pa'i sa/ khyi 'brug gnyis kyi sa shed nas/ pho rog bsdongs pa sdod 'dra na/ nor god chen po 'ong ba'i sa/ glang lug gnyis kyi sa shed nas/ rmog byi 'dra ba'i ri byung na/ bran gyis nor khyer 'bros pa'i sa/

58   See for instance Meyer and Jest 1987; Dollfus 1994; Harrison and Ramble 1998.

59   lHa mo tshul khrims, *dPag bsam ljon shing* 2000, 25f.; see Tseng, *Divinationskalkulation*, 130.

60   For further methods of calculating *gnam sgo* and *sa sgo* see Maurer, forthcoming.

Calculating the *gnam sgo* with the signs of the zodiac, one starts—whatever *rus khams* a person has—for a male person from the fire-tiger-year (*me stag*)[61] and counts down (*thur du*), for a female person from the water-monkey-year (*chu sprel*) and counts up (*gyen du*) the number of years, the age of the person. If, counting for the male person, the diviner reaches a dog-year (*khyi lo*), and counting for the female person a dragon-year, these are called *gnam sgo*. If he reaches a pig-year (*phag lo*) while counting for the male person and a snake-year, counting for the female person, these are called *sa sgo*.[62]

A similar explanation is found in chapter 28 of the *Vaiḍūrya dkar po*, although the distinction in gender calculation is less clear. The designation of the male is, as one would expect, always given first:

> The identification of *gnam sgo* and *sa sgo*: the years are dog- and dragon-years, the *spar kha* in the [element] relation mother (*ma*) and *khen*, the *sme ba* three [blue], five [yellow] and six [white] are *gnam sgo*. *Sa sgo* are the pig- and snake-year, the *spar kha khon* and in the [element] relation "son" (*bu*), the *sme ba* two black and [four] green. The bad *sa bdag* is the house of a *'dre*-demon. The *gnam sgo* is rough for men when they are aged, the *sa sgo* is bad for women when they are younger.[63]

7 *Sa dpyad* Temporal Relationships in Practice

These short explanations might clarify how the construction of houses was or still is understood to face many hindrances, especially if someone with a large family were really to consider all factors mentioned. To mitigate these potential problems and prevent any kind of possible obstructions, the pragmatic Tibetans invented a great variety of rituals, from quite simple to complex

---

61 Sangs rgya rgya mtsho, *Vaiḍūrya dkar po, stod cha*, 387.3, gives only the tiger year and omits the element: *brtsi bya'i lo khams gang yin gyi/ skyes pa bu 'dod stag thog nas / du lon lo grangs thur du 'dren/ bud med ma yi sprel thog nas/ gyen du lo grangs brtsis pa yis/ khyi 'brug gnyis ni gnams sgo lnga/ phag sbrul gnyis ni sa sgo lnga / pho gnam khyi la sa sgo ni/ phag lngar brjod do mo yi yang/ gnam sgo 'brug la sa sgo sbrul/.*

62 See Tseng, *Divinationskalkulation*, 130 f.

63 Sangs rgyas rgya mtsho, *Vaiḍūrya dkar po, smad cha*, 42.11–13: *gnam sa'i sgo yi ngos 'dzin ni / lo ni khyi 'brug spar kha ma / khen thog sme ba gsum lnga drug /gnam gyi sgo yin sa sgo ni /phag sbrul spar kha khon dang bu / sme ba gnyis nag ljang gu yin / sa bdag ngan pa 'dre yi khyim / gnam sgo skyes pa yar rgan rtsub /sa sgo bud med mar gzhon ngan/.*

ones. These rituals could help create a site suitable for construction or clear the negative calculated influences on an already constructed house. One simple procedure—I was told by the present oracle of Nechung (*gnas chung*)[64]—is the use of a flag to change directions. South is connected with fire and the related color red. So if a building faces in the wrong direction, say north, one could place a red flag to the north and, together with certain prayers, change north into south.

Rituals that enable alterations are also found in the Regent's text. These include: *sa dgra* rituals for an unsuitably shaped construction site, rituals when constructing a cemetery, rituals for the well-being and wealth of a building's inhabitants, the well-being of their cattle, and rituals against calculated hindrances as *gnam sgo* and *sa sgo*. The most complex ritual is the one used to placate the Sa bdag lTo 'phye, a *klu* or *klu mo* thought to inhabit the ground. He is regarded as the main Sa bdag of a site and Sangs rgyas rgya mtsho explicitly describes in chapter 32 of the *Vaiḍūrya dkar po* how his position should be calculated before the construction of a building can start. It is very important to start digging the ground at the right place in order not to hit the Sa bdag lTo 'phye as wounding his body would result in the damage for the construction and its inhabitants. Here, Sangs rgyas rgya mtsho also describes his shape,[65] but more detailed in the preceding chapter 31 on *sa bdag* in general, where we learn that he is of blue color and that his shape is not definite as his head might be the one of an ox (*glang*). According to both passages (in chapter 31 and 32), his upper body resembles the one of a man and his lower part the one of a snake.[66]

Interestingly enough, this Sa bdag lTo 'phye seems to be omnipresent in the world, wherever one constructs a building his or her—some astrologers call the *sa bdag* Sa yi lha mo and consider her to be female—position can be calculated exactly on the construction site. To prevent him or her from disturbing the construction and harming the inhabitants, a ritual to appease this *klu* should be performed before any undertaking is started. Yet, as the Secretary of the Department of Religion in Dharamsala and some astrologers informed me, secularization and time constraints in modern life have led to a simplification of this ritual. Quite often it is not performed anymore, and only the simple libation offering (*gser skyems*) or the offering of the "three whites" (*dkar gsum*, i.e.

---

64   The interviews mentioned here were conducted in Dharamsala and Sikkim in 2000 and 2001.

65   See Maurer, *Grundlagen der tibetischen Geomantie*, 282.

66   The detailed description of the Sa bdag lTo 'phye is found in Sangs rgya rgya mtsho, *Vaiḍūrya dkar po, smad cha*, 214.8–215.5.

milk, curd and butter) and the "three sweets" (*mngar gsum* i.e. sugar, honey and molasses) is carried out to prevent any harm in the future.

8   Conclusions: *sa dpyad* in Place and Time

The *sa bdag* ritual makes the connection between the place and the time very obvious. The exact position of the *sa bdag* depends on the time, and only when the diviner has calculated its position can he determine the exact place for the first spade cut. It seems that they structure these temporal dimensions and also constitute an interrelationship between past, present, and future as well as place.

Time in general, and more specifically time of birth or the time of birth in relation to the present time, influence the place: the birth year determines the place to build, and gives advice concerning the mountain behind the house, the growth of trees and so on. The right time for construction depends on the time of birth, while the time of birth, the past, determines the relationship between the present and the future. For a successful outcome, the elements thought to be active during birth should be in a positive relationship with those of the day on which the activities take place. This clearly shows that according to Chinese divination time and space are not independent of each other but interrelated.

When we look at the Buddhist concept of karma, with its idea that actions in the past will influence present and future, it seems quite logical that nothing stood in the way of integrating these concepts of Chinese divination that were primarily introduced from China into Buddhism. Time in the context of divination and, more specifically, geomancy, seem to have several aspects. First of all, it is not considered as a continually flowing abstract as *time*: here it rather means something like *timing* or *period of time*.

Time as an abstraction seems to be constituted as a kind of multi-layered mesh. The components are the above-mentioned dimensions: the twelve signs of the zodiac, the five elements, the *sme ba*, the *spar kha*, and the *rus khams*. The net has a flexible structure and becomes fixed with personal dates, the starting point being birth. As the right (or wrong) time, the timing of an undertaking depends on a person's constellation in the past. Time in geomancy is a private, personal time and would therefore correspond to the Tibetan term *tshe*: it exists in relation to a personal point of reference that is the year of birth and the time of one's activity, here the construction of a building.

The third aspect lies in its connection with the place for construction. The time of birth determines the topography of an area suitable for the construction of buildings, the shape of a mountain or an area suitable for building, the direction and growth of trees. The connection between the three times is implied: the year of birth as the past is relevant for the present, the time of building, and both of these influence the future. The "net" of the dimensions gives the coordinates for the future, and since the relations between the years, the months and the days and so on are given, humans have freedom of activity within this frame and might restrain themselves from action to prevent greater damage.

The term *sa dpyad* uses and is framed by all these approaches to time. Time is linked to place, to relationships with time and place, and therefore time is an important aspect of investigating place. *Sa dpyad* involves not only the examination of the place but the calculation of time to find the right time and place for construction. Moreover, as *sa dpyad* provides an opportunity to prevent unsuitable events by prescribing preventative measures, it not only reflects the past and the present but it affects the future.

The Buddhist world has preserved various incompatible concepts of time. However, although *sa dpyad* and *nag rtsis* are influenced by several different cultural and not only Buddhist concepts, the connection between the three times that has been established above accords best with the well-known Buddhist concept of time established by Nāgārjuna. He regards his own requirement that the present and the future already exist in the past as a paradox, as only something that exists simultaneously can be interrelated. In *sa dpyad* and *nag rtsis*, time as an abstract philosophical concept in itself is not important: what is significant are time's aspects, the *timing* and *the period of time* in which an event occurs. It is important to find *the right time* and *the right place*. This corresponds to Nāgārjuna's concept of time and the interpretation of the Indian term for time, *kāla*. When Nāgārjuna talks about time, he considers it in the same way quite specifically as a certain time, that is as the moment, the *timing* of an event and a *period of time*.[67]

Even in the contemporary period, single moments or events, the *right setting of time* or the *timing* and *periods of time* are significant aspects of human lives. They are irreversible and do matter as nothing, not a single moment can be repeated. In *sa dpyad* and *nag rtsis*, the past meets with the present through certain aspects of time, when the *sme ba* of the birth year coincides with the *sme ba* of the current year, for example; or when the zodiac sign or the personal element assigned to the birth year coincides with those assigned to the current year. This, the relation between past, present, and future, and especially the relation between time and place require further reflection. In this regard, how-

---

67   Weber-Brosamer, Bernhard and Dieter M. Back: *Die Philosophie der Leere*, 70 f.

ever, it seems important to note that in various constructions of temporality, the significance of time depends on the fact that it is nothing but a collection, a suite of moments and fragments.

References

Aris, Michael. *Bhutan. The Early History of a Himalayan Kingdom.* Warminster: Aris and Phillips, 1979.

Beckwith, Christopher I. *The Tibetan Empire in Central Asia: A History of the Struggle for great Power among Tibetans, Turks Arabs and Chinese during the Early Middle Ages.* Princeton: University Press, 1993.

Conboy, Kenneth and Morrison, James. *The CIA's Secret War in Tibet.* Kansas: University Press of Kansas, 2002.

Cüppers, Christoph and Sørensen, Per K. *A Collection of Tibetan Proverbs and Sayings. Gems of Tibetan Wisdom and Wit.* Stuttgart: Franz Steiner Verlag, 1998.

Dollfus, Pascale. "Porte de la Terre, Porte du Ciel, un rituel de Rançon au Ladakh." In *Tibetan Studies. Proceedings of the 6th Seminar of the International Association for Tibetan Studies, Fagernes 1992,* ed. Per Kvaerne, Vol. 1, pp. 178–196. Oslo: The Institute for Comparative Research in Human Culture, 1994.

van Donzel, Elizabeth, Lewis, Bernard and Pellat, Charles. eds. *The Encyclopaedia of Islam.* New Edition, Vol. IV, Iran-KhA. Leiden: Brill, 1978.

dPag bsam ljon shing: see lHa mo tshul khrims.

Ekvall, Robert. *Religious Observances in Tibet: Patterns and Function.* Chicago and London: The University of Chicago Press, 1964.

Feuchtwang, Stephan. *An Anthropological Analysis of Chinese Geomancy.* Vientiane: Editions Vithagna, 1974.

Fraser, Julius T. Die Zeit. *Auf den Spuren eines vertrauten und doch fremden Phänomens.* München: Dtv, 1998.

Goldstein, Melvyn C. ed. *The New Tibetan-English Dictionary of Modern Tibetan.* Berkeley, Los Angeles and London: University of California Press, 2001.

Gurney, O.R. "The Babylonians and Hittites." In *Divination and Oracles,* ed. M. Loewe and C. Blacker. London: George Allen & Unwin, 1981.

Harrison, John and Ramble, Charles. "Houses and Households in Southern Mustang." In *Ancient Nepal* 140, pp. 23–37. Kathmandu: Nepal Times Press, 1998.

Henning, Edward. *Kālacakra and the Tibetan Calendar.* New York: American Institute of Buddhist Studies, 2007.

Huber, Toni. *The Cult of Pure Crystal Mountain. Popular Pilgrimage and Visionary Landscape in Southeast Tibet.* New York / Oxford: Oxford University Press, 1999.

Jacobi, Hermann. "Einteilung des Tages und Zeitmessung im alten Indien." In *Zeitschrift*

LANDSCAPING TIME, TIMING LANDSCAPES

der Deutschen Morgenländischen Gesellschaft 74, pp. 247–263. Wiesbaden: Franz-Steiner Verlag, 1920.

Jäschke, Heinrich August. *A Tibetan-English Dictionary*. London and Henley: Routledge & Paul Kegan, 1985 [1. ed. 1881].

Kern, Stephen. *The Culture of Time and Space 1880–1918*. London: Harvard University Press, 2003.

mKhas grub Karma chags med. "Sa dpyad rin chen gter mdzod." In *mKhas grub Karma chags med kyi gsung 'bum*, 60 vols., vol. Si (58), pp. 175–186. Nang chen rdzong: gNas mdo gsang sngags chos 'phel gling gi dpe rnying nyams gso khang, 2010.

Kong sprul blo gros mtha' yas. "Tsi na'i sa dpyad gsar 'gyur lugs kyi sgo 'byed 'phrul gyi lde'u mig." In *bKa' mdzod*, Section Ta, Dieter Schuh 1976, personal copy.

Kuznetsov, I.B. ed. *rGyal rabs gsal ba'i me long*. (The Clear Mirror of Royal Genealogies). Tibetan Text in Transliteration with an Introduction in English. Leiden: Brill, 1966.

Lhamo Pemba. *Bod kyi gtam dpe. Tibetan Proverbs*. Dharamsala: Library of Tibetan Works and Archives, 1996.

lHa mo tshul khrims. ed. *Nag rtsis rdel 'grem 'bras bshad dpag bsam ljon shing zhes bya ba bzhugs so*. Dharamsala: Bod gzhung sman rtsis khang, 2000.

Loewe, Michael and Blacker, Carmen. eds. *Divination and Oracles*. London: George Allen & Unwin, 1981.

Marasinghe, Eugene Walter. *The Vāstuvidyā Śāstra ascribed to Mañjuśrī*. Delhi: Sri Satguru Publications, 1989.

Maurer, Petra. "Ein Thangka zur sino-tibetischen Divination." In Münchner Beiträge zur Völkerkunde 15, pp. 218–243. München: Verlag des Staatlichen Museums für Völkerkunde, 2012/2013.

Maurer, Petra. "*Sa dpyad* and the concept *of bla ri*." In *This World and the Next: Contributions on Tibetan Religion, Science and Society* ed. Charles Ramble and Jill Sudbury, pp. 67–69. Andiast: International Institute for Tibetan and Buddhist Studies GmbH, 2012.

Maurer, Petra. *Die Grundlagen der tibetischen Geomantie dargestellt anhand des 32. Kapitels des Vaiḍūrya dkar po von sde srid Sangs rgyas rgya mtsho (1653–1705)*. Halle: International Institute for Tibetan and Buddhist Studies, 2009. (Beiträge zur Zentralasienforschung 21).

Meyer, Fernand and Jest, Corneille. "Milieux, Matériaux et Techniques." In *Demeures des Hommes, Sanctuaires des Dieux*, ed. Paola Mortari Vergara and Gilles Béguin, pp. 146–167. Roma / Paris: Università di Roma / Reunion des Musées Nationaux. 1987.

Monier-Williams, Sir Monier. *A Sanskrit-English Dictionary. Etymologically and Philologically Arranged with Special Reference to Cognate Indo-European Languages*. New Delhi, 1986 [1. ed. 1899].

de Nebesky-Wojkowitz, René. *Oracles and Demons of Tibet. The Cult and Iconography of the Tibetan Protective Deities.* Kathmandu: Tiwari's Pilgrims Book House, 1993 (reprint of 1956).

Oldenberg, Hermann. *The Grihya-Sūtras.* Rules of Vedic Domestic Ceremonies, Part II, Gobhila, Hiranyakesin, Āpastamba, Yagña-Paribhāshā-Sūtras translated by F. Max Müller. Oxford: Clarendon Press, 1982. (Sacred Books of the East XXX).

Paton, Michael John. *Five Classics of Fengshui. Chinese Spiritual Geography in Historical and Environmental Perspective.* Leiden: Brill, 2013.

Pingree, David. *Jyotiḥāstra.* Astral and Mathematical Literature. Wiesbaden 1981 (A History of Indian Literature VI, Fasc. 4).

Sangs rgyas rgya mtsho. *Phug lugs rtsis kyi legs bshad bai ḍūrya dkar po,* 2 vols. Pe cin: Krung go'i bod rig pa dpe skrun khang, 1997.

Schwieger, Peter. *Ein tibetisches Wunschgebet in der Sukhāvatī.* St. Augustin: VGH Wissenschaftsverlag, 1978. (Beiträge zur Zentralasienforschung Band I).

Schuh, Dieter. *Grundlagen tibetischer Siegelkunde. Eine Untersuchung über tibetische Siegelaufschriften in 'Phags-pa-Schrift.* St. Augustin: VGH Wissenschaftsverlag, 1981.

Schuh, Dieter. *Tibetische Handschriften und Blockdrucke.* Part 6 (Gesammelte Werke des Koṅ-sprul Blo-gros mtha'-yas). Wiesbaden: Franz Steiner Verlag, 1976.

Schuh, Dieter. "Grundzüge der Entwicklung der tibetischen Kalenderrechnung." In *Zeitschrift der Deutschen Morgenländischen Gesellschaft,* ed. Wolfgang Vogt, Suppl. II, pp. 554–566. Wiesbaden: Franz Steiner Verlag, 1974.

Schuh, Dieter. *Untersuchungen zur Geschichte der tibetischen Kalenderrechnung.* Wiesbaden: Franz Steiner Verlag, 1973. (Verzeichnis der orientalischen Handschriften in Deutschland Supplementband 10).

Skinner, Stephen. *The Living Earth Manual of Feng-Shui.* London, Boston, Melbourne and Henley: Routledge & Keagan Paul, 1982.

Skorupski, Tadeusz. *Kriyāsaṃgraha. Compendium of Buddhist Rituals. An abridged Version.* Tring: 2002. (Buddhica Britannica, Series Continua X).

Sørensen, Per. *Tibetan Buddhist Historiography: The Mirror Illuminating the Royal Genealogies. An Annotated Translation of the XIVth Century Tibetan Chronicle: rGyal-rabs gsal-ba'i me-long.* Wiesbaden: Harrassowitz Verlag, 1994. (Asiatische Forschungen 128).

Sørensen, Per and Hazod, Guntram. *Thundering Falcon. An Inquiry into the History and Cult of Khra-'brug, Tibet's First Buddhist Temple.* Wien: Österreichische Akademie der Wissenschaften, 2005. (Philosophisch-historische Klasse, Denkschriften 333).

Schama, Simon. *Landscape and Memory.* New York: Alfred A. Knopf, 1995.

Stein, Rolf. A. *L'épopée tibétaine de Gesar dans la version lamaique de Ling.* Paris: Presses Universitaire de France, 1956. (Annales du Musée Guimet, Bibl. d'Études 61).

Tseng, Te-ming. *Sino-tibetische Divinationskalkulationen (Nag rtis). Dargestellt anhand des Werkes dPag-bsam ljon-shing von Blo bzang tshul-khrims rgya mtsho.* Halle: International Institute for Tibetan and Buddhist Studies, 2005. (Beiträge zur Zentralasienforschung 9).

TTC: Zhang, Yisun. *Bod rgya tshig mdzod chen mo*. Krang dbyi sun [i.e. Zhang Yisun] gyis gtso 'gan bzhes nas rtsom sgrig byas pa. Pe cin: Mi rigs dpe skrun khang, 1985.

Vogel, Claus. "On Tibetan Chronology." In *Central Asiatic Journal*, Vol. IX, pp. 224–238. Wiesbaden: Otto Harrassowitz, 1964.

Weber-Brosamer, Bernhard and Back, Dieter M. *Die Philosophie der Leere. Nāgārjunas Mūlamadhyamaka-Kārikās Übersetzung des buddhistischen Basistextes mit kommentierenden Einführungen*. Wiesbaden: Harrassowitz-Verlag, 2005 (Beiträge zur Indologie 28).

WtS: *Wörterbuch der tibetischen Schriftsprache*. In Auftrag der Kommission für zentral- und ostasiatische Studien der Bayerischen Akademie der Wissenschaften, herausgegeben von Herbert Franke, Jens-Uwe Hartmann und Thomas O. Höllmann, bearbeitet von Petra Maurer, Jampa L. Panglung, Samyo Rode, Johannes Schneider, Nikolai Solmsdorf und Helga Uebach. München: Verlag der Bayerischen Akademie der Wissenschaften in Kommission beim Verlag C.H. Beck.

Zhang, Juwen. *A Translation of the Ancient Chinese "The Book of Burial (Zang shu) by Guo Pu (276–324)."* New York and Ontario: The Edwin Mellen Press, 2004.

CHAPTER 6

Signs and Portents in Nature and in Dreams: What They Mean and What Can Be Done about Them

Charles Ramble

1 Introduction

Divination is a way of discovering the causes of events that would otherwise remain unknown, and more generally to find out what lies in store for us. The techniques that are used reveal the visible component of a constellation of forces that underlie past and future events, thereby revealing to us the natural or supernatural agents of past incidents (such as death or theft) and also enabling us to make provision for anticipated crises.

Tibet offers a wide range of techniques for revealing past causes and future events. The purpose of all these methods is to establish a threshold at which the boundary between the everyday world and the realm that holds this knowledge is infringed, and the information that we seek can be communicated to us. More often than not, the technique entails an element of chance, since it is through randomly generated numbers and configurations that the gods or other powers convey their message, or whereby, in more impersonal schemes, we may discern the general pattern of the nature of things by extrapolation from the fragment that is revealed to us at this threshold. Such techniques include the use of dice, sticks, pebbles—a method discussed in this volume by Alexander K. Smith—and knotted strings, though others could be added to this list. In most cases the answer sought is based on a succession of binary oppositions—yes/no—whereas the outcome of certain other forms of divination requires interpretation; and such cases require either prior knowledge or the use of sophisticated manuals. But thresholds do not always need to be generated by artifice: There are, in fact, signs all around us that serve as portals onto the knowledge we require, if only we knew how to recognize and interpret them. These indications do not demand any preparation on our part, but only careful observation and an understanding of the significance of what it is we are perceiving. Certain types of divination that fall into this category have already been the subject of fine scholarly studies. Perhaps the best known of these are ornithomancy (Laufer 1914; Mortensen 2013) and geomancy (Maurer 2009, 2012), but there are others besides, and this contribu-

© KONINKLIJKE BRILL NV, LEIDEN, 2020 | DOI:10.1163/9789004410688_007

SIGNS AND PORTENTS IN NATURE AND IN DREAMS

tion will briefly examine Tibetan procedures for the analysis of certain other types of natural signs that have not yet been the subject of detailed studies.

2 Analyzing the Divination Environment

Certain observations may provide a 'meta-divination' associated with procedures that do require preparation and active intervention on the part of a specialist. A case in point is the set of preliminary observations that must be made before the performance of the type of divination known as *ju thig*, that entails the interpretation of the patterns formed by knotted strings that are cast onto a surface. The technique is described in several sources, among them *Zhang zhung gi ju thig*, by the Bonpo scholar Kun grol grags pa (b. 1700). While the technique itself does not concern us here, the preliminary observations are worth consideration since they involve the analysis of the ambient environment of the divination.

The first thing to be examined, according to the author, is the condition of the surface on which the strings are to be cast. This is referred to as the *gzhi*, the 'base.' This base has considerable importance in several ritual contexts: certain rituals for summoning good fortune (*g.yang 'gugs*), for example, are accompanied by a charter myth (*smrang*) that explains the origin of the rite. One such account, from a work entitled *Mu ye pra phud*, is set in the land of Phywa yul snang ldan, which is experiencing hardships because the ruler, Phywa Yab lha bdal drug, is bereft of a *phya* base (*phya gzhi*).[1] Srid pa Sangs po explains that the absence of the base is due to demons that dispersed the five *srid pa* gods. The requisite base must be sought, and the hero who is charged with accomplishing this task is Prince sGam po, the son of 'Od de gung rgyal (*sic*) and Phywa lcam lo ma. The goddess gNam phyi gung rgyal advises the prince that the *phya* base should be made from a certain deer, which he then sets off to hunt. After many adventures the deer is found, and it agrees to give its body to be used for the ritual, and the goddess Srid pa'i lha mo explains how the various parts of its body are transformed into the requisites. First of all, "from the hide of that deer there came into being the white conch felt mat. First, that was the substance

---

1 Although the base is intended to serve for both *phya* and *gzhi*, it is only ever described as a *phya gzhi*, and never *g.yang gzhi*, probably the latter term has been appropriated by tantric vocabulary to denote a human skin.

from which it was made. Next it was set up as a support for the *phya*. It is there today for the sake of the *phya* and the *g.yang*" (*Mu ye pra phud*, cited in Ramble 2015: 514).

The *gzhi* that is usually used by diviners is a small white felt mat, but the myth recounted here implies that the original item was a deerskin. Skins are used in certain ritual procedures related to divination. Cassinelli and Ekvall, for example, describe a murder investigation in Sakya in the 1940s, in which the law officials ordered that a yak be killed and flayed, and the accuser and the accused required to roll dice on the inner surface to determine the validity of their respective claims (1969: 176). Freshly-flayed yak hides and goatskins are also used in certain oath-swearing ceremonies. In the former case the parties to the oath must be seated, naked, on the hide. The significance of using skins in such contexts is nowhere clearly explained. However, a clue may be found in the point made earlier, that divination entails the creation of a threshold between the ordinary world and the divine or preternatural realm. It is also worth noting that when oaths between adjacent communities are sworn, the location for the ceremony is of crucial importance: The ritual must take place at the boundary between the two communities, in a designated no-man's-land. In early Bon myths, it is at margins, and especially at the margin of dark and light, being and non-being—as opposed to the void favored by the tantric Buddhist tradition—that things come into being. It may not be too far-fetched to suggest that a hide is the liminal surface *par excellence*, insofar as it constitutes the boundary between the interior of any creature and the outside world, and therefore symbolic of both neutral territory and also the margin at which two worlds meet.

According to *Zhang zhung ju thig*,[2] before beginning his divination, the first thing the diviner must assess is the appearance of the base. A white base is ideal; the presence of darkness indicates that there will be harm from the *the'u rang*; ruggedness indicates an empty center, a sign that there will be a theft; a yellow tint is a presage of harm resulting from curses emitted by Buddhist monks; red betokens defilement or a cerebral stroke (*grib*); if the base is worn and threadbare, there is the likelihood of shortages in the community; and an eddy of wind on the surface of the base is also a sign of *grib*.

The next thing the diviner must consider is the nature of the payment made by the client for the divination (*mo yon*). An offering of butter is the best of

---

2   The text of the passage paraphrased here is provided at the end of this article, under "Texts cited". I am indebted to Alexander Smith for drawing my attention to this work.

SIGNS AND PORTENTS IN NATURE AND IN DREAMS   121

all; barley indicates an increase in people and livestock; wool is a sign of great
wealth; dairy products—milk and curd—mean long life, while a gift of meat
is a warning that livestock will be lost to disease. Worst of all is a presentation
of tea, which denotes malicious gossip and also warns that the country's cattle
will be depleted.

Thirdly, close attention must be paid to the 'divination barley' (*mo nas*)
that is spread on the surface of the base. Fragments of bone are an indication that clouds will gather, while charcoal is a warning of impurity and incest.
White stones reveal a threat of obstructions and inauspicious death caused by
demonesses, and the presence of salt and coarse grass presages an epidemic
among cattle. Barley that cannot germinate is a sign of predators;[3] metal shards
are a harbinger of enemies.

The fourth thing the diviner must observe is the body-language of the client,
and his or her self-presentation. This section is gender non-specific, and we
may assume that the following remarks refer to clients of either sex. If, when
the client first approaches the diviner, she first places her right knee on the
ground and presents her left cheek, this bodes ill for the elderly, whereas the
opposite—placing her left knee first and presenting her right cheek—is a bad
sign for the young generation. A covered head is an inauspicious sign, an indication of a contamination (*mu khab*) that veils the five divinities that surround
our bodies (*'go ba'i lha*). Reciting mantras is an inauspicious form of behavior, and singing songs indicates future suffering. A client who presents herself
square on, facing the diviner and showing respect, is a very favorable sign.

The text then proceeds to the divination itself, which is beyond the scope of
this article. All the phenomena listed above may be classified as 'natural' in the
sense that they entail observations of the environment surrounding the actual
rite of prognostication, and are not directly generated by the diviner.

3   The Meaning of Dreams

A particularly fertile arena for the observation of unprovoked signs is the realm
of dreams. The topic of dreaming in the Tibetan tradition is a vast one, not
least because any serious investigation of the subject must entail an examination of the probably even vaster Indic literature from which much of it

---

3   Translation tentative: *rgyund* [*rgyun chad*] *byung na gcan ngo yin*. The protasis of this clause
    may also mean "if there is an interruption [in the presentation of the barley]"—for example,
    if the client should break off the process of pouring it from her container into that of the
    diviner and then resume after a pause.

is derived. The subject of dreaming in Tibet has been discussed at length by Serinity Young (1999), and although the work is primarily concerned with the Buddhist context, attention is also given to the more popular aspects of dream divination (ibid.: 56–59). As the author notes, the pioneering—and indeed, as so often, almost the only—treatment of the subject is to be found in Nebesky-Wojkowitz's *Oracles and Demons of Tibet* (1956), and she cites parts of the author's translations. Nebesky-Wojkowitz's source here is a work by Klong rdol bla ma Ngag dbang blo bzang (1719–1794), entitled *rMi ltas sna tshogs brtag thabs*, "Methods for interpreting a variety of signs in dreams".[4]

Since this work has already been treated in some detail, it will be enough here to give a brief outline of its contents. The night should be divided into three periods: dusk, night proper, and dawn. The dreams that one has in these periods fall into different categories. The first relates to experiences from past lives, and the dreams will be about such things as food, conversation and friends to whom one was attached. These are likely to be recurring dreams, with many uncertain features. Dreams experienced in the middle of the night are the result of illusions generated by the various demons—*bdud* and *srin*—that are on the move at that time, and should not be taken seriously. It is the dreams that one has at dawn that are to be given close attention, since it is these that foretell the future. A few examples of these dreams and their significance may be listed here:

– Climbing a high mountain: The dreamer will achieve greatness
– Cloudless day: Happiness
– Abundant harvest and fruits: Prosperity, cattle and grain, fine clothes
– Wearing fine clothes: Respect from others
– Wearing armor: Protection from illness and harm
– Carrying weapons: Absence of enemies
– Riding lions and dragons: The way to greatness

Other auspicious signs include sitting on a throne, eating well and enjoying good company.

Inauspicious signs and their significance include the following:
– Walking through a storm or mud, being in a dirty place, eating poor food, wearing shabby clothes: Various forms of pollution (*grib* and *mi gtsang*)
– Wearing clothes with a collar, crying, being hatless, looking in a mirror: Future suffering

---

4   There are several published versions of this work. The version used here is from *Mo dpe*: 138–144.

SIGNS AND PORTENTS IN NATURE AND IN DREAMS

- Being attacked by wolves, wearing rags, being infested by parasites: Illness
- Empty grain containers, bows and arrows: Malicious gossip
- Being struck with weapons or chased by soldiers; blood, lightning, hail: Curses (*phur ka*) from others
- Being bound, being underground, being mutilated in prison: Attack by *'dre* demons
- Being naked and riding south on a donkey, or dreaming of all red flowers: Obstructions to one's life

Then follows a list of signs that are indicators of the presence and influence of different demons:

- Snakes, blue women, meadows: *Klu*
- Rocks, trees, mounted soldiers: *bTsan*
- Monks, donkeys, monkeys, cats, horses, dogs: *rGyal po*

Dreams also provide an arena in which one might see portents of one's own impending death. These include: Black women with no belongings or food; riding a camel southward, a donkey eastward, or a monkey northward; wearing red clothes and gathering red flowers; crossing a plateau wearing a turban; drinking beer and dancing with the dead.

There is also a section about motifs that are likely to occur as an indication that one's spiritual practice is becoming effective, but since these belong rather to the soteriological aspect of dreaming, they do not concern us here. Although references to divinities such as the *btsan* are obviously a Tibetan inflection, it is clear that this work owes a considerable debt to Indian Āyurvedic works, presumably via the chapter on dream prognosis in the *rGyud bzhi*.

Before leaving the topic of dream divination, it is worth considering one short fourteenth-century work that provides instructions on how to determine the whereabouts of one's future rebirth through dreams. The work is by sGra tshad pa Rin chen rnam rgyal (1318–1388), but the author traces the transmission through a succession of Tibetan scholars back to an Indian source whom he names as Paṇḍita Bikhyu Ta de ba. The work is entitled simply *rMi lam brtag pa*, "Dream analysis" (*Mo dpe*: 134–138).[5] The work is divided into two parts: The main text, and the author's comments on how the procedure should be performed (*zin ris*). The order of the activities is not quite the same in the two sections, and the following paraphrase presents a synthesis of the work as a whole.

---

5   Since this published work is quite readily available, the Tibetan text of the paraphrased and translated passages is not provided here.

The enquirer should go to an extremely remote place on the first day of a given month, and thoroughly clean the place and purify himself. He should give up such things as meat, alcohol, and garlic, and then on the second day, he should desist from eating altogether. He should set up a mandala with an abundance of flowers, other offerings, and sacred relics, and in the middle of it, he should place an image of one of the Buddhas. After praying that there should be no obstructions, he should make offerings of *tormas* to the elemental spirits, and then imagine that the sky is filled with the Buddha and his entourage. He should recite the appropriate mantra ten thousand times (the *zin ris* increases this figure considerably), and again 108 times before going to sleep. The procedure should be repeated the following day—indeed, the more times this exercise is performed, the better the results will be. The *zin ris* adds that, just before going to sleep, the enquirer should recite the mantras 108 times over a vessel of clean water and then drink the contents. After performing ablutions, reciting prayers and making *torma* offerings, and ensuring that nothing and no one occupies the space between him and the shrine, he should wish for good dreams and entreat the *jina*s to reveal to him where he will be reborn. With this earnest wish in mind, he should assume the posture of the reclining lion and then go to sleep. Having done this, if he does not receive the various auditory and visual indications of his future rebirth, he should repeat the exercise until the signs do appear. If, when they do manifest, they reveal that he is to be born in one of the three lower realms, he should take appropriate action by abandoning unvirtuous actions. Although the text does mention that sounds and tactile sensations experienced in dreams can provide a clue, the only specific examples given relate to the colors of the visual images that may appear, corresponding to the future location of rebirth. White signifies rebirth in the divine realm; green: human; yellow: *asura*s; blue: animals; red: *preta*s, and black: the hell realms.

4 Portents of Death and Miscellaneous Portents

The collected works of Klong rdol contain a number of other short treatises on divination that are worth our attention insofar as they involve the observation and analysis of phenomena that have not been produced by the diviner. The section on dream divination is immediately followed by one entitled *'Chi ba'i mtshan ma brtag pa*, "An analysis of portents of death." The signs in question are more redolent of medical symptoms, but we may briefly list a selection. In each case the feature is followed by a rather precise indication of the period of time after which death is likely to occur.

SIGNS AND PORTENTS IN NATURE AND IN DREAMS

- Diarrhea and paralysis: One month
- Absence of blood beneath the fingernails: Six months
- Suffering paralysis during sexual intercourse: One month
- The appearance of a black spot in the middle of the tongue: Two days
- Loss of sense of taste: Five days
- Loss of sense of smell: Three days

As in the case of many such works, this one clearly has Indian antecedents. The source here is likely to be one or another of the 'death deception' (*'chi bslu*) rituals that appear in the Buddhist bKa' 'gyur, most of which, as Irmgard Mengele points out, "are short versions of Vāgīśvarakīrti's *Mṛtyuvañcanopadeśa*" (2010: 105).[6]

Klong rdol continues with a summary of another work from the bsTan 'gyur, entitled *lTas brtag pa rgyas pa*, "An extensive analysis of signs", a compilation that he was encouraged to complete by the Seventh Dalai Lama.[7] The first of these deals with divinations based on the appearance of rainbows (*Nam mkha'i 'ja' ltas brtag pa*). Each of the different forms and configurations carries a different message: Their significance is to be determined from their location, the time at which they appear, and the shape they assume.

Generally, where there are many rainbows in a land, it will not endure long but will be destroyed. When a town is surrounded by an army, if there is a rainbow at the same time as there is a circle around the sun, the two sides will slaughter each other. When joining battle, if there are rainbows to both the right and the left, that means the attackers will be destroyed. A rainbow just before nightfall signifies that the king will die, the country will succumb to conflict, and illness and famine will prevail. Regarding their shape: Rainbows that have the form of a parasol, a victory banner, a chariot or a wheel are good omens, indicating a good harvest and victory for the king. If they resemble a stake, a spear or a bow, the town will be destroyed. If they look like crocodiles, turtles and so forth, there is a danger from fire and water. The appearance of a rainbow on an auspicious day signifies that the king will flourish and brigands will be defeated.

The next section concerns "Methods of analyzing the occurrence of loud noises" (*sGra chen 'byung ba brtag pa bya tshul*). The loud noises in question are presumably a reference to thunder. The variables, in this case, relate to the

---

6 For a book-length study of this work see Schneider 2010.

7 This is indicated in the title of the work: *bsTan 'gyur nang gi drang srong gharga'i ltas brtag pa rgyas pa bskal bzang rgya mtshos legs pa yin gsungs pas de'i gces bsdus 'ga' zhig*, "A selection of quotations from the 'Extended analysis of signs' by Ṛṣi Gharga, from the bsTan 'gyur, because bsKal bzang rgya mtsho said this would be a good thing".

time, the direction and the quality of the sounds. A loud noise in the morning foretells the destruction of the realm. In the morning, such a sound bodes ill for Shudras, at noon for Brahmans, at sunset for Kshatriyas, and at dawn for slaves.

A loud noise that comes from two different directions simultaneously presages the loss of cattle and goats, whereas a protracted sound from an unidentifiable direction is a sign that disaster will befall the army.

Klong rdol then adds a section entitled "The consequences of miscellaneous signs" (*sNa tshogs ltas kyi 'bras bu*). Here, too, a selection of the omens listed—all inauspicious, and all foreboding calamity for the king, his realm and his subjects—will serve our purpose.

- Dogs and crows barking and cawing at a crossroads: An armed attack
- A crow building its nest in a beehive colony (*bung ba grong*): Imminent danger
- Rats, crows and other animals mating at inappropriate times: The destruction of the king and his realm
- Breech birth among animals: Internecine conflict and the death of the king
- A white crow: Inauspicious
- The sight of a murder of crows plunging their beaks into the ground, then making a dreadful noise and flying off together: Thorough defeat of the army
- A piece of meat falling from the bill of a passing bird: The punishment of that community by the king
- A vulture or other carrion bird sitting on top of the house and calling: The death of the owner
- An owl calling from the midst of a herd of cows in broad daylight: Danger for the king
- Crows frolicking in a wood or ducks frolicking on open ground: The destruction of that land
- Fruit growing on trees out of season: The death of the king and his entourage
- Leaves growing on a dead branch: Conflict among the people of that land

These miscellaneous signs include a list of unnatural or monstrous births. A cow giving birth to a human baby signifies that harm will befall women; unborn children speaking, crying or laughing from inside the womb signal the destruction of the land; babies born with one leg, or three or four legs, signify the death of the king or famine in the land, and the same is true of hermaphrodite births. Hatchlings with several beaks and heads herald the country's demise; a land in which a child is born with one body, two faces and three eyes will come to a swift end—it is said that it will be overcome by an army; a land where a child is born with the head of a pig, or with a set of teeth, or missing its head or an arm will suffer extensive destruction.

SIGNS AND PORTENTS IN NATURE AND IN DREAMS

The work concludes with the following signs: Sap dripping from blossom or fruit on trees indicates harm for the regent. If the fruits on a tree are constantly of a color that indicates that they are ripe, or if they drip juice like blood, that is a sign of impending illness and famine. Saplings that resemble humans forebode the destruction of that land. If earthly gods happen to speak or to smile when offerings are being made to them, this means that the king will abandon his realm, which will consequently come to grief.

5 Indigenous or Indigenized Interpretations

Whether or not they may be ultimately of Indian inspiration, like the examples listed above, certain collections of natural portents have a large component of distinctively Tibetan features, suggesting at least a considerable degree of indigenization. The most extensive such collection of which I am aware is to be found embedded in the text of a ritual that is itself very probably an entirely Tibetan development. This the "Three-Headed Man of the Black Rituals" (*gTo nag mgo gsum*),[8] an exorcistic rite that is widely performed by Buddhist and Bonpo tantric lamas in the Himalayan region, as well as in parts of Tibet.

The background to the ritual is given in the myth (*smrang*) that precedes the performance. In brief, the Old Man of the Sky (associated with the trigram *khen*) and the Old Woman of the Earth (*khon*) couple, and in due course the woman bears a child with the body of a human and three animal heads, those of a bull, a tiger and a pig, as well as the attributes of other creatures. They place it in a roasting pan that they then deposit at a crossroads, where it proceeds to devour everyone and everything it meets. It is eventually overcome by Kong tse 'Phrul gyi rgyal po, who induces it to apply its powers against evil, using each of its distinctive features to destroy a different category of demon or misfortune. In this way, the creature becomes a sort of panacea against all ills, including inauspicious signs, and we are informed at the very beginning that "of all curses and maledictions or calamities, or of illnesses and epidemics that might inflict the land, or of evil omens, there is nothing that cannot be

---

8 The full title of the text referred to here is *Srid pa'i gto nag mgo gsum*, the "Three-Headed Man of the Black *Srid pa* Rituals" (short title *gTo nag*). The noun *srid pa* may denote the phenomenal world or a category of gods, and the term *srid pa bon* is sometimes used as an epithet of the so-called 'lower vehicles' of Bon in the well-known nine-vehicle classification. Although it is clear in many places in the text which of these particular meanings it carries, its application to the *gto* category of rituals is more diffuse, and I have therefore left it untranslated.

128 RAMBLE

repulsed by this ritual" (fol. 1v).[9] Later in the text we are given an extensive list of the omens that the Three-Headed Man is able to repel, and this passage is worth quoting at length.

"(fol. 13r) Repel evil signs and magical manifestations. Prevent us from [encountering] people carrying corpses. Keep us from having to eat tasteless wretched fare; ward off sudden death; prevent disturbances from coming to our communities. Keep us from the sight of stags locking antlers at the head of the valley, of fish fighting with their tails in the valley floor, and crows fighting with their claws in the middle. (fol. 13v) The horse whinnying at midnight; the dog at the door howling at dawn; the cock crowing at dusk; these are dreadful omens for our patron, but these, too, are reversed by this ritual. The mouse squeaking in its hole; the weasel carrying off a mouse in its mouth—these are harbingers of drought, but they, too, are reversed by this *srid pa* ritual. A woman behaving erratically, or missing her monthly period, are portents of the end of a family line, but they, too, are reversed by this *srid pa* ritual. Wild birds descending onto the fields, or a cuckoo alighting at the top of a ladder, are omens of the approach of different enemies, but they, too, are reversed by this *srid pa* ritual. The owl hooting or the owlet crying during the daytime foretell an epidemic, but they, too, are reversed by this *srid pa* ritual. (fol. 14r) A cow with a prolapsed uterus[10] is an omen of an impending epidemic, but this, too, is reversed by this *srid pa* ritual. The wolf howling above, and the fox yelping below are signs that vampires of decline are stirring, but they, too, are reversed by this *srid pa* ritual. Black birds fighting with their talons, and a black snake entering one's house are omens that the demons of the rocks are active, but they, too, are reversed by this *srid pa* ritual. The sight of stags locking antlers at the peak of the high mountain is a sign that *btsan* of bad death are on the move, but they, too, are reversed by this *srid pa* ritual. The sight of fish fighting with their tails in the Manasarovar[-like] lake down below is a warning of disease borne by the serpent-spirits, but they, too, are reversed by this *srid pa* ritual. Seeing a black bird attacking a striped tiger with its claws is a sign that demonesses are stirring, but they, too, are reversed by this *srid pa* ritual. Whatever is summoned by this ritual will be repelled by it. Repelling the affliction of the *btsan* can be accomplished by means of this ritual, which repels and diverts all inaus-

---

9   *byad kha phur kha chag che nyams nga dang / yul du nad yam byung ba dang / ltas ngan thamd (thams cad) gto 'di yi mi bzlog gang yang med /* (fol. 1v).

10 The translation is highly tentative: *ba la grod pa skyes pa* would literally mean "a cow that gives birth to its/a stomach," which could possibly signify a uterine prolapse, as proposed here, or some sort of teratoma. It might also mean "*grod pa* that appear(s) on a cow", where *grod pa* could be the name of a cattle disease (see the following footnote).

SIGNS AND PORTENTS IN NATURE AND IN DREAMS   129

picious signs. (fol. 14v) The owl that calls at dusk; the owlet that is ashamed in front of the gods; untimely clashes between crows and between deer; deer at the head of the valley locking antlers; fish down below fighting with their tails; dead birds in the middle being carried away by the wind; the cock crowing at dusk; wormholes appearing in the fields; *ro bkal* appearing on sheep; *dkar chags* appearing on goats; the she-wolf howling at midnight; *sogs dkar* appearing on livestock; *drug phrom* appearing on horses; *gtsed pa* appearing on dogs;[11] a decaying bird's-nest in the three summer months; a decaying mouse-nest in the three winter months; the swollen (lit. pregnant) corpse of a bull in the three spring months; the bloated corpse of a dead fox in the three autumn months; the sight of ducklings leaving the nest; a large coiled serpent in the three winter months—these evil portents and manifestations, too, are repelled by this *srid pa* ritual."

6   Conclusion: More Than Just Signs?

In the examples considered before *gTo nag*, the signs that are analyzed are precisely that—indications of the events they betoken, and not the predicted blessings or afflictions themselves. In the case of the procedures for foretelling one's future birth through dreams, for instance, the prognosis of incarnation in the lower realms can be addressed by engagement in virtuous acts. This is also true of astrological and divination manuals, which recommend measures—such as the recitation of specified texts or the performance of particular rituals—to counteract any likely consequences.

In the *gTo nag*, by contrast, it is not just the calamities presaged by the signs but *the signs themselves* that are to be repelled. It seems that the distinction between the signifiers and what they signify has been erased, and that the omens are conflated with what they portend. In the passage cited above, it is sometimes uncertain whether it is the signs that the Three-Headed Man is being entreated to repel, or the afflictions that they warn of, but there are enough unambiguous passages to leave no doubt that, more often than not, it is the former, the portents themselves, that are the target. This is made explicit in several places. In addition to the very first citation from the text at the beginning of the last section, there are assertions such as: "Continually repulse evil

---

11   The terms *ro bkal, dkar chags, sogs dkar* and *drug phrom* are unknown to me. The first could conceivably mean "a corpse being carried on a sheep", which is possible but unlikely; the context suggests rather that they are all types of diseases to which the respective animals are susceptible.

omens that may come" (*rtag tu ltas ngan yong ba bsgyur*, fol. 12v); "divert inauspicious prognostications and bad dreams" (*mo ngan rmi ngan bsgyur du gsol*, fol. 8v), and numerous other examples that might be cited. The signs that the *gTo nag* is exhorted to repel are not confined to inauspicious sights in the natural world, but also include adverse configurations belonging to the realm of elemental divination. This is to be seen in an earlier section that gives a list of thirteen specific targets: "... Fourth, repel *bzhi gshed*; fifth, repel *bye bral* (*recte: bye brag*); ... seventh, repel *bdun zur*; ... tenth, repel *dur mig*; twelfth, repel *lag sbrel* (*recte: lag 'bres*) ...".[12] In this excerpt, the terms *bzhi gshed, bye bral, bdun zur, dur mig* and *lag 'bres* are all inauspicious configurations of years and trigrams. Although the precise nature of these combinations does not concern us here, explanations of each can be found in Tseng 2005.[13]

A significant feature of many of the natural signs is that they involve *combinations* of components. All the examples in the last set, by their very nature, entail inauspicious associations; but even in the case of signs from the world of animals, it is not the animal itself that is inauspicious but the fact of the animal being in a particular place or engaging in a particular activity, often at a specified time. In *gTo nag*, this includes owls calling during the daytime; wolves howling above the hearer's location, and foxes yelping below it; horses whinnying at midnight, dogs howling at dawn, a cuckoo alighting on a ladder; and in *rMi ltas sna tshogs*, certain animals mating at unusual moments, owls calling from the midst of a herd of cows in broad daylight, and so on. It is worth considering these coincidences in the light of another ritual that is not ostensibly concerned with the interpretation of signs. The text in question, entitled *Kong rtse bla glud*, is concerned with the procedure for the retrieval and restoration of lost souls. The passage of the text that is of particular relevance to the present study is a section that lists a series of causes that might have led to the loss of the patient's soul. Each of the eight causes listed is a combination of three factors: one of the eight trigrams, a particular activity, and the circumstance in which the activity occurred. The structure of this passage may be illustrated by two examples:

"*Kyai!* Upon the *zon* trigram of the southeast, if you, *rgyal po* and '*gong po* demons and demons of madness acting in unison, accused [the patient] of sleeping in a frightening place and, at the time of the solstice, when the sun

---

12   *bzhi pa bzhi gshed* [*bsgyur du gsol*] / *lnga pa bye brag* (< *bye bral*) [*bsgyur du gsol*] ... *bdun pa bdun zur* [*bsgyur du gsol*] / ... *bcu pa dur mig gto* [*yis bsgyur*] / ... *bcuis* (*bcu gnyis*) *lag sbrel* (< *lag 'bres*) [*bsgyur du gsol*] / (fol. 8v).

13   For each of the configurations, see respectively pp. 122 (for *bzhi gshed*), 130 (for *bye bral*), 109 (for *bdun zur*) and 118 (for *dur mig*) and 243 (for *lag 'bres*).

SIGNS AND PORTENTS IN NATURE AND IN DREAMS 131

had reached its limit and was turning back, you stole or harmed the soul of this little one, our precious patron, I offer you this soul-ransom that is [as vast as] the glorious sky, as well as these precious splints and fine pendant banners, these ransom effigies (*ngar mi*) with their adorned human forms, the effigies of males and females, this beer and food and these dough buttons (*theb kyu*), these *torma*s and this food—these things I offer you as a ransom. Free your captive! (fol. 6v) *Kyai!* Upon the *li* trigram in the south, if you, *btsan* and sorcerers, acting in unison, accused her of [polluting] the stove and producing a smell of scorching, and, while she was on a meadow with a yellow surface, you stole or harmed the soul of this little one, our precious patron, I offer you this soul-ransom ... (etc.)."

Other combinations include: the trigram *khon* together with the activity of incest and the circumstance of sitting on a green hill or in a green valley; the trigram *kham*, the activity of fratricide and the state of widowhood, and the circumstance of opening an irrigation channel.[14]

In a sense, this text is the opposite of a divination manual: Instead of analyzing combinations of events in the human and natural world to determine what they portend, it takes the outcome as the point of departure and looks back to the signs that could possibly have presaged it. But if the combinations listed are not exactly the causes of soul loss, neither are they merely passive indications; they are, rather, the set of conditions necessary to enable a particular category of demons to capture souls. These conditions are ambiguous concepts that are neither purely neutral signs nor unequivocal agents. It may be that, on entering the cultural arena represented by works such as *gTo nag*, the Indian science of signs underwent a process of indigenization whereby signs came to lose their neutrality and were assimilated into a pre-existing hybrid category of secondary causes.

Texts Cited

Note: In the following transliterations, the original texts have not been edited. Contractions (*bskungs yig*) are represented by an approximate representation of the form that appears in the text, followed by the expanded form in brackets. In *gTo nag mgo gsum* and *Kong rtse bla glud*, the punctuation "=/" stands for the *shad* that signifies "etc."; in the former, the missing text is usually

---

14   For the other combinations, see Ramble 2009: 210. The text of the extract cited here is given below in the final section, "Texts cited".

bsgyur du gsol, and in a few cases *bzlog*; in the latter, the missing text is supplied in the first example.

Zhang zhung gi ju thig

(p. 473) *Zhang zhung gi ju thig bsdus pa mo bya drug 'phrul gyi lde mig bzhugs pa legso (legs so) / (p. 474) [...] dang po mo gzhi brtags pa ni / dkar po byung na bzang / nag po byung na the'u rang gdon / bug ral byung na snying stong yin / rkun ngo yin / ser po byung na ben dhe'i gdon / byad ngo yin / dmar po byung na grib ngo yin / zad pa byung na nor zas yul bud 'ong / mo gzhi'i steng du rlung dmar bu yug byung na grib ngo yin / mo yon mar byung na shin tu bzang / nas byung na mi nor 'phel / bal byung na longs spyod che / 'o zho phruṃ gsum byung na tshe ring / sha byung na yang god kha 'ong / ja byung na mi (p. 475) kha 'ong / sa la god kha 'ong ngo yin / da ni mo nas spyad pa la / rus pa byung na mug 'dus pa'i ngo / sol ba byung na rtsog nal yong / mkhar rgong byung na 'dre mo 'gag gri gdon / tsha dang ram pa byung na god kha 'ong / nas 'bru bzang na mi 'bru bzang / gro byung na bu mo mang / rgyund (rgyun chad) byung na gcan ngo med / byad ngo yin / lcags rigs byung na dgra ngo yin / da ni mo rmod mi spyad la / pus mo g.yas btsug na 'graṃ pa g.yon bstan na che rgyud la ngan / pus g.yon btsug 'graṃ pa g.yas bstan na chung rgyud la ngan / stong pa khum nas stong pa yin pas dbul po 'ong / mgo btuṃ na ngan / zha gyon na dmu gab yin / yang na 'og la rkyen ngo (p. 476) yin / sngags pa bsgrang na ngan / glu blang na mya ngan 'ong / mdun bstan na gus tshul byung na bzang /*

gTo nag mgo gsum

(fol. 13r) *lhas (< ltas) ngan cho 'phrul yong ba =/ mi theg ro khur byed pa =/ mi zhim sdug zas za ba =/ blo bur shi chad yong ba =/ yul la phog 'chug yong ba =/ phu yi sha ba ru 'dzing bsgyur/ mda' yi nya mo rnga 'dzing =/ bar gyi nag mo'i sder 'dzing =/ (fol. 13v) 'og rta nam phyed 'tsher ba =/ tho rangs sgo khyi ngu ba da =/ srod la bya pho 'tshe ba 'di/ bdag po 'jigs pa'i ltas ngan yin/ de yang srid pa gto 'dis bzlog/ phugsu (phugs su) byi ba mkhun pa dang/ sri mong kha nas byi khyer yang/ than ngan yong ba'i ltas ngan yin/ de yang srid pa gto yi =/ bumed (bu med) smyo spyod byed pa dang/ zla zhig khrag ral byed pa de/ rab chad yong ba'i ltas ngan yin/ de yang srid =/ ri bya sno^gs (sna tshogs) klung du 'babs/ khu byug skras mgo bab pa 'di/ dgra sna yong ba'i ltas ngan yin/ de yang srid pa =/ 'ug pa nyin mo rgod pa dang/ srin bya nyi mo kus 'debs des/ dal yam yong ba'i ltas ngan yin/ de yang sri =/ khyi la sgo nga skyes pa dang/ ba la (fol. 14r) grod pa skyes pa de/ god kha yong ba'i ltas =/ de yang srid =/ gong du spyang ku ngu ba dang/ 'og tu wa mo brgyal ba de/ phung sri g.yos pa'i =/ de yang srid =/ bya nag sdero (sder mo) 'dzing ba dang/ khyim du sbrul nag sleb pa de/ drag srin g.yos pa'i ltas =/ de yang srid =/ phu'i lha ri rtse mtho la/ sha pho ru 'dzing mthong ba*

SIGNS AND PORTENTS IN NATURE AND IN DREAMS

de/ gri btsan g.yos pa'i =/ de yang =/ mda'i ma phang g.yu mtsho/ nya mo rnga 'dzing mthong ba de/ klu nad yong pa'i =/ de yang srid =/ bar gyi stag ri khra bo la/ nag mo'i sder 'dzing mthong ba de/ bdud mo g.yos pa'i ltas =/ de yang srid =/ gto 'dis 'bod pa gto 'dis bsgyur/ btsan khram bsgyur byed gto 'dis bsgyur/ ltas ngan thaṃd (thams cad) bzlog cing bsgyur/ btsan khram (fol. 14v) 'ug pa srod la rgod pa bzlog/ srin bya lha la gnong pa =/ dus min pho rog sha 'dzing =/ phu ru sho pho ru 'dzing =/ mda' ru nya mo rnga 'dzing/ bar gyi bya ro rlung khyer =/ srod pa bya pho 'tshe ba =/ tho rang sgo khyi ngu ba =/ zhing la 'bu khung byung ba =/ lug la ro bkal byung =/ ra la dkar chags byung ba =/ rnam gung spyang mo ngu ba =/ nor la sogs dkar byung =/ rta la drug phrom byung ba =/ khyi la gtsed pa byung ba =/ dbyar gsum bya tshang rul ba =/ dgun gsum byi'u tshang rul =/ dpyid gsum glang ro sbrum pa =/ ston gsum wa ro bam pa =/ ngang phrug tshang nas gyes mthong =/ dgun gsum sbrul chen 'khyil =/ ltas ngan than dang cho 'phrul rnams/ de yang srid pa gto'dis (gto 'dis) bzlog //

Kong rtse bla glud

kyai lhogs (lho phyogs) spar kha zon steng na / rgyal 'gong bsnyo 'dre bsdong pa yin / 'jigs par nyal ba snyad btags nas / rdod cig nyi ma log 'tshaṃs na / yon+g (yon bdag) mi'u rien (rin chen) la / bla la brkuṃs (brkus sam) bzhoms srid na // bla glud naṃkha' (nam mkha') rien (rin chen) dang / rien (rin chen) rgyang bu 'phan bzang dang / ngar gyi mi mo rgyan dang / pho tho mo thong bshos [bu dang] / 'thib brkyu chang zan rnaṃs ni glud du ['bul] / bzung ba thong la bcings pa khrol// mnan pa theg la bsdam pa slod / zhi ba cheo'i (chen po'i) ngang la bzhugs / kyai lho phyogs spar kha li steng na / btsan dang dri po bsdongs pa yi / thabs gzhob gnyis la snyad btag nas / rtod cig spang po kha ser la / yon+g (yon bdag) mi'u =/ bla la brkuṃs (brkus sam) =/ naṃkha' (nam mkha') rien (rin chen) =/ naṃkha' (nam mkha') rien (rin chen) rgyang bu =/ ngar gyi mi mo rgyan =/ pho thong mo thong =/ 'theb brkyu chang zas rnaṃs ni =/ bzung pa thong la =/ mnan pa theg la bsdam =/ zhi ba cheo'i (chen po'i) =/

References

Works in Tibetan (listed by short title)

gTo nag

Srid pa'i gto nag mgo gsum bzhugs pa legs+hō. Anonymous manuscript in *dbu med*, 31 folios, owned by Lama Tshultrim of Lubrak, Mustang, Nepal.

Kong rtse bla glud

Kong rtse 'phrul rgyal gyis mdzad pa'i bla glud dbus phyogs. Anonymous manuscript in *dbu med*, 8 folios, owned by Lama Tshultrim of Lubrak, Mustang, Nepal.

lTas brtag pa rgyas pa

bsTan 'gyur nang gi drang srong gharga'i ltas brtag pa rgyas pa bskal bzang rgya mtshos legs pa yin gsungs pas de'i gces bsdus 'ga' zhig, by Klong rdol bla ma Ngag dbang blo bzang (1719–1794). In *Mo dpe*, pp. 144–150.

Mo dpe

Mo dpe dang sa dpyad rmi lam brtag thabs bzhugs so, compiled by Tshe ring and 'Brug mkhar. Kan su'u mi rigs dpe skrun khang, 1997.

Mu ye pra phud

Mu ye pra phud phya'i mthar thug bzhugs s+ho. *dBu med* manuscript, 36 fols, transcribed in *dbu can* in Karmay and Nagano (eds.) 2002, *The Call of the Blue Cuckoo: An Anthology of Nine Bonpo Texts of Myths and Rituals*. Osaka: National Museum of Ethnology, pp. 35–90.

rMi lam brtag pa

rMi lam brtag pa bzhugs so, by sGra tshad pa Rin chen rnam rgyal (1318–1388). In *Mo dpe*, pp. 134–137.

rMi ltas sna tshogs

rMi ltas sna tshogs brtag thabs bzhugs so, by Klong rdol bla ma Ngag dbang blo bzang (1719–1794). In *Mo dpe*, pp. 138–144.

Srid pa yab lha bdal drug gis phya gzhung chen mo gzhugs s+ho. Anonymous manuscript, owned by Lama Tshultrim of Lubrak, Mustang, Nepal.

Zhang zhung gi ju thig

Zhang zhung gi ju thig bsdus pa mo bya drug 'phrul gyi lde mig bzhugs pa legs so, by Kun grol grags pa (b. 1700). In *'Chi med mgon po tshe dpag med dań ma gśin gñis kyi sgrub chog mo yig sna tshogs bcas kyi gsuń pod*. A collection of ritual and divinational texts of the "New" Bon (Bon-gsar) tradition, chiefly work by Rig-'dzin Kun-grol-grags-pa and Mi-śig-rdo-rje. Reproduced from a manuscript brought from Rgyal-ri Dgon in Koń-po by Tenzin Namdak. New Thobgyal, P.O. Ochghat (via Solan): Tibetan Bonpo Monastic Centre, 1973, pp. 473–520.

Works in European Languages

Cassinelli, C.W. and R.B. Ekvall. *A Tibetan Principality: The Political System of Sakya*. Ithaca: Cornell University Press, 1969.

Karmay, S and Y. Nagano. eds. *The Call of the Blue Cuckoo: An Anthology of Nine Bonpo Texts of Myths and Rituals*. Osaka: National Museum of Ethnology, 2002.

Laufer, B. "Bird divination among the Tibetans: notes on document Pelliot No. 3530, with a study of Tibetan phonology of the ninth century." *T'oung Pao* 14, 1914, pp. 786–787.

Maurer, P. *Die Grundlagen der tibetischen Geomantie dargestellt anhand des 32. Kapitels des Vaiḍūrya dkar po von sde srid Sangs rgyas rgya mtsho (1653–1705)*. Halle (Saale): IITBS, 2009.

SIGNS AND PORTENTS IN NATURE AND IN DREAMS

Maurer, P. "*Sa dpyad* and the concept of *bla ri.*" In *This World and the Next: Contributions on Tibetan Religion, Science and Society*, ed. C. Ramble and J. Sudbury, pp. 67–80. Andiast: IITBS, 2012.

Mengele, I. "*Chilu* (*'Chi bslu*): Rituals for 'deceiving death'." In *Tibetan Ritual*, ed. J. Cabezón, pp. 103–130. New York: Oxford University Press, 2010.

Mortensen, E.D. *Raven augury in Tibet, Northwest Yunnan, Inner Asia, and circumpolar regions: A study in comparative folklore and religion*. PhD thesis, Harvard University, 2003.

Nebesky-Wojkowitz, R. de. *Oracles and Demons in Tibet. The Cult and Iconography of the Tibetan Protective Deities*. The Hague: Mouton, 1956.

Ramble, C. "The deer as a structuring principle in certain Bonpo rituals: a comparison of three texts for the acquisition of good fortune (*g.yang*)." In *Cultural Flows across the Western Himalaya*, ed. Patrick Mc Allister, Helmut Krasser† and Cristina Scherrer-Schaub, pp. 499–528. Vienna: Verlag der Österreichischen Akademie der Wissenschaften, 2015.

Ramble, C. "Playing Dice with the Devil. Two Bonpo Soul-retrieval Texts and Their Interpretation in Mustang, Nepal." In *Bon. The Everlasting Religion of Tibet. Tibetan Studies in Honour of Professor David L. Snellgrove*, ed. S.G. Karmay and D. Rossi, pp. 205–232. Special issue of *EAST AND WEST*, vol. 59, nos. 1–4, 2009.

Schneider, J. *Vāgīśvarakīrtis Mṛtyuvañcanopadeśa, eine buddhistische Lehrschrift zur Abwehr des Todes*. Vienna: OeAW, 2010.

Tseng Te-ming. *Sino-tibetische Divinationskalkulation* (Nag-rtsis), *dargestellt anhand des Werkes dPag-bsam ljon-šiṅ von Blo-Bzaṅ tshul-khrims rgya-mtsho*. Halle (Saale): International Institute for Tibetan and Buddhist Studies, 2005.

Young, S. *Dreaming in the Lotus: Buddhist Dream Narrative, Imagery and Practice*. Boston: Wisdom Publications, 1999.

CHAPTER 7

Identifying the Magical Displays of the Lords of the World: The Oneiromancy of the *gSal byed byang bu**

Donatella Rossi

Once Zhuang Zhou dreamed he was a butterfly, a butterfly flitting and fluttering around, happy with himself and doing as he pleased. He didn't know he was Zhuang Zhou. Suddenly he woke up, and there he was, solid and unmistakable Zhuang Zhou. But he didn't know if he were Zhuang Zhou who had dreamed he was a butterfly or a butterfly dreaming he was Zhuang Zhou. Between Zhuang Zhou and a butterfly, there must be some distinction! This is called the Transformation of Things.[1]

∴

1 Introduction

The above-mentioned story attributed to Master Zhuang (莊子 ca. fourth century BCE) is perhaps one of the most famous Taoist pearls of wisdom; it is symbolical of the dream state and of dreaming, sometimes welcomed, sometimes feared, ethereal and evanescent yet so real and concrete when events and emotions are therein experienced. Master Zhuang wonders about the necessity of a differentiation in the identity of things; the answer is inscribed in their everlasting mutability and transience.[2]

---

* This chapter is based on a paper presented at the Tibetan Divination Panel organized by Petra Maurer and myself in occasion of the Fourteenth Seminar of the International Association for Tibetan Studies (IATS) (Bergen, 19–25 June, 2016).

1 *Zhuang zi* Inner Chapter Two, section 14; see trans. Burton Watson, *The Complete Works of Zhuangzi*, (New York: Columbia University Press, 2013), 18. 昔者莊周夢為胡蝶，栩栩然胡蝶也，自喻適志與！不知周也。俄然覺，則蘧蘧然周也。不知周之夢為胡蝶與，胡蝶之夢為周與？周與胡蝶，則必有分矣。此之謂物化, accessed March 19, 2017, http://ctext.org/zhuangzi/adjustment-of-controversies#n2732.

2 For a study of dreams in Chinese culture see Richard E. Strassberg, *Wandering Spirits: Chen Shiyuan's Encyclopedia of Dreams* (Berkeley: University of California Press, 2008).

© KONINKLIJKE BRILL NV, LEIDEN, 2020 | DOI:10.1163/9789004410688_008

Dreamtime is for the Australian Aboriginals an era that precedes creation, a time before time when the world already existed, albeit in a kind of indistinct form; the chanted myths of the *Dreamtime* define the cultures of the Aboriginals with particular regard to the geographical characteristics of their space, in the belief that a sacred relation exists between each living being and its own place.[3]

Interpretation of dreams was practiced, along with other mantic forms, by Mesopotamian civilizations: the Assyrian King Ashurbanipal (r. 668–627 BCE) collected divination texts in what has been reckoned as the first systematized library of the ancient Near East, which he created in the capital city of Niniveh.[4]

Egyptians believed that the human soul would be released through sleep into a different life and for that reason the interpretation of dreams was highly esteemed and constituted the prerogative of priests, as demonstrated by a hieratic book dating back to the Nineteenth Dynasty (1292–1189 BCE) known as the *Ramesside Dream Manual*, which is contained in the Papyrus Chester Beatty 3 preserved at the British Museum (EA10683,3).[5]

Around the seventh century BCE, a religious movement which came to be known as Orphism emerged in the Hellenistic world; its views about the soul and metempsychosis influenced several successive philosophers and dramatists, such as Pythagoras (c. 570–495 BCE), Aeschylus (525–456 BCE), and Plato (429?–347 BCE). The term Orphism has been used to indicate a series of cosmogonic myths and beliefs geared towards the pursuit of a virtuous life, prohibition of sanguinary offerings, the notion of a soul trapped in the physical body to expiate errors, practices concerning purity, avoidance of meat, and faith in deities hence in the immortality of the soul. Eric R. Dodds maintains that their origin is to be looked for in the Greek colonization of the Black Sea (occurred around the seventh century BCE), which allowed the Greek civilization to get in touch with the shamanic cultures of Central Asia, especially the Scythian one.[6] Eighty-seven hymns have been associated with the Orphic tradition; they were most likely composed between the second and the third century CE, an epoch

---

3 See e.g. Alexander W. Reed, *Aboriginal Myths: Tales of the Dreamtime* (Chatswood: New Holland Publishers, 2006).

4 Cf. Leo, A. Oppenheim, *The Interpretation of Dreams in the Ancient Near East, with a Translation of an Assyrian Dream-book* (Philadelphia: American Philosophical Society, 1956).

5 Cf. Scott B. Noegel and Kasia Szpakowska, "'Word Play' in the Ramesside Dream Manual", in *Studien zur Altägyptischen Kultur* 35 (2007), 193–212.

6 Eric R. Dodds, *The Greeks and the Irrational* (Berkeley: Sather Classical Lectures Series 25, University of California Press, 2004 [1951]), *passim*. Helmut Hoffmann pointed out the affinity of Bonpo myths with the Orphic cosmogony; see *Tibet. A Handbook* (Bloomington: Indiana University Publications, 1975), 108.

during which the cult of Dionysus was flourishing in western Asia Minor and nearby islands. They are attributed to Orpheus (Ὀρφεύς), a semi-divine bard and shaman, son of Calliope (Καλλιόπη), the mythological Muse of epic poetry. The last three of those hymns (85, 86, 87) are respectively dedicated to the deities Ýpnos (ὕπνος, Sleep), Óneiros (ὄνειρος, Dream), and Thánatos (θάνατος, Death). Each of the eighty-seven hymns had to be recited with the accompaniment of fumigation offerings, with a different scent for each divinity. The one prescribed for Óneiros is Aromatics.[7] The hymn of the deity of Dream recites:

> Thee I invoke, blest pow'r of dreams divine, Angel of future fates, swift wings are thine. Great source of oracles to human kind, When stealing soft, and whisp'ring to the mind, Thro' sleep's sweet silence, and the gloom of night, Thy pow'r awakes th' intellectual sight; To silent souls the will of heaven relates, And silently reveals their future fates. Forever friendly to the upright mind, Sacred and pure, to holy rites inclin'd; For these with pleasing hope thy dreams inspire: Bliss to anticipate, which all desire. Thy visions manifest of fate disclose, What methods best may mitigate our woes; Reveal what rites the Gods immortal please, And what the means their anger to appease; For ever tranquil is the good man's end, Whose life, thy dreams admonish and defend. But from the wicked turn'd averse to bless, Thy form unseen, the angel of distress; No means to check approaching ill they find, Pensive with fears, and to the future blind. Come, blessed pow'r, the signatures reveal Which heav'n's decrees mysteriously conceal, Signs only present to the worthy mind, nor omens ill disclose of monstrous kind.[8]

---

7   Those for sleep and death are poppy (*Papaverum somniferum*) and manna (the lymph of the *Fraxinus ornus*).

8   Thomas Taylor, *The Mystical Hymns of Orpheus, Translated from the Greek, and Demonstrated to be the Invocations which were used in the Eleusinian Mysteries* (London: Bertram Dobell, 1896), 160–161; for the Greek text cf. ed. Gabriella Ricciardelli, *Inni Orfici* (Segrate: Fondazione Lorenzo Valla / Arnoldo Mondadori Editore, 2000), 212. The oldest Greek text extant on the interpretation of dreams is the *Oneirocritica* (Ὀνειροκριτικά), a five-volume encyclopedic work compiled by Artemidorus (Ἀρτεμίδωρος) of Daldis in the second century BCE; see transl. and comm. Robert J. White, *The Interpretation of Dreams: The Oneirocritica of Artemidorus* (Park Ridge: Noyes Press, 1975); cf. Patricia Cox Miller, *Dreams in Late Antiquity: Studies in the Imagination of a Culture* (Princeton: Princeton University Press, 1997). In medieval times, the most important and influential source for dream interpretation was the *Oneirocriticon of Achmet*, a tenth century's Byzantine work compiled in Greek when the Macedonian dynasty ruled the Byzantine Empire (867–1056); see transl. and ed. Steven M. Oberhelman, *The Oneirocriticon of Achmet. A Medieval Greek and Arabic Treatise on the Interpretation of Dreams* (Lubbock: Texas Tech University Press, 1991) and Idem, *Dreambooks in Byzantium. Six Oneirocritica in Trans-*

Marcus Tullius Cicero (106–43 BCE), in his *De Divinatione*, a treatise in which he examines various aspects of the Stoic doctrine elaborated by Chrysippus (279–206 BCE), establishes a difference between 'natural' and 'artificial' divination and ascribes the interpretation of dreams to the first kind. He relates the definition of the Stoic philosopher on divination, *Uim cognoscentem et uidentem et explicantes signa quae a dis hominibus portendantur* (a faculty of knowing, recognizing, and explaining the signs which are shown by the gods to men), and affirms that *Ea quibus bene percepta sunt ii non saepe falluntur; male coniecta maleque interpretata falsa sunt non rerum uitio sed interpretum inscientia* (those who can understand those signs correctly are rarely mistaken; prophecies and interpretations inaccurately accomplished are ineffective not because reality is faulty but because of the ignorance of the interpreters).[9]

There is no need to emphasize here the fact that dreams, as in the instances delineated above, represent a significant facet of the Tibetan mantic arts, just as significant is the value attributed to dreams in the assessment of diagnoses in medical procedures or in terms of spiritual activities. The interrelation of divination in general, and oneiromancy in particular, with specifically identified apotropaic liturgies and medical praxes testifies to the value and importance attributed to the first and contributes to define and confirm the efficacy of the latter.

As is well-known, Buddhist and Bonpo literature abounds of similes involving dreams that expose the illusory quality of life, the inconsistency and worthlessness of all human tensions and longings vis-à-vis impermanence, the briefness of life, and the unexpectedness of the time of death. At the Tantric level, they are the object of specific bio-spiritual techniques which aim at their conscious recognition and at their utilization as a skillful medium for the advancement of one's praxis—which in such a state is reputed to evolve much more swiftly because the mind is not weighted by the function of the senses—thus becoming a path of liberation in their own right.[10] In David Germano's words:

---

    lation, with Commentary and Introduction (London: Routledge, 2008); cf. Maria Mavroudi, *A Byzantine Book on Dream Interpretation. The Oneirocriticon of Achmet and Its Arabic Sources* (Leiden: Brill 2002).

9   Cf. ed. Georg Luck, *Arcana Mundi, Magia e Occulto nel Mondo Greco Romano, Volume II, Divinazione, Astrologia, Alchimia* (Segrate: Fondazione Lorenzo Valla / Arnoldo Mondadori Editore, 1999), *passim*.

10   For a study about dreams related to sacred biographies in Indo-Tibetan Buddhism see Serenity Young, *Dreaming in the Lotus. Buddhist Dream Narrative, Imagery & Practice* (Boston: Wisdom Publications, 1999). Cf. Dylan Esler, "Note d'Oniromancie Tibétaine: Réflexions sur le Chapitre 4 du *bSam-gtan mig-sgron* de gNubs-chen sangs-rgyas ye-shes," *Acta Orientalia Belgica* 25 (2012), 317–328.

Dream yoga thus could be said, in a sense, to be the overcoming of karmic dreams to open the vast new vistas of the dreaming of a buddha, a gnostic dreaming that takes place within "the vast sky of originally pure emptiness." [... L]ucid dreaming also incarnates the key principle of self-recognition (*rang ngo shes*), which constitutes the threshold between *saṃsāra* and *nirvāṇa*, between the path of an ordinary being and a path of a buddha.[11]

According to traditional Tibetan medicine, the subtle wind element (*rlung*) in the physical body is the power-force that acts as a carrier for the consciousness, making it circulate in all the channels. When the consciousness enters the channels pushed by the subtle wind, various dreams appear; the consciousness is influenced by the state of the channels, that is, whether they are healthy and uncluttered or blocked and polluted, so that the quality of dreams changes together with the symbolic elements that they display; a doctor can analyze those symbols and use them as a component to establish diagnoses or adapt the treatment, since dreams are also revealing of the course of illness itself:

> There are six types of dreams mentioned in Tibetan Medicine that can be generally interpreted: dreams of what was seen the previous days, dreams of what was heard the previous days, dreams of what was experienced the previous days, dreams of fulfilling the spiritual wishes, dreams of fulfilling the normal wishes, dream omens or illness prognosis.[12]

In that regard, a Bonpo metaphysical text equates the body to a sanctuary where the Wisdom of Enlightenment abides:

> O, son of Noble Clan! The sanctuary that is complete with its three channels, six kind of Wheels, trunk, branches, limbs, and secondary limbs is the pure realm of the perfect Wheel of Letters; in that sanctuary, the Wisdom of one's Awareness (is endowed with a) dynamism that emerges in the six objects of the six consciousnesses; the fact that it performs the manifold activities of body, speech, and mind (means that) the Emanation Body emerges within oneself and consequently that the pure realms

---

11   Cf. David Germano, "Food, Clothes, Dreams, and Karmic Propensities," in *Religions of Tibet in Practice*, ed. Donald S. Lopez, Jr. (Princeton: Princeton University Press, 1997), 299–300.

12   Dream Interpretation in Tantra and Tibetan Medicine (http://www.tibetanmedicine-edu.org, accessed 14 March 2017).

of the Emanation Body abide within oneself. But if they are not realized (as such), they arise as the manifestation of the six destinies.[13]

The *gSal byed byang bu*, a Bonpo text on the interpretation of dreams, will now be introduced and translated, followed by some hermeneutical remarks which will take into account the text's emic implications in an attempt to contextualize it in the broader framework of the Tibetan divination discourse.

2 Presentation of the *gSal byed byang bu*

The *gSal byed byang bu* or *Exegetic Guide* is a very brief text. It is the forty-fourth in a group of forty-six works contained in Volume 514, one of the seventy-eight volumes featuring Bonpo sources preserved in the Giuseppe Tucci Tibetan Fund of the ex IsIAO Library.[14]

Volume 514 features a heterogeneous number of works including many teachings and visions by Khyung po sPrul sku Blo ldan sNying po (fourteenth century) on O rgyan cemeteries or the country of sTag gzigs, as well as various dream visions, dream dialogues, and prophecies involving *ḍākinīs*. The *Byang bu* is written in *dbu med*, with no abridged syllables (*bsdus yig*); it consists of 3 folia (1a–2a), eight lines per folio with seven sentences of seven syllables each; it has no title page and no colophon.

Judging from the style and the final exhortation, it would appear to be a compilation mostly intended for a monastic establishment. However, given its succinct style, it could also be considered as a quick reference manual for medical or retreat purposes. The text is not written in verses. Hence it would not seem intended as a manual to be learned by heart. It presents a list of manifestations that may be encountered in dreams as well as in real life or as meditative experiences—characterized by specific symbolic components, animals, colors, and circumstances—and elucidates the meaning of those manifestations by identifying the forces or entities responsible for those occurrences. Such entities, in virtue of their own nature, are believed to govern the anatomies of the

---

13 Jean-Luc Achard, *The Six Lamps. Secret Dzogchen Instructions of the Bön Tradition* (Somerville: Wisdom Publications 2017), 83–84.

14 See ed. Elena De Rossi Filibeck, *Catalogue of the Tucci Tibetan Fund in the Library of IsIAO*. Vol. 2 (Rome: Istituto Italiano per l'Africa e l'Oriente, 2003), 291, *gSal byed byang bu zhes bya ba*. As of May 2017, the Giuseppe Tucci Fund has been incorporated into the National Library, Rome.

FIGURE 7.1 Folio 1 (first half, *recto*) of the *gSal byed byang bu*, cm. 60×9
PHOTOGRAPH BY DONATELLA ROSSI, GRATEFULLY REPRODUCED WITH PERMISSION OF THE ISIAO PRESIDENT, PROF. GHERARDO GNOLI (1937–2012)

Universe as their emblematic protagonists, populating the Bonpo *Weltanschauung* and its mythological culture.[15]

The *Byang bu* makes specific reference to the magical displays of the Eight Haughty Classes (*sDe brgyad dregs pa'i cho 'phrul*), examining a total of sixteen instances. However, it only portrays allegorical manifestations without providing any clue as to the ensuing effects of those displays, and above all, how to neutralize them; one may presume that the interested recipient may already be knowledgeable of those aspects or able to access congruous information and help. Furthermore, it does not omit to stipulate from the very beginning that the necessity itself of identifying and reversing the workings of those entities—even if undertaken with the intention of benefiting people and

---

15   Cf. Rolf A. Stein, "The Indigenous Religion and the *Bon po* in Dunhuang Manuscripts", in *Rolf Stein's Tibetiqua Antica*, transl. and ed. Arthur P. McKeown (Leiden: Brill's Tibetan Studies Library 24, 2010), 231–271 and also "Bonpo Accounts on the First Men", *ivi*, 307–313; Samten G. Karmay, *The Arrow and the Spindle: Studies in History, Myths, Rituals and Beliefs in Tibet*. Vol. I and Vol. II (Kathmandu: Mandala Book Point, 1998 and 2005); Samten G. Karmay, "A Historical Overview of the Bon Religion", in *Bon The Magic Word. The Indigenous Religion of Tibet*, eds. Samten G. Karmay and Jeff Watt (New York: Rubin Museum of Art & London: Philip Wilson Publishers, 2007), 55–81.

IDENTIFYING THE MAGICAL DISPLAYS OF THE LORDS OF THE WORLD

FIGURE 7.2   Folio 1 (first half, *recto*) of the *gSal byed byang bu*, cm. 60×9
PHOTOGRAPH BY DONATELLA ROSSI, GRATEFULLY REPRODUCED WITH PERMISSION OF THE ISIAO PRESIDENT, PROF. GHERARDO GNOLI (1937–2012)

beings—belongs to the restricted sphere of the conceptual mind: one should always be aware of the real essence of things, symbolized by the Condition of Kun tu bZang po.

3   Text

Folio 1. (*recto*)

[1r-1] *gSal byed byang bu zhes bya ba* / dngos dang nyams dang rmi lam du / cho' 'phrul ston pa byung pa rnams / gang yin ngos bzung par bya / 'jig rten mgon po'i cho 'phrul ni / gsal byed me long bstan pa ni / mi thar [...]

[1r-2] g.yang la lus pa dang / me 'bar chu dang gcan zan nyer / nam mkha' lding dang lce 'bab mtshon / mun sros thog du ri 'gyel dang / dgra'am zun du rdzu 'phrul ston / lus la mtshon zug cham [phyam] du ltung / me rlung brag dang chu bos 'gogs /

[1r-3] mi theg khur dang thag lag sgrog / dmig so snying dang rkang 'byin dang / gos med 'thur rgyug 'dam rdzab zhugs / gdul bya gang byung gdul dka' dang / re lde zhabs ma'i gos gon dang / dpung med btsan khang zhig pa rnams / 'jig rten [...]

[1r-4] *mgon po lcam dral gyis / yid kyi rdzu 'phrul g.yos nas kyang / 'jig rten log pa'i bar chod rnams / gab pa dngos su bstan pas na / phyi nang dge ba'i las spyad cing / rdzu 'phrul zlog pa'i 'khor lo bya / me la chu rgyab ci bzhin* [...]

[1r-5] *du / pha rol stobs ni 'byil bar byed / lta sgom dmigs pa'i gur khang bca' / rgyun sbyin tshogs 'khor bshags pa bya / bar mi chod dang zhi ba ni / nam mkha' lding la zhon pa dang / 'byung pa gnyen pos sad pa dang / 'thur 'babs gyen* [...]

[1r-6] *la log gin 'jigs / gcer bus gos gon rgyan rnams btags / de rnams bar chad zhi rtags yin / bar chad cho 'phrul log pa yang / rnam rtog sems kyi dri ma ste / rtog tshogs lha dang lha mor gsal / lha yang ye shes sems* [...]

[1r-7] *su dag / mtshon med ye shes kun bzang ngang / tha snyad 'bad rtsol bcas bcos med / ma g.yos bde ba'i ngang la bzhag / sde brgyad dregs pa'i cho 'phrul ni / mun pa nag pos 'thibs pa dang / na bun smugs pas* [b]*tibs pa dang / phug* [...]

[1r-8] *run* [ron] *'phur zhing lding pa ni / dmu'i cho 'phrul ston pa yin / mi nag rta nag dar nag 'phyar / nub nas khrom nag rgyu ba dang / drib ma nag pos g.yogs pa dang / bya nag lding zhing khyi nag nyer / g.yag rog rdung gyin 'phra ba rdeg /*

Folio 1 (*verso*)

[1v-1] *bdud kyi cho 'phrul gtong pa yin / ri dmar lung dmar brag dmar dang / mi rta dmar po dar dmar 'phyar / khra 'ug lding zhing gcan zan 'khrol / skyes pa mthogs 'khor gyis bskor / rta dmag khrom chen rgyu ba ni / btsan gyi cho 'phrul yin* [...]

[1v-2] *par bshad / bar snang 'khams nas gzugs ston dang / yid dam lha'i bkar sdus nas / spro ba'i tshig gis slu byed pa / lha'i cho 'phrul ston pa yin / mi lus gcan zan lpags pa gon / lus la me stag 'phro ba dang / skya shar* [...]

[1v-3] *rme po spyang khu dang / skad rigs mi cig skad bsgyur ba / gnod sbyin 'byung po'i cho 'phrul yin / mi rta dkar po dar dkar 'phyar / bya dkar khyi dkar btsad po dang / btsun mo skya bshar 'khor gyis bskor / rgyal po'i cho 'phrul ston pa yin / shan* [...]

[1v-4] *pa gri thogs dred kyi gzugs / gcan zan gdug pas bskor nas ni / bdag la 'gran tshol phod 'dzugs na / srin po'i cho 'phrul ston pa yin / sbrul dang chu rta 'khyag rum dang / gcan zan ngang skya ba glang rnams / gnyan gyi cho* [...]

IDENTIFYING THE MAGICAL DISPLAYS OF THE LORDS OF THE WORLD 145

[1v-5] *'phrul yin par bshad / sbal pa phyi ba khyi lug ser / sdom dang sdig pa kha brgyad rnams / sa bdag cho 'phrul yin par bshad / mtsho dang ne [g]sing chu dmig dang / nya dang lcong mo ngur pa rnams / klu'i cho 'phrul yin par bshad / mtsho dang [...]*

[1v-6] *bud med mang po dang / sbra gar [sic, gur] phub gyin sngo khrag 'tshod / bdag la skyo dang g.yo spyod dang / bud med mdzo dre zhon pa rnams / ma mo'i cho 'phrul ston pa yin / bud med mi sdug yugs sa mo / mon mo nag mo gdug rtsub ston /*

[1v-7] *btsun pa sgom ma dam nyams rnams / dam sri mo'i cho 'phrul yin / mi shar gcan zan khyi spyang rgol / byi la spra spre'u rdzu 'phrul ston / 'byung po rnams kyi cho 'phrul yin / lha khang sku gzugs mchod rten dang / 'bag [...]*

[1v-8] *seng 'phan gdugs btsun pa dang / ban nag bon nag dar nag 'phyar / dkor skyong rgyal po'i cho 'phrul yin / sprang po hrul po glang mkhar can / spra spre byi la bu chung sogs / the rang 'gong po'i cho 'phrul yin / thog 'bab sgyogs [...]*

Folio 2. (*recto*)

[2r-1] *'phen mda' rdo 'phen / ser ba 'bab cing rlung dmar 'tshub / gza' rdong cho 'phrul ston pa yin / gyer nyams dun nyams mu stegs dang / btsad po mi nag bud med sogs / lta log dam nyams brtag cing [...]*

[2r-2] *gzir [gzigs] / mi gnod gzir [gzigs] na rnam smin che / gang gnod nyams rtags bstan pa'i / gsal byed byang bu zhes bya ba / sMar ro / ? tso / gces pa'i yang khol bon 'di rnams / dmar [sic] la zab pas snying dang 'dra / phyi rabs bus [...]*

[2r-3] *kyang gces par zung / kun la spel na rnam smin che / de phyir gtang gzhag shes par gyis / ces gsungs ste sbas so //*

4 Translation

Folio 1. (*recto*)

[1r-1] *Exegetic Guide.* All magical performances of the Lords of the World, in whatever mode they arise, whether in reality, as an experiential sign [of the practice], or in dreams, should be identified. According to the criteria of this *Guide,*

[1r-2] the Brothers and Sisters Masters of the World enjoy creating havoc with their magic, which they enact through death, decline in prosperity (*g.yang*), fires, floods, suffering animals, sky turbulence and lightning, landslides occurring at night, enemies and friends, sharp pains of the body, continuously tripping over/falling down, impediments provoked by rivers, rocks, water, and fire,

[1r-3] unbearable loads to be carried as well as binding ropes and chains, the extraction of the eyes, the teeth, the heart, and the cutting out of the legs, running wildly without clothes [and] entering muddy waters, difficulty in managing whatever needs to be under control, wearing felt undercoats, and destruction of demilitarized royal residences.

[1r-4] Nevertheless, if the secrets about the [cause of the] obstructions that upset the mundane sphere are explicitly disclosed, the magic can be exorcised, and the effect in terms of inner and outer happiness can be enjoyed.

[1r-5] Just like throwing water on the fire, the power of the adversary is nullified. Prepare the tent where to focus on the View and Meditation, repeatedly perform sacred offerings and confession. Indications that the obstacles have been blocked and are pacified will be riding an eagle, the elemental forces becoming one's allies,

[1r-6] the withdrawing and abating of the disturbances, wearing garments and ornaments on the naked body. However, even reversing magic obstacles is a distortion of the conceptual mind: thoughts mirror the assemblies of male and female deities; as for the deities, they are perfected in the noetic sphere of Primordial Wisdom.

[1r-7] Ineffable Primordial Wisdom rests in the undisturbed condition of bliss, the immutable, relaxed, transcendent Condition of Kun tu bZang po.

The Eight Haughty Classes and the way in which they manifest their magic antagonism:

[1r-8] Enveloping darkness, thick mist, a flying and soaring pigeon are magical displays of the dMu [1]. A black man on a black horse raising a black banner; black multitudes of people arriving from the western direction; being covered in black filth; a black bird soaring or a suffering black dog; and black-colored yaks fighting [hitting and kicking]

IDENTIFYING THE MAGICAL DISPLAYS OF THE LORDS OF THE WORLD

Folio 1. (*verso*)

[1v-1] are magical displays [indicating obstructions] sent by the bDud [2]. Red mountains, rocks and valleys, a red man on a red horse raising a red banner, soaring hawks and owls and carnivorous animals[16] making noises, men gathering together surrounded by followers and attendants, a large number of mounted troops coming and going are said to be magical displays [indicating obstructions] sent by the bTsan [3].

[1v-2] Forms materializing in midair and personal sacred deities gathered together making alluring proclamations with pleasant words are magical displays [indicating obstructions] sent by the lHa [4]. People wearing the skin of carnivorous animals, sparks of fire emanating from the body, gray spotted wolves, [and]

[1v-3] [a person] speaking different languages are magical displays of the gNod sbyin 'Byung po [5]. A white man riding a white horse and raising a white banner, a white bird, a white dog, a white king and queen surrounded by a retinue are magical displays [indicating obstructions sent by] the rGyal po [6].

[1v-4] A butcher holding a knife, the image of a hyena [or of a] bear, and wild dangerous animals going around contending with one another for [killing] oneself are magical displays [indicating obstructions sent by] the Srin po [7]. Snakes, *chu rta* [?], ice fields, ferocious animals, gray teals, and oxen are said to be magical displays [indicating obstructions] sent by the gNyan [8].

[1v-5] Yellow frogs, marmots, dogs, and sheep, spiders, scorpions, and octopodes are said to be magical displays [indicating obstructions] sent by the Sa bdag [9]. Expanses of water, meadows, springs, fishes, tadpoles, and ducks are said to be magical displays [indicating obstructions] sent by the Klu [10].

[1v-6] Waters, numerous female persons pitching a tent and boiling greens [with] blood, who appear deceitfully sorrow toward oneself, and female persons riding *mdzo* and mules are said to be magical displays [indicating obstruc-

---

16   Cf. Cathy Cantwell and Rob Meyer, "The Winged and the Fanged", in *From Bhakti to Bon. Festschrift for Per Kværne*, eds. Hanna Havnevik and Charles Ramble, (Oslo: Novus Press, 2015), 153–170.

tions] sent by the Ma mo [11]. Repulsive women, widows, black Mon females with a ferocious expression,[17] [and]

[1v-7] monks in training[18] spoiling their vows are magical displays [indicating obstructions sent by] the female Dam Sri [12]. Wild beasts, dogs, and wolves fighting for human flesh as well as cats and monkeys displaying magical behavior [indicate obstructions sent by] the 'Byung po [13]. Temples, statues and images, stupas,

[1v-8] lion masks, ribbons, parasols, monks, and black Bonpos and Buddhists raising black banners are magical displays of the dKor skyong rGyal po [14]. Ragged beggars, ox-shaped clouds, monkeys, cats, small children and the like are magical displays of the The rang 'Gong po [15]. Lightning descending, catapults

Folio 2. (*recto*)

[2r-1] hurling, arrows cast and stones thrown, hailstorms and hurricanes are magical displays [indicating obstructions sent by] the gZa' rdong [16].[19] One should examine and evaluate [the accuracy of one's] practice [in terms of] recitations [and] assiduity; [eschew] extreme views; [understand one's position with regard to] the king, lay people, women, and so on; [recognize one's] wrong ideas and [one's] violations of vows.

[2r-2] When one considers the [potential] harm [for] people [deriving from one's wrong behavior, one is also aware of the] heavy [implications of] karmic

---

17 Cf. Toni Huber, "Descent, Tutelaries and Ancestors. Transmission among Autonomous, *Bon* Ritual Specialists in Eastern Bhutan and the Mon-yul Corridor", in *From Bhakti to Bon. Festschrift for Per Kværne*, eds. Hanna Havnevik and Charles Ramble, (Oslo: Novus Press, 2015), 271–289.

18 Cf. Ulrike Roesler, "The Vinaya of the Bon Tradition", in *From Bhakti to Bon. Festschrift for Per Kværne*, eds. Hanna Havnevik and Charles Ramble, (Oslo: Novus Press, 2015), 431–448; Toni Huber, "Contributions on the Bon religion in A-mdo (1): The monastic tradition of Bya-dur dGa'-mal in Shar-khog," in ed. Alex McKay, *The History of Tibet. The Medieval Period: c. 850–1895. The Development of Buddhist Paramountcy*, vol. 2 (London: Routledge-Curzon, 2003), 675–709.

19 For the different types of specific disturbances, illnesses, and so on caused by the various Classes see for example Réne De Nebesky-Wojkowitz, *Oracles and Demons of Tibet. The Cult and Iconography of the Tibetan Protective Deities* (Kathmandu: Pilgrims Book House, 1993), *passim*; cf. Lin, Shen-Yu, "The Fifteen Great Demons of Children" (*byis pa'i gdon chen bco lnga*), in *Revue d'Études Tibétaines* 26 (2013), 5–33.

IDENTIFYING THE MAGICAL DISPLAYS OF THE LORDS OF THE WORLD

retribution. The *Exegetic Guide* dealing with experiential indications about that which [may] cause harm [is hereby completed]. Fortune! These very succinct, valuable teachings are good and profound like [one's] own heart.

[2r-3] May also the lads of future generations hold them dear! If they will be spread everywhere, [the positivity of] karmic retribution [will be] significant. That is why one should know [what to] take [and what to] let go. So it was said [and the teachings] were concealed.

5   Remarks on the Text

The *Byang bu* is focused upon the recognition of signs that let one identify which class of nonhuman beings is manifesting and is ready to attack. There is no mention of any sort of compromise in terms of compassionate attitude to be adopted in their regard. The purpose of recognizing those signs is that of nullifying their damaging efforts towards all aspects of human and animal life. In order to accomplish that, the practitioner is requested to create a sacred space where first of all he should focus the mind on the view and meditation [1r-5]; given the content of the lines immediately following such statement [1r-6,7], they should correspond to the view and meditation associated with *rDzogs chen* tenets. For a sketchy definition we can quote a Bonpo *gter ma* text, belonging to the *Yang rtse klong chen* cycle, which reads:

lTa ba thag bcad	The View [is] definitely ascertained.
rTogs pa yid ches	Realization [dwells in] confidence.[20]
bsGom pas nyams su myong	Through Meditation [one has access to] the experience [of the Primordial State].
sPyod pas la bzla	Through Conduct [limitations are] transcended.
'Bras bu rang sa zin pa	The Fruit [is] abiding in the natural condition.[21]

In the *rDo rje sems dpa' nam mkha' che'i rgyud*, the Buddha Kun tu bZang po describes the way of understanding the meaning of *rDzogs chen* as follows:

---

20   That is to say, confidence of one's knowledge of the Primordial State.

21   *lTa ba'i stong thun bzhugs pa dge'o*. In *Bla med rdzogs pa chen po yaṅ rtse kloṅ chen gyi khrid gźuṅ cha lag daṅ bcas pa'i gsuṅ pod*, vol. 1, ed. Sherab Wangyal (New Thobgyal: Tibetan Bonpo Monastic Centre, 1973), 431–451, (449, line 5). The discovery of the cycle is attributed to *gter ston* gZhod ston dNgos grub Grags pa (eleventh century), also renowned by the rNyingmas as gTer ston Grub thob dNgos grub, since he retrieved Buddhist treasure texts.

This sphere of experience of the Buddhas
Is not a place to be found by searching,
And like phenomena of the six senses, it is not an object:
Those who search for it are like the blind reaching for the sky.
The path of purity that leads higher and higher
Does not correspond with the nature beyond action.
Were there really a path to thread,
Just like the boundaries of the sky, one would never arrive.[22]

At the beginning of the *Guide* we find a generic reference to the malicious tricks of the Lords of the World ('Jig rten mGon po) that the *Byang bu* intends to expose [1r-1]; then comes the list of the signs connected to the so-called Eight Haughty Classes (sDe brgyad dregs pa) [1r-7 up to 2r-1]; nevertheless, the number of entities mentioned amounts to a total of sixteen, appearing in the following order: 1. dMu; 2. bDud; 3. bTsan; 4. lHa; 5. gNod sbyin 'Byung po; 6. rGyal po; 7. Srin po; 8. gNyan; 9. Sa bdag; 10. Klu; 11. Ma mo; 12. Dam Sri; 13. 'Byung po; 14. dKor skyong rGyal po; 15. The rang 'Gong po; 16. gZa' rdong. René de Nebesky-Wojkowitz dedicates an entire chapter to the Haughty Ones.[23] He affirms (253, 254):

[T]he expression *dregs pa* [...] had been used as the title of higher-ranking *dharmapālas*. More frequently, however, this term was applied as a general appellation of a multitude of gods and goddesses (*dregs pa pho mo*) occupying a lower rank. Most of these were originally members of the Bon pantheon. There are several subdivisions of the *dregs pa*: some texts of the *rNying ma pa* sect speak about [...] the "sixteen *dregs pa*", but it remains obscure who the members of these groups are. [...] An important group of *dregs pa* frequently invoked in the course of magic ceremonies is that of the *Dregs pa sde brgyad*, which comprises the following six subdivisions: *Phyi yi sde brgyad; Nang gi sde brgyad; gSang ba'i sde brgyad; mChog gi sde brgyad; sPrul pa sde brgyad; sNang srid sde brgyad* [...]

and continues by listing the respective eight members or group of deities. Out of the *Byang bu*'s list, the Eight Classes that fall into one or more of the cate-

---

22 See Adriano Clemente, *rDo rje Sems dpa' Nam mkha' che'i rGyud. An Analysis of the Tantra of the Total Space of Vajrasattva*, in *Sharro. Festschrift for Chögyal Namkhai Norbu*, eds. Donatella Rossi and Charles Jamyang Oliphant of Rossie (Schongau: Garuda Verlag, 2016), 52–74.

23 De Nebesky-Wojkowitz, op. cit., Chapter XVI, The Dregs pa, 253–317.

gories quoted above are: 2. bDud (*gSang sde, mChog sde*); 3. bTsan (*Nang sde, gSang sde, mChog sde*); 4. lHa (*Phyi yi sde*); 5. gNod sbyin (*Phyi yi sde, gSang sde*); 6. rGyal po (*mChog sde, sNang srid*); 9. Sa bdag (*sNang sde*); 10. Klu (*Phyi yi sde, gSang sde, mChog sde, sNang srid*); 11. Ma mo (*Nang sde, gSang sde, mChog sde*); and 16. gZa' (*mChog sde*).

Per Kværne, in his *The Bon Religion of Tibet. The Iconography of a Living Tradition*,[24] reproduces two *thang ka* of sTag la Me 'bar,[25] the *yi dam* associated with the transmission of Phur pa teachings;[26] the first one is especially interesting in this context because it depicts Eighteen Dregs pa (Dregs pa bco brgyad) surrounding the ferocious deity. Here we find ten classes out of the *Byang bu*'s list: 1. dMu; 2. bDud; 3. bTsan; 4. lHa; 6. rGyal po; 8. gNyan; 9. Sa bdag; 10. Klu; 11. Ma mo; and 15. The rang ('Gong po depicted as a separate figure).

Samten G. Karmay, in his "Une Note sur l'Origine du Concept des Huit Catégories d'Esprits",[27] states that the conceptual genesis and the epoch in which Tibetans began to talk about the eight categories called *lha klu sde brgyad*, and later on *lha srin sde brgyad*, remains unknown; in reference to the work of de Nebesky-Wojkowitz, he remarks that the expression *dregs pa sde brgyad* is an appellation found in late Tibetan sources (67, n. 1). He further elaborates upon the topic, by presenting and analyzing categories of entities mentioned in Pelliot tibétain 1047,[28] that is to say, *lha* and *sku bla* (68–69),[29] *gnyan*[30] and *klu* (69–70),[31] *dri* and *btsan*,[32] concluding that, "aucun concept de classification en

---

24   London: Serindia Publications, 1995.

25   Per Kværne, op. cit., Plates 38 and 39, 122–123 and 124–125.

26   For a description of the *yi dam* see *ivi*, 117–118; cf. Idem, "Bonpo Tantric Deities", in *Bon The Magic Word. The Indigenous Religion of Tibet*, eds. Samten G. Karmay and Jeff Watt (New York: Rubin Museum of Art & London: Philip Wilson Publishers, 2007), 165–179.

27   *Revue d'Études Tibétaines* 2 (2003), 67–80; see also Brigitte Steinmann, "Les *lHa srin sde brgyad* et le Problème de leur Catégorisation. Une Interprétation", *ivi*, 81–91.

28   See Ariane Macdonald, "Une Lecture des Pelliot Tibétain 1286, 1287, 1038, et 1290. Essai sur la Formation et l'Emploi des Mythes Politiques dans la Religion Royale de Sroṅ-bcan sgam-po", in *Études Tibétaines Dédiées à la Mémoire de Marcelle Lalou* (Paris: Adrien Maisonneuve, 1971), 272 et seq.

29   Ariane Macdonald, *ivi*, 301 et seq. Cf. Nathan W. Hill, "The sku-bla Rite in Imperial Tibetan Religion", in *Cahiers d'Extrême-Asie* 24 (2015), 49–58.

30   Cf. Daniel Berounský, "The Nyen Collection (Gnyan bum) and Shenrab Miwo of Nam", in eds. J. Ptackova and Adrian Zenz, *Mapping Amdo*. Supplementa of the *Archiv Orientální* (2017): forthcoming.

31   Cf. Agata Bareja-Starzyńska, "A Bonpo Text on the Propitiation of Serpent Deities (*Klu 'bum dkar po*) in Mongolian", in *From Bhakti to Bon. Festschrift for Per Kværne*, eds. Hanna Havnevik and Charles Ramble, (Oslo: Novus Press, 2015), 39–52.

32   On the association of bTsan with the deer and connected apotropaic rituals cf. Samten G. Karmay, *cit.* (2003): 70; Katsumi Mimaki and Samten G. Karmay, *Bon sgo gsal byed*.

listes des différentes catégories d'esprits ne se dégage de ce manuscrit. La catégorie des *srin*, qui joue un rôle important [...] n'y est même pas mentionnée (70–71)." Turning his attention to PT 16,[33] Karmay posits that PT 16 may be the oldest text he found in which the expression *lha klu sde brgyad* appears; and in his *Conclusion* he deliberates that the expression

> renvoie aux huit catégories des esprits énumérées dans le *Suvarnabhasa* et le *Saddharmapundarika*. La liste contenue dans ces sutra est certainement la première et à l'origine du concept de systématisation en liste des esprit en huit catégories. [...] C'est, à notre avis, le modèle de ce qu'on appelle les *lha srin sde brgyad*, fréquemment traités dans la littérature bonpo et rnying ma pa à partir du 11e siècle.[34]

With respect to the *Byang bu* and its taxonomy, there are some questions which remain unanswered at the time of this writing and which necessitate further investigation:

- why the text introduces the manifestations as being those of the Eight Haughty Classes (*sde brgyad dregs pa'i cho 'phrul ni*, 1r-7), and then presents sixteen instances.
- What is the justification for the order in the sequence: is the order meant to be for reasons of relevance (which, however, cannot be deduced from the context) because it implies a hierarchy in potency; or is it just randomized because the *Guide* is fundamentally concerned with identifying those classes as the most dangerous ones.
- Is the sequence drawing from mythological notions or considerations: for instance, the thirteenth century's *gter ma* titled *Srid pa las kyi gting zlog gi rtsa rgyud kun gsal nyi zer sgron ma*[35] places the 1. dMu; 2. bDud; 3. bTsan; and 4. lHa in the group of the g.Yar g.yen gNyen po bCu gsum (Thirteen Mighty Ones of the Higher Sphere) and the 10. Klu; 8. gNyan; 6. rGyal; 11. Ma mo (sMan); 15. The (Ther) rang; 7. Srin po; and 12. (Dam) Sri in the group of the Sa g.yen Che ba bCu gcig (Eleven Great Beings of the Earthly Sphere).

Two Tibetan Manuscripts in Facsimile Edition of A Fourteenth Century Encyclopedia of Bon po Doxography (Tokyo: The Toyo Bunko, 1997), 84 (114a); Daniel Berounský, "A Dialogue between the Priest and the Deer", in *From Bhakti to Bon. Festschrift for Per Kværne*, eds. Hanna Havnevik and Charles Ramble, (Oslo: Novus Press, 2015), 97–112.

33   See Samten G. Karmay, *cit.* (2003), 71–72, n. 18 and n. 19.

34   *Ivi*, 77–78.

35   Discovered by Bra bo sGom nyag, alias Bra bo rGyal ba Grags pa. See ed. and transl. Samten G. Karmay, *The Treasury of Good Sayings. A Tibetan History of Bon* (Delhi: Motilal Banarsidass 2001 [1972]), 173.

These nonhuman beings, together with the Bar g.yen gTod po dgu (Nine Inflexible Ones of the Intermediate Space), were believed to dominate the tripartite dimension of the world and were said to be controlled by specific hierophants, as can be inferred by perusing the *'Dus pa rin po che dri ma med pa gzi brjid rab tu 'bar ba'i mdo*.[36] These classes are dealt with in the *sNang gshen Theg pa*, the second of the Nine Vehicles.[37]

- How should the sixteen classes be correlated or grouped within the *sDe brgyad Dregs pa*?
- Are these the sixteen *dregs pa* that de Nebesky-Wojkowitz mentions in relation to rNying ma texts; a reworking of that group; or perhaps some kind of inspirational source for that group?

At the same time, it seems arduous to determine whether the *Byang bu* is intended as a synthesis of the most salient *cho 'phrul* gleaned from texts explicitly dealing with one or possibly the totality of the Eight Haughty Classes as they are envisaged in the *Guide*; or if it represents a generic, perhaps discretionary, narrative. In any case, although the *sDe brgyad* in both their noxious (*nag phyogs*) and protective (*dkar phyogs*) aspects[38] are not the object of this paper, I will submit an obviousness by saying that additional in-depth and *ad hoc* studies will be valuable to further assess and understand the role played by local and regional cults vis-à-vis the ontogenesis of the Tibetan cultural identity in its broadest spatio-temporal sense, just as the research carried out by numerous Tibetologists has already demonstrated so far.[39]

---

36 The longest, 12 volume hagiography of sTon pa gShen rab received in a vision by mChog sprul Blo ldan sNying po (fourteenth century). Cf. Samten G. Karmay, *cit.*, (2001 [1972]), 182, 185; Per Kværne, "Tonpa Shenrab Miwo: Founder of the Bon Religion", in *Bon The Magic Word. The Indigenous Religion of Tibet*, eds. Samten G. Karmay and Jeff Watt (New York: Rubin Museum of Art & London: Philip Wilson Publishers, 2007), 83–97.

37 Cf. David L. Snellgrove, *The Nine Ways of Bon. Excerpts from the gZi-brjid edited and translated* (London: Oxford University Press, 1967), 78–79.

38 Cf. Samten G. Karmay, "The Protector Deities of a Bonpo Funeral Rite", in *From Bhakti to Bon. Festschrift for Per Kværne*, eds. Hanna Havnevik and Charles Ramble, (Oslo: Novus Press, 2015), 303–323; Charles Ramble, "Fearless Dawn, Bloodless Demon: Literary and Iconographic Manifestations of a Little-known Bonpo Protector", in *From Bhakti to Bon. Festschrift for Per Kværne*, eds. Hanna Havnevik and Charles Ramble, (Oslo: Novus Press, 2015), 409–430.

39 Cf. e.g. Samten G. Karmay, "Myths and Rituals", in *Bon The Magic Word. The Indigenous Religion of Tibet*, eds. Samten G. Karmay and Jeff Watt (New York: Rubin Museum of Art & London: Philip Wilson Publishers, 2007), 147–163; Charles Ramble, "Tsewang Rigdzin. The Bon Tradition of Sacred Geography", in *Bon The Magic Word. The Indigenous Religion of Tibet*, eds. Samten G. Karmay and Jeff Watt (New York: Rubin Museum of Art & London: Philip Wilson Publishers, 2007), 125–145; John Vincent Bellezza, *Spirit-Mediums, Sacred Mountains and Related Bon Textual Traditions in Upper Tibet: Calling Down the Gods* (Lei-

6 Conclusions

Within the vast array of mantic tools that characterize the discernment and clarification of hidden circumstances in the Tibetan culture, oneiromancy occupies a revered position and plays a specific role. According to indications contained in copious textual sources, the dream state can represent the vehicle for visions of pure fields, prophetic encounters, suggestive appearances of totemic animals and messengers of powerful entities, to name just a few instances.

In the classification of the *Theg pa dgu* contained in the above-mentioned *gZi brjid*, dreams are included in the first rubric of the first of the Nine Vehicles, the Vehicle of the *Phywa gShen*, the hierophant entrusted with methods for attracting prosperity and for prognostication in general. The *Phywa gshen theg pa* is the first of the so-called four vehicles of the Cause (*rgyu'i theg pa bzhi*). It deals with methods of divination (*pra ltas mo*), astrological reckoning (*snang mthong rtsis*), rituals for healing diseases (*na gso gto*), and diagnostic methods for death ransom ('*chi bslu dpyad*).[40] In the *pra ltas mo* series, dreams form the third category, which is mythopoetically styled *Ye rje smon pa'i rmi lam* (the Dream of the Lord of Primordial Aspiration).[41]

It is interesting to perceive a parallelism between the reference contained in the *gZi brjid* on the relativity of methods, such as those expounded in the *Phywa gshen theg pa*,[42] and the *Byang bu*'s emphasis attributed to merit and retribution but also to the recipient's position within society, something that would

---

den: Brill, 2005); Katia Buffetrille, "Reflections on pilgrimages to sacred mountains, lakes and caves", in ed. Alex McKay, *The History of Tibet. The Medieval Period: c. 850–1895. The Development of Buddhist Paramountcy*, vol. 2 (London: RoutledgeCurzon, 2003), 233–246; Robert B. Ekvall, "The Tibetan Self-Image", in ed. Alex McKay, *The History of Tibet. The Modern Period: 1895–1959. The Encounter with Modernity*, vol. 3 (London: RoutledgeCurzon, 2003), 629–634; Alex McKay, "Tibet. The myth of isolation", *ivi*, 635–645.

40   In the doxography of the Nine Vehicles belonging to the Southern Treasury (*lho gter gyi theg pa dgu*) presented in the fourteenth century's *Bon sgo gsal byed*, the Phya gShen Vehicle consists of the teachings of five sciences (*phyi, nang, bzo, sgra,* and *gso ba rig pa'i gnas lnga*); the text states that divination is an External Science (*mo yang phyi rig te*); it does not mention dreams but it does mention cord-based divination (*zhang zhung gi ju thig*), scapulimancy (*mi nyag gi sog pa*), and pebble divination (*ma sangs kyi mde'u*); see Katsumi Mimaki and Samten G. Karmay, op. cit., 84 (112a,5–112b,4); Katsumi Mimaki and Samten G. Karmay, "Nine Vehicles of the Southern Treasury (*lho gter gyi theg pa dgu*) as Presented in the *Bon sgo gsal byed* of Tre ston rGyal mtshan dpal, Part One: First Four Vehicles," in *Memoirs of the Faculty of Letters, Kyoto University* 48 (2009), 38–47.

41   Cf. Snellgrove, op. cit., 24–41.

42   *Ivi*, 26 and 27.

corroborate the assumption that the text is indeed designed for a male member of the monastic establishment: "One should examine and evaluate [the accuracy of one's] practice [in terms of] recitations [and] assiduity; [eschew] extreme views; [understand one's position with regard to] the king, lay people, women, and so on (*btsad po mi nag bud med sogs*); [recognize one's] wrong ideas and [one's] violations of vows. When one considers the [potential] harm [for] people [deriving from one's wrong behavior, one is also aware of the] heavy [implications of] karmic retribution" [2r-1 and 2r-2].

Equally poignant and pertinent is the succinct reminder about absolute reality as being the receptacle of both wisdom and phenomena, a principle that an adept should always keep in mind when performing spiritual exercises:

> [1r-6] However, even reversing magic obstacles is a distortion of the conceptual mind: thoughts mirror the assemblies of male and female deities; as for the deities, they are perfected in the noetic sphere of Primordial Wisdom.

> [1r-7] Ineffable Primordial Wisdom rests in the undisturbed condition of bliss, the immutable, relaxed, transcendent Condition of Kun tu bZang po.

Deconstruction of the anatomies of the universe in terms of identification of pathogenic entities is flavored by the most ancient and perhaps best possible (emotional) choice at the disposal of human beings, that is to say, deification or sublimation of inexplicable and awesome phenomena. Let us consider for example the Etruscans first, and the Romans later, who entitled malaria to the female deities Febris and Mephitis who, like all other deities, had to be propitiated, and whose intermediaries, the haruspices, were expert in divination with birds[43] and sanguinary divinations with entrails, especially liver, and so on.[44] In this regard the Roman Stoic philosopher Lucius Annaeus Seneca (4 BCE–65 CE) wrote:

---

43   Cf. Daniel Berounský, "Bird Offerings in the Old Tibetan Myths of the Nyen Collection (*Gnyan 'bum*)", in *Archiv Orientální* 84 (2016), 527–559; Ai Nishida (愛西田), "Bird Divination in Old Tibetan texts," in *Current Issues and Progress in Tibetan Studies: Proceedings of the Third International Seminar of Young Tibetologists, Kobe 2012. Journal of the Research Institute of Foreign Studies* 51, 317–341. Kobe: Kobe City University of Foreign Studies, 2013.

44   Cf. Giovanni Feo, *La Religione degli Etruschi. Divinità, Miti e Sopravvivenze* (Arcidosso: Effigi Edizioni, 2011); Idem, *Ninfe, Sibille, Lase. Storia e Leggende del Sacerdozio Femminile Etrusco* (Arcidosso: Effigi Edizioni, 2016).

The difference between us and the Etruscans, who master the science of interpreting lightning at the highest degree, is this: we believe that because clouds collide lightning is emitted; they think that clouds collide so that lightning may be emitted. (In fact, since they bring everything back to the divinity, they are convinced that lightning provide omens not because they occur, but that they occur in order to provide omens). [...][45]

The *gSal byed byang bu*—with its evocative semiotic fields, the totemic role of animals, the ethics of respect and reverence, the acknowledgement of the good aspects of life and the awareness of the interdependence of all beings—can be appreciated, in a religious-comparative perspective, as a peculiar native case within the transversal phenomenon of divination, whose tangible applications and intangible significance participate throughout history in defining the cultural facets of most civilizations including the Tibetan one.

References

Achard, Jean-Luc. *The Six Lamps. Secret Dzogchen Instructions of the Bön Tradition.* Somerville: Wisdom Publications, 2017.

Bareja-Starzyńska, Agata. "A Bonpo Text on the Propitiation of Serpent Deities (*Klu 'bum dkar po*) in Mongolian." In *From Bhakti to Bon. Festschrift for Per Kværne*, eds. Hanna Havnevik and Charles Ramble, pp. 39–52. Oslo: Novus Press, 2015.

Bellezza, John Vincent. *Spirit-Mediums, Sacred Mountains and Related Bon Textual Traditions in Upper Tibet: Calling Down the Gods.* Leiden: Brill, 2005.

Berounský, Daniel. "A Dialogue between the Priest and the Deer." In *From Bhakti to Bon. Festschrift for Per Kværne*, eds. Hanna Havnevik and Charles Ramble, pp. 97–112. Oslo: Novus Press, 2015.

Berounský, Daniel. "Bird Offerings in the Old Tibetan Myths of the Nyen Collection (*Gnyan 'bum*)." *Archiv Orientální* 84 (2016), pp. 527–559.

Berounský, Daniel. "The Nyen Collection (Gnyan 'bum) and Shenrab Miwo of Nam." In

---

45 *Naturales quaestiones* Liber II, 32, 2: *Hoc inter nos et Tuscos, quibus summa est fulgurum persequendorum scientia, interest: nos putamus quia nubes collisae sunt fulmina emitti; illi existimant nubes collidi ut fulmina emittantur (nam cum omnia ad deum referant, in ea opinione sunt tamquam non quia facta sunt significent, sed quia significatura sunt fiant).* Cf. e.g. ed. Piergiorgio Parroni, *Seneca, Ricerche sulla Natura*, Segrate: Fondazione Lorenzo Valla / Arnoldo Mondadori Editore, 2000, 128–129; transl. Harry M. Hine, *Seneca: Natural Questions* (Chicago and London: University of Chicago Press, 2010), 163 et seq.

Mapping Amdo, eds. J. Ptackova and Adrian Zenz. Supplementa of the *Archiv Orientální* (2017): forthcoming.

Buffetrille, Katia. "Reflections on Pilgrimages to Sacred Mountains, Lakes and Caves." In *The History of Tibet. The Medieval Period: c. 850–1895. The Development of Buddhist Paramountcy*, ed. Alex McKay, vol. 2, pp. 233–246. London: RoutledgeCurzon, 2003.

Cantwell, Cathy and Meyer, Rob. "The Winged and the Fanged." In *From Bhakti to Bon. Festschrift for Per Kværne*, eds. Hanna Havnevik and Charles Ramble, pp. 153–170. Oslo: Novus Press, 2015.

Clemente, Adriano. *rDo rje Sems dpa' Nam mkha' che' i rGyud. An Analysis of the Tantra of the Total Space of Vajrasattva*. In *Sharro. Festschrift for Chögyal Namkhai Norbu*, eds. Donatella Rossi and Charles Jamyang Oliphant of Rossie, pp. 52–74. Schongau: Garuda Verlag, 2016.

De Nebesky-Wojkowitz, Réne. *Oracles and Demons of Tibet. The Cult and Iconography of the Tibetan Protective Deities*. Kathmandu: Pilgrims Book House, 1993.

De Rossi Filibeck, Elena. ed. *Catalogue of the Tucci Tibetan Fund in the Library of IsIAO* vol. 2. Rome: Istituto Italiano per l'Africa e l'Oriente, 2003.

Dodds, Eric R. *The Greeks and the Irrational*. Berkeley: Sather Classical Lectures Series 25, University of California Press, 2004 [1951].

Ekvall, Robert B. "The Tibetan Self-Image." In *The History of Tibet. The Modern Period: 1895–1959. The Encounter with Modernity*, ed. Alex McKay, vol. 3, pp. 629–634. London: RoutledgeCurzon, 2003.

Esler, Dylan. "Note d'Oniromancie Tibétaine: Réflexions sur le Chapitre 4 du *bSamgtan mig-sgron* de gNubs-chen sangs-rgyas ye-shes." *Acta Orientalia Belgica* 25 (2012), pp. 317–328.

Feo, Giovanni. *La Religione degli Etruschi. Divinità, Miti e Sopravvivenze*. Arcidosso: Effigi Edizioni, 2011.

Feo, Giovanni. *Ninfe, Sibille, Lase. Storia e Leggende del Sacerdozio Femminile Etrusco*. Arcidosso: Effigi Edizioni, 2016.

Germano, David. "Food, Clothes, Dreams, and Karmic Propensities." In *Religions of Tibet in Practice*, ed. Donald S. Lopez, Jr., pp. 293–118. Princeton: Princeton University Press, 1997.

Hine, Harry M. transl. *Seneca: Natural Questions*. Chicago and London: University of Chicago Press, 2010.

Hoffmann, Helmut. *Tibet. A Handbook*. Bloomington: Indiana University Publications, 1975.

Huber, Toni. "Contributions on the Bon Religion in A-mdo (1): The Monastic Tradition of Bya-dur dGa'-mal in Shar-khog." In *The History of Tibet. The Medieval Period: c. 850–1895. The Development of Buddhist Paramountcy*, ed. Alex McKay, vol. 2, pp. 675–709. London: RoutledgeCurzon, 2003.

Huber, Toni. "Descent, Tutelaries and Ancestors. Transmission among Autonomous,

Bon Ritual Specialists in Eastern Bhutan and the Mon-yul Corridor." In *From Bhakti to Bon. Festschrift for Per Kværne*, eds. Hanna Havnevik and Charles Ramble, pp. 271–289. Oslo: Novus Press, 2015.

Karmay, Samten G. "The Protector Deities of a Bonpo Funeral Rite." In *From Bhakti to Bon. Festschrift for Per Kværne*, eds. Hanna Havnevik and Charles Ramble, pp. 303–323. Oslo: Novus Press, 2015.

Karmay, Samten G. ed. and transl. *The Treasury of Good Sayings. A Tibetan History of Bon*. Delhi: Motilal Banarsidass 2001 [1972].

Karmay, Samten G. *The Arrow and the Spindle: Studies in History, Myths, Rituals and Beliefs in Tibet*. Vol. I and Vol. II. Kathmandu: Mandala Book Point, 1998, 2005.

Karmay, Samten G. "A Historical Overview of the Bon Religion." In *Bon The Magic Word. The Indigenous Religion of Tibet*, eds. Samten G. Karmay and Jeff Watt, pp. 55–81. New York: Rubin Museum of Art & London: Philip Wilson Publishers, 2007.

Karmay, Samten G. "Une Note sur l'Origine du Concept des Huit Catégories d'Esprits." *Revue d'Études Tibétaines* 2 (2003), pp. 67–80.

Kværne, Per. *The Bon Religion of Tibet. The Iconography of a Living Tradition*. London: Serindia Publications, 1995.

Kværne, Per. "Bonpo Tantric Deities." In *Bon The Magic Word. The Indigenous Religion of Tibet*, eds. Samten G. Karmay and Jeff Watt, pp. 165–179. New York: Rubin Museum of Art & London: Philip Wilson Publishers, 2007.

Kværne, Per. "Tonpa Shenrab Miwo: Founder of the Bon Religion." In *Bon The Magic Word. The Indigenous Religion of Tibet*, eds. Samten G. Karmay and Jeff Watt, pp. 83–97. New York: Rubin Museum of Art & London: Philip Wilson Publishers, 2007.

Lin, Shen-Yu, "The Fifteen Great Demons of Children." *Revue d'Études Tibétaines* 26 (2013), pp. 5–33.

Luck, Georg. ed. *Arcana Mundi. Magia e Occulto nel Mondo Greco Romano. Volume II, Divinazione, Astrologia, Alchimia*. Segrate: Fondazione Lorenzo Valla / Arnoldo Mondadori Editore, 1999.

Macdonald, Ariane. "Une Lecture des Pelliot Tibétain 1286, 1287, 1038, et 1290. Essai sur la Formation et l'Emploi des Mythes Politiques dans la Religion Royale de Sroń bcan sgam po." In *Études Tibétaines Dédiées à la Mémoire de Marcelle Lalou*, pp. 190–391. Paris: Adrien Maisonneuve, 1971.

Mavroudi, Maria. *A Byzantine Book on Dream Interpretation. The Oneirocriticon of Achmet and Its Arabic Sources*. Leiden: Brill, 2002.

McKay, Alex. "Tibet. The Myth of Isolation." In *The History of Tibet. The Modern Period: 1895–1959. The Encounter with Modernity*, vol. 3, ed. Alex McKay, pp. 635–645. London: Routledge Curzon, 2003.

Miller, Cox Patricia. *Dreams in Late Antiquity: Studies in the Imagination of a Culture*. Princeton: Princeton University Press, 1997.

Mimaki, Katsumi and Karmay, Samten G. *Bon sgo gsal byed. Two Tibetan Manuscripts in*

Facsimile Edition of A Fourteenth Century Encyclopedia of Bon po Doxography. Tokyo: The Toyo Bunko, 1997.

Mimaki, Katsumi. "Nine Vehicles of the Southern Treasury (*lho gter gyi theg pa dgu*) as presented in the *Bon sgo gsal byed* of Tre ston rGyal mtshan dpal. Part One: First Four Vehicles." In *Memoirs of the Faculty of Letters, Kyoto University* 48 (2009), pp. 33–172.

Nishida, Ai. 西田愛. "Bird Divination in Old Tibetan Texts." In *Current Issues and Progress in Tibetan Studies: Proceedings of the Third International Seminar of Young Tibetologists, Kobe 2012. Journal of the Research Institute of Foreign Studies* 51: 317–341. Kobe: Kobe City University of Foreign Studies, 2013.

Noegel, Scott B. and Szpakowska, Kasia. "'Word Play' in the Ramesside Dream Manual." *Studien zur Altägyptischen Kultur* 35 (2007), pp. 193–212.

Oberhelman. Steven M. transl. and ed. *The Oneirocriticon of Achmet. A Medieval Greek and Arabic Treatise on the Interpretation of Dreams*. Lubbock: Texas Tech University Press, 1991.

Oberhelman. Steven M. *Dreambooks in Byzantium. Six Oneirocritica in Translation, with Commentary and Introduction*. London: Routledge, 2008.

Oppenheim, Leo, A. *The interpretation of dreams in the ancient Near East, with a translation of an Assyrian dream-book*. Philadelphia: American Philosophical Society, 1956.

Parroni, Piergiorgio. ed. *Seneca, Ricerche sulla Natura*. Segrate: Fondazione Lorenzo Valla / Arnoldo Mondadori Editore, 2000.

Ramble, Charles. "Fearless Dawn, Bloodless Demon: Literary and Iconographic Manifestations of a Little-known Bonpo Protector." In *From Bhakti to Bon. Festschrift for Per Kværne*, eds. Hanna Havnevik and Charles Ramble, pp. 409–430. Oslo: Novus Press, 2015.

Ramble, Charles. "Tsewang Rigdzin. The Bon Tradition of Sacred Geography." In *Bon The Magic Word. The Indigenous Religion of Tibet*, eds. Samten G. Karmay and Jeff Watt, pp. 125–145. New York: Rubin Museum of Art & London: Philip Wilson Publishers, 2007.

Reed, Alexander Wyclif. *Aboriginal Myths: Tales Of The Dreamtime*. Chatswood: New Holland Publishers, 2006.

Ricciardelli, Gabriella. ed. *Inni Orfici*. Segrate: Fondazione Lorenzo Valla / Arnoldo Mondadori Editore, 2000.

Roesler, Ulrike. "The Vinaya of the Bon Tradition." In *From Bhakti to Bon. Festschrift for Per Kværne*, eds. Hanna Havnevik and Charles Ramble, pp. 431–448. Oslo: Novus Press, 2015.

Sherab Wangyal. ed. *lTa ba'i stong thun bzhugs pa dge'o*. In *Bla med rdzogs pa chen po yaḍ rtse kloḍ chen gyi khrid gźuḍ cha lag daḍ bcas pa'i gsuḍ pod* vol. 1, pp. 431–451. New Thobgyal: Tibetan Bonpo Monastic Centre, 1973.

Snellgrove, David L. *The Nine Ways of Bon. Excerpts from the* gZi-brjid *edited and translated*. London: Oxford University Press, 1967.

Stein, Rolf A. "The Indigenous Religion and the *Bon po* in Dunhuang Manuscripts." In *Rolf Stein's Tibetiqua Antica*, transl. and ed. Arthur P. McKeown, pp. 231–271. Leiden: Brill's Tibetan Studies Library 24, 2010.

Stein, Rolf A. "Bonpo Accounts on the First Men." In *Rolf Stein's Tibetiqua Antica*, transl. and ed. Arthur P. McKeown, pp. 307–313. Leiden: Brill's Tibetan Studies Library 24, 2010.

Steinmann, Brigitte. "Les *lHa srin sde brgyad* et le problème de leur catégorisation. Une Interprétation." *Revue d'Études Tibétaines* 2 (2003), pp. 81–91.

Strassberg, Richard E. *Wandering Spirits: Chen Shiyuan's Encyclopedia of Dreams*. Berkeley: University of California Press, 2008.

Taylor, Thomas. *The Mystical Hymns of Orpheus, Translated from the Greek, and Demonstrated to be the Invocations which were used in the Eleusinian Mysteries*. London: Bertram Dobell, 1896.

Watson, Burton. transl. *The Complete Works of Zhuangzi*. New York: Columbia University Press, 2013.

White, Robert J. transl. and comment. *The Interpretation of Dreams: The Oneirocritica of Artemidorus*. Park Ridge: Noyes Press, 1975.

Young, Serenity. *Dreaming in the Lotus. Buddhist Dream Narrative, Imagery & Practice*. Boston: Wisdom Publications, 1999.

CHAPTER 8

Vibhūticandra's *Svapnohana* and the Examination of Dreams

Rolf Scheuermann

1 Introduction

Techniques aimed at coping with the uncertainties of the future are found in both premodern and modern cultures and can be regarded as a constant in the history of mankind. Following the European Enlightenment and the radical departure from the medieval world-view that it propagated, traditional forms of prognostication, particularly mantic practices, have been widely stigmatized as "superstition" in the West. A quick glance at the Tibetan cultural context reveals that divinatory practices do not only play a role in the secular or private context but are deeply rooted in the religious practices of Buddhism and Bon. They range from astrology, oracles, and prophecies to different techniques that involve coins, dice, rosaries, mirrors, ropes, scapulimancy, and the drawing of lots.[1] Yet a further category of divinatory techniques examines and interprets natural signs, such as coincidences in the meeting of individuals, natural phenomena, or the behavior of animals, but may also cover the practice of *sa dpyad* or geomancy.[2] This category also includes the examination of signs in dreams, which is the focus of this article that centers on a short oneiromantic text contained in the *bsTan 'gyur*, the *Svapnohana* by Vibhūticandra (12th–13th cent.).

---

1 For a comprehensive overview of the different practices, see Nebesky-Wojkowitz, *Oracles and Demons of Tibet*, 409–466.

2 For a presentation of the chapter on geomancy of the *Vaiḍūrya dkar po*, see Maurer, *Die Grundlagen der tibetischen Geomantie dargestellt anhand des 32. Kapitels des* Vaiḍūrya dkar po *von* sde srid *Sangs rgyas rgya mtsho* (1653–1705).

© KONINKLIJKE BRILL NV, LEIDEN, 2020 | DOI:10.1163/9789004410688_009

2   Remarks about the Taxonomy of Tibetan Divinatory Techniques[3]

Starting with the famous differentiation in the "two kinds of divination, the one involving a technique, the other involving nature"[4] found in Cicero's *De Divinatione* (1.11), taxonomies of different traditional forms of prognostication in the West evolved. So far, I did not come across a written record of a traditional Tibetan Buddhist taxonomy for different divinatory practices, but a certain hierarchy can be deduced from Buddhist thought.[5] Quite naturally, prophecies are considered to have sprung forth from a direct perception of reality of a religious adept who is considered to be a person of authority (*tshad ma'i skyes bu*),[6] such as the Buddha, a wisdom deity or certain revered masters. Constituting a means of valid cognition in themselves, they are hence deemed to possess a supreme type of foreknowledge. By definition, such prophecies are then defined as being untainted by ignorance and worldly motives.

In contrast, other divinatory practices—with the exception of spirit-mediumship—depend on different types of inferential or second-hand knowledge. However, from a Buddhist doctrinal stance, spirit-mediumship should be considered as being inferior to most other methods as the information received is not based on a person of authority, such as a dharma guardian or *dharmapāla* that is believed to have transcended the world (*'jig rten las 'das pa'i srung ma*), but on a worldly deity (*'jig rten pa'i lha*) or worldly *dharmapāla* (*'jig rten pa'i srung ma*).[7] As René de Nebesky-Wojkowitz noted, "none of these high-ranking guardians of religion would condescend to interfere with more or less mundane affairs by speaking through the mouth of a medium,"[8] and a prediction cast by

---

3   The following observations are reflections based on my own examinations and a discussion with the contemporary Tibetan Buddhist master, Trehor Lama Thubten Phuntsok. The interview took place at the Bodhi Path Buddhist center, Renchen-Ulm, Germany, December 9, 2016.

4   Wardle, *Cicero: on Divination. Book 1*, 49.

5   While divination plays an important role in Tibetan Buddhist practice, its role in Buddhist soteriology is generally neither defined nor addressed in Tibetan presentations of the Buddhist path. This is quite different in the Bon tradition, where divination is presented in the first of the nine vehicles (*theg pa dgu*), the *Phywa gshen theg pa*. See Snellgrove, *The Nine Ways of Bon*.

6   Steinkellner, *Tshad ma'i skyes bu. Meaning and Historical Significance of the Term*.

7   An interesting example is the gNas chung oracle, which involves the *dharmapāla* Pe har (or related deities such as *rDo rje grags ldan*), a previously local Tibetan spirit believed to have been tamed and turned into the protector of bSam yas monastery by Padmasambhava. Even though Pe har is categorized as a worldly deity, it ascended to a central position as the state oracle of Tibet with an influence on political decision-making. For a presentation of the evolution of Pe har, see Shen-Yu, *Pehar: A Historical Survey*.

8   Nebesky-Wojkowitz, *Oracles and Demons of Tibet*, 409.

a spirit-medium invoking a worldly deity is deemed fallible since its source of information is not trustworthy. Such a deity may have either its personal motif to cast a wrong prediction or its capacity of foreknowledge is flawed or limited.[9] On the contrary, the majority of Tibetan cleromantic practices involve invocations of the blessing and inspiration of the Buddha, revered Buddhist deities and/or Buddhist masters,[10] which is meant to guarantee the efficacy of the divination. The assumed efficacy of the practice is grounded in the doctrine of *pratītyasamūtpāda* or dependent arising, the notion that things do not manifest randomly, but occur due to an interplay of causes and conditions. It is believed that through the application of cleromantic practices by a skilled diviner, in combination with divine intervention, one can tap into the current state of affairs of causes and conditions, which allows a prediction of what is to come.

Oneiromancy, the examination of dreams (*rmi lam brtag pa*), however, has a special status among the divinatory practices in Buddhism. While a certain hierarchy can be established among the different divinatory techniques, the main criterion safeguarding the efficacy of a prediction remains the religious authority of the person that employs the method or other agents that are involved in the process. In the case of oneiromancy, it is believed that an experienced Buddhist master skilled in dream yoga has the capacity to correctly interpret signs in dreams. As Torricelli noted, dreams can become a path, and "being a 'Path' where tantric practices are involved, it would be more correct to designate the purified dream as a 'direct experience' (*mngon sum*) instead of 'valid cognition' (*tshad ma*)."[11] Furthermore, oneiromancy occurs frequently as a theme in hagiographies of important religious figures, foreboding important events or developments, as has been addressed already by Alexander Wayman.[12]

There is, for example, the famous account of the dream of Māyādevī, the mother of Prince Siddhārtha or the Buddha, which is found in various canonical Buddhist scriptures and has frequently been depicted in Buddhist art. In this dream, Māyādevī sees how a white elephant circumambulates her three times and enters her body from the right side. This dream is then brought

---

9   For a presentation of the origin of spirit-mediumship in Bon and Tibetan Buddhism, see Bellezza, *Spirit-Mediums, Sacred Mountains and Related Bon Textual Traditions in Upper Tibet.*

10 Cf. the cleromantic practices contained in the following collections of divination manuals: *Mo dpe dang sa dpyad rmi lam brtag thabs* (BDRC W21880) and *Mo dpe sna tshogs* (BDRC W23716).

11 Torricelli, *Tibetan Literature on Dreams*, 62.

12 Wayman, *Significance of Dreams in India and Tibet*, 2–3.

before the Brahmins for examination, who consequently produce the famous prediction that her future son, the Prince Siddhārtha, will either become a great saint or a universal monarch.[13] A well-known episode from the life-story of sGam po pa bSod nams rin chen (1079–1153), one of the founding fathers of the bKa' brgyud tradition of Tibetan Buddhism, also attests to this. It recounts a prophetic dream of a man wearing white clothes imparting *Mahāmudrā* teachings to bSod nams rin chen, which foretells the meeting with his later teacher Mi la ras pa.[14]

Furthermore, some Tibetan Buddhist religious writings describe the Buddhist path as a process, which aims at awakening from the sleep of ignorance due to understanding that all phenomena resemble dream-illusions, and that one thus comes to see ultimate reality (*paramārthasatya, don dam gyi bden pa*).[15] From a Buddhist doctrinal point of view, Tibetan Buddhist oneiromantic texts are associated with the level of apparent reality (*saṃvṛtisatya, kun rdzob kyi bden pa*) and its workings, where dream appearances can be understood as omens foreshadowing events or circumstances in this or future lifetimes. Still, oneiromancy is not only used to predict the future. Concerning pathogenesis in the context of Tibetan medicine, it also occurs, for example, as a diagnostic technique, particularly if it is suspected that the patient suffers from a disease that has been caused through the influence of a potentially harmful spirit (*gdon nad*).[16]

3   Vibhūticandra's *Svapnohana*

3.1   *The Text and Its Author*

The *bsTan 'gyur* preserves Tibetan versions of two short stand-alone oneiromantic texts that present reference lists of omens along with guidelines for their interpretation: the *Svapnohana* (Tôh. no. 1749)[17] attributed to Vibhūtican-

---

13   See Nidānakathā in Jā I. For a translation of the relevant passage, see Rhys, *Buddhist Birth Stories*, 149–151. See also Young, *Dreaming in the Lotus*, 21–24.

14   Trungram Gyaltrul Rinpoche, *Gampopa, the Monk and the Yogi*, 50.

15   See, e.g., the *Chos bzhi mdor bsdus pa legs* by sGam po pa bSod nams rin chen. For the Tibetan text and its English translation, see Scheuermann, *When Sūtra Meets Tantra*, 193–199.

16   Chapters 77–81 of the medical treatise *rGyud bzhi* deals with diseases caused by demonic forces, and chapter 73 discusses the same topic from the perspective of pediatrics.

17   For the sDe dge-edition, see *bsTan 'gyur*, BDRC W23703, vol. 28, 266–269. For the dPe bsdur ma-edition of the *bsTan 'Gyur*, see BDRC W1PD95844, vol. 14, 1301–1305.

dra (12th–13th cent.), and the *Svapnekṣā* (Tôh. no. 2100)[18] attributed to Maitrī-pāda (11th cent.). The titles of both works have been rendered in Tibetan as *rMi lam brtag pa* or the *Examination of Dreams*.[19] With a length of merely four folios, the *Svapnohana* is a concise text, but it is still slightly longer than the *Svapnekṣā*. Nevertheless, both works form an essential link between the Indian and the Tibetan tradition of dream examination. While Serenity Young already discussed and partially translated the *Svapnekṣā*,[20] the *Svapnohana* has so far not been treated by Western scholars. This article will therefore shortly introduce the work and discuss as well as analyze some of the notions described therein. It further presents translations of some excerpts of selected stanzas, which have been prepared on the basis of the Tibetan *sDe dge*-edition that has been read against the comparative *dPe bsdur ma*-edition.

The author of the *Svapnohana*, the Bengalese Buddhist master Vibhūtican-dra, was a tantric master active during the later spread of the doctrine in Tibet during the second half of the 12th century. According to Cyrus Stearns, he studied Buddhist and non-Buddhist subjects at Vikramaśīla under his teacher Śākyaśrībhadra, accompanied the latter to Tibet for the first time in 1204, and played an important role in the Tibetan Kālacakra transmission.[21] Acting as Śākyaśrībhadra's translator, he came in contact with several Tibetan Buddhist masters of his time, such as 'Bri gung 'Jig rten mgon po (1143–1217). All in all, he visited Tibet three times and spent around fifteen years there.[22]

---

18   For the sDe dge-edition, see *bsTan 'gyur*, BDRC W23703, vol. 49, 261–262. For the dPe bsdur ma-edition of the *bsTan 'Gyur*, see BDRC W1PD95844, vol. 25, 354–357.

19   While *svapna-* means dream, the Sanskrit *īkṣa-* in *Svapnekṣā* can be translated as "examination," but *ūhana-* would more literally correspond to "inferring" or "reasoning." Furthermore, it should be noted here that there are a few later Tibetan works on dream examination that carry the same title. Thus, it rather seems to be a genre classification than an actual title. One of these works, the *rMi lam brtag pa* by sGra tshad pa Rin chen rnam rgyal (1318–1388), has been introduced in this volume by Charles Ramble. The lineage of this work could be related to that of Vibhūticandra as it can be traced back to Vikhyātadeva, teacher of Vibhūticandra's teacher Buddhaśrī (Stearns, *Life and Tibetan Legacy of Vibhūticandra*, 129–130). Still, it focuses on omens that indicate future rebirths, a subject that is not at all addressed by Vibhūticandra.

20   Young, *Dreaming in the Lotus*, 137–146.

21   Stearns, *Life and Tibetan Legacy of Vibhūticandra*, 127–129.

22   Even though a superficial examination of works by 'Jig rten mgon po and his early disciples does not suggest that dream divination features prominently in his writings, a brief work on how to avert bad dreams and bad portents is attributed to him. See 'Jig rten mgon po, *rMi lam ngan pa dang mtshan ma ngan pa 'jig pa byed pa* [*The Elimination of Bad Dreams and Bad Omens*].

While there are controversies about the authenticity of other works attributed to Vibhūticandra,[23] the *Svapnohana* occurs in an enumeration of texts composed by Vibhūticandra authored by the scholar bCom ldan Rig pa'i ral gri (1235–1315?).[24] Hence, it has been considered a work by Vibhūticandra since at least the late 13th or early 14th century. This attribution of authorship is further reflected in its colophon that states:

> This concludes the "Examination of Dreams." The East Indian Paṇḍita Vibhūticandra has translated it himself.[25]

Unfortunately, time and location of its composition in Sanskrit and/or the Tibetan translation are not known, and the Sanskrit version is not available.

3.2 *The Structure of the* Svapnohana

The *Svapnohana* is a short poetic work that consists of thirty-six stanzas of mostly four lines and seven syllables each, but this is not applied consistently.[26] This gives the impression that the work is indeed a translation of a poetic Sanskrit work, and that its translator struggled to maintain a homogeneous style, but was not able to do so in all instances. The stanzas are framed by, at the beginning, a very brief salutation and a statement of composition, and at the end, a colophon. The salutation consists of a line of paying homage to the Buddha,[27] and a statement of the composition of two lines. The latter informs the reader that the work will elaborate on the examination of a multitude of dreams that can occur.[28] The main part begins with a short discussion of the time of dreaming that spans over two stanzas. This is then followed by thirty-three stanzas that deal with descriptions of good and bad omens, i.e., dreams caused by virtuous or non-virtuous *karman*, adhering to the Indian classification of auspicious (*śubha*) and inauspicious (*aśubha*) omens.[29] It is succeeded by a stanza that briefly elaborates on the benefits of reciting the famous *Gāyatrī* mantra,[30] particularly highlighting its apotropaic capacity to prevent bad

---

23 Stearns, *Life and Tibetan Legacy of Vibhūticandra*, 129–130.
24 Ibid., 150–151, particularly fn. 83. According to Cyrus Stearns, the work has probably been authored before 1283.
25 *Svapnohana*, bsTan 'gyur, vol. 28, 269, 4: *rmi lam brtag pa rdzogs so|| ||rgya gar shar phyogs kyi paṇ ḍi ta bi bhū ti candras rang 'gyur du mdzad pa'o||*.
26 The fourth and six stanzas, for example, consist of four lines with eleven syllables each.
27 Ibid., 266₄: *sangs rgyas la phyag 'tshal lo.*
28 Ibid., 266₄: *rmi lam sna tshogs las byung ba| |de yi brtag pa bshad par bya||.*
29 Alexander Wayman, *Significance of Dreams in India and Tibet*, 3.
30 The famous *Gāyatrī* mantra is a part of the important rite of passage indicating the begin-

VIBHŪTICANDRA'S SVAPNOHANA AND THE EXAMINATION OF DREAMS   167

dreams when recited at home. The work then concludes with the earlier cited brief colophon.

3.3   *On the Time of Dreaming*
The explanation concerned found in the *Svapnohana* is actually very brief so that it can be quoted here in full:

> If the dream occurs in the first watch (of the night), a result is brought forth within one year. One will undoubtedly come to see [the result] during eight months, [if the dream occurs] in the second watch, during three months, [if it occurs] in the third watch, or during half a month [if it occurs] during the fourth watch. [If it occurs] at the time when dawn breaks, a result is brought forth within ten days.[31]

Interestingly, an almost identical presentation is found in an extensive Indian oneiromantic work, the *Svapnacintāmaṇi* of Jagaddeva (12th cent.).[32] The corresponding passage differs only in the suggested periods needed for a result to arise, which also starts out with one year, but then varies slightly, in that the second watch indicates that the result will occur within half a year, the third watch three months, the fourth watch one month, the last forty-eight minutes of the night ten days, and sunrise indicates that the result will occur immediately.[33]

The afore-mentioned *Svapnekṣā* attributed to Maitrīpāda, however, shares a very different view on the subject. It suggests that the time during which a dream occurs indicates whether a related omen is more or less meaningful or

---

      ning of a student's vedic studies, the *upanayana*. The mantra is generally believed to represent the essence of the vedas.

31   *Svapnohana*, *bsTan 'gyur*, vol. 28, 266$_{4-5}$: *dang po'i thun la rmi lam byung| |lo gcig nang du 'bras bu 'byin| |thun gnyis zla ba brgyad bar la| |thun gsum zla ba gsum gyi bar| |thun bzhi zla ba phyed bar du| mthong bar 'gyur ba the tshom med| |skya rengs shar ba'i dus nyid la| |zhag bcu'i nang du 'bras bu 'byin||.*

32   For the Sanskrit text along with a German translation, see Negelein, *Der Traumschlüssel des Jagaddeva.*

33   Ibid., 1.15–17: "Ein Traum, der in der ersten Nachtwache gesehen wird, geht nach einem Jahre in Erfüllung; in einem halben Jahre erfüllt sich ein Traum, der in der zweiten Nachtwache gesehen ist." ... 1.16: "Nach Ablauf dreier Monate erfüllt sich für die Menschen sicherlich ein Traum der dritten Nachtwache; nach einem Monate muß ein in der vierten Nachtwache gesehener Traum zur Wirklichkeit werden." ... 1.17: "Ein in der Zeit der letzten beiden ghaṭikā (= der letzten 48 Minuten) der Nacht geträumter Traum geht sicherlich innerhalb 10 Tagen in Erfüllung. Ein Traum aber, der bei Sonnenaufgang gesehen ist, verwirklicht sich sofort."

trustworthy, a notion that is already present in the *Caraka Saṃhitā*,[34] but also in later Tibetan works on the examination of dreams.[35] According to the presentation of the *Svapnekṣā*, it is mainly the dreams that occur at dawn that are considered to be very significant. Here, the relevant passage of the *Svapnekṣā* in the translation of Serenity Young:

> In the first part of the night habitual propensities (*bag chags*) are agitated; in the second part of the night ghosts are active; so examine the dream that comes in the third part of the night.[36]

The view taken in the *Svapnohana* is, however, quite different in that dreams that occur during all of the four parts of the night are considered meaningful and are believed to convey information on future circumstances—if interpreted correctly. In this work, the time of dreaming is not treated as an indicator for the question whether an information is reliable or not, but relevant for determining the time that remains until the predicted circumstance will occur.

3.4 *Omens Described in the* Svapnohana

3.4.1 Auspicious Omens

The following section presents a list of omens that indicate future circumstances, which are the result of virtuous and non-virtuous deeds or *karman* along with an explanation of their meaning. While the *Svapnohana* is a brief text, the signs described are still varied. The text commences with a couple of typical auspicious omens that foretell future good circumstances caused by good deeds, such as obtaining wealth, qualities, positions, a son, a partner or combinations of these. A few examples that show how the *Svapnohana* addresses these subjects are given below. Please note that in each case, passages in the *Svapnacintāmaṇi* of Jagaddeva that closely correspond or are related to them are referenced in the footnotes.

---

34 Young, *Dreaming in the Lotus*, 67.

35 For example, the *rMi ltas sna tshogs brtag thabs* by Ngag dbang Blo bzang, which has been discussed by Charles Ramble in this volume.

36 Young, *Dreaming in the Lotus*, 138. Svapnekṣā, bsTan 'gyur, vol. 49, 261_{2-3}: *dang po'i cha ni bag chags 'khrug| |gnyis par yi d[w]ags rgyu bar 'gyur| |tha mar rmi lam brtags la nyal||*.

VIBHŪTICANDRA'S SVAPNOHANA AND THE EXAMINATION OF DREAMS

3.4.1.1   *Obtaining wealth*

If a person [dreams of] climbing trees with milk and fruits alone or [of] sitting on them when waking up, [the person] will quickly obtain wealth.[37]

If someone's left hand has been seized by a white snake [in a dream], that [person] is thus certain to obtain riches within truly ten [days].[38]

3.4.1.2   *Obtaining Qualities*

(Dreaming of) drinking a blood beverage, or else, drinking a beer completely—if [the person] is a Brahmin, (it indicates that) [he or she] will obtain intelligence, and [for] all others [that they] will obtain riches.[39]

---

[37]   *Svapnohana*, *bsTan 'gyur*, vol. 28, 267₁: *shing ljon 'o ma 'bras bu can| |gang gis gcig pu de la 'dzegs| |de la 'dug na gnyid sad na| |myur du nor ni 'thob par 'gyur*. Negelein, *Der Traumschlüssel des Jagaddeva*, 93, 1.86: "Wer im Traume einen Baum mit Milchsaft, vielen Früchten und dichtem Schatten besteigt und auf demselben (noch stehend) erwacht, der erlangt Schätze." If one wonders what such a tree with milk or a tree emitting milk is, an answer is again found in Jagaddeva's *Svapnacintāmaṇi*, where several trees that emit milky fluids are listed, among others the Ficus religiosa or Bodhi tree. Ibid., 156, 1.146: "Die Gewächse: Ficus Tjakela Burm., Ficus religiosa, Aegle Marmelos, Ficus indica, Feronia elephantum oder ein anderer Baum mit milchartigem Saft sind für denjenigen, der sie im Traume sieht, bekommt oder von ihnen genießt, glückbringend."

[38]   *Svapnohana*, *bsTan 'gyur*, vol. 28, 268₆: *gang zhig khrag gi btung ba 'thungs| |yang na chang ni rab tu 'thungs| |bram ze yin na rig pa thob| de las gzhan ni nor thob 'gyur||*. An exact correspondence is again found in a stanza of the *Svapnacintāmaṇi*. Negelein, *Der Traumschlüssel des Jagaddeva*, 44, 1.109: "Wer von einer weißen Haubenschlange in seinen rechten Arm gebissen wird, erlangt in 5 Tagen 1000 Goldstücke." Cf. also Ibid., 115–116. That "to be bitten by a snake in a dream generally indicates great wealth (蛇蛟人主得大財)" can also be found in the context of dream examination in Chinese Chan Buddhism. Smith, *Meditation, Divination and Dream Interpretation*, 15.

[39]   *Svapnohana*, *bsTan 'gyur*, vol. 28, 268₆: *gang zhig khrag gi btung ba 'thungs| |yang na chang ni rab tu 'thungs| |bram ze yin na rig pa thob| de las gzhan ni nor thob 'gyur||*. Dreaming of drinking blood generally points to obtaining wealth, as is indicated also by two verses found in the *Svapnacintāmaṇi*. Negelein, *Der Traumschlüssel des Jagaddeva*, 52, 1.37: "Wer Urin, das semen virile oder Blut genießt und vor diesen keinen Ekel empfindet, wer es anblickt und sich damit besudelt,—auch dieser dürfte einen Zuwachs erfahren." A further verse discusses drinking alcoholic beverages, and suggests that a brahmin who dreams this, will obtain the drink of soma, which grants extraordinary powers, and all others will obtain wealth. Ibid., 68, 1.60: "Wenn ein Mann ein Getränk von einer Flüssigkeit, die nicht getrunken werden darf, zu sich nimmt, oder, wenn er gefesselt ist, wieder loskommt, so

Listen! If someone eats human flesh in a dream—cooked or raw, either is fine—the qualities of that person will abound. [40]

3.4.1.3   Obtaining Positions

Whose intestines (magically) bind a village or a town, will become a local ruler if a village was bound, or a king if a town was bound.[41]

3.4.1.4   Obtaining a Partner

Someone who awakens from sleep after dreaming that [he or she] obtains a mare, a domestic fowl or a sarus crane,[42] will thereby then obtain a sweetheart. [This] is called "a spouse is close-by."[43]

---

bedeutet dies für ihn, wenn er Priester ist, Somatrank, anderenfalls aber soll der Erfolg in Geld und Wohlstand bestehen."

40 *Svapnohana, bsTan 'gyur*, vol. 28, 267$_3$: *mi dag gi ni sha rnams ni| |btsos sam ma btsos gang yang rung| |rmi lam du ni gang gis zos| |nyon cig de yi yon tan gang||*. Eating human flesh is also mentioned as an auspicious omen in the *Svapnacintāmaṇi*, however, it is restricted there to raw flesh and is said to indicate offspring and rulership. *Der Traumschlüssel des Jagaddeva*, 48, 1.32: "Wer Menschenfleisch oder sein eigenes Fleisch in (noch) rohem Zustande im Traume nach Herzenslust genießt, erlangt Nachkommenschaft und Herrschaft." Cooked meat is generally described in the *Svapnacintāmaṇi* as a bad omen. Cf. Ibid., 226, 2.27.

41 *Svapnohana, bsTan 'gyur*, vol. 28, 267$_4$: *gang gi rgyu mas grong dang ni| |yang na grong khyer dkris pa ni |grong gcig dkris na rgyal phran thob| |grong khyer dkris na rgyal po thob|*. Again, an almost identical description is found in the *Svapnacintāmaṇi*. Negelein, *Der Traumschlüssel des Jagaddeva*, 70, 1.62: "Wer im Traume mit seinen Eingeweiden als mit Zaubermitteln eine Stadt oder ein Dorf umgarnt, wird in der Stadt Fürst, im Dorf Provinzoberhaupt."

42 The Tibetan term *kra uñtsi* probably refers to a bird that in Sanskrit is called *krauñca-* or *kruñca-*. According to Julia Leslie, this refers to the Indian sarus crane, but different dictionaries suggest that it refers to the curlew, heron or snipe. See Leslie, *The Identity and Significance of Vālmīki's Krauñca*.

43 *Svapnohana, bsTan 'gyur*, vol. 28, 268$_{3-4}$: *rgod ma khyim bya kra uñtsi| |thob nas gang gi gnyid sad na| |de yis de dus snying sdug 'thob| chung ma nye du smra ba can||*. The *Svapnacintāmaṇi* contains an almost identical verse. Negelein, *Der Traumschlüssel des Jagaddeva*, 109, 1.104: "Wer im Traume eine Stute, ein Brachvogelweibchen oder eine Henne empfing und wach wird, findet ein Mädchen mit Geld oder eine süß redende Schöne."

VIBHŪTICANDRA'S SVAPNOHANA AND THE EXAMINATION OF DREAMS   171

3.4.1.5 *Obtaining a Son*

Someone who has been captured and bound, or else, whose hands are tied with a rope, will thus obtain a son. Alternatively, [he or she] will become someone in a high position.[44]

Travel is a further subject that is addressed in the *Svapnohana*, and dreaming of riding a boat is considered a good sign for travelers:

Someone who rides a boat, and will be rescued even if [he or she] shipwrecks, is known to travel his or her path. He or she is also certain to return quickly.[45]

Signs that offer indications for those who inquire about sickness or health are also found in the *Svapnohana*:

If a person perceives an orb of the sun in a dream, or else, [an orb] of the moon, the sick person will be freed from sickness, and if [the person] has no sickness, [he or she] will become a Glorious One.[46]

3.4.2 Inauspicious Omens

While all of the portents introduced up to this point were auspicious ones, the *Svapnohana* offers also descriptions of inauspicious omens. However, since only six of the thirty-three stanzas that make up the section that discusses

---

44   *Svapnohana, bsTan 'gyur*, vol. 28, 268$_4$: *gang gis bzung nas bcings pa dang| | yang na lag pa zhags pas btab| |de las bu ni thob par 'gyur| |yang na gnas pa chen por 'gyur||*. Again, an almost verbatim identical stanza is found in the *Svapnacintāmaṇi*. Negelein, *Der Traumschlüssel des Jagaddeva*, 69, 1.61: "Sollte einer mit festen, bis zu den Knieen reichenden Banden oder Armfesseln gebunden werden, so erlangt er einen Sohn, soziale Stellung und Position ohne Mühe."

45   *Svapnohana, bsTan 'gyur*, vol. 28, 267$_5$: *gang zhig gru la zhon nas ni| |zhig pa yin yang yang dag sgrol| |de yi lam bgrod shes par bya| |de yang myur du ldog par nges||*. A closely related stanza is again found in the *Svapnacintāmaṇi*. Negelein, *Der Traumschlüssel des Jagaddeva*, 57, 1.44: "Wer ein Boot besteigt und auf diesem, ohne daß es zerbricht, gut übersetzt, kehrt, nachdem er eine Reise unternommen hat, alsbald erfolgreich zurück."

46   *Svapnohana, bsTan 'gyur*, vol. 28, 268$_{2-3}$: *nyi ma'i dkyil 'khor rmi lam du| |yang na zla ba gang gis mthong| |nad can nad las grol ba dang| |nad med yin na dpal ldan 'gyur||*. Once again one finds a corresponding stanza in the *Svapnacintāmaṇi*, where seeing sun and moon discs in a dream is said to indicate fortune. Negelein, *Der Traumschlüssel des Jagaddeva*, 107, 1.101: "Wer Sonne und Mond im Traume mit vollen Scheiben neu aufgegangen sieht, an diesem erfreut sich die Göttin des Fürstenglückes."

172   SCHEUERMANN

omens are concerned with inauspicious omens, they represent a significant yet comparatively smaller proportion of the work. Inauspicious omens presented in the *Svapnohana* address the following subjects:

- financial loss and sickness (omens: a crevice or an earthquake occurs),[47]
- danger caused by a person of authority (omens: animals with horns or fangs, monkeys, and pigs),[48]
- sickness (omens: to apply sesame butter, milk or butter),[49] and death being imminent (omens: mounting a chariot with a donkey or a camel and waking up while being on it,[50] being embraced by a red woman[51]).

3.4.3   Colors

In general, color plays an important role in the *Svapnohana*, and particularly red, white, black and yellow are discussed. Black and white, as one might expect, are respectively considered as inauspicious and auspicious omens:

> (Dreaming of) black (things) other than Brahmins, cattle, ox, and deities is very bad. (Dreaming of) white (things) other than skull cups, cotton wool, ashes, and bones is truly excellent.[52]

There are also four stanzas[53] that discuss dreaming of women with attributes of different colors. Here, red is considered inauspicious in that dreaming of being embraced by a woman with a red dress, red garland and red talc indicates that

---

47   The *Svapnacintāmaṇi* also lists crevices (e.g. Ibid., 262, 2.60) and earthquakes (e.g. Ibid., 311, 2.94) among the inauspicious omens.

48   Cf. Ibid., 370, 2.151: "Wenn im Traume ein Tier mit langen Hörnern. oder großen Zähnen, ein Affe oder ein wilder Eber jemanden anrennt, so erfährt er Heimsuchung durch das Fürstenhaus."

49   Cf. Ibid., 325, 2.107: "Salbung der Glieder oder Trinken von sauerem Reisschleim, Honig, flüssiger Butter, Sesamöl, (mit Wasser vermischter) Buttermilch und anderen fettigen Substanzen bringt den Menschen Unglück."

50   Cf. Ibid., 273, 2.68: "Wenn ein einzelner Mann einen von Eseln oder Kamelen gezogenen Wagen besteigt, und, auf demselben stehend, erwacht, bedeutet dies sicherlich seinen Tod."

51   See also the following discussion of colors.

52   *Svapnohana, bsTan 'gyur*, vol. 28, 268₄₋₅: *bram zer phyugs dang glang chen lha| |gzhan dag nag po shin tu ngan| |thod pa ras bal thal ba rus| |gzhan rnams dkar po mngon par dga'||*. This corresponds again to a stanza of the *Svapnacintāmaṇi*, which informs one in stanza 150 that everything black indicates misfortune, except for cattle, kings, horses, elephants and gods, and that everything which is white indicates fortune, except for cotton, salt, bones and ashes. Negelein, *Der Traumschlüssel des Jagaddeva*, 160, 1.150: "Alles Schwarze bedeutet Unglück mit Ausnahme von Rindern, Königen, Pferden, Elefanten und Göttern; dagegen alles Weiße Glück mit Ausnahme von Baumwolle, Salz, Knochen und Asche."

53   Ibid., 268₁₋₃.

VIBHŪTICANDRA'S SVAPNOHANA AND THE EXAMINATION OF DREAMS   173

one will die within one day.[54] On the contrary, being embraced by a woman with the identical attributes in white (every splendor will occur),[55] yellow (one will obtain political authority), or black (an increase of splendor) is presented as auspicious. These four stanzas are puzzling and show some inconsistencies in that the occurrence of the color black in relation to an auspicious omen is in stark contrast to the explanation that black is usually considered an inauspicious omen in the stanza presented above.[56]

While the explanations of omens discussed so far were all more or less in line with those found in the *Svapnacintāmaṇi*, this part deviates clearly from the explanation found therein. Contrary to what we find here, Jagaddeva describes dreaming of a woman with a black dress as an inauspicious omen indicating death[57] and dreaming of a woman with a yellow dress as an inauspicious omen indicating sickness.[58]

3.5 Specifically Indian Dream Images Found in the Svapnohana
Some of the omens described in the *Svapnohana* may not have been very common to the daily life of the majority of people living on the Himalayan plateau and are witnesses of an interesting facet of cultural exchange processes between India and Tibet. Lotus ponds, for instance, may not have been very frequent in Tibet:

> Someone who (dreams that he or she) sits within large lotus petals in the center of a pond, eating yogurt or milk soup, will undoubtedly become a landlord.[59]

---

54   Cf. Ibid., 266, 2.62: "Wenn eine schöne Frau mit rotgeschminkten Gliedern, rotem Gewand und rotem Kranz im Traume jemanden umarmt, so bedeutet dies sicherlich Brahmanenmord."

55   A corresponding stanza is found in the Svapnacintāmaṇi. Ibid., 75, 1.68: "Wen eine schöne junge Frau umarmt, die mit weißen Salben geschmückt ist und ein weißes Kleid trägt, einem solchen ist die Glücksgöttin immer wie eine Freundin zugewandt."

56   This could, of course, be explained by understanding the different women as representing female deities, which has been defined as an exception. However, dreaming of black women has also been described as a sign foreboding one's death in the *rMi ltas sna tshogs brtag thabs* presented by Charles Ramble in this volume. Cf. Nebesky-Wojkowitz, *Oracles and Demons of Tibet*, 465.

57   Ibid., 267, 2.63: "Wenn ein junges Mädchen, deren (am) Körper (getragene) Schlingpflanzen (oder: deren Glieder, die Schlingpflanzen gleichen) trocken sind, die mit schwarzen Salben geschmückt ist und ein schwarzes Gewand trägt, im Traume jemanden umarmt, so ist ihm der Gang in das Haus des Todes nahe."

58   Ibid., 268, 2.64: "Wenn eine junge Frau mit schrecklichen Augenbrauen und gelber Kleidung und Salbe im Traume jemanden umarmt, dann dürfte mannigfache Krankheit entstehen."

59   *Svapnohana, bsTan 'gyur*, vol. 28, 267₂: *gang zhig rdzing bu'i dkyil du ni| |padma'i 'dab ma*

174 SCHEUERMANN

This also holds true for elephants:

> [Dreaming of being] a rider, riding on the mount of an ox or an elephant, being [in] a mansion, [at] a mountain peak, [on top of a] majestic forest tree or in a boat, holding a lute, and eating food [indicates that] one will continuously obtain material goods.[60]

Brahmins, elephants, lotus ponds and the like, are images that originally belong to a different cultural sphere characterized by very different circumstances of life. Nevertheless, through a process of cultural appropriation in literature, art, and religious practice, they seem to have found their way into Tibetan dreams.

4   Some Related Dream Images in Tibetan and Indian Works on Buddhist Religion

A comparison with two short passages of the *Phyag chen rgyas pa nges don rgya mtsho* or the *Extensive Treatise on Mahāmudrā, the Ocean of Definitive Meaning*,[61] by Karmapa dBang phyug rDo rje (1556–1601/3), shows some apparent similarities. This work is a very influential commentary on the preliminary practices of *Mahāmudrā (phyag chen sngon 'gro)* of the Karma bKa' brgyud tradition of Tibetan Buddhism and serves as an example for how the exami-

---

chen po'i nang| |zho dang 'o thug za byed pa| |sa bdag 'thob par the tshom med||. Again, one finds the almost exact same wording in the *Svapnacintāmaṇi*. Ibid., 53, 1.38: "Wer, auf einem Lotusblatte sitzend, mitten in einem Teiche Reis, in Milch gekocht, mit flüssiger Butter und feinem Zucker genießt, wird eine Respektsperson und erlangt die Königsherrschaft."

60   *Svapnohana, bsTan 'gyur*, vol. 28, 266₆: *bzhon pa ba lang dang ni glang chen zhon pa dang| |khang bzangs ri rtse dang ni nags kyi ljon shing dang| |gru nang 'dug ste pi wang 'dzin par byed pa dang| |kha zas za zhin du byed rtag par dngos po 'thob||.* For these lines, we again find a closely related stanza in the *Svapnacintāmaṇi*. Negelein, *Der Traumschlüssel des Jagaddeva*, 79, 1.38: "Wer im Traum auf einem Stier, einem Menschen einem Elefanten, einem Pferd, einem Palast oder einer Bergspitze das Meer austrinkt, und dann erwacht, der wird Fürst werden." Here, however, the lute is not mentioned and instead of eating food, one is to drink the ocean. Negelein quotes here also an older dream manual, which resembles our text more closely, but does not specify the source further. This text also refers to the playing of the lute and mentions eating food instead of drinking the ocean as Jagaddeva does here.

61   For the Tibetan, see dBang phyug rDo rje, *Nges don rgya mtsho*. For a general English translation, see Havlat, *Mahamudra. The Ocean of True Meaning*.

VIBHŪTICANDRA'S SVAPNOHANA AND THE EXAMINATION OF DREAMS   175

nation of dreams is presented in a Tibetan Buddhist meditation manual. Up to this day, this commentary is used by both Tibetan and Western followers of the tradition as a guideline for conducting the associated meditation practices of the four uncommon preliminary practices, a set of four times 100.000 repetitions. The set consists of the following four practices: (1) recitation of a sixfold refuge-formula accompanied by physical prostrations, (2) recitation of the hundred-syllable mantra of Vajrasattva along with the meditation on the deity, (3) recitation of a short offering prayer along with the act of offering extensive *maṇḍalas*, and (4) recitation of a prayer to the guru in combination with the practice of guru-yoga.

The second practice, the Vajrasattva practice, is conducted in order to purify negative imprints in a practitioner's mind. Therefore, at the very end of the section, one finds a short list of signs in dreams meant to indicate that the process of purification from the imprints of negative deeds was successful. The list reads as follows:

> If the following [omens] occur in one's dreams, it is a sign that one has purified the negativities and defilements:
>
> One washes oneself, becomes naked, blood and pus drips from one's body, one has diarrhea, one vomits, wears white clothes, vomits bad food, drinks yogurt or milk, looks at the sun and moon, moves through the sky, one subdues a blazing fire, a buffalo or a black man, sees an assembly of monks or nuns, climbs on trees that emit milk, elephants or lordly bulls, a mountain, a lion throne or a mansion, or listens to the Dharma.[62]

The second short list found in this work concludes the section that deals with the third of the four practices, the *maṇḍala*-offerings. It is a ritual meant to let the practitioner accomplish the two accumulations of merit and wisdom that are needed to attain Buddhahood in accordance with the Mahāyāna.

> [If the following signs occur] also in one's dreams [it is a sign that one has accomplished the two accumulations]:

---

62   dBang phyug rDo rje, *Nges don rgya mtsho*, 46–47: *rmi lam du khrus byas pa| gcer bur thon pa| lus la rnag khrag 'dzag pa| 'khru pa| skyug pa| gos dkar po gyon pa sogs rmi'o|| gzhan yang zas ngan skyug pa| zho dang 'o ma 'thung ba| nyi zla mthong ba| nam mkha' la 'gro ba| me 'bar ba| ma he dang mi nag po thub pa| dge slong dang dge slong ma'i dge 'dun mthong ba| 'o ma 'byung ba'i shing dang glang po che dang khyu mchog dang| ri dang seng ge'i khri dang khang bzang rnams kyi steng du 'dzeg pa| chos nyan pa sogs rmis na sdig sgrib dag pa'i rtags so||.*

Many girls are serving food and drinks, sun and moon are shining, one walks uphill, walks through a flowery meadow and plucks flowers, one puts on new clothes or jewelry, one crosses a water and gets rescued on the other shore, one launches a boat or builds a bridge, one wipes a maṇḍala or a mirror and looks at it, one blows a conch, beats a big drum, plays music or visits a temple and so on.[63]

These lists may have their origin in Indian Buddhist works such as the following enumeration found in Śāntideva's *Śikṣāsamuccaya* that shows many similarities. There, Śāntideva instructs a practitioner to purify negative karmic imprints through reciting the *dhāraṇī* of the Buddhist goddess Cundā:

Or let him recite the Cundādhāraṇī until he sees in the sleep the tokens of the destruction of sin: namely, when he dreams of uttering various cries, or partaking of milk and whey and so forth, vomiting, staring at sun and moon, passing through the air, overcoming a black man, a bull, or blazing fire, beholding a congregation of Brethren and Sisters, climbing upon milk-trees, elephants, bulls, mountains, thrones, palaces, boats, by hearing the Law, the annulling of sin is to be indicated.[64]

This list is undoubtedly derived from oneiromantic works as well and similarities with some of the examples presented above are recognizable. However, it is noteworthy that a shift occurs concerning the temporal perspective of the divination. Dream examination in general, as found in manuals like the *Svapnohana*, focuses on predicting future events. Still, it is often also concerned with clarifying uncertainties with respect to the past (e.g., in the context of Tibetan medicine, mainly when used for etiological inquiries), or is applied to

---

63   Dbang phyug Rdo rje, *Nges don rgya mtsho*, 53: *rmi lam du'ang bud med mang pos zas skom ster ba dang| nyi zla shar ba| gyen la 'gro ba| me tog gi thang la 'gro zhing me tog 'thu ba| gos gsar gyon pa| rgyan btags pa| chu brgal bas pha rol du sgrol ba| chu la gru'am zam pa btsugs pa| maṇḍala dang me long phyi zhing lta ba| dung 'bud pa | rnga po che brdung ba| rol mo dkrol ba| lha khang lta ba sogs rmi'o||.*

64   Bendall and Rouse, *Śikshā-Samuccaya. A Compendium of Buddhist Doctrine*, 169. For the Sanskrit, see Bendall/Braarvig/Mahoney, *Śikṣāsamuccaya of Śāntideva: cundādhāraṇīṃ vā tāvaj japed yāvat pāpakṣayanimittāni paśyati svapne| tad yathā krandanādichardanadadhikṣīrādibhojanāt tu vigatapāpo bhavati| vamanād vā candrasūryadarśanād ākāśagamanāj jvalitânalamahiṣakṛṣṇapuruṣaparājayād bhikṣubhikṣuṇīsaṃghadarśanāt kṣīravṛkṣagaja vṛṣagirisiṃhâsanaprāsādanâvarohaṇād dharmaśravaṇāc ca pāpakṣayaḥ saṃlakṣayitavyaḥ ||.* Bendall, *Çikshāsamuccaya. A Compendium of Buddhist Teaching*, 173₄–7.

the present (e.g., in order to evaluate the efficacy of the current religious practice in the context of Buddhist meditation as in the two examples above).

5   Conclusions

The *Svapnohana* attributed to Vibhūticandra is a work on the examination of dreams that clearly stands in an Indian tradition of oneiromantic texts. The visible familiarity with the Indian oneiromantic tradition is a further indication that its author has been trained in India, which supports the claim that Vibhūticandra is indeed its author. Furthermore, it is apparent that the *Svapnohana* is based on the much more extensive *Svapnacintāmaṇi* of Jagaddeva or a work that is closely related to it, and may have been conceived as a summary of some of its important points. It shares a similar presentation of the time of dreaming (3.3) and mostly agrees with it concerning the explanation of omens (3.4).[65]

The focus of the *Svapnohana* is mundane topics such as health, wealth, political power, travel, marriage, sickness, death and so on. In contrast to many of the prevalent Tibetan divination practices that involve techniques such as dice divination, Buddhist rosary (*māla, 'phreng ba*) divination and the like,[66] the *Svapnohana* does not suggest remedies along with the description of bad omens. The only reference of this type is found towards the end, with the aforementioned suggestion to rely on the *Gāyatrī* mantra to prevent bad dreams. There is also nothing that characterizes the text as Buddhist, and religious practice does not seem to be the focus of this work. Still, as the excerpts of the *Phyag chen rgyas pa nges don rgya mtsho* and the *Śikṣāsamuccaya* show, omens that occur in the *Svapnohana* and other oneiromantic texts found their way also into Buddhist literature, both in India and Tibet. These two examples show how a method designed to predict future circumstances can undergo a reinterpretation, turning it into a method for inquiring into uncertain past or present circumstances. In this case, the same dream images that occur as a general indicator of a future event are then used to evaluate religious progress, which is also a further example for the deep interconnection between divinatory techniques and religious practice in Tibetan Buddhism.

---

65   In section 3.4, corresponding stanzas of the *Svapnacintāmaṇi* have been referenced in a footnote for each of the translated excerpts of the *Svapnohana*.

66   For examples of suggested remedies related to death predictions found in three manuals of different cleromantic practices, see Scheuermann, *One will quickly die!*, 119–122 (rosary divination), 124 (crow divination), and 126 (dice divination).

References

Works in Tibetan or Sanskrit (listed by title)

bsTan 'gyur

bKa' 'gyur dang bstan 'gyur (Sde dge pha phud). Delhi: Delhi Karmapae Chodhey Gyalwae Sungrab Partun Khang, 1982–1985 (BDRC W23703, 213 vols.). Cf. bsTan 'gyur dpe bsdur ma. Pec in: Krung go'i bod rig pa'i dpe skrun khang, 1994–2008 (BDRC W1PD95844, 120 vols.).

rMi lam brtag pa (Svapnekṣā, Tôh. no. 2100)

Maitrīpāda, "rMi lam brtag pa." In: bsTan 'gyur (Sde dge pha phud), vol. 49, 259–260 (BDRC W23703). Cf. bsTan 'gyur dpe bsdur ma, vol. 25, 354–357 (BDRC W1PD95844).

rMi lam brtag pa (Svapnohana, Tôh. no. 1749)

Vibhūticandra, "rMi lam brtag pa." In: bsTan 'gyur (Sde dge pha phud), vol. 28, 266–269 (BDRC W23703). Cf. bsTan 'gyur dpe bsdur ma, vol. 14, 1301–1305 (BDRC W1PD95844).

rMi lam ngan pa dang mtshan ma ngan pa 'jig pa byed pa

'Jig rten mgon po, "rMi lam ngan pa dang mtshan ma ngan pa 'jig pa byed pa." In: 'Bri gung bka' brgyud chos mdzod chen mo. Lhasa: ?, 2004 (BDRC W00JW501203; 151 vols.), vol. 24, 187.

Nges don rgya mtsho sogs

dBang phyug rDo rje [Karmapa IX. (1556–1601/03)], Phyag chen rgyas pa nges don rgya mtsho 'bring po ma rig mun sel bsdus pa chos sku mdzub tshugs bcas so. Varanasi: Vāṇa Vajravidyā dpe mdzod khang, 2006.

Śikṣāsamuccaya

Śāntideva. Bendall, Cécile, Braarvig, Jens, and Mahoney, Richard. eds. Śikṣāsamuccaya of Śāntideva. Oxford, North Canterbury: Indica et Buddhica, 2003. Accessed May 18, 2017. http://indica-et-buddhica.org/repositorium/santideva/siksasamuccaya-sanskrit-digital-text. Cf. Śāntideva, Bendall, Cecile. ed. Çikṣāsamuccaya. A Compendium of Buddhist Teaching Compiled by Çāntideva. Chiefly from Earlier Mahāyāna-Sūtras. St.-Pétersbourg: Imperial Academy of Sciences, 1902.

Works in European Languages

Bellezza, John V. Spirit-Mediums, Sacred Mountains and Related Bon Textual Traditions in Upper Tibet: Calling Down the Gods. Leiden: Brill, 2005.

Cicero, Marcus Tullius. Cicero on divination. De divinatione, book 1. Translated with Introduction and Historical Commentary by David Wardle. Oxford: Clarendon Press, 2006.

Havlat, Henrik (tr.). Mahamudra, the Ocean of True Meaning. The Profound Instructions on Coexistent Unity, the Essence of the Ocean of True Meaning, and Light Radiating Activity. Münster: Monsenstein und Vannerdat, 2009.

Jagaddeva, and Negelein, Julius von. Der Traumschlüssel des Jagaddeva. Ein Beitrag zur *indischen Mantik.* [Religionsgeschichtliche Versuche und Vorarbeiten XI., Heft 4.] Giessen: A. Töpelmann, 1912.

Leslie, Julia. "A Bird Bereaved. The Identity and Significance of Vālmīki's Krauñca." In *Journal of Indian Philosophy* 26 (1998): 455–487.

Maurer, Petra. *Die Grundlagen der tibetischen Geomantie dargestellt anhand des 32. Kapitels des* Vaiḍūrya dkar po *von* sde srid *Sangs rgyas rgya mtsho* (1653–1705). Ein Beitrag zum Verständnis der Kultur- und Wissenschaftsgeschichte Tibets zur Zeit des 5. Dalai Lamas Ngag dbang blo bzang rgya mtsho (1717–1682), Halle: International Institute of Tibetan and Buddhist Studies (Beiträge zur Zentralasienforschung 21), 2009.

Nebesky-Wojkowitz, René de. *Oracles and Demons of Tibet. The Cult and Iconography of the Tibetan Protective Deities.* The Hague: Mouton & Co. 1956.

Śāntideva, Bendall, Cécile, and Rouse, W.H.D. eds. *Śikshā-Samuccaya. A compendium of Buddhist doctrine. Compiled by Śāntideva chiefly from earlier Mahāyāna Sutras.* [Indian Texts Series]. London: John Murray, 1921.

Scheuermann, Rolf. *When Sūtra Meets Tantra—sGam po pa's Four Dharma Doctrine as an Example for his Synthesis of the bKa' gdams- and Mahāmudrā-Systems.* Ph.D. Thesis, University of Vienna, 2015. Accessed February 28, 2018. http://othes.univie.ac.at/38587/1/2015-04-26_0507668.pdf.

Scheuermann, Rolf. "'One will quickly die!'—Predictions of Death in Three Tibetan Buddhist Divination Manuals." In *Fate, Longevity, and Immortality*, eds. Agostino Paravicini Bagliani, Michael Lackner, Fabrizio Pregadio, pp. 113–130. Firenze: Sismel Edizioni del Galluzzo (Micrologus XXVI), 2018.

Shen-Yu, Lin. "Pehar: A Historical Survey." In Revue d' Etudes Tibétaines 19 (2010): 5–26.

Smith, Richard J. "Meditation, Divination and Dream Interpretation. Chan/Zen Buddhism, the I Ching (Book of Changes), and Other Chinese Devices for Jungian Self-Realization." Accessed May 12, 2017. http://chaocenter.rice.edu/uploadedFiles/Chao_Center/Yijing/C.%20Meditation,%20Divination%20and%20Dream%20Interpretation.pdf.

Snellgrove, David L. *The Nine Ways of Bon. Excerpts from the* gZi-brjid *edited and translated.* London: Oxford University Press, 1967.

Stearns, Cyrus. "The Life and Tibetan Legacy of the Indian Mahapaṇḍita Vibhūticandra." In *Journal of the International Association of Buddhist Studies* 19, no. 1 (1996): 127–171.

Steinkellner, Ernst. "Tshad ma'i skye bu: Meaning and Historical Significance of the term." In *Proceedings of the Csoma de Kőrös Symposium held at Velm-Vienna, Austria, 13–19 September 1981*, eds. Ernst Steinkellner and Helmut Tauscher, vol. 2, pp. 275–284. Wien: Arbeitskreis für Tibetische und Buddhistische Studien, 1983.

Torricelli, Fabrizio. "Tibetan Literature on Dreams: Materials for a Bibliography." In *The Tibet Journal* 22, no. 1 (1997): 58–82.

Trungram Gyaltrul Rinpoche, S. "Gampopa, the Monk and the Yogi. His Life and Teachings." PhD dissertation. Sanskrit and Indian Studies, Harvard University, 2004. Accessed May 12, 2017. http://vajrayana.faithweb.com/Gampopa.pdf.

Wayman, Alexander. "Significance of Dreams in India and Tibet." *History of Religions* 7, no. 1 (1967): 1–12. Accessed May 12, 2017. http://www.jstor.org/stable/1061861.

Young, Serinity. *Dreaming in the Lotus: Buddhist Dream Narrative, Imagery and Practice.* Boston, London [etc.]: Wisdom Publications, 1999.

CHAPTER 9

Prognosis, Prophylaxis, and Trumps: Comparative Remarks on Several Common Forms of Tibetan Cleromancy*

Alexander K. Smith

In traditional Tibetan imaginaries, as is well known, human beings are considered to be subject to a host of influences, both natural and supernatural, among which are counted the planets and stars, as well as a dizzying variety of gods, demons, demi-gods, and regional spirits. On the one hand, the interrelationship of these myriad forces, whether harmonious or inharmonious, is believed to exert a considerable amount of control over individual human lives and to affect the functioning of society at large. On the other hand, these forces can themselves be influenced through various forms of ritual action, which differ dramatically in their scope and sophistication, ranging from daily *bsang mchod* offerings, for example, to the construction of elaborate mandalas in preparation for the the birthday of the Dalai Lama. Within this framework, divination provides a mechanism through which individuals are able to gain insight into the nature and disposition of the various elemental, social, or supernatural forces that could potentially affect their lives.

Despite the growing number of specialist studies on the subject of Tibetan divination practices, a variety of divinatory techniques, including divination by rice, salt, and fingernails, as well as the interpretation of dreams and forms of Tibetan physiognomy remain almost entirely unknown to Western academic literature. Like any complex ritual system, Tibetan divination practices are often highly composite, displaying elements from different divinatory traditions which have been cobbled together over long periods of time. Neverthe-

---

* It should be noted that sections of this paper follow closely remarks that I published in a separate article in 2015 (Alexander K. Smith, "Prognostic Structure and the Use of Trumps in Tibetan Pebble Divination" in *Magic Ritual and Witchcraft* Vol. 10, No. 1 [Summer, 2015]). I would like to thank Professor Donatella Rossi and the staff of the "Divination in Tibet and Mongolia" workshop (December, 2014) for their generous support and for the opportunity to rework some of these materials in a format that was not only more satisfying to write, but also hopefully more interesting and informative to my readers.

© KONINKLIJKE BRILL NV, LEIDEN, 2020 | DOI:10.1163/9789004410688_010

less, building upon the extant literature, there is room for several guarded generalizations to be made, particularly when discussing divination practices in their textual forms.

To begin with, the performance of divination, particularly forms of mechanical divination falling under the rubric of *mo* or *mo rtsis*, has been described by a number of authors as a pan-Tibetan phenomenon.[1] A cursory survey of the literature reveals that there are many different forms of divination practiced in Tibetan cultures, both past, and present. A number of these are outlined in Ekvall 1963[2] and Lama Chime Radha 1981,[3] which discuss a variety of divinatory techniques, including divination by dice, stones, songs, rosaries, mirrors, arrows, butter-lamps, and the burning of sheep scapulas. Several studies have also been published on the subjects of divination by bird-call, aviary flight patterns, and augury.[4] At present, divination by ropes and strings (including the performance of *ju thig*) remains largely unstudied in Tibetan milieus, though some cursory remarks can be found in publications.[5] Furthermore, the quasi-divinatory selection of hierarchs through various aleatoric processes, sometimes involving the mediation of major and minor deities, is not entirely

---

1 Lama Chime Radha, Rinpoche, "Tibet" in Michael Loewe and Carmen Blacker, eds., *Oracles and Divination* (Boulder: Shambhala, 1981), 3–37; Robert B. Ekvall, "Some Aspects of Divination in Tibetan Society" in *Ethnology* 2 (1963), 31–39; Barbara Gerke, *Long Lives and Untimely Deaths: Life-Span Concepts and Longevity Practices Among Tibetans in the Darjeeling Hills, India* (Leiden: Brill, 2011); A. Róna-Tas, "Tally-Stick and Divination-Dice in the Iconography of the Lha mo" in *Acta Orientalia Hungaricae* 62 (1965), 163–168.

2 Ekvall, "Some Aspects of Divination in Tibetan Society".

3 Lama Chime Radha "Tibet".

4 In particular: Berthold Laufer, "Bird Divination Among the Tibetans: Notes on Pelliot No. 3530, with a Study of Tibetan Phonology of the Ninth Century" in *T'oung Pao or Archives Concernant l'Histoire, les Langues, la Géographie et l'Ethnographie de l'Asie Orientale* Vol. xv (Leiden: Brill, 1914); F.W. Thomas, *Ancient Folk-Literature From North-Eastern Tibet* (Berlin: Akademie-Verlag, 1957); Carol Morgan, "La Divination d'après les Croassements des Corbeaux dans les Manuscrits de Dunhuang" in *Cahiers d'Extême-Asie*, Vol. 3 (1987), 55–76; Eric Mortensen, *Raven Augury in Tibet, Northwest Yunnan, Inner Asia, and Circumpolar Regions: A Study in Comparative Folklore and Religion* (PhD Thesis: Harvard University, 2003).

5 See: Giuseppe Tucci, *The Religions of Tibet* (Berkely: Routledge & Kegan Paul Ltd., 1988 [1970]), 228. It is also worth noting that *ju thig* is the subject of my current post-graduate research at Friedrich-Alexander Universität, as well as a previous research project conducted by Donatella Rossi at the same institution. Perhaps the most notable aspect of Professor Rossi's work on *ju thig* is the release of a short documentary film on the subject of Bon divination practices, in which the head educator of sMan ri Monastery, the sMan ri Slob dpon 'Phrin las nyi ma, discusses the performance of *ju thig* at great length. The film is freely available on the IKGF website at the following address: http://ikgf.fau.de/videos/documentaries/practice -of-divination-rinpoche.shtml.

unknown.[6] The election of the abbot of sMan ri Monastery and the Junior Tutor of the Dalai Lama by *rtags ril*, for example, are perhaps the most widely known examples of election through such aleatoric processes.[7] Other forms of divination are also attested to in Dunhuang literature, where one finds manuscripts outlining coin divination,[8] canine divination,[9] and divination by leather lots[10] along with many other divination practices.

To speak very generally, many of the divination practices encountered in Tibetan cultures can be understood (along etic taxonomic lines) as forms of cleromancy. Cleromantic divinations make use of mobile elements, such as dice, stones, lots, ropes, or runes, which are cast by the diviner in order to randomly generate a pattern, a set of symbols, or a particular numerical signifier. The diviner then refers to some type of an interpretive catalog, either textual or memorized, in order to make ineligible the results of the casting and to generate a response to the client's query. For example, in the African case of Ndembu *ng'ombu yakesekula*, which is studied at length by Victor Turner,[11] the diviner begins by placing twenty to thirty objects into a shallow, open-topped basket. The basket is then shaken, randomizing the distribution of the objects and maneuvering them into a heap from which the diviner examines the top three or four objects. In this instance, the interpretive catalog could be said to be rooted in Ndembu oral culture, in that the interpretation of *ng'ombu yakesekula*'s mobile elements depends upon the memorization of an enormous body of rigidly defined symbols, which are communicated orally from diviner to apprentice and not recorded in textual form. By way of contrast, some cleromantic traditions like the *I Ching*[12] and Yoruba *Ifá* divination[13] are

---

6 Charles Ramble, "Rule by Play in Southern Mustang" in Charles Ramble and Martin Brauen, eds., *Anthropology of Tibet and the Himalaya* (Vajra Publications: Kathmandu, 1993); Charles Ramble, *The Navel of the Demoness: Tibetan Buddhism and Civil Religion in Highland Nepal* (New York: Oxford University Press, 2008).

7 Sherpa Tulku, "The Structure of the Ge-lug Monastic Order" in *The Tibet Journal* 2(3) (1977), 68–69; Krystina Cech, *The Social and Religious Identity of the Tibetan Bonpos with Special Reference to a North-West Himalayan Settlement* (DPhil Thesis: Oxford University, 1993), 112. See also: Marcia Calkowski "Contesting Hierarchy: On Gambling as an Authoritative Resource in Tibetan Refugee Society" in Ramble and Brauen, *Anthropology of Tibet and the Himalaya*, 30–39.

8 See, for example: IOL Tib J 741.1, IOL Tib J 741.2, IOL Tib J 744, PT 1055, PT 1056.

9 See: PT 3601.

10 See: IO 742.

11 Victor W. Turner, *Revelation and Divination in Ndembu Ritual* (Oxford: Clarendon, 1975).

12 See, in particular: Stephen Feuchtwang, *An Anthropological Analysis of Chinese Geomancy* (Bangkok: White Lotus Co. Ltd., 2002 [1972]).

13 See, for example: W. Abimbola, *Ifa: an Exposition of Ifa Literary Corpus* (Ibadan: Oxford

expressly textual, whereas other forms of cleromancy, like Nyole *lamuli* divination,[14] combine both written and memorized verses.[15]

Returning to the Tibetan cultural sphere, it is important to note that many forms of cleromantic divination are textually oriented, which is to say that they involve the mediation of an interpretive textual catalog. For instance, in one form of dice divination widely practiced in Tibetan speaking communities in Himachal Pradesh, the diviner requires a set of three six-sided dice, as well as a divination manual affiliated, in many cases, with the goddess dPal ldan dmag zor rgyal mo.[16] Following the prerequisite rites and invocations, the dice are cast once, twice, or several times. In each instance, the casting provides a single, randomly generated numerical result numbering three through eighteen. A cursory glance at the prognosticatory section of the associated divination manual reveals that the manuscript is composed of sixteen sections, correspondingly numbered three through eighteen, each of which is further divided into a series of eleven sub-sections, the topics of which range from mercantile activities and travel to various health, spiritual, and domestic concerns. In this sense, the dice divination in question can be seen to make use of a mechanical randomness generator (i.e. the set of three six-sided dice), the results of which are then keyed into an interpretive textual catalog that serves as a guideline from which the diviner is able to distill a response to the clients' queries.

Looking at a cross-section of divinatory literature, one of the genera's most distinctive qualities is that—structurally speaking—divination manuals display a high degree of homogeneity, which is particularly evident in the composition of divinatory prognostics. Though I could not hope to exhaust the available witnesses, I would like to move on to provide a number textual examples in order to illustrate several of the basic structural features encountered when reading cleromantic manuscripts.

To begin with, Tibetan textual prognostics are often composed of cryptic, sometimes poetic sections of prose that are frequently supplemented by

---

University Press, 1976); William Bascom, *Ifa Divination: Communication Between Gods and Men in West Africa* (Bloomington: Indiana University Press, 1969).

14   Susan Reynolds Whyte, *Questioning Misfortune: The Pragmatics of Uncertainty in Eastern Uganda* (Cambridge: University of Cambridge Press, 1997).

15   For an excellent general study of text-based divination and, in particular, a thorough discussion of the roles played by the diviner during the interpretation of divination manuals in African milieus, see: David Zeitlyn, "Finding Meaning in the Text: The Process of Interpretation in Text-Based Divination" in *Journal of the Royal Anthropological Institute* 7 no. 2 (June 2011), 225–240.

16   [author unknown] *dPal ldan dmag zor rgyal mo'i sgo nas rno mthong sgrub tshul de'i 'grol bshad dang bcas pa zhes bya ba bzhugs so* (Delhi: *Bod gzhung shes rig dpar khang*, 1997).

PROGNOSIS, PROPHYLAXIS, AND TRUMPS

qualitative statements classifying each casting as either excellent (*rab*), good (*bzang*), mediocre (*'bring*), or bad (*ngan*). For example, the following excerpt is taken from IOL Tib J 744, a short coin divination manual (10th c.) recovered from cave seventeen in Dunhuang. The manuscript and its relationship to other Dunhuang divination materials is the subject of a recent article by Ai Nishida, published in *Old Tibetan Studies*.[17]

> If six coins are obverse (*gan*), the omen of water and gold is cast. If this is cast for *khyim phya*, *srid phya*, or *srog phya*, it is good. If this is cast for *dgra phya*, there will be no enemies. If someone has been taken as a prisoner, they will go free. If the charge is disputed (*brtsod*?), they will win. If there is a wound (*rmas*), it will be cleansed. If there is a sick person, s/he will recover. If someone strives for the sake of profit, it will be attained. [This casting] is an omen of the Pleiades constellation[18] in the sky. It is a sign that [the Pleiades constellation] is surrounded by many stars. For whatever is cast, this divination is excellent.
>
> IOL Tib J 744, lines 23–26

> *dong tshe drug gan na / chu dang gser gI ngo la bab ste / khyIm phya srId phya srog phyar btab na bzang / dgra phyar btab na dgra myed / btson tu bzung na thar / yus brtsod / na thob / gyod rmas na 'byang / nad pa na gsos so / dog gnyer na 'grub / gnam la skar ma smyIn drug gI ngo ste / skar ma mang pos bskor ba'I ngo / mo 'di ci la btab kyang rab bo /*

We find similar basic structures in our second example. The excerpt is taken from a short discussion of physiognomy, which appears in the *Zhang zhung gi ju thig bsrus pa mo bya drug 'phrul gyi lde mig*, a brief 18th century commentary on rope divination (*ju thig*).

> Now, if the divination is slandered, it is bad for all concerned (*mi spyid*). If the [client's] right knee is planted down and the left cheek is presented, it is bad for adults. If the left knee is planted and the right cheek is presented, it is bad for children ... If the [client's] head is covered [when he enters], it is bad. If a hat is worn, the *dmu* is covered. If one enters recit-

---

17   Ai Nishida, "An Old Tibetan Divination with Coins" in Cristina Scherrer-Schaub, ed., *Old Tibetan Studies. Dedicated to the Memory of R.E. Emmerick. Proceedings of the Tenth Seminar of IATS, 2003* (Leiden: Brill, 2012).

18   As a point of reference, the Pleiades constellation (Messier 45), which is visible with the naked eye, is an open star cluster in the Taurus constellation.

ing mantras, it is bad. If one sings songs, it is an omen of sorrow. If [the client's] front is presented and [s/he] adopts a reverential posture, it is good.

> folio 3, line 3–folio 4, line 1

da ni mo smad mi spyid la / pus mo g.yas btsug na 'gram pa g.yon bstan na che rgyud la ngan / pus g.yon brtsug 'gram pa g.yas bstan na chung rgyud la ngan / ... mgo btum na ngan / zhwa gyon na dmu gab yin / yang na 'og la rkyen ngo yin / sngags pa bsgrang na ngan / glu blang na mya ngan 'ong / mdun bstan na gus tshul byung na bzang /

In the case of negative, ostensibly undesirable results, textual prognostics are frequently followed by highly specific lists of rites that the client may perform in order to stem any of the undesirable events outlined within the text. However, divination manuals typically describe the nature of any current or pending misfortunes in vague terms, leaving a great deal of room for *ex post facto* elaborations on part of the diviner. The following excerpts, for example, are taken from the *sMra seng rdel mo gsal ba'i me long*, an 18th century pebble divination manuscript written by Kun grol grags pa.

> (411) Six stones arranged like this is a heart filled with regret. Debates and confrontations will arise with one's superiors. The people will be unsettled. A plague will spread. To avoid this, perform a great enemy-burying rite (*dgra brub*). Nonetheless, for whatever is cast, this is bad. (141) Six stones arranged like this is misery. It is wild leopards, jackals, and dogs. Of the two, which will strike first: spears or arrows? A din of humiliated voices, it is a sign of turmoil.[19] Perform as well as possible an enemy-burying rite and a demon-suppressing rite (*dgra mnan*). [This casting indicates] the malevolent influence of the king of the knife demons (*rgyal*

---

19   I have taken great liberties with this passage, *kha sma 'ur zing 'byung ngo yin*. First of all, I have used the term *'ur zing* twice: (1) "a din (*'ur zing*) of humiliated voices (*kha sma*)"; and (2) "it is a sign (*ngo*) of turmoil (*'ur zing*)," or rendered literally, "it is a sign (*ngo*) that turmoil (*'ur zing*) will arise (*'byung*)." Nonetheless, it is a beautiful passage and I feel that it merits a slightly liberal treatment of the prose. With that said, the passage could also be rendered in a very different fashion. To begin with, *'ur zing* may not be an attributive noun (i.e. a noun adjunct) and the phrase *kha sma 'ur zing* may not be a compound noun at all (as the seven syllable verse does not allow here for the associative particle *dang*). If this is the case, the passage would read something like: "It is a sign that humiliated voices (*kha sma*) and unrest/turmoil (*'ur zing*) will arise (*'byung*)."

PROGNOSIS, PROPHYLAXIS, AND TRUMPS

po gri mo) and the gdon demons. Make a rgyal mdos offering and tie down the mo gri. It is a sign that the sick person will not recover and die. Nonetheless, for whatever is cast, it is said that this is a moderate result. (222) Six stones arranged like this is lamentation. It is a sign of injury caused by the btsan and the rgyal po demons. [This casting indicates] malevolent spirits (gdon) [associated with] fresh meats, wild animals, perpetuators of incest, and comely women. Whichever star underlies [the relevant misfortune must be identified] and [exorcised] with a mdos rite.

> folio 451, line 1–folio 452, line 1

(411) 'di 'dra'i rdel drug snying 'gyod yin / rang bas che dang tsod pa 'byung / yul pa mi bde nad yams dar / zlog pa dgra brub stebs chen bya / ci la tab kyang ngan pa yin / (141) 'di 'dra'i rdel drug mya ngan yin / khyi dang spyang ku gung rgod yin / mda' dang mdung gnyis gang snga yin / kha sma 'ur zing 'byung ngo yin / dgra brub dgra mnan gang drag sgrub / gdon du rgyal po gri mo'i gdon / rgyal mdos 'bul zhing gri mo bkar / nad pa mi sos 'chi ngo yin / ci la tab kyang 'bring du bshad / (222) 'di 'dra'i rdel drug ngu 'bod yin / btsan dang rgyal po'i gnod ngo yin / bud med kha so mi sang dang / dme bo ri dwags sha rlon gdon / gza' rkyen gang yin gza' mdos bya /

If a one is cast here, it is a sign of companionship. Having heard good news, guests and helpers will come. The lady of the house will be free from disease. If a two is cast here, the bdud demons will run off with the divination medicine. This is a sign of thieves, of disputes, and of sickness. It is a sign that the sleeping place will be empty and the sick person unfulfilled. Recite myriad Sutra verses to placate the family-afflicting demon (khyim mtshes 'dre). Perform victorious wealth sadhanas (nor sgrub) and make sacrifices to secure prosperity (g.yang skyabs). If a three is cast, the curdled milk of g.yang is enclosed. This is excellent for all cattle and livestock. It is a sign that friends will come. It is good for making beer and terrible for making yogurt. If a four is cast, it is a sign that four houses will be built. What will come? Who will be met? What will be achieved? It is a sign that whatsoever occurs, events will be delayed.

> folio 444, line 5–folio 445, line 4

'di ru gcig bab grogs ngo yin / gtam snyan thos shing 'gron mgon 'ong / khyim bdag mo nad med cing / gnyis bab mo sman bdud kyis khyer nad dang kha 'chu rkun ma'i ngo / nad pa mal sa stong ba'i ngo / knyims mtshes 'dre gdon mdo 'bum 'don / rnam rgyal nor sgrub g.yang skyabs bya / gsum bab g.yang *gi ru ma skyil / bud med nor phyugs kun la bzang / zho than chang yags grogs yang ngo / bzhi bab khyims bzhi tshugs pa'i ngo / e 'ong e 'phod e 'grub dang / gang yang phyi dal che ba'i ngo /*

Taking these examples as a baseline, we see that textual prognostics often open with relatively ambiguous statements, such as metaphors, similes, or references to folkloric fragments. Additionally, following their ambiguous opening lines, it appears that prognostics offer a series of brief, case-specific passages. In the third excerpt, for example, the appearance of three stones in a particular location is taken to be excellent for cattle and livestock, good for the manufacture of beer, but terrible for making yogurt. Negative results are typically coupled with highly specific lists of rites intended to avert or to appease demonic forces. Similar structures, coupling an ambiguous negative portent with a highly specific series of rites, have been discussed by several authors as a central feature underlying the perceived efficacy of divination practices in Tibetan milieus.[20] To my knowledge, Lama Chime Radha was the first to discuss the point at length in his contribution to Loewe and Blacker's 1981 *Oracles and Divination*.[21] In extreme brief, Lama Chime Radha notes that ambiguity is a recurring feature of Tibetan divinatory prognostics; however, he contends that this ambiguity is intentionally added to the prognostics by the diviners themselves "in order to minimize the possibility of error."[22] This is necessary, he contends, because the career of a professional diviner is a "somewhat insecure way of supporting oneself" and a single false prediction could lead to a diviner "quickly loos[ing] his reputation."[23] As such, Chime Radha writes that both a "high degree of tact and diplomacy," as well as a willingness "to express ... predictions with some degree of ambiguity and inexactitude" are necessary elements of a successful diviner's repertoire.[24]

Whether or not we agree with his remarks, it may be instructive to note that Lama Chime Radha's characterization of prognostic ambiguity is reflected in a number of prevalent, contemporaneous discourses on religion and social theory, including discussions of subjective validation and the Forer effect in the

---

20   Lama Chime Radha, "Tibet;" Gerke, *Long Lives and Untimely Deaths: Life-Span Concepts and Longevity Practices Among Tibetans in the Darjeeling Hills, India*; Alexander K. Smith, "Prognostic Structure and the Use of Trumps in Tibetan Pebble Divination" in *Magic Ritual and Witchcraft* Vol. 10, No. 1 (Summer, 2015).

21   Lama Chime Radha, "Tibet."

22   Ibid, 7.

23   Ibid.

24   Ibid.

cognitive sciences,[25] as well as, broadly speaking, much of the so-called rationality debate in social and cultural anthropology. Leaving these issues aside, for the time being, I think that we can locate a more critical assessment of the ambiguity of Tibetan divinatory prognostics in Barbara Gerke's recent book, *Long Lives and Untimely Deaths*.

In her fourth chapter, Gerke studies several contemporary astrological almanacs in the exile community, as well as a well-known, recently published dPal ldan lha mo dice divination manual. Comparing these source materials, one of Gerke's first observations is that the predictions offered in astrological and divinatory compendia do not often come true. Considering this, Gerke puzzles over the fact that, during her fieldwork, she rarely encountered Tibetans who expressed reservations regarding the efficacy of astrological and divinatory practices.[26] She concludes that this data mediates in favor of the interpretation of textual prognostics being, for the diviner and/or astrologer, "more a matter of style and interpretation, in which actors are quite free to interpret … [textual] predictions within their larger cosmological frameworks, involving karma, merit, blessing, (in)auspiciousness, as well as obstacles."[27] In the case of *mo*, Gerke argues that an important feature of this interpretive flexibility is the generally vague or poetic nature of the responses offered by the divination manuals themselves. The ambiguity of divinatory prognostics serves, she writes, "to leave space for the diviner's intuitive interpretation concerning the client's personal situation."[28] Another important feature of this process is that it serves to draw the client into the divinatory consultation in such a way that "the client becomes an active agent in shaping his/her vital force and life-span."[29]

It is worth noting that similar themes have been extensively explored by a number of authors writing on the subject of divination in African and East-Asian milieus. This is particularly true of studies characteristic of Rene Devisch's "internal semiotic and semantic" mode of analysis, which, in more recent configurations, emphasizes the dialogic relationship expressed between both the client and the diviner, as well as between the diviner and the div-

---

25   See: Bertram R. Forer, "The Fallacy of Personal Validation: A Classroom Demonstration of Gullibility" in *Journal of Abnormal and Social Psychology* 44 (1) (January, 1949), 118–123; Paul Meehl, "Wanted—A Good Cookbook" in *The American Psychologist* Vol. 11 (6) (June, 1956), 263–272. See also: David F. Marks, *The Psychology of the Psychic* (Amherst, New York: Prometheus Books, 2000).

26   Gerke, *Long Lives and Untimely Deaths: Life-Span Concepts and Longevity Practices Among Tibetans in the Darjeeling Hills, India*, 37.

27   Ibid.

28   Ibid, 221.

29   Ibid.

ination text.[30] Several of the contributors to Phillip Peek's watershed *African Divination Systems*,[31] for instance, stress the interpretive and collaborative work that occurs during divinatory séances.[32] In these studies, divination is represented as proceeding from ambiguity to clarity or, in Parkin's terminology, from "chaos to order."[33] This is seen, on the one hand, as the diviner interpreting and contextualizing a randomly selected result, transforming otherwise incomprehensible sections of text into case-specific prognostics; and, on the other hand, it can be seen as the diviner mediating a therapeutic discussion with the client, clarifying the client's questions, concerns, hopes, fears, and so forth, ultimately settling upon a course of action that may resolve the issues underlying the client's initial query. In this sense, as Whyte writes, divination often involves "a three-way conversation, with the diviner mediating ... between the client and the authoritative book."[34]

Returning for a moment to the above examples, we saw that negative prognostics are often followed by detailed lists of rites, which are typically apotropaic or prophylactic in nature. Though the issue is under-represented in the literature, it is important to note that this aspect of prognostic structure has been characterized by several authors as a structural feature of Tibetan ritual economies.[35] Barbara Gerke, for example, not only notes the frequency with

---

30 See, in particular: Niyi F. Akinnaso, "Bourdieu and the Diviner: Knowledge and Symbolic Power in Yoruba Divination" in Wendy James, ed., *The Pursuit of Certainty: Religions and Cultural Formulations* (London/New York: Routledge, 1995), 234–257; Rene Devisch, "Perspectives on Divination in Contemporary Sub-Saharan Africa" in W.M.J. van Binsbergen and J.M. Schoffeleers, eds., *Theoretical Explorations in African Religion* (London/Boston: Kegan Paul International, 1985), 50–83; Rosalind Shaw, "Splitting Truths from Darkness: Epistemological Aspects of Temne Divination" in Philip M. Peek, ed., *African Divination Systems* (Bloomington & Indianapolis: Indiana University Press, 1991), 137–152; David Parkin, "Straightening the Paths from Wilderness: the Case of Divinatory Speech" in *JASO* 10 (3) (1979), 147–160; R.P. Werbner, "Tswapong Wisdom Divination" in *Ritual Passage, Sacred Journey* (Washington D.C.: Smithsonian Institution Press, 1989), 19–60; Susan Reynolds Whyte, "Knowledge and Power in Nyole Divination" in Peek, *African Divination Systems*; David Zeitlyn, "Professor Garfinkle Visits the Soothsayers: Ethnomethodology and Mambila Divination" in *Man* (N.S.) 25 (1990), 654–666; Zeitlyn, "Finding Meaning in the Text: the Process of Interpretation in Text-Based Divination."

31 Peek, *African Divination Systems.*

32 David Parkin, "Simultaneity and sequencing in the oracular speech of Kenyan diviners" in Peek *African Divination Systems*; Shaw, "Splitting Truths from Darkness: Epistemological Aspects of Temne Divination;" Whyte, "Knowledge and Power in Nyole Divination."

33 Parkin, "Straightening the Paths from Wilderness: the Case of Divinatory Speech"; Parkin, "Simultaneity and Sequencing in the Oracular Speech of Kenyan Diviners."

34 Whyte, "Knowledge and Power in Nyole Divination."

35 G.E. Clarke, "Ideas of Merit (*bsod-nams*), Virtue (*dge-ba*), Blessing (*byin rlabs*) and Mate-

PROGNOSIS, PROPHYLAXIS, AND TRUMPS 191

which divination manuals offer lengthy lists of rites, but also that the correct performance of these rites would sometimes require the intercession of a ritual specialist. As a consequence, in her second chapter, Gerke characterizes the relationship between divination and ritual (as well as between diviners and monastic communities) as one that is symbiotic in nature. "Both reap rewards," she writes, "[t]he diviners provide the monastery with clients and detailed instructions on what kind of practices to perform, and the monasteries provide the body of sophisticated religious practices.[36] The client usually 'pays' for the [diviner's] services in the form of donations."[37] This same dynamic is characterized by Graham Clarke, in his ethnographic study of the Yolmo people, as a form of "religious capitalism" in which divination serves to economically subsidize hegemonic institutions and, in return, the diviners' clientele receive types of symbolic capital in the form of *bsod nams* and *byin rlabs*, or meritorious action and religious blessing.[38] In my opinion, this particular aspect of Tibetan divination warrants a great deal of further study. With that said, however, I would now like to move on to briefly address a separate, though also understudied aspect of prognostic structure: the appearance of trumps in cleromantic prognoses.

In a recent article published by the University of Pennsylvania,[39] I discuss the usage and function of trumps in *lde'u 'phrul*, a form of Tibetan pebble-divination. It is important to stress, however, that prognostic trumps also feature in a number of other divinatory practices, including rope-divination, dice-divination, and forms of Tibetan physiognomy. To illustrate how these trumps operate and could be incorporated into a divinatory casting, I would like to present a fragment of the *Srid rgyal dus drug mngon shes gsal ba'i me long* (hereafter *Srid rgyal dus drug*), a short treatise on dice-divination that was generously given to me by a young Bon monk during a recent trip to Himachal Pradesh. The text is 24 folios in length and is handwritten in a clear *dbu med* script. According to the colophon, the text was penned in an iron-horse year

---

     rial Prosperity (*rten-'brel*) in Highland Nepal" in *JASO* 21 (2) (1990), 165–184; Gerke, *Long Lives and Untimely Deaths: Life-Span Concepts and Longevity Practices Among Tibetans in the Darjeeling Hills, India*; Smith, "Prognostic Structure and the Use of Trumps in Tibetan Pebble Divination."

36   Gerke, *Long Lives and Untimely Deaths: Life-Span Concepts and Longevity Practices Among Tibetans in the Darjeeling Hills, India*, 104.

37   Ibid.

38   Clarke, "Ideas of Merit (*bsod-nams*), Virtue (*dge-ba*), Blessing (*byin rlabs*) and Material Prosperity (*rten-'brel*) in Highland Nepal," 182.

39   Smith, "Prognostic Structure and the Use of Trumps in Tibetan Pebble Divination."

(possibly 1870–1871) by a priest of the rGya clan. Furthermore, the author stipulates that the text should be classified as *gter ma*, though the colophon fails to mention when, where, or by whom the text was discovered.

Broadly speaking, dice-divination is one of the most common and relatively straightforward cleromantic practice encountered in Tibetan milieus. The rites that I have observed make use of three dice, the set of which may be cast up to three separate times in a single session. As noted above, each individual casting yields a numerical result that corresponds to a particular entry in a divination text. The prognostications provided by the text are then collated and woven into a response for the diviner's client.

The excerpt that follows is a short addendum that has been added to the final folios of the *Srid rgyal dus drug*. The passage provides a set of prognostics that govern the interpretation of divination sessions that are extended to a full three throws of the dice. In reading the excerpt, it may be noted that the entries are somewhat formulaic. Essentially, the passage boils each of the three primary castings down to a good or bad result and, depending upon the order of the castings in question, it then provides a meta-response, or trump that supersedes the disparate results of each individual casting.

> Furthermore, it is excellent if the divination is decided all at once (*thang gcig*) ... If all three [castings] are good, it is of an extremely superior quality. If both the former and the later are good, but the middle is bad, whatever is cast is good. If the first is bad and the following two are good, it is an omen of illness. It will be necessary to perform a *tshe sgrub* and a *tshe dbang*. If the first two are good but the last is bad, the *lha mo* is displeased. Make prayers and offerings to the *lha* and the *srung* ... If the first and the last are bad, but the middle is good, it is an omen of enemies and thieves. Perform a *dgra grub* and a *dgra zlog*. Suppress the *dgra sri*. If all three are bad, it is extremely bad. If the first is good but the following two are bad, it is an average result. One must make innumerable offerings to the *nor lha*, praise the *sgra bla*, and perform a *g.yang sgrub*. If the first two are bad, but the last is good, it is good.
>
> folio 23, line 3–folio 24, line 1

> *gsum ka bzang na shin tu yag nyes che / snga phyi gnyis bzang bar ma ngan na gang btab kyang bzang sa yin / dang po ngan phyi ma gnyis bzang na nang ngo tshe sgrub tshe dbang dgos / snga ma gnyis bzang na phyis ma ngan na lha mo ma dga' lha srung gsol mchod / ... snga phyi ngan bar ma bzang na dgra krun ngo / dgra grub dang dgra zlog bya / dgra sri mnan / gsum ka ngan na shin tu ngan / snga ma bzang phyi ma gnis ngan na 'bring*

tsa yin / g.yang sgrub sgra bla dpa' bstod nor lha mchod gsol grangs mang dgos / dong gnyis ngan phyi ma bzang na bzang ba yin /

In many respects, this excerpt is similar to the examples that we have already seen. The prognostics offer simple conditional statements with a *protasis* (an "if x" clause) and an *apodosis* (the "then y" clause). Generally, the *apodosis* is somewhat vague and is supplemented by a qualitative statement, which tallies the results of three separate castings and classifies the outcome as being either good (*bzang*) or bad (*ngan*). Once again, in the case of negative results, lists of specific rites are offered, each of which is intended to avert or appease potentially malign supernatural forces.

Leaving these basic structural features aside, the appearance of trumps in cleromantic texts raises a number of interesting questions, chief among which is, perhaps, the issue of authorial intention vs. contemporary ethnographic usage. How far, for example, do diviners actually diverge from their texts in offering responses to their clients? And how, for that matter, do different diviners understand and interpret textual prognostics in order to adapt them to changing social and economic conditions? For my part, in observing the performance of pebble divination during my doctoral fieldwork at sMan ri Monastery in Himachal Pradesh, I noted that similar kinds of trumps, or meta-prognostics which appear (textually) to supersede lower-order prognostics, are rarely used in practice to replace them.[40] In other words, passages like the excerpt from the *Srid rgyal dus drug* are rarely used to actually trump the results of individual castings. Though I still lack the data to argue the case deductively, prognostic trumps appear to be used to enhance the results of lower-order prognostics, to add a kind of tone and depth to the casting that the diviner can draw from in crafting a customized response to the clients' queries. This (very limited) observation, however, only scratches at the surface of what is, in fact, a tremendously complex issue.

Divination manuals, as with many other forms of Tibetan ritual literature, are often composed in environments far removed—temporally, geographically, and linguistically—from the contexts in which they are used today. To recall Nicolas Sihlé's remarks in *Tibetan Ritual*,[41] this gives many divination manuscripts an exogenous or partially exogenous character, which serves to draw both the ethnographer and textual scholar into the evolving discourse on

---

40 Ibid.

41 Nicolas Sihlé, "Written Texts at the Juncture of the Local and the Global: Some Anthropological Considerations on a Local Corpus of Tantric Rituals (Lower Mustang, Nepal)" in José Ignacio Cabezón, ed., *Tibetan Ritual* (New York: Oxford University Press, 2010), 35.

the ritual-textual interface in Tibetan cultures. This is an issue, I believe, that the study of Tibetan divination is very well suited to address. As we have already seen, a number of scholars have observed that divination practices are closely related to overarching medical and ritual systems and, as Graham Clarke[42] and Barbara Gerke[43] have noted, divination also plays a role in the regulation of Tibetan ritual economies. To this I would add that divinatory traditions also serve to articulate (and, perhaps, to validate) many epistemological and cosmological ideas. In this paper, I have attempted to show that not only are these features evidenced by the contemporary performance of divination, but also— and in particular—that they are articulated in the structure of cleromantic textual prognostics as well. In order to advance our understanding of the roles played by divination in contemporary Tibetan communities, this demands that researchers continue to work towards uncovering the local, ethnographic relevance of the divination manuals that they scrutinize.

One of the virtues of a library investigation is that it allows us to focus on divination practices in a static and idealized form.[44] As with other ritual traditions in the Tibetan cultural sphere, however, the performance of divination in variable ethnographic contexts is much more diverse than a comparative textual study might suggest. Nonetheless, a basic understanding of the structure and semantic patterning of divinatory prognostics is required in order to address the more complex issues that inform the usage and perception of divination manuals in contemporary Tibetan communities. Through my examples and my brief analyses, I hope to have shown that divination practices sit at a critical juncture, mediating multiple ritual traditions, as well as a number of social and economic structures. I also hope to have shown that, despite their simplistic structure, divinatory prognostics provide a unique perspective on the performance of divination, which remains largely unexplored in Western academic literature.

---

42 Clarke, "Ideas of Merit (*bsod-nams*), Virtue (*dge-ba*), Blessing (*byin rlabs*) and Material Prosperity (*rten-'brel*) in Highland Nepal."

43 Gerke, *Long Lives and Untimely Deaths: Life-Span Concepts and Longevity Practices Among Tibetans in the Darjeeling Hills, India.*

44 Feuchtwang, *An Anthropological Analysis of Chinese Geomancy*, 11–12.

References

Abimbola, W. *Ifa: an Exposition of Ifa Literary Corpus*. Ibadan: Oxford University Press, 1976.

Akinnaso, Niyi F. "Bourdieu and the Diviner: Knowledge and Symbolic Power in Yoruba Divination." In *The Pursuit of Certainty: Religions and Cultural Formulations*, ed. Wendy James, pp. 234–257. London/New York: Routledge, 1995.

[author unknown]. [nineteenth century] *Srid rgyal dus drug mngon shes gsal ba'i me long*.

[author unknown]. *dPal ldan dmag zor rgyal mo'i sgo nas rno mthong sgrub tshul de'i 'grol bshad dang bcas pa zhes bya ba bzhugs so*. Delhi: Bod gzhung shes rig dpar khang, 1997.

Bascom, William. *Ifa Divination: Communication Between Gos and Men in West Africa*. Bloomington: Indiana University Press, 1969.

Calkowski, Marcia. "Contesting Hierarchy: On Gambling as an Authoritative Resource in Tibetan Refugee Society." In *Anthropology of Tibet and the Himalaya*, eds. Charles Ramble and Martin Brauen, pp. 30–39. Vajra Publication: Kathmandu, 1993.

Cech, Krystina. *The Social and Religious Identity of the Tibetan Bonpos with Special Reference to a North-West Himalayan Settlement*. DPhil Thesis: Oxford University, 1993.

Clarke, G.E. "Ideas of Merit (*bsod-nams*), Virtue (*dge-ba*), Blessing (*byin rlabs*) and Material Prosperity (*rten-'brel*) in Highland Nepal." In *JASO* 21 (2) (1990), pp. 165–184.

Devisch, Rene. "Perspectives on Divination in Contemporary Sub-Saharan Africa." In *Theoretical Explorations in African Religion*, eds. W.M.J. van Binsbergen and J.M. Schoffeleers, pp. 50–83. London/Boston: Kegan Paul International, 1985.

Ekvall, Robert B., "Some Aspects of Divination in Tibetan Society." In *Ethnology* 2 (1963), pp. 31–39.

Feuchtwang, Stephen. *An Anthropological Analysis of Chinese Geomancy*. Bangkok: White Lotus Co. Ltd., 2002 [1972].

Forer, Bertram R. "The Fallacy of Personal Validation: A Classroom Demonstration of Gullibility." In *Journal of Abnormal and Social Psychology* 44(1) (1949): 118–123.

Gerke, Barbara. *Long Lives and Untimely Deaths: Life-Span Concepts and Longevity Practices Among Tibetans in the Darjeeling Hills, India*. Leiden: Brill, 2011.

Kun grol grags pa. [eighteenth century] *sMra seng rdel mo gsal ba'i me long*, reprinted in *'Chi med mgon po tshe dpag med dang ma gshin gnyis kyi sgrub chog mo yig sna tshogs bcas yi gsung pod: A Collection of ritual and divinational texts of the "New" Bon (Bon-gsar) tradition chiefly works by Rig-'dzin Kun-grol-grags-pa and Mi-shig-rdo-rje*. Tibetan Bonpo Monastic Centre, New Thobgyal, P.O. Ochghat, H.P., 1997.

Kun grol grags pa. [eighteenth century] *Zhang zhung gi ju thig bsrus pa mo bya drug 'phrul gyi lde mig* reprinted in *'Chi med mgon po tshe dpag med dang ma gshin gnyis kyi sgrub chog mo yig sna tshogs bcas yi gsung pod: A Collection of Ritual and Div-*

inational Texts of the "New" Bon (Bon-gsar) Tradition Chiefly Works by Rig-'dzin Kun-grol-grags-pa and Mi-shig-rdo-rje. Tibetan Bonpo Monastic Centre, New Thobgyal, P.O. Ochghat, H.P., 1997.

Lama Chime Radha, Rinpoche. "Tibet." In *Oracles and Divination*, eds. Michael Loewe and Carmen Blacker, pp. 3–37. Boulder: Shambhala, 1981.

Laufer, Berthold. "Bird Divination among the Tibetans: Notes on Pelliot No. 3530, with a Study of Tibetan Phonology in the Ninth Century." In *T'oung Pao or Archives Concernant l'Histoire, les Langues, la Géographie et l'Ethnographie de l'Asie Orientale* XV (1957).

Marks, David F. *The Psychology of the Psychic.* Amherst, New York: Prometheus Books, 2000.

Meehl, Paul. "Wanted—A Good Cookbook." In *The American Psychologist* Vol. 11,6 (1956): 263–272.

Morgan, Carol. "La Divination d'après les Croassements des Corbeaux dans les Manuscrits de Dunhuang." *Cahiers d'Etrême-Asie* 3 (1987), pp. 55–76.

Mortensen, Eric. *Raven Augury in Tibet, Northwestern Yunnan, Inner Asia, and Circumpolar Regions: A Study in Comparative Folklore and Religion.* Ph.D. Thesis. Harvard University, 2003.

Nishida, Ai. "An Old Tibetan Divination with Coins." In *Old Tibetan Studies. Dedicated to the Memory of R.E. Emmerick. Proceedings of the Tenth Seminar of IATS, 2003*, ed. Cristina Scherrer-Schaub, pp. 315–327. Leiden: Brill, 2012.

Parkin, David. "Straightening the Paths from the Wilderness: the Case of Divinatory Speech." In *JASO* 10,3 (1979), pp. 147–160.

Parkin, David. "Simultaneity and Sequencing in the Oracular Speech of Kenyan Diviners." In *African Divination Systems*, ed. Philip M. Peek, pp. 171–191. Bloomington & Indianapolis: Indiana University Press, 1991.

Ramble, Charles. "Rule by Play in Southern Mustang." In *Anthropology of Tibet and the Himalaya*, eds. Charles Ramble and Martin Brauen. Kathmandu: Vajra Publications, 1993.

Ramble, Charles. *The Navel of the Demoness: Tibetan Buddhism and Civil Religion in Highland Nepal.* New York: Oxford University Press, 2008.

Róna-Tas, A. "Tally-Stick and Divination-Dice in the Iconography of the Lha mo." *Acta Orientalia Hungaricae* 62 (1965), pp. 163–168.

Shaw, Rosalind. "Splitting Truths from Darkness: Epistemological Aspects of Temne Divination." In *African Divination Systems*, ed. Philip M. Peek, pp. 137–152. Bloomington & Indianapolis: Indiana University Press, 1991.

Sihlé, Nicolas. "Written Texts at the Juncture of the Local and the Global: Some Anthropological Considerations on a Local Corpus of Tantric Rituals (Lower Mustang, Nepal)." In *Tibetan Ritual*, ed. José Ignacio Cabezón, pp. 35–52. New York: Oxford University Press, 2010.

Smith, Alexander K. "Prognostic Structure and the Use of Trumps in Tibetan Pebble Divination." In *Magic Ritual and Witchcraft* 10,1 (2015).

Tucci, Giuseppe. *The Religions of Tibet*. Berkley: Routledge & Kegan Paul Ltd., 1988 [1970].

Tulku, Sherpa. "The Structure of the Ge-lug Monastic Order." In *The Tibet Journal* 2,3 (1977), pp. 67–71.

Turner, Victor. *Revelation and Divination in Ndembu Ritual*. Oxford: Clarendon, 1975.

Werbner, R.P. "Tswapong Wisdom Divination." In *Ritual Passage, Sacred Journey*, pp. 19–60. Washington D.C.: Smithsonian Institution Press, 1989.

Whyte, Susan Reynolds. "Knowledge and Power in Nyole Divination." In *African Divination Systems*, ed. Philip M. Peek, pp. 153–172. Bloomington & Indianapolis: Indiana University Press, 1991.

Whyte, Susan Reynolds. *Questioning Misfortune: The Pragmatics of Uncertainty in Eastern Uganda*. Cambridge: University of Cambridge Press, 1997.

Zeitlyn, David. "Professor Garfinkle Visits the Soothsayers: Ethnomethodology and Mambila Divination." In *Man* (N.S.) 25 (1990), pp. 654–666.

Zeitlyn, David. "Finding Meaning in the Text: The Process of Interpretation in Text-Based Divination." In *Journal of the Royal Anthropological Institute* 7,2 (2011), pp. 225–240.

CHAPTER 10

The Role of Lamyn Gegeen Blo bzang bstan 'dzin rgyal mtshan in the Dissemination of Tibetan Astrology, Divination and Prognostication in Mongolia

Agata Bareja-Starzyńska

1 Introductory Notes on Mongolian Terminology

In Tibet, the 'science of astrology and divination' is called *rtsis kyi rig gnas*,[1] where *rtsis*—in the most general sense—can be understood as 'calculations'. In the Mongolian language, similar to Tibetan, *rtsis* was conveyed by the term *toγ-a* (Modern Mong. *too*), meaning 'number, figure'. However, other terms were also in use.[2] One of the most widely employed Mongolian terms has been *jiruqai* in Class. Mong. (Modern Mong. *zurkhai*), meaning 'mathematics, calculations, astrology, horoscope'. The term may be further specified as *odny zurkhai*, referring then to 'planet calculations', or 'astronomy', from the Tibetan *skar rtsis*. However, in Tibetan, it is sometimes rendered also by the term *dkar rtsis*,[3] 'Indian calculations', lit. 'white [domain] calculations'. It was

---

1 According to Leonard J.W. van der Kuijp, "in the Indian subcontinent as well in Tibet, astronomy with its rigorous mathematics and astrology fell under the rubric of *rtsis rig pa* (**jyoti-hvidyā*), that is, what can be called 'astral science', and it was in turn included in the so-called 'eighteen domains of knowledge' (*rig gnas chung ba bco brgyad*)." See van der Kuijp, Leonard J.W., "From *Chongzhen lishu* 崇禎曆書 to *Tengri-yin udq-a* and *Rgya rtsis chen mo*," in *Tibetan Printing: Comparisons, Continuities and Change*, eds. Diemberger, Hildegard, Ehrhard, Franz-Karl and Kornicki, Peter, p. 55. Leiden, Boston: Brill, 2016. On *rtsis* see Schuh, Dieter, *Zur Geschichte der tibetischen Kalenderrechnung*, Wiesbaden: Franz Steiner Verlag GmbH, 1973; Schuh, Dieter, "Politik und Wissenschaft in Tibet im 13. und 17. Jahrhundert," ZAS 33 (2004): 1–23. More popular presentation by Alex Berzin: https://studybuddhism.com/en/advanced-studies/history-culture/tibetan-astrology/tibetan-astro-sciences (accessed 5 January 2017).

2 Such as Modern Mong. *merge tölög* 'divination', *mergelekh* or *mereglekh*—'to divine, to do divination'.

3 Dieter Schuh translates this term into German as 'Astronomie', see http://www.tibet-encyclopaedia.de/astronomie.html (accessed 5 January 2017).

© KONINKLIJKE BRILL NV, LEIDEN, 2020 | DOI:10.1163/9789004410688_011

THE ROLE OF LAMYN GEGEEN BLO BZANG BSTAN 'DZIN RGYAL MTSHAN   199

translated accordingly into Mongolian as *tsagaan zurkhai*, i.e. 'white calculations'. Both terms are understood to refer to a science associated with the *Kālacakra-tantra*.[4] Modern astronomy can be rendered as *odzüi* or *odon orny sudlal*. The Tibetan term *nag rtsis*, 'Chinese calculations' (in which *nag* comes from *rgya nag*, i.e. China, but lit. means 'black domain') was translated as *khar zurkhai*, i.e. 'black calculations'.[5] It refers to 'elemental divination' in Mongolian, also called *makhbodyn zurkhai*.[6] The 'broad Chinese calculations and calendar', also lunisolar, that developed later, are called, in Tibetan, *gser rtsis*,[7] lit. 'yellow calculations'. However, the term 'yellow calculations'[8] may have a different meaning in Mongolia today. The Mongolian term *shar zurkhai* ('yellow calculations') may also refer to calculations used by Mongols during the period of the Mongolian Empire and so might be claimed to be a Mongolian tradition.[9] Another Tibetan term, *'bras rtsis*—lit. 'result calculations', "the Tibetan system of horary and electional astrology"[10]—is translated as *üriin zurkhai*. A 'diviner' is usually called *zurkhaich*. It should be emphasized that it is relatively com-

---

4   On the Kālacakra Calendar, see Henning, Edward: http://www.kalacakra.org/calendar/kcal.htm; on Tibetan calendar see Janson, Svante: http://www2.math.uu.se/~svante/papers/calendars/tibet.pdf (both accessed 22 June 2016).

5   Sharnuud ovogt Dondogjalyn Mönkh-Ochir, in the monograph devoted to the history of astronomy and astrology/divination in Mongolia *Mongolyn odon oron, zurkhai sudlalyn tüükh*, Ulaanbaatar (no editor) 2012, on p. 26, explains that 'white' and 'black' were associated with the colors of the clothes worn by Indian and Chinese commoners. However, the same color designation is present in the Tibetan terms for India—*rgya dkar, rgya gar*—and China—*rgya nag*—as well as 'Indian', 'Chinese', etc.

6   See Mönkh-Ochir 2012, p. 26, with more information on pp. 27–28.

7   On *gser rtsis*, see the explanations on the website of the Tibetan Men-tsee-khang in Dharamsala http://www.men-tsee-khang.org/tibastro/origin_classification.htm.

8   On the meaning of the term 'yellow calculations', Mönkh-Ochir (2012), on pp. 28–29, writes that the Chinese word *huang* referred to 'yellow' and also to 'the Emperor of China' (p. 29), and adds that Mongols used to refer to this method using the Chinese term *khuanli*.

9   It is impossible to present here all of the arguments of the proponents of *shar zurkhai* in Mongolia. On the history of the system, see, for example, Sharnuud ovogt Dondogjalyn Mönkh-Ochir, *On tsag toolol ba myanga khorin jiliin shar zurkhain tsaglabar*, Ulaanbaatar (no editor), 2014, pp. 54–57. He emphasizes that *shar zurkhai* should not be understood as 'Chinese calculations', but as a Mongolian tradition originating from the time of Kubilai Khan (pp. 56–57). An alternative position is adopted by L. Terbish, who regards *shar zurkhai* and *khuanli* as referring to calculations which were used during the Qing dynasty—"Mongol zurkhain yosny tsaglavar tüüniig khereglekh irsen tüükhen ulamjlal" —in *Önöödör* newspaper, No. 16, 21.01.2004.

10   Gerke, *Long Lives and Untimely Deaths: Life-Span Concepts and Longevity Practices*, Leiden, Boston: Brill, 2012, p. 95.

mon to translate Mong. *zurkhai* into English as 'astrology', even when this term actually refers to practices of divination which are unconnected to planetary observation.[11]

2   Lamyn Gegeen or Khanchin Choijal (Tib. mkhan chen chos rgyal), Blo bzang bstan 'dzin rgyal mtshan (1639–1704)

There is no comprehensive *namthar* (*rnam thar*), i.e. 'biography of an exemplary life' of Blo bzang bstan 'dzin rgyal mtshan, called here Lamyn Gegeen.[12] There exists, however, a short, versified autobiography.[13] More information on his life can be obtained from a biography written by the Khalkha Zaya Pandita Luvsanprinlei (Blo bzang 'phrin las, 1642–1715), a disciple of Lamyn Gegeen, which is included in his famous work, *Sha kya'i btsun pa blo bzang 'phrin las kyi zab pa dang rgya che ba'i dam pa'i chos kyi thob yig gsal ba'i me long* in vol. IV (*nga*), folios 147a–165b2, abbreviated further as ZP.[14] Lamyn Gegeen was regarded as the reincarnation (*sku skye*) of the *mahāsiddha* (*grub chen*) Legs tshogs lhun grub (ZP f. 147b1–2, 149a3). He had five previous reincarnations in India and six in Tibet. Panchen Lama, when asked about him, replied in a letter that he was a reincarnation of Blo bzang don grub, called *mahāsiddha* Legs tshogs lhun grub (ZP f. 149a3–4). Blo bzang don grub (1505–1566) was an eminent dGe lugs pa master, the founder of the dBen sa monastery, who was given the posthumous title of Panchen Lama (III). He was a famous yogi.

In Zaya Pandita's work, a connection was also made to Chinggis Khan to whom Lamyn Gegeen was related and descendants up to Khöndlön Tsökhür

---

11   On the problems related to the translation of terms referring to 'mathematics', 'astrology', 'astronomy' and 'divination' into European languages and the actual comprehension of the subject(s) they cover, see also Brian G. Baumann, *Divine Knowledge: Buddhist Mathematics according to the Anonymous Manual of Mongolian Astrology and Divination*, Leiden, Boston: Brill, 2008. Baumann decided to use the word 'mathematics'. See, for example, "Preface", pp. IX–X and the beginning of Chapter Seven, "Divination," pp. 175–177.

12   Terbish, Lkhasran published a monograph about him: *Lamyn Gegeen Luvsandanzanjantsan, tüünii zurkhain büteel tuurvil*, Ulaanbaatar: Mongol Ulsyn Ikh Suguul', 2004 as well as Byambaa, Ragchaagiin, and Ganzorig, Davaa-Ochiryn, *Erdene Bandida Khutagt Lamyn gegeen Luvsandandzinjaltsangiin Namtar khiigeed Sunbumiin Garchig*, Ulaanbaatar: Mongol Bilig, 2009. Other Mongolian authors who wrote about Lamyn Gegeen: Sh. Bira, L. Khürelbaatar, Sh. Soninbayar and Sh. Choimaa, are mentioned by Byambaa, Ganzorig 2009, p. 25. The date of Lamyn Gegeen's death is usually given as 1704, although in Byambaa, Ganzorig 2009 it is 1703, while in TBRC P4113 the date is not provided.

13   Reproduced in Byambaa, Ganzorig 2009, pp. 170–173, translated into Mong. on pp. 38–42.

14   Reproduced in Byambaa, Ganzorig 2009, pp. 175–184, translated into Mong. on pp. 45–69.

THE ROLE OF LAMYN GEGEEN BLO BZANG BSTAN 'DZIN RGYAL MTSHAN   201

were mentioned (ZP f. 147b3).[15] Khöndlön Tsökhür's reincarnation was the Khalkha Zaya Pandita, previously mentioned famous dGe lugs pa monk-scholar (ZP f. 147b3–4).

Khöndlön Tsökhür's son, Loyag Erkhe Tsökhür (Blo yag Er khe Tshos khur), was Lamyn Gegeen's father. His mother also belonged to Chinggis Khan's descendants (ZP f. 148b1-2). Lamyn Gegeen was four years younger than the First Khalkha Jetsundampa Zanabazar (1635–1723), his teacher, and three years older than the Khalkha Zaya Pandita, who became his disciple. Those three reincarnations were the most influential masters of Tibetan Buddhism in Khalkha Mongolia in the 17–18th centuries. It seems that the Tibetan important dGe lugs pa master, dBen sa sprul sku mKhas grub III, Blo bzang bstan 'dzin rgya mtsho (1605–1643/44), was involved in the recognition of all three of them. It may be speculated that, with their help, he planned to strengthen dGe lugs pa's position in Khalkha Mongolia.[16]

According to his autobiography and the account by Zaya Pandita, the five-year-old[17] Lamyn Gegeen was given a secret name, Chos kyi rdo rje, by Nam mkha' bsod nams grags pa, the tutor of the First Khalkha Jetsundampa Zanabazar, who delivered a prophecy (*lung bstan*) on the basis of the *bKa' gdams glegs bam* (ZP f. 149a1–2).[18] Lamyn Gegeen's recognition had been foreseen by mNga' ris dKa' chen Chos rje Blo bzang yar 'phel (ZP f. 149a2–3)[19] and later confirmed by the First/Fourth Panchen Lama Blo bzang chos kyi rgyal mtshan (1570–1662) (ZP f. 149a3–4). When Lamyn Gegeen was seven years old, he was ordained as a monk and given the name of Blo bzang bstan 'dzin rgyal mtshan (ZP ff. 149a6–149b1).

---

15   Also in his autobiography, Lamyn Gegeen points to his origin from the lineage of the holy Chinggis Khan: *lha rigs jing gir rgyal po'i rigs* | see f. 2a2, Byambaa, Ganzorig 2009, p. 170.

16   See Smith, Gene, *The Autobiography of the First Panchen Lama Blo-bzang chos-kyi-rgyal-mtshan edited by Ngawang Gelek Demo with an English Introduction by E. Gene Smith*, Gedan Sungrab Minyam Gyuphel Series, vol. 12, New Delhi 1969, p. 12.

17   Autobiography of Lamyn Gegeen, f. 2a4, Byambaa, Ganzorig 2009, p. 170.

18   The *bKa' gdams glegs bam pha chos bu chos* ("Scriptures of the bKa' gdams pa, Father and Sons"), the collected teachings and stories of the Indian master Atiśa and his Tibetan disciples on the practice of the bKa' gdams pa tradition, was used for creating prophecies. See, for example, a prophecy regarding Zanabazar's teacher, Nam mkha' bsod nams grags pa: Bareja-Starzyńska, Agata, *The Biography of the First Khalkha Jetsundampa Zanabazar by Zaya Pandita Luvsanprinlei*, Warsaw: Faculty of Oriental Studies, University of Warsaw, 2015, footnote 12 on p. 80.

19   In his autobiography, Lamyn Gegeen mentioned only the arrival of Chos rje Blo bzang yar 'phel from the bKra shis lhun po monastery ff. 2a4–2b1, Byambaa, Ganzorig 2009, pp. 170–171. He stayed in Khalkha for the next six years, see Byambaa, Ganzorig 2009, p. 47, footnote 127.

Initially, he studied in Mongolia. According to Zaya Pandita, the eleven-year-old Lamyn Gegeen began his medical studies under Kun dga' byang chub zer ba (ZP f. 149b3–4),[20] a physician from 'Phan yul, and when he was fourteen, he continued these studies (ZP f. 149b5). When he was fifteen, he received important empowerment and instructions from Klu 'bum chos kyi rgyal po 'Phrin las rgya mtsho (ZP ff. 149b5–150a1).[21] When he was seventeen, he went to Tibet (ZP f. 150a1), where he remained for the period 1655–1661. At first, he paid visits to the sKu 'bum and Bya khyung monasteries and later went to Rwa sgreng and then to sTag lung (ZP f. 150a4–6). After visiting dGa' ldan, he finally reached Lhasa (ZP f. 150b2) and visited the Se ra and 'Bras spungs monasteries (ZP f. 150b5). Then he proceeded to gTsang to the bKra shis lhun po monastery (ZP f. 150b6), where he stayed for over three years. He studied in Tibet under many important masters, including the First/Fourth Panchen Lama (ZP f. 151a1) and the Fifth Dalai Lama (ZP f. 150b3). At the rGyud college of the bKra shis lhun po monastery, he studied the *Kālacakra* (ZP f. 151a5 and following folios).[22]

After returning from Tibet to Khalkha in 1661 (ZP f. 154b4), Lamyn Gegeen must have been busy organizing his own monastery.[23] In 1686, he participated in the translation of *Dag yig za ma tog* (ZP f. 157a2)[24] on Tibetan orthography by Zha lu lo tsā ba chos skyong bzang po (1441–1528). In the years after 1688, due to the Oirat-Khalkha war, Lamyn Gegeen was forced to flee from Khalkha. He spent several years in Ordos, at Khatan gol (ZP ff. 157a6). In 1691, he traveled to Beijing to meet the Manchu Emperor (ZP f. 157b1). Together with the First

---

20   The teacher was described as *'Phan yul pa'i em chi gser mgon po'i slob ma em chi Kun dga' byang chub zer ba.* He is mentioned in TBRC but there are no details pertaining to him: P6422.

21   According to Byambaa, Ganzorig 2009, p. 49, footnote 146, 'Phrin las rgya mtsho was the eighteenth abbot of the Bya khyung monastery and he was called Lunbum Nomun khan, i.e. Klu 'bum Chos kyi rgal po. Byambaa also points to the hymn composed by Lamyn Gegeen and devoted to this teacher: *Bya khyung mkhan po 'phrin las rgya mtsho dpal bzang po la bstod pa dus gsum rgyal ba,* Byambaa, Ganzorig 2009 No. 0006, p. 74. 'Phrin las rgya mtsho is mentioned as well in Byambaa, Ganzorig 2009 p. 21. On the eighteenth abbot of Bya khyung monastery, see TBRC P8LS12214.

22   According to Byambaa, Ganzorig 2009, p. 16 he received the title of *sman rams pa.* ZP f. 153a5 writes about *a rgham pa,* perhaps for *sngags rams pa.*

23   Since Zaya Pandita was studying in Tibet in 1662–1679 he was unable to follow Lamyn Gegeen's biography closely. ZP f. 155b5–6, Byambaa and Ganzorig 2009, p. 56.

24   Mönkh-Ochir 2000, p. 90 wrote about Lamyn Gegeen's translation of the Chinese work on divination, *The Jade Box,* in 1686. Perhaps he confused two titles which contained the word *qayurcay,* i.e. 'basket, box'. The information was repeated by Baumann 2008, p. 12, who stated that the Chinese text *Xuan ze guang yu xia ji* was translated by Lamyn Gegeen in 1686. Mönkh-Ochir did not include this detail in his later works.

Khalkha Jetsundampa, he also participated in the funeral rites for the Empress Xiaozhuang, where he met the Emperor's astrologer, Chos 'byor (ZP f. 157b5).[25] He traveled to Beijing again in 1693 (ZP f. 158a1). He met the Emperor also in 1697 (ZP f. 158a2–3) and 1699 (ZP f. 158b6). In 1694, the First Khalkha Jetsundampa bestowed on him the title *mkhan po no mon khāng* (ZP f. 158a3), rendered in Tibetan as *mkhan chen chos rgyal*, and pronounced in Mongolian as *Khanchin choijal*.[26] He had many disciples who became important Buddhist figures in Mongolia.[27] Since the biography of Lamyn Gegeen by Zaya Pandita was written in 1698–1702, there is no information available about the last years of his life, 1702–1704. After his passing, his line of reincarnations called Lamyn Gegeen began.[28]

3 Works on *rtsis* by Lamyn Gegeen

Lamyn Gegeen acquired fame as a physician, astrologer, and author of religious texts as well as scholarly treatises devoted to medicine[29] and astrology. His scholarly works comprise four volumes of his "Collected Works" (*gsung 'bum*). They were reprinted in *pothi* form by Byambaa Ragchaa in 2008,[30] while the Catalog of the Collected Works of Lamyn Gegeen was published by Byambaa and Ganzorig in 2009.[31] The main works on astrology/divination

---

25 According to Mönkh-Ochir 2012, p. 363 Lamyn Gegeen received many teachings from him. On the First Khalkha Jetsundampa and Chos 'byor, see Bareja-Starzyńska 2015, pp. 155 and 166.

26 Byambaa, Ganzorig 2009, p. 61, footnote 282, stated that the biography of Zanabazar by Luvsandondov (Tib. Blo bzang don grub, written in 1874) explained that, since that time, Lamyn Gegeen had been called by this title. The title was mentioned in the Tibetan fashion by Zaya Pandita on f. 161a3.

27 Zaya Pandita lists sixteen names, see ZP f. 160b2–6, transl. by Byambaa, Ganzorig 2009, pp. 64–65.

28 Currently, the eighth incarnation, born in Mongolia, recognized by the Fourteenth Dalai Lama and enthroned in 2010, is studying Buddhism in India.

29 Seven works of Lamyn Gegeen are regarded as medical in nature. They appear in vol. IV (*nga*) of his *gsung 'bum*, and are also briefly described in the catalog by Byambaa, Ganzorig 2009, on p. 23 and on pp. 145–147, Nos. 0210–0216. See also Jam'yangarav, "Lamyn Gegeen Luvsandanzanjantsany anagaakh ukhaany bütelüüd," *Lavain Egshig*, MBSHTöv Gandantegchenlin khiid (2009): 51–58.

30 Byambaa, Ragchaagiin (ed.), *Khalkhyn Erdene Bandida Khutagt Lamyn Gegeen Luvsandanzanjaltsany büren zokhioluudyn emkhtgel*, Ulaanbaatar: Mongol Bilig, Mongol Bilig Sünbüm Series, 2008.

31 See above, footnote 14.

by Lamyn Gegeen are included in his "Collected Works" (*gsung 'bum*) in vol. *nga*:

1. *rTsis gzhung blang dor gsal ba'i 'od zer*[32] "Light Illuminating 'Acceptance and Rejection' in Calculations," composed in 1687 (Byambaa ed., 2008, pp. 157–215);

2. *'Bras rtsis legs bshad kun 'dus*[33] "Collection of Writings on Prognostication," composed in 1689 (Byambaa ed., 2008, pp. 217–292);

3. *rTsis gzhung mun sel sgron me*[34] "The Lamp Illuminating the Darkness of Calculations," composed in 1687 (Byambaa ed., 2008, pp. 335–350);

4. *Grub rtsis sogs kyi lag len gsal bar bkod pa*[35] "Practical Instructions to Clarify *grub rtsis* Calculations etc.," i.e. the Siddhānta system based on *Kālacakra* (Byambaa ed., 2008, pp. 315–334);

5. *rTag longs sogs re'u mig*[36] "Diagram of the Planets" (Byambaa ed., 2008, pp. 293–314).

Of those five works, the first two had probably the biggest influence on the development of Tibetan astrology/divination among the Mongols.

3.1 rTsis gzhung blang dor gsal ba'i 'od zer

Lamyn Gegeen explains how to calculate the dates of important Buddhist events, lists astrological treatises, and presents methods for composing calendars. In the colophon of the *rTsis gzhung blang dor gsal ba'i 'od zer*,[37] he refers to his origins as a descendant of Chinggis Khan and provides a date counted as 2642 years from the time of the birth of the Buddha as well as the year 1687 (*me yos*). In this year, in the eleventh month, he began composing his text in Ikh Khüree, the main seat of the First Khalkha rJe btsun dam pa Zanabazar, and he completed it on the fifteenth [day] of the middle spring month at a new monastery, dGa' ldan bkra shis dge 'phel.

---

32 Terbish 2004 on p. 23 translated the title into Mongolian as: *Zurkhain gol avch, ogoorokhyg todotgogch gerel*, while Byambaa, Ganzorig 2009, No. 0217, p. 147: *Zurkhain gol avakh geekhiig todruulagch gerel*.

33 Terbish 2004, p. 23: *Üriin zurkhai sain nomlol bükhnii khuraangui*; Byambaa, Ganzorig 2009, No. 0218, p. 148: *Üriin zurkhai sain nomlol bükhen khursan*.

34 Terbish 2004, p. 23: *Zurkhain gol kharankhuig arilgagch zul*; Byambaa, Ganzorig 2009, No. 0221, p. 149.

35 Terbish 2004, p. 23: *Büteeliin zurkhai tergüütnii garyn avlag*; Byambaa, Ganzorig 2009, No. 0220, p. 148: *Büüteeliin zurkhain garyn avlagyg todorkhoilon bichsen*.

36 Byambaa, Ganzorig 2009, No. 0219, p. 148: *Mönkh, tögs edlel tergüütnii khüsnegt*.

37 Byambaa ed., 2008, pp. 214–215. See also L. Terbish 2004, p. 9 and his translation of this section of the text into Mongolian.

At the beginning of his text, in the verses with prayers,[38] Lamyn Gegeen mentioned several Tibetan masters including the First (or Fourth) Panchen Lama (1570–1662);[39] Ye shes rdo rje, i.e. the First Khalkha rJe btsun dam pa Zanabazar; Rang byung rdo rje, i.e. the Third Karmapa (1284–1339);[40] Bu ston rin chen grub (1290–1368);[41] mKhas grub Nor bzang rgya mtsho (1423–1513), the teacher of the First Dalai Lama dGe 'dun rgya mtsho;[42] Phug pa Lhun grub rgya mtsho (15th cent.),[43] creator of a new calendar; Mi bskyod rdo rje, the Eighth Karmapa (1507–1554);[44] dPa' bo gtsug lag phreng ba (1504–1564/66);[45] and (Ngag dbang) Blo bzang rgya mtsho, the Fifth Dalai Lama (1617–1682). He probably wished to honor those masters whose works have influenced his own text. Moreover, he referred to the seven and twenty-five kings of Śambhala and to the *Kālacakra-tantra*.[46]

In his text, Lamyn Gegeen mentioned Buddhist chronology (*bstan rtsis*) and explained the methods employed by different traditions to start their calculations, i.e. the years of the animal cycle from which they began counting. For example, Atīśa's tradition is described as the one which starts from the Wooden Ox year; the system of Sa skya from the Earth Dragon year; the one of Karmapa Rang byung rdo rje from the Wooden Rat, etc. The dates of certain events, such as the composition of several texts on astrology and divination, are mentioned in this work by Lamyn Gegeen as well.[47]

---

38   Byambaa ed., 2008, pp. 158–159.

39   Blo bzang chos kyi rgyal mtshan. See also Terbish 2004, p. 174.

40   TBRC P66. Author of (inter alia) *rTsis kyi bstan bcos kun las btus pa'i rtog pa*, see TBRC W00EGS1016802.

41   TBRC P155. Author of (inter alia) *rTsis kyi bstan bcos mkhas pa dga' byed* TBRC W1KG21838.

42   TBRC P75, Terbish 2004, pp. 176–177, footnote 18. Author of (inter alia) *Dus 'khor spyi don dri med 'od rgyan*, a commentary on the *Kālacakra-tantra*, TBRC W686.

43   TBRC P8101, Terbish 2004, p. 177, footnote 19. Author of (inter alia) *rTsis gzhung pad dkar zhal lung*, TBRC W687.

44   TBRC P385, Terbish 2004, p. 177, footnote 20.

45   TBRC P319, Terbish 2004, pp. 178–179, footnote 21. Author of (inter alia) *rTsis kyi bstan bcos rin chen gter mdzod* TBRC W7503 and works on medicine which might have interested Lamyn Gegeen.

46   Byambaa ed., 2008, p. 159.

47   Terbish 2004 summarizes the text on pp. 7–8.

3.2 'Bras rtsis legs bshad kun 'dus

One even more important work by Lamyn Gegeen is his *'Bras rtsis legs bshad kun 'dus*, a text on prognostication,[48] written in the Earth Female Snake year (*sa mo sbrul*), i.e. 1689.[49] It was translated into Mongolian by L. Terbish in 1991.[50] Terbish wrote that the text was compiled at the time when sde srid Sangs rgyas rgya mtsho (1653–1705) composed his treatise entitled *Vaidūrya dkar po*,[51] which took place between 1683 and 1685.[52] After providing a short comparison of selected excerpts from several texts, Terbish concluded, since the information regarding the five main subjects[53] is presented in Tibetan texts in a similar fashion and the same is also to be found in the work of sde srid Sangs rgyas rgya mtsho, that Lamyn Gegeen must also have followed this work.[54] However, the *Vaidūrya dkar po* by Sangs rgyas rgya mtsho is not mentioned in the work of Lamyn Gegeen and there are no traces that he used it when writing his text on prognostication. Lamyn Gegeen left Tibet in 1661, and he might not have had access to any Tibetan compositions which appeared subsequent to that date.

Judging even simply by the length of the two texts, the *Vaidūrya dkar po* and the *'Bras rtsis legs bshad kun 'dus*, the latter cannot be a translation of the former, since the text by Lamyn Gegeen is considerably shorter (38 folios) and cannot cover the same amount of information as the *Vaidūrya dkar po*. It is also probably not a summary of it, since the author mentioned the following as his sources: *rGyud rdo rje mkha' 'gro*,[55] *mDo sde nyi ma'i snying po* (Skt. *Sūrya-garbha*),[56] *sTag sna'i mdo*, i.e. *sTag rna'i rtogs pa brjod pa* (Skt. *Śārdula-*

---

48   It should be stressed that this is a preliminary study of the text.

49   Byambaa ed., 2008, p. 291, Tibetan original f. 38a5.

50   The book, *Mongol zurkhain tsag toony bichig*, published in 1991 in Ulaanbaatar by L. Terbish, is not available today even in antiquary collections due to its popularity and wide use by diviners. In his monograph on Lamyn Gegeen (2004), L. Terbish summarized the contents of this text on pp. 15–23 and offered again the full translation into Modern Mongolian on pp. 24–76.

51   Full title: *Phug lugs rtsis kyi legs bshad Vaidūrya dkar po*. See TBRC W2CZ8040 and TBRC W30116.

52   See D. Schuh: http://www.tibet-encyclopaedia.de/vaidurya-dkar-po.html.

53   Terbish 2004, p. 14 states that these are called in Mong. *tavan khuraangui* and they cover dates, planets, constellations, conjunctions, and actions. See further explanation below.

54   Terbish 2004, p. 15.

55   Terbish 2004, p. 14: *Dorjkhandyn dander*, p. 76: *Ochir daginisyn ündes*.

56   Terbish 2004, p. 14: *Narny shim*, p. 76: *Sudryn aimag narny zürkhen*. Mahāyāna Sūtra included in the Tibetan *bKa' 'gyur* (in different editions, see TBRC). See Baumann 2008, pp. 100–101 on its importance for *nakṣatras*.

THE ROLE OF LAMYN GEGEEN BLO BZANG BSTAN 'DZIN RGYAL MTSHAN   207

karna-avadāna),[57] *rTsis kun 'dus pa*,[58] *Lu gu gdong rtsis*,[59] *rTsis 'go brgya pa*,[60] *'Bras rtsis rin chen 'phreng ba*,[61] and *sDong po dgu 'dus*,[62] *Khrom rtsis*.[63] The main topics which are discussed in *'Bras rtsis legs bshad kun 'dus* by Lamyn Gegeen are presented in eight chapters:[64] 1) dates (*tshes*);[65] 2) planets (*gza'*);[66] 3) constellations (*rgyu skar*);[67] 4) conjunctions [of the planets and stars] (*sbyor ba*, Skt. *karaṇa*);[68] actions [of the planets and stars] (*byed pa*) and encounters [of the seven planets with one of the stars] (*'phrod*); 5) dependent origination

---

57   Terbish 2004, p. 14, p. 76: *Barsyn khamryn sudar*, a Buddhist work in which early Indian astronomy and astrology are mentioned. Lamyn Gegeen points to this source on f. 15b3 in the chapter on constellations (*rgyu skar*).

58   Terbish 2004 translates this on p. 14 as: *Bükhnii khuraasan zurkhai*, while on p. 76 as: *Zurkhai bükhnii khuraangui*. Perhaps it refers to the text entitled *rTsis kyi bstan bcos kun las btus pa'i rtog pa* by the Third Karmapa Rang byung rdo rje. It was also mentioned by Lamyn Gegeen on f. 9a1 in the chapter on planets (*gza'*), on f. 17b1 in the chapter on conjunctions of the planets and stars, etc. (*'phrod dang sbyor byed rnams*), as well as on f. 24b4 in the chapter on dependent origination (*rten 'brel*).

59   Probably *rDo rje lu gu rgyud ma'i rgyud kyi rtog pa*, see TBRC W22703. Terbish 2004, p. 14: *Khurgany khonshooryn sudar*, p. 76: *Khurgany niguuryn zurkhai*. Mentioned also by Lamyn Gegeen on f. 13b5 in the chapter on constellations (*rgyu skar*).

60   Terbish 2004, p. 14, p. 76: *Zuun ekht zurkhai*.

61   Terbish 2004, p. 14, p. 76: *Üriin zurkhai erdeniin erikh*. Mentioned also by Lamyn Gegeen on f. 8b4 in the chapter on planets (*gza'*) and on f. 13b2 in the chapter on constellations (*rgyu skar*).

62   Terbish 2004, p. 15: *Gol modon yesdiin tüüver*, p. 76: *Yesön modny khuraangui*. Dieter Schuh lists *nag rtsis* sources of the *Vaidūrya dkar po*, including the *Thugs rgyud sDong dgu 'dus*; see Schuh, Dieter, "Zwischen Großreich und Phyi-dar: Eine dunkle, kulturlose Zeit? Das Beispiel des Lehrsystems von sinotibetischen Divinationskalkulationen (nag-rtsis), Geomantie (sa-dpyad), gTo-Ritualen und Erdherrengeister (sa-bdag)," ZAS 45 (2016), p. 5.

63   Terbish 2004, p. 15, p. 76: *Zeeliin zurkhai*. Mentioned also by Lamyn Gegeen on f. 15a5 in the chapter on constellations (*rgyu skar*).

64   Summarized in the colophon as: *tshes | gza' | rgyu skar | sbyor ba | byed pa | 'phrod | rten 'brel | dus sbyor | nyi ma | spar sme | sa bdag rnams kyi 'bras bu*, Tib. original f. 38a2, Byambaa ed. 2008, p. 291.

65   Terbish 2004, pp. 24–30, *ödriin ür*, see Tib. original ff. 2a1–6b5, Byambaa ed. 2008, pp. 219–228.

66   Terbish 2004, pp. 31–33, *garagiin ür*, Tib. original ff. 6b5–9a4, Byambaa ed. 2008, pp. 228–233.

67   Terbish 2004, pp. 34–42, *byadagch odny ür*, Tib. original ff. 9a4–16a4, Byambaa ed. 2008, pp. 233–247.

68   *sByor ba, byed pa* and *'phrod* are discussed together (*'phrod dang sbyor byed rnams*), see Terbish 2004, pp. 42–46 as *uchral, barildlaga and üilchnii ür*, Tib. original ff. 16a4–19a5, Byambaa ed. 2008, pp. 247–253.

(*rten 'brel*, Skt. *pratītyasamutpāda*);[69] 6) year deities (*lo bdag*);[70] 7) the twelve divisions of the day or the twelve gods of the Sun (*nyi ma bcu gnyis*) and tri-grams and diagrams (*spar sme*, i.e. *spar kha* and *sme ba*);[71] as well as 8) lords of the earth (*sa bdag*).[72] Those subjects appeared in the *Vaiḍūrya dkar po*, as well, but in a different sequence.

4 Epilogue

We ought to mention briefly that another great master who was regarded by the Mongols as a person significant for the popularization of Tibetan astrology/divination among the Mongols was Sum pa mkhan po Ye shes dpal 'byor (1704–1788), a Mongolian (Oirat-Jungar) scholar from Amdo.[73] He reformed the calendar (called then the *dge ldan rtsis gsar*,[74] Modern Mong. *tögs buyant shine zurkhai*, "New Virtuous Calculations").[75] This was commented on by several scholars.[76] In 1911, it was officially recognized by the Bogd Khan (the Eighth Jetsundampa, 1870–1824) and introduced in Mongolia.[77]

---

69   Tib. *rten 'brel* translated in Terbish 2004 as *shüten barildlaga, geriin ür* on pp. 46–54, see Tib. original ff. 19a5–25a1, Byambaa ed. 2008, pp. 253–265.

70   Mong. *jiliin ezen tergüünii ür*, Terbish 2004, pp. 54–61, Tib. original ff. 25a1–29a6, Byambaa ed. 2008, pp. 265–273.

71   Tib. *nyi ma bcu gnyis dang spar sme*, in Mong. *arvan khoyor ödör, khölöl, mengenii ür*, Terbish 2004, pp. 61–65, Tib. original ff. 29a6–32b2, Byambaa ed. 2008, pp. 273–280. No sources are mentioned by Lamyn Gegeen for this part of his work.

72   Terbish 2004, pp. 65–75, *gazryn ezen*, Tib. original ff. 32b2–37b5, Byambaa ed. 2008, pp. 280–290. On *sa bdag* divination see D. Schuh: http://www.tibet-encyclopaedia.de/erdherren-sa-bdag.html.

73   TBRC P339. See also Erdenibayar "Sumpa Khenpo Ishibaljur: A great Figure in Mongolian and Tibetan Cultures." In *The Mongolia-Tibet Interface. Opening New Research in Inner Asia. PIATS 2003: Tibetan Studies: Proceedings of the Tenth International Seminar of the International Association for Tibetan Studies, Oxford, 2003*, eds. Uradyn E. Bulag and Diemberger, Hildegard G.M., pp. 303–314, Leiden, Boston: Brill, 2007.

74   Tib. *rTsis kyi bstan bcos kun gsal me long gi gzhung zla bsil rtsi sbyor dge ldan rtsis gsar*, vol. 7 of his *gsung 'bum*.

75   See Salmi, Olli *Mongolian calendar*. http://www.uusikaupunki.fi/~olsalmi/Mongolian%20Calendar.html (accessed 22 June 2016); Mönkh-Ochir 2014, pp. 41–42.

76   On critical remarks, see Mönkh-Ochir 2012, pp. 317–333, Mönkh-Ochir 2014, pp. 41–42.

77   Mönkh-Ochir 2014, p. 43. However, Mönkh-Ochir argues that the new method and calendar were not followed strictly and that there are documents suggesting that even the Bogd Khaan was in favor of using another method of calculation, i.e. the *shar zurkhai*, as confirmed by the document issued in 1915. See Mönkh-Ochir 2012, pp. 317–333, esp. p. 333, Mönkh-Ochir 2014, pp. 43–44.

The two aforementioned masters, Lamyn Gegeen and Sum pa mkhan po, are by no means the only ones who had an impact on popularizing astrological calculations and practices of divination and prognostication based on the Tibetan model in the Mongolian lands. According to Terbish, there exist approximately three hundred works on these topics, written in Tibetan by over eighty Mongolian authors.[78] Terbish mentions five features which characterize these Mongolian works: the replication of books of Indian and Tibetan scholars; the adjustment of the calculation methods in accordance with the Mongolian climate etc.; the simplification of the calculation methods; the development of methodologies to identify the movement and location of certain planets; and the identification of local events caused by nature and the climate.

Since 1990, democratization and religious freedom in Mongolia have led to the revitalization of Buddhism. Together with this, *zurkhai* i.e. divination has also been practiced in almost every Buddhist monastery, while some of them primarily focus on this activity.[79] An annual ritual—prognosis for a New Year and remedy against past failures—is performed during Tsagaan Sar, i.e. the Mongolian New Year celebrations, by all who visit temples at that time. It is called in Mongolian *zasal*, meaning lit. 'treatment, therapy' which corresponds to the Tibetan *bcos thabs* i.e. 'remedy, cure, help'. One way of performing it is to provide a diviner with the date of birth. The diviner, called *zurkhaich* in Mongolian, calculates the number and, according to this, provides instructions on what needs to be done in order to secure good health, wealth and prosperity in the New Year. Sometimes, other rituals, the recitation of certain texts, and bringing offerings are also necessary to remove obstacles. Frequently, diviners consult Terbish's book (with the translation of Lamyn Gegeen's work on prognostication) and the calendar for the current year in order to tell the fortune.[80] It should be stressed, however, that while Tibetan practices which have been

---

78   Terbish, 2013, p. 154.

79   On the revival of Buddhism in Mongolia, see Bareja-Starzyńska, Agata and Havnevik, Hanna "A Preliminary Study of Buddhism in Present-day Mongolia," in *Mongolians from Country to City. Floating boundaries, Pastoralism, and City Life in the Mongol Lands*, eds. Ole Bruun, Li Narangoa, pp. 212–236, Copenhagen: NIAS (Nordic Institute of Asian Studies), 2006; Havnevik Hanna, Byambaa Ragchaa, Bareja-Starzyńska, Agata "Some Practices of the Buddhist Red Tradition in Contemporary Mongolia." in *The Mongolia-Tibet Interface. Opening New Research in Inner Asia. PIATS 2003: Tibetan Studies: Proceedings of the Tenth International Seminar of the International Association for Tibetan Studies, Oxford, 2003*, eds. Uradyn E. Bulag and Diemberger, Hildegard G.M., pp. 223–237, Leiden, Boston: Brill, 2007.

80   Information based on the fieldwork research by the author in Ulan Bator in 2009.

developed by the Mongols since the seventeenth century are being revitalized today, they are, by no means, the only methods of divination which are widely practiced currently in Mongolia.

5   Conclusions

The impact of *zurkhai* on the life of Mongols today should not be underestimated; for example, astrological calculations help to set a date for each New Year. As mentioned above, today, two systems are the most popular in Mongolia: the Tibetan system and the so-called *shar zurkhai*.[81] In 2017, calculations based on those two systems resulted in a gap of one month. The official line follows the Tibetan calculations of Sum pa mkhan po with the beginning of the Bird Year on 27th February 2017. According to the 'yellow calculations', however, the New Year's date was calculated as 28th January. The discrepancy of a whole month is considerable and creates problems starting with the issue of children born within the thirty days which belong, according to the two systems, to two different years, the Monkey or the Bird. Since the prognostication is based on the animal calendar, calculations made on the basis of the wrong year of birth may have fatal results. Those are the concerns and therefore there is a hot debate regarding the superiority of one system over the other.[82]

There is no direct connection between the introduction of the Tibetan methods of calculation, *rtsis*, to Mongolia by Lamyn Gegeen in the 17th century and the activity of Sum pa mkhan po, the Buddhist scholar from Amdo. However, the practical implementation of Lamyn Gegeen's works, such as on prognostication, combined with Sum pa mkhan po's calendar, can be observed in use in modern Mongolia, showing some results of the process of "Tibeto-Mongolica," which is understood as the adaptation of Tibetan practices by the Mongols.

---

81 Explained at the beginning of the paper. It can be added that the 'yellow calculation' system is preferred by Mongols in Inner Mongolia.

82 In the interview for the newspaper *Önöödör* (15.11.2016) the *shar zurkhai* specialist M. Namsrai, the Chair of the Mongolian National United Association of Free Astrologists, strongly criticized Sum pa mkhan po's calendar and emphasized that due to its implementation in the period between 1807–2016 the New Year was wrongly celebrated 134 times and properly celebrated 75 times. http://unuudur.mn/article/91870 (accessed 5 January 2017).

References

Bareja-Starzyńska, Agata. *The Biography of the First Khalkha Jetsundampa Zanabazar by Zaya Pandita Luvsanprinlei.* Warsaw: Faculty of Oriental Studies, University of Warsaw, 2015.

Bareja-Starzyńska, Agata and Havnevik, Hanna. "A Preliminary Study of Buddhism in Present-day Mongolia." In *Mongolians from Country to City. Floating Boundaries, Pastoralism, and City Life in the Mongol Lands,* eds. Ole Bruun, Li Narangoa, pp. 212–236. Copenhagen: NIAS (Nordic Institute of Asian Studies), 2006.

Baumann, Brian, G. *Divine Knowledge: Buddhist Mathematics According to the Anonymous Manual of Mongolian Astrology and Divination.* Leiden, Boston: Brill, 2008.

Baumann, Brian G. "Nakshatra astrology." In *The Black Master. Essays in Central Eurasia,* pp. 11–20. Wiesbaden: Otto Harrassowitz, 2005.

Baumann, Brian G. "By the Power of Eternal Heaven: The Primacy of Astral Allegory to the Government of the Pre-Buddhist Mongols." *Extreme-orient Extreme Occident:* "The Stars and Fate. Astrology and Divination in East Asia," No. 35 (1), 2013, pp. 233–284.

Berzin, Alex. https://studybuddhism.com/en/advanced-studies/history-culture/tibetan-astrology/tibetan-astro-sciences (accessed 5 January 2017).

Byambaa, Ragchaagiin, ed. *Khalkhyn Erdene Bandida Khutagt Lamyn Gegeen Luvsandanzanjaltsany büren zokhioluudyn emkhtgel.* Ulaanbaatar: Mongol Bilig, Mongol Bilig Sünbüm Series, 2008.

Byambaa, Ragchaagiin and Ganzorig, Davaa-Ochiryn. *Erdene Bandida Khutagt Lamyn gegeen Luvsandandzinjaltsangiin Namtar khiigeed Sunbumiin Garchig.* Ulaanbaatar: Mongol Bilig, 2009.

Erdenibayar. "Sumpa Khenpo Ishibaljur: A great Figure in Mongolian and Tibetan Cultures." In *The Mongolia-Tibet Interface. Opening New Research in Inner Asia. PIATS 2003: Tibetan Studies: Proceedings of the Tenth International Seminar of the International Association for Tibetan Studies, Oxford, 2003,* eds. Uradyn E. Bulag and Diemberger, Hildegard G.M., pp. 303–314. Leiden, Boston: Brill, 2007.

Gerke, Barbara, *Long Lives and Untimely Deaths: Life-Span Concepts and Longevity Practices,* Leiden, Boston: Brill, 2012.

Havnevik Hanna, Byambaa Ragchaa, Bareja-Starzyńska, Agata. "Some Practices of the Buddhist Red Tradition in Contemporary Mongolia." In *The Mongolia-Tibet Interface. Opening New Research in Inner Asia. PIATS 2003: Tibetan Studies: Proceedings of the Tenth International Seminar of the International Association for Tibetan Studies, Oxford, 2003,* eds. Uradyn E. Bulag and Diemberger, Hildegard G.M., pp. 223–237. Leiden, Boston: Brill, 2007.

Henning, Edward. *Kālacakra Calendar.* http://www.kalacakra.org/calendar/kcal.htm (accessed 22 June 2016).

Ho Kai-lung. "Spread and Preservation of Chinese Divination in Mongolian, 14th–17th centuries: the Documents of Dunhuang, Turfan, Qara Qota and Xarbuxyn Balgas." *Central Asiatic Journal*, vol. 56 (2012/2013), pp. 133–153.

Janson, Svante. http://www2.math.uu.se/~svante/papers/calendars/tibet.pdf (accessed 22 June 2016).

Jam'yangarav, "Lamyn Gegeen Luvsandanzanjantsany anagaakh ukhaany bütelüüd." *Lavain Egshig*, MBSHTöv Gandantegchenlin khiid (2009), pp. 51–58.

van der Kuijp, Leonard J.W. "From *Chongzhen lishu* 崇禎曆書 to *Tengri-yin udq-a* and *Rgya rtsis chen mo*". In *Tibetan Printing: Comparisons, Continuities and Change*, eds. Diemberger, Hildegard; Ehrhard, Franz-Karl and Kornicki, Peter, pp. 51–71. Leiden, Boston: Brill, 2016.

Mostaert, Antoine. *Manual of Mongolian Astrology and Divination*. Cambridge: Harvard University Press, 1969.

Mönkh-Ochir, Sharnuud ovogt Dondogjalyn. *Mongolyn odon oron, zurkhai sudlalyn tüükh*. Ulaanbaatar (no editor) 2012.

Mönkh-Ochir, Sharnuud ovogt Dondogjalyn. *On tsag toolol ba myanga khorin jiliin shar zurkhain tsaglabar*. Ulaanbaatar (no editor) 2014.

Namsrai, M. http://unuudur.mn/article/91870 (accessed 5 January 2017).

Salmi, Olli. *Mongolian calendar*: http://www.uusikaupunki.fi/~olsalmi/Mongolian%20 Calendar.html (accessed 22 June 2016).

Schuh, Dieter. *Zur Geschichte der tibetischen Kalenderrechnung*. Wiesbaden: Franz Steiner Verlag GmbH, 1973.

Schuh, Dieter. "Politik und Wissenschaft in Tibet im 13. und 17. Jahrhundert." ZAS 33 (2004), pp. 1–23.

Schuh, Dieter. "Zwischen Großreich und Phyi-dar: Eine dunkle, kulturlose Zeit? Das Beispiel des Lehrsystems von sinotibetischen Divinationskalkulationen (nag-rtsis), Geomantie (sa-dpyad), gTo-Ritualen und Erdherrengeister (sa-bdag)." ZAS 45 (2016), pp. 361–396.

Schuh, Dieter. http://www.tibet-encyclopaedia.de/vaidurya-dkar-po.html (accessed 5 January 2017).

Smith, E. Gene. *The Autobiography of the First Panchen Lama Blo-bzangchos-kyi-rgyalmtshan edited by Ngawang Gelek Demo with an English Introduction by E. Gene Smith*. New Delhi: Gedan Sungrab Minyam Gyuphel Series, vol. 12, 1969.

Terbish, Lkhasran. *Lamyn Gegeen Luvsandanzanjantsan, tüünii zurkhain büteel tuurvil*. Ulaanbaatar: Mongol Ulsyn Ikh Surguul', 2004.

Terbish, Lkhasran. "Mongol zurkhain yosny tsaglavar tüüniig khereglekh irsen tüükhen ulamjlal." *Önöödör* newspaper, No. 16, 21.01.2004.

Terbish, Lkhasran. "Mongolian Renown Scholars That Introduced Astrology as a Science in Mongolia." In *The Study of Mongolian Literature in Tibetan*, ed. B. Enkhtuvshin, pp. 153–159. Ulaanbaatar: Mongolian Academy of Sciences, Institute of Language and Literature, 2013.

Index

A.H. Francke   12, 14–15, 49
Aeschylus   137
Ajitanātha   75
Alexander K. Smith   81
Amdo   208, 210
apparent reality (*saṃvṛtisatya*)   164
art of dotting   90, 91
Artemidorus   138n8
Ashurbanipal   137
astragalos   19–20, 23, 24
asura   124
Atiśa   80–81, 84–85, 201n18
auspicious omens   166, 168–173

'bras rtsis   199
'Bras rtsis legs bshad kun 'dus   204, 206
'Bras rtsis rin chen 'phreng ba   207
'Bras spungs monastery   202
'Bri gung 'Jig rten mgon po   165
'byung po   148, 150
balance of fortune   35–40
Bar g.yen gTod po dgu   153
bCom ldan Rig pa'i ral gri   166
bcos thabs   209
bdud   122, 133, 147, 150, 151, 152, 187
Beijing   32, 202, 203
bKa' mdzod   91
bKa' gdams glegs bam   201
bKra shis lhun po monastery   201n19, 202
Bla bo bla sras   65
Blo bzang bstan 'dzin rgyal mtshan   200–201
Blo bzang don grub   200
(Ngag dbang) Blo bzang rgya mtsho   205
Bogd Khan, Khalkha Jetsundampa VIII   208
Bon   2–7, 7–9, 62–64, 120, 127n8, 134
Bonpo   139, 140, 141, 148, 149
Bower Manuscript   12, 24, 29–31, 32, 33, 34, 36, 41, 42, 44
Bra bo sGom nyag   152n35
Brahmans   126
breech birth   126
bsang mchod   181
bsdus yig   141
bsod nams   191
bstan rtsis   205

bsTan 'gyur   25, 125, 161, 164
btsan   123, 128, 131, 147, 150, 151, 152, 187
Bu ston rin chen grub   205
Buddha   9, 162–163, 166, 204
Bya khyung monastery   202
byin rlabs   191

Calliope   138
Caraka Saṃhitā   168
Catherine the Second   77
Central Asia   137
charter myth   119
chi bslu dpyad   154
Chinggis Khan   200, 201, 204
Chos 'byor   203
Chos kyi rdo rje   201
Chos rje blo bzang yar 'phel   201
Chrysippus   139
chu tshod   99, 102, 103
Churchillian drift   85
cleromancy   163, 183
colors   79, 124, 141, 172–173
Confucius   85

Dag yig za ma tog   202
*ḍākinī*s   141
Dalai Lama V   202, 205
Dalai Lama VII   125
Daldis   138n8
dam sri   148, 150, 152
Dampa Sangyé   78
dar gud   101
dBang phyug rDo rje, Karmapa IX   174
dBen sa monastery   200
dBen sa sprul sku mKhas grub III, Blo bzang bstan 'dzin rgya mtsho   201
dbu med   141, 191
dbugs   103
dependent arising (*pratītyasamūtpāda*)   163
dGa' ldan monastery   202
dGe 'dun rgya mtsho, Dalai Lama I   205
dgu mig   96
dharma guardian (*dharmapāla*)   150, 162
Dionysus   138
divination   118, 119, 120, 121, 122, 123, 124, 129, 130, 131, 162–163, 181–182, 189

arrow divination   77
dice   118
five finger divination   77
knotted strings   118
lot (*chouqian* 抽籤)   22, 40
mo (divination)   94, 95, 182
rosary   77, 79–81, 84, 177
sixty pebble divination   85
sticks   118
stones, pebbles   77, 85, 118
dkar rtsis   198
dKor skyong rGyal po   148, 150
dmu   146, 150, 151, 152, 185
dPa' bo gtsug lag phreng ba   205
dPag bsam ljon shing   98, 102n39, 105, 109
dPal ldan dmag zor rgyal mo   184
dPal ldan lha mo   23, 189
Dran pa Nam mkha'   3–10
dregs pa bco brgyad   151
dregs pa sde brgyad   150, 151
dri   151
Druglha ('Brug lha)   82
Duchy of Württemberg   77
Dunhuang   11, 24, 29, 32, 35, 44, 49, 51, 65
dur mig   96, 130
dus   95, 96, 97, 98, 99
'Dus srong   65
dus tshod   95, 98, 99

Empress Xiaozhuang   203
Eternal Bon (*g.yung drung bon*)   3
Examination of dreams (*rmi lam brtag pa*)   123, 163, 165, 168

Fālnamāh   18, 22, 25, 26, 27, 31, 36
Febris   155
Female divinities/ goddesses   11, 40
feng shui   90
Blo bzang chos kyi rgyal mtshan, Panchen Lama I/IV   201, 202, 205
Fortune (*phya*)   11
fratricide   131

'go ba'i lha   121
'Gong po   130, 151
g.yang 'gugs, summoning good fortune   119
g.yang gzhi   119n1

g.yang   120, 146
g.Yar g.yen gNyen po bCu gsum   152
games
   chess   18
   nard   18
   pachisi and *caupur*   18, 19, 41
geomancy   89, 90, 91, 92, 94, 106, 112
Gesar   78
Giuseppe Tucci   141
gNam phyi gung rgyal   119
gnam sgo   96, 109, 110, 111
gnod sbyin 'byung po   147, 150
gnod sbyin   151
gnyan   147, 150, 151, 152
Grags pa gling grags   3, 7, 9
grib   120, 122, 132
Grub rtsis sogs kyi lag len gsal bar bkod pa   204
gSal byed byang bu   136, 141, 142, 156
gser rtsis   199
gter ma   149, 152, 192
gTer ston Grub thob dNgos grub   149n21
gTsang   202
gza' rdong   148, 150
gza'   151, 207
gzhi, 'base'   36–39, 43, 119, 120, 132
gZhod ston dNgos grub Grags pa,   149n21

hermaphrodite   126
Hidden *mahdī*   9
Himachal Pradesh   184, 191, 193

Ikh Khüree   204
inauspicious omens   68–69, 166, 171–173
Irq Bitig   12, 24, 32, 35, 41, 42

'Jig rten mGon po   150
Jagaddeva   167–174, 177
Jan Assmann   76, 85
Jeremiah   1
Jesus   2
Joseph Smith   2
ju thig   119, 120, 132, 134, 182, 185

Kālacakra-tantra   199, 202, 205
Kamalaśīla   75
Kamalaśrī   75
Karuṇasiddhi   75
Kāśyapa   9

INDEX

215

keg 94, 96
keg rtsis 95, 109
Khalkha 201, 202
Khalkha Zaya Pandita 201
Khalkha Zaya Pandita Luvsanprinlei (Blo
  bzang 'phrin las) 200
kham (trigram) 131
Khams ston Shes rab dpal 84
khar zurkhai 199
Khatan gol 202
khen (trigram) 110, 127
khon (trigram) 110, 127, 131
Khöndlön Tsökhür 200, 201
Khotan
  Niya 15
  Mazār Tāgh 11, 14, 35, 44
Khri srong lDe btsan (742–c. 800 CE) 3
Khrom rtsis 207
khyim zhag 99
Khyung po sPrul sku Blo ldan sNying po 141
Kitāb al-Bulhān 25, 32
Kitāb al-Fāl 18, 22, 25, 26
Klu 'bum chos kyi rgyal po 'Phrin las rgya
  mtsho 202
klu 147, 150, 151, 152
Kong rtse bla glud 130, 131, 133
Kong sprul blo gros mtha' yas 91, 106
Kong tse 'Phrul gyi rgyal po 127
Kshatriyas 126
Kun dga' byang chub zer ba 202
Kun tu bZang po 143, 146, 149

Lam lha 58
Lamyn Gegeen (Blo bzang bstan 'dzin rgyal
  mtshan) 198, 200–205, 207–210
Langkhor (Glang 'khor) 83
Legs tshogs lhun grub 200
lHa bla ma Ye shes 'od, king of Pu hrangs 6
lHa bu ru la skyes 66
lHa dByar mo thang 65
lha klu sde brgyad 151, 152
lHa Mu tsa myed(/med) 65
lHa myI mgon mched bun 66
lha srin sde brgyad 151, 152
lha 147, 150, 151, 152
Lhasa 202
lHe'u rje zin tags 65
li (trigram) 131
Lingqi jing 26, 33

Loyag Erkhe Tsökhür (Blo yag Er khe Tshos
  khur) 201
Lu gu gdong rtsis 207
Lucius Annaeus Seneca 155
Lunbum Nomun khan 202
lung bstan 73
lung ma bstan pa 73

ma mo 148, 150, 151, 152
Mahāmudrā 164, 174
Maitreya 9
Maitrīpāda 165, 167
makhbodyn zurkhai 199
Manasarovar 128
Manchu Emperor 202, 203
mandala 181
Maṇi Mantra 80
Mani 2
Mañjuśrī 26
Marcus Tullius Cicero 139
Maudgalyāyana 79
Māyādevī 163
mDo sde nyi ma'i snying po 206
medicine 84
Mephitis 155
Mi bskyod rdo rje, Karmapa VIII 205
Mi la ras pa 164
mi tshe 98
Michel Strickmann 12, 23, 25
Mkhan chen Chos rgyal 200
mKhas grub Nor bzang rgya mtsho 205
mnemohistory 85
mNga' ris dKa' chen Chos rje Blo bzang yar
  'phel 201
mo, female 100, 102
mo rtsis 25, 31, 32, 36, 94, 95, 182
Mohammed 2, 7
Mount Kukkuṭapāda 9
Moxishouluo bu (*Maheśvara's Method of Div-
  ination*) 24, 33, 34, 35, 36
mu khab 121
mu sman 61–62
Mu ye pra phud 119, 120, 134

na gso gto 154
nag rtsis 90, 91, 92, 93, 99, 113, 199
nakṣatra 103
Nam mkha' bsod nams grags pa 201
Namkhai Norbu 82

216 INDEX

ngar mi 131, 133
Niniveh 137
nirvāṇa 140
nyin zhag 99

'O [l]de gung rgyal 65, 119
O rgyan 141
Oneirocritica 138n8
Oneirocriticon of Achmet 138n8
Oneiromancy 163–164, 167, 176–177
Óneiros 138
orality 34–35, 43
Ordos 202
ornithomancy 118
Orpheus 138
Orphism 137
Otani 6004 51, 55

'Phan yul 202
'phreng mo 95
Padampa 74
Padampa Sangyé 75–76
Panchen Lama III 200
Pāśaka dice 11, 13–19, 21–22, 24–25, 41–44
Pāśakakevalī 12, 22, 24, 29, 30–31, 36, 41–42
Person of authority (*tshad ma'i skyes bu*)
    162, 172
Peter Simon Pallas 78
pho, male 100, 102
Phug pa Lhun grub rgya mtsho 205
phya 119, 120, 134
Phyag chen rgyas pa nges don rgya mtsho
    174–175, 177
Phywa gshen theg pa, 154
Phywa lcam lo ma 119
Phywa Yab lha bdal drug 119
Plato 137
pra ltas mo 154
preliminary practices of *Mahāmudrā* (*phyag
    chen sngon 'gro*) 174–175
preta 124
'Chi ba'i mtshan ma brtag pa 124
Mṛtyuvañcanopadeśa 125
Vāgīśvarakīrti 125
lTas brtag pa rgyas pa 125, 134
Nam mkha'i 'ja' ltas brtag pa 125
Old Man of the Sky 127
Old Woman of the Earth 127
Paṇḍita Bikhyu Ta de ba 123

probability 35–39, 41, 43
prophecy 3–10, 161–162
prophet 1–2
pseudepigrapha 76
PT 1047 39
Punktierkunst 91
Pythagoras 137

Quran 7

rainbows 125
Ralph Waldo Emerson 85
Ramesside Dream Manual 137
Rang byung rdo rje, Karmapa III 205, 207
rang ngo shes 140
rDo rje sems dpa' nam mkha' che'i rgyud
    149, 150n22
rDzogs chen 149
Rene Devisch 189
resistance 40
Revelation of Saint John 7
rgyal po 123, 127, 130, 147, 150, 151, 152
rgyu skar 99, 103
rgyu'i theg pa bzhi, 154
rGyud bzhi 123
rGyud rdo rje mkha' 'gro 206
ritual system 181, 194
rMa lineage 83, 84
rMi ltas sna tshogs brtag thabs 122
rTsis 'go brgya pa 207
rTsis gzhung blang dor gsal ba'i 'od zer 204
rTsis gzhung mun sel sgron me 204
rTsis kun 'dus pa 207
rtsis mkhan 91
rtsis pa 92, 93, 95
rtsis 198, 203, 210
rtsub 96
rus chen 96, 102, 104–108
rus khams 90, 96, 102, 104–107, 110, 112
Rwa sgreng monastery 202

sa bdag 110–112, 147, 150, 151, 208
Sa dpyad nyung ngu rin chen kun 'dus 92
sa g.yen che ba bcu gcig 152
sa sgo 96, 109, 110, 111
Sa skya monastery 7
Saddharmapundarika 152
Sakya 120
Śākyaśrībhadra (11th–12th cent.) 165

INDEX

217

saṃsāra 140

Sangs rgyas rgya mtsho 91, 93–94, 96, 101, 103–106, 108, 111, 206

Śāntideva 25, 26, 42, 176

Śārdula-karṇa-avadāna 206–207

Śāriputra 79

sde brgyad 152

sde brgyad dregs pa 150

sde brgyad dregs pa'i cho 'phrul 142

sDong po dgu 'dus 207

Se ra monastery 202

sGam po pa bSod nams rin chen 164

sGra tshad pa Rin chen rnam rgyal 123, 134

Sha kya'i btsun pa blo bzang 'phrin las kyi zab pa dang rgya che ba'i dam pa'i chos kyi thob yig gsal ba'i me long 200

shar zurkhai 199, 210

Shudras 126

Śikṣāsamuccaya 176–177

sKu 'bum monastery 202

sku bla 151

Sla bo sla sras 65

sMan ri Monastery 183, 193

sMan 61–63, 64

sMra seng rdel mo gsal ba'i me long 186

smrang 119, 127

sNang gshen Theg pa 153

snang mthong rtsis 154

sog mo 95

Sortes Sanctorum 23–24, 28

soul retrieval 130

spirit-mediumship 162–163

srid pa 119, 127n8, 128, 129, 132

Srid pa las kyi gting zlog gi rts rgyud kun gsal nyi zer sgron ma 152n35

Srid pa Sangs po 119

Srid pa'i gTo nag mgo gsum 127, 133

Srid pa'i lha mo 119

Srid rgyal dus drug mngon shes gsal ba'i me long 191

srin 122, 132, 133

Srong btsan sgam po 90

St. Petersburg 77

sTag gzigs 141

sTag la Me 'bar 151

sTag lung monastery 202

sTag rna'i rtogs pa brjod pa 206

sTag sna'i mdo 206

Stuttgart 77

Sum pa mkhan po Ye shes dpal 'byor 208, 209, 210

Sūrya-garbha 206

Svapnacintāmaṇi 167–174, 177

Svapnekṣā (rMi lam brtag pa) 165, 167–168

Svapnohana (rMi lam brtag pa) 161, 164–177

Tārā 80

Taxila 16–17

taxonomy 152, 162

Thánatos 138

Thang lha ya bzhur 65

The rang 'Gong po 148, 150

the('u) rang 120, 132, 152

theb kyu, dough buttons 131

Three-Headed Man of the Black Rituals 127

thunder 125

Tingrian Couplets 83

topomancy 90

torma (gtor ma) 124, 131

trigram 127, 130, 131

tsagaan zurkhai 199

tshe 97, 98, 99, 112

tshes zhag 99

Tsi na'i sa dpyad gsar 'gyur lugs kyi sgo 'byed 'phrul gyi lde'u mig 91, 106

Turfan 11, 14, 35, 44

ultimate reality (*paramārthasatya*) 164

Vaiḍūrya dkar po 91, 93, 95–96, 98, 106, 109, 110, 111, 206, 208

Vibhūticandra 161, 164–166, 177

Victor Turner 183

Vikramaśila monastery 75, 165

widowhood 131

world ages (*yuga-s*) 19, 30, 43

Xuan ze guang yu xia ji 202

Yang rtse klong chen 149

Yar lha sham pho 65

Ye shes rdo rje 205

yi dam 151

Yijing 22, 26, 27, 28

Ýpnos 138

Zanabazar, Khalkha Jetsundampa I 201, 203, 204

Zarathushtra 2

zasal 209

Zaya Pandita 200, 201, 202, 203

Zha lu lo tsā ba chos skyong bzang po 202

Zhancha shan'e yebao jing (Zhancha jing) 20–21, 27

Zhang zhung gi ju thig bsrus pa mo bya drug 'phrul gyi lde mig 185

Zhang zhung ju thig 119, 120, 132, 134

Zhijé Collection 75

Zhuang Zhou 136

zon (trigram) 130, 133

zurkhai 198, 209, 210

zurkhaich 199

Printed in the United States
By Bookmasters